“THE SHOWY TOWN OF SAVANNAH”

The Story of the Architect William Jay

MERCER UNIVERSITY

MERCER UNIVERSITY PRESS

Endowed by

TOM WATSON BROWN
and
THE WATSON-BROWN FOUNDATION, INC.

"THE SHOWY TOWN OF SAVANNAH"

The Story of the Architect William Jay

John D. Duncan and Sandra L. Underwood

MERCER UNIVERSITY PRESS
Macon, Georgia
1979–2019
40 Years of Publishing Excellence

MUP/ H965

Published by Mercer University Press
1501 Mercer University Drive
Macon, Georgia 31207

9 8 7 6 5 4 3 2 1

Books published by Mercer University Press are printed on acid-free paper that meets the requirements of the American National Standard for Information Sciences—Permanence of Paper for Printed Library Materials.

Printed and bound in Canada.

This book is set in Adobe Caslon.

ISBN 978-0-88146-689-8
Cataloging-in-Publication Data is available from the Library of Congress

To Virginia Duncan and John Underwood

CONTENTS

ABOUT THE TITLE

The word "showy" (or "shewy") first made its appearance in England in the mid-eighteenth century. With the growth of wealth and prestige brought by the successes of industry and empire, "showy" defined what was desirable in matters of display. Dress or furnishings or architecture were most admired when they appeared to be of very fine quality, opulent even ostentatious, but also refined and tasteful. By the early nineteenth century, the word had come to embody the social and artistic aspirations of the Regency, that very lively era of the prince regent who became George IV.

By the mid-1820s, Savannah, Georgia, was frequently described as a remarkably lovely place. In 1828 Basil Hall, retired from long service in the Royal Navy and the author of a number of popular accounts of his travels, attached a description to Savannah that still has meaning. He called it "the showy town of Savannah."[1]

---

[1] Hall, 3:202.

INTRODUCTION

"ALMOST PERFECT TASTE"

> [William] Jay was one of the most original architects of the period [the early nineteenth century], inventive and with almost perfect taste, a man who has remained—as his city of Savannah, with its remarkable early parks and avenues, has remained—too little known and studied.... He was gifted with a remarkable fertility of mind.
>
> —Talbot Hamlin, *Greek Revival Architecture in America*, 1944[1]

In 1817, when there were few trained architects in the United States to tend to the important business of building a new nation, William Jay arrived in Savannah, Georgia, from London, England. He was young and anxious for work, and he had been well trained in the craft and the art of architecture. His practical experience had come in the office of a busy architect and surveyor, and he had access to the lectures of the professor of architecture at the Royal Academy where one could learn the history and theory of the art. He had accomplished the design and construction of one building in London, which was well received. But his efforts to gain additional commissions in England failed, so he set off for Savannah where family ties could be traced to Georgia's colonial beginning.

Jay had gathered sufficient intelligence about Savannah to know that in 1817 the city was very prosperous and leading citizens had an appetite for building. He found abundant work immediately. In Savannah he is known to have designed several prominent public buildings and private residences. Only three of the houses survive, but these are now gracious settings for museums of art and history. And these are structures of such elegance and ingenuity that they have come to be the very symbols of Savannah, a remarkably beautiful place. Jay would also make his mark on Charleston, South Carolina, although for complicated reasons he was less successful there. Then, just four and a half years later, he was gone, back to England.

For decades, the work that Jay accomplished in the American South

[1] Hamlin, *Greek Revival Architecture*, 201.

went largely unnoticed except by Savannahians who understood how the city had benefited from the labors of this young English architect. Then, in the early twentieth century, Jay began to catch the attention of some of the most important scholars of American architecture. The evidence of the surviving buildings in Savannah suggested that the designer was an extraordinary talent, but very little was known of the circumstances of his life.

The first important figure to contemplate Jay was Fiske Kimball, who would come to be called the dean of American architectural historians. In 1920 he gave a series of lectures at the Metropolitan Museum in New York City, published two years later as *Domestic Architecture of the American Colonies and of the Early Republic*. In this book, there was no mention of Jay, but included was a photograph of one of the architect's most ingenious designs, the portico of the Bulloch-Habersham House. Kimball made the quick observation that the composition appeared to be "after the manner of Soane."[2] The reference was to John Soane, the professor of architecture at the Royal Academy during Jay's time as a student in London. A few years later, Kimball replied to an inquiry from a Savannahian about Jay by saying, "The question about Jay is one that has often perplexed me, and so far from being able to solve it I wish very much that you could solve it for me."[3]

By 1940 Jay had come to the attention of Talbot Hamlin. In a survey of world architecture, he referred to "an English architect, Jay" in Savannah and Charleston who accomplished "exquisite work…perhaps more original in detail than the work in other parts of the country."[4] In *Greek Revival Architecture in America* (1944), the first important study of that style in American architecture, Hamlin offered the remarkable praise of Jay's work cited at the beginning of this introduction. He would see Jay's achievements for himself when he visited Savannah in 1954, here reported in a local newspaper, "Mr. Hamlin spoke of the unusual quality of Jay's work and mentioned particularly the beauty of detail and originality of conception 'which touched everything he did.'"[5]

---

[2] Kimball, 222–23.

[3] "Is Jay a Myth," Dec. 8, 1927.

[4] Hamlin, *Architecture Through the Ages*, 570.

[5] "Hamlin Lauds Owens-Thomas Restoration," *Savannah Morning News* (hereafter *SMN*), Oct. 24, 1954.

By 1957 Jay had gained a third important admirer in the person of Frederick D. Nichols. In *Early Architecture of Georgia*, Nichols focused on Jay's houses, declaring, "William Jay was, unquestionably, one of the most important architects practicing anywhere in America in the early part of the nineteenth century. No one else had his feeling for plain surfaces...for curves and movement...or his conviction that architecture is based on the creative use of space." Of the entry hall at the Scarbrough House, Nichols claimed that it was "one of the grandest spacial compositions in American domestic architecture."[6]

These three important early scholars of American architectural history came to know the work of Jay, and they were struck by its special character. As in the record of all fine art, the work could speak for itself. Still, what was missing was the notice of Jay's life—his origins, his training, his struggles, and the complete record of his accomplishments.

GATHERING AND CORRECTING THE RECORD OF THE LIFE AND WORK OF JAY

By the early years of the twentieth century, a certain rudimentary understanding of Jay's history had been acquired, particularly through the efforts of his Savannah admirers. A legend of the architect was forged when it was remembered that he had been born in Bath, England, as the eldest son of a quite famous evangelical preacher. His father's autobiography included some comment about this child and established the family's Savannah connections. But these findings led to some odd conclusions about Jay's character and the means by which he had been persuaded to journey to Georgia.

In 1950 and 1983, there were two academic reports of Jay's work. The first was a dissertation by James Vernon McDonough, who focused on the architect's labors in Georgia and South Carolina. McDonough was preparing what would have been a welcome book on Jay at the time of his death in 1959. The second report was by Hanna Hryniewiecka Lerski, a professor of art history at Georgia State University, who provided some evidence of what Jay had accomplished in the years after he left the United States. Both of these studies advanced an understanding of Jay's work, but both were addressed to specialists, and neither one was widely distributed.

[6] Nichols, 33, 40.

Recognition of Jay has come slowly. To date, none of the reviews of his work have surveyed all of the projects that can now be attributed to him, and none have been able to paint a convincing portrait of his life. Unsurprisingly, there is much to be learned from the story of Jay, particularly in the context of these themes:

THE TIMES

Jay was born in 1792 into an England that had been transformed by an industrial revolution. Great wealth had come to a rapidly expanding class of manufacturers, managers, and merchants; grinding poverty was the condition of those who labored in the mines, mills, and factories. In the tumult of this era, some men and women of means and station in life saw these disparities and sought to transform society by addressing the physical and spiritual needs of the poor, the disenfranchised, and the enslaved. Jay's father stood in the wake of these events, recruited as a mere lad by followers of John Wesley and George Whitefield to pursue an evangelical ministry.

A FAMOUS FATHER

Jay's life was marked by the circumstance of his birth as the eldest son and namesake of perhaps the most popular preacher of the day. The Reverend William Jay, the Dissident Divine of Bath, was admired by both dissenters and Evangelical Anglicans in an era of Anglican angst when membership in the Church of England was said to be less than that of nonconformist assemblies. He was known throughout England, Scotland, Ireland, and the United States for his captivating invocations of faith from the pulpit and in the large number of books written by him or about him. He spoke to gatherings of hundreds and thousands, regularly in his chapel in Bath and for several weeks each year in London at Surrey Chapel, one of the largest congregations in the metropolis. Through a ministry lasting seven decades, the Reverend Jay gained as friends and followers some of the most influential figures of the age.

THE PROFESSION OF ARCHITECTURE

From Jay's experiences, there is much to learn about the beginnings of the profession of architecture in England and America. By the early nineteenth century, an "architect" was understood to be someone trained in the methods and materials of construction *and* tutored in the history and theory of architecture as an art. The education of an architect included an apprenticeship in a working office and a course of study at an academy. In London, the Royal Academy of Arts, founded in 1768, provided a program for architectural students including lectures and annual exhibitions. These joined experiences of practice and theory formed a preparation quite unlike that of ordinary builders, such as stonemasons and bricklayers, who had simply been taught a trade.

Jay claimed to be an "architect," not a builder. There is some quarrel about how he achieved this status, but there is no dispute that he was competent in practical skills and well informed about the history and theory of the art of architecture. He understood himself to be an artist. He came to a project with his own clear notions of what a building should look like to suit its function and be a credit to the community, sometimes suffering the consequences of patrons unwilling to pay the surcharge the services of an "architect" required.

Jay came of age at a time of opportunity for his art. His career unfolded in the context of two very important but quite different developments. In England, and particularly in London, this was the time of "metropolitan improvements," a rush to build grand structures that would be worthy of England's expanding role in world politics and commerce. An ambitious prince regent, later George IV, took as his own initiative to promote the art of architecture, to serve the nation and embellish his own reign. In the United States, in the aftermath of the War of 1812, buildings were needed to provide for federal, state, and district governance, and for the interests of commerce and culture in a country just beginning to take its place on the world stage.

THE PLACES

Jay lived and worked in several of the most interesting locations of the era. First, he was a child of Bath, the great spa town of the eighteenth century. This was a place made so lovely by nature and by architecture that it is still claimed as the most beautiful city in England. Further, at Bath one could see the importance of the built environment for the prosperity of the town. It is easy to imagine that the character of this place might prompt a young man to become an architect.

Jay took his training in London, the greatest metropolis of the day and a place that was busy building. When efforts to establish a practice in London failed him, he sought opportunities elsewhere. He had been born into a world made small by sailing ships prompted by the adventures and misadventures of wars and commerce. Seeking work, Jay traveled to far-flung places. His first venture abroad was to Georgia, founded in 1733 as the last of the English colonies and in 1817 still remembered as one of the most audacious experiments of the age.

When America failed him, Jay made his way back to England, to Cheltenham, the new spa destination just then eagerly building to take the place of fading Bath. When Cheltenham failed him, Jay's next adventure was to Mauritius in the Indian Ocean. This very small island was one of England's most important colonial holdings, playing a vital role in protecting the lucrative shipping trade from the East.

The trajectory of Jay's career has bewildered some. In 1983 Lerski titled her study *William Jay: Itinerant English Architect 1792–1837*, suggesting that he moved from place to place because he was peripatetic by nature. The truth is that he went where he expected to find work, and he stayed there until something, usually a poor economy, forced him out. In these several places, Jay met extraordinary opportunities and made the most of them. But, at the end of it all, the place in which he found the greatest measure of success was Savannah.

SAVANNAH

Jay is linked to Savannah as to no other place, but these questions linger: Why did he come to Savannah? The usual response is that he came to build a house for the brother-in-law of the husband of his eldest sister. But that house had been in construction for at least a year before Jay arrived in Georgia, an inadequate reason for him to make such an arduous journey. Why did he achieve such success in Savannah? Few architects realize the opportunity to impart a particular aesthetic to a whole town, and Jay's imprint on Savannah was so profound that it endures to this day. And, why on the heels of his success in Savannah did he return to England after only four and a half years in America? These are all questions for which answers reside in the telling of Jay's story.

JAY'S PLACE IN AMERICAN ARCHITECTURE

There is still a question about the role Jay played in the early history of American architecture. Here was an architect of remarkable abilities working in this country at a time when talent and professionalism were much needed, yet his timc hcrc was brief. He made a very good showing in Savannah, but he realized only a modest success in Charleston and left no mark at all in the rapidly developing areas of the Mid-Atlantic and the Northeast.

The problem of determining what Jay means to the early history of American architecture rests with two particularly knotty issues. First, early scholarship concerning the beginnings of architecture in this country was occupied primarily with developments in the Northeast, and the South was often ignored. Next, Jay's designs have been counted as the best examples in the United States of the Regency style and among the earliest evidence in this country of the Greek Revival. But the Regency was a particular flower of England in the time of a flamboyant prince regent, and it was an uncongenial blossom on American soil. And the Greek Revival, with its unassailable English origins, came by the early twentieth century to be embraced as the quintessential American style, catching the reputation of a young English architect in the snare of the politics of American art.

Jay has been an elusive figure. He continues to be much misunderstood in the context of the history of American art, and he is still hardly known in England. This story of Jay is an effort to understand just who he was and how he made his way in the difficult early years of the profession of architecture and in the extraordinary circumstances of the early nineteenth century.

PART ONE

BEGINNING THE PATH OF AN ARCHITECT

CHAPTER 1

THE WILLIAM JAYS OF TISBURY

Why did the eldest son and namesake of the Dissident Divine of Bath take up the difficult art of architecture? There is no evidence that Jay was turned in that direction by his famous father. The Reverend Jay loved the arts of poetry and music, admired some sorts of painting and sculpture, shunned the tawdry spectacle of the theater, and offered no comment at all on the wondrous art of architecture. Bath was the home of this family, and growing up in that beautiful place may have played a role in Jay's choice of occupation. But other circumstances surely contributed to set him on his course.

Jay's father and grandfather, both William Jays, had their roots in the stony soil of Wiltshire in the south of England. Here in the Nadder River Valley folds of ancient chalk downs expose ridges of limestone. The village of Tisbury, home of the William Jays, is just seventeen miles southwest of the prehistoric monument of Stonehenge. At fourteen miles west is the Gothic Cathedral of Salisbury made of Tisbury limestone. Building stone had been quarried in this region since Roman times. By the twelfth century, Tisbury was a village of small homesteads of quarrymen and farmers who owned their own land.

A part of the renown of the Reverend Jay was the wonder of his humble beginnings. It was often told that as a lad he had been apprenticed to his father, a stonemason, as they both labored at Fonthill Abbey, an architectural folly in the Gothic style prompted by a fellow of enormous wealth who would waste it all on this project. As it happens, this father and son could not have worked together at Fonthill Abbey, because construction on that structure did not begin for some years after the mason's son had left home. Still, this old story reminds us to consider what the architect Jay may have inherited from his grandfather and from the region of Wiltshire.

LESSONS FOR AN ASPIRING ARCHITECT

Some have suggested that Jay was drawn to the art of building because his grandfather was a stonemason, and there would be reason to find that true. The profession of architect was still in its infancy when Jay took his training in London and began his work. Before that time, builders were often the sons and grandsons of stonemasons and bricklayers. From his grandfather, Jay could learn about the materials and modes of construction, and he surely heard accounts of three unique structures raised in the near countryside in the late eighteenth and early nineteenth centuries. The Reverend Jay named these places when he referred to his father's dwelling as "situated about an equal distance from Lord Arundel's, Wardour Castle; Pithouse [*sic*], the seat of Mr. Bennet [*sic*]; and Fonthill, then the splendid mansion of Mr. Beckford."[1] These were three singular projects, each one having elements that could catch the interest of a boy and prompt a fascination with the art of building.

Further there was someone present in this place who might have given Jay some special access to these three great country houses and encouraged him in the pursuit of his life's work. This was a Mr. Coombes, the husband of the Reverend Jay's favorite sister, "a man of property" and a specialist in the geology of the region. Cyrus Jay, William's younger brother, remembered that the home of this uncle was the favorite retreat of his father, observing, "I and my late brother William (then both of us young) were often his companions there."[2] Coombes knew the proprietors of these estates. All three structures were built of the local stone. They represented traditional and modern styles as well as old and new techniques of construction, matters of considerable interest to a lad who would later come to the work of designing buildings.

New Wardour Castle was built in 1768–1776 by Henry Arundell, the 8th Lord Arundell of Wardour. Jay's family was tied to this estate. The Reverend Jay described his father as "the son of a small farmer" who had become "a mechanic…a stone-cutter and mason," providing a comfortable home for his wife, four daughters, and one son. The dwelling and its gardens were "my father's own property" granted by Lord Arundell.[3] It was here that the Reverend Jay was born in 1769.

Built in the Palladian style then popular in England, the most remarkable feature of New Wardour Castle is an entry hall designed as a rotunda with flying curved stairs at two sides of the room. This chamber came to be known as the "Pantheon," named for the great domed sanctuary of ancient Rome. A

---

[1] Rev. Jay, *Autobiography*, 19–20. Citations are to the 1854 edition unless otherwise noted.

[2] Ibid., 18; C. Jay, *Recollections*, 202–03.

[3] Rev. Jay, *Autobiography*, 17, 19.

guidebook of 1820 observed that this remarkable stairway was "an unrivaled specimen of modern architectural ornament."[4] It is an audacious conception of sculptural space of the sort Jay would later explore in his compositions.

Pythouse is a fine building in the contemporary mode that would come to be called the "Regency villa." This was the home of John Benett, a wealthy farmer and member of the House of Commons, who designed and built Pythouse in 1805. It is a block form, two stories over a high basement, exactly like Jay's Savannah houses. The exterior is almost entirely free of applied ornament, relying instead on volume to achieve the effect of stateliness, as Jay would do in his own work. On the interior, the entry hall ceiling is embellished with an anthemion frieze (a pattern of lotus or honeysuckle blossoms) that would come to be a hallmark of Jay's style; and this hall contains an imposing central staircase with cantilevered returns, another feature favored by Jay.

Fonthill Abbey, built in 1796–1813, could not have escaped the notice of young Jay. It was one of the most fantastic projects of the age. Now only a ruin, it is still legendary in accounts of architectural history. In 1736 Fonthill, an estate of five thousand acres, was purchased by a William Beckford, whose great-grandfather had made an immense fortune from sugar in Jamaica. In 1755 he began building a new mansion designed by a London bricklayer in the Palladian style. This house, which came to be known as Fonthill Splendens, was still incomplete in 1770 when it came into the hands of his son, also a William Beckford, when he was only ten years old.

Work on Fonthill Splendens continued, and it was during 1783–1785 that the stonemason Jay and his son worked together at this estate. By 1794 Beckford had made the decision to turn a garden structure into a folly as a medieval ruin with a great tower. As the project evolved, he was taken with the notion of building an ersatz abbey, and in 1796 he gained the services of James Wyatt, a popular architect of the day and a favorite of George III. By 1801 Beckford had resolved to occupy his abbey. Built on a monumental scale with a majestic central tower, the structure was raised quickly to satisfy an impatient patron, with the regrettable consequence that the tower collapsed twice during construction. It was completed in 1813, but Beckford lived there for only a few years. By 1822 his fortune was much diminished by his own

[4] Leigh, 549.

extravagant spending on the abbey, his extensive art collecting, and the neglect of his Jamaican holdings. He sold Fonthill Abbey and moved thirty miles northwest to Bath.

In 1825 the great tower of Fonthill Abbey fell, leaving the place a ruin as it had begun. According to the Reverend Jay, "On a very clear day…my two nephews [the sons of Mr. Coombes] were riding on horseback; and whilst looking at the elegant structure at the distance of two miles, and expressing their mutual admiration of it, they saw its very high tower fall instantaneously, and vanish like a dream. They thought they had lost their senses, the shock being so sudden.… [M]y father, who worked at it, told me that the masons who were employed in erecting it predicted its sudden downfall."[5]

What was the worth of knowing Fonthill Abbey to the stonemason's grandson? As long as it stood, this structure was an emblem of the Gothic Revival. The Regency was besotted by classical styles, but one of its most engaging characteristics was its affection for the flourishes of the Gothic and various Oriental styles. Jay's houses occasionally featured the Gothic motifs of pointed arches and the play of light through colored glass. And, on at least one occasion, Jay may have turned his hand to the design of a house in the Gothic style. This structure, now lost, was advertised for sale in January 1821 as "A Marine Villa" on Sullivan's Island near Charleston, South Carolina, "erected in the Gothic order" and represented by "Mr. Wm. Jay, Architect."[6]

THE LEGEND OF BILLY JAY THE BOY PREACHER

The village of Tisbury also counts in the story of the architect Jay because it was here that the fortunes of his father were changed in remarkable ways. Of his own inheritance, the Reverend Jay said,

> I have not to trace a long and proud lineage.…Lord [Francis] Bacon has remarked that they who derive their worth from their ancestors resemble "potatoes, the most valuable part of which is under ground."…My parents were very respectable, that is, they were *poor* and *religious*: *religious*, not precisely according to the theory and discipline of a particular party…but really and practically religious…*poor*, not abjectly and dependently, but able, by frugality and diligence, to support themselves, and to bring up a

[5] C. Jay, *Recollections*, 306

[6] W. Jay, arch., attrib., "A Marine Villa," Jan. 3–5, 1821.

family in the decencies and even comforts of village life.[7]

The Reverend Jay recalled that his family attended a church in the village of Tisbury which had "a very dry and dull preacher, but a lovely character...exceedingly tender-hearted, kind, and generous." When Billy Jay was fourteen years of age and an apprentice stonemason, this preacher made him aware of a Methodist who was coming to the village to speak. Billy had never heard of a Methodist, but he attended the service and was moved to tears by the singing and by the speaker's message and manner.[8] His response was noticed by organizers of the event, and, in the following year, he was invited by the Reverend Cornelius Winter to enter his academy at Marlborough in Wiltshire, some forty miles north of Tisbury, to train for the evangelical ministry.

His letter of acceptance survives, and its awkward language reveals what the Reverend Jay later declared as the sure foundation for his subsequent great success, that his faith was earnest and pure and unencumbered by any formal education. Years later, he said, "[N]o one could have gone to an academy more destitute of many advantages than myself. But I had a thirst for knowledge, and a valuation of it." The training at Winter's academy was on-the-job. Just as soon as the students seemed fit, they were sent out to preach in homes and at outdoor gatherings. The Reverend Jay remembered, "The spiritual condition of many of the villages was deplorable, and the people were perishing for lack of knowledge. No one cared for their souls." From the age of sixteen until he left Winter's academy three years later, Billy Jay the Boy Preacher preached over one thousand times.[9]

What would next assure the fame of Billy Jay was an invitation to speak at Surrey Chapel in London, the largest of the nonconformist meeting halls in the city, planned for two thousand but often accommodating many more. The pulpit was open to Church of England ministers and dissenters by the design of its rather extraordinary patron, Rowland Hill. Hill was the sixth son of Sir Rowland Hill, the 1st Baronet of Hawkstone, in Shropshire, in the West Midlands. At Cambridge University, this son succumbed to Methodist influence and began preaching in the open air, much to the horror of his family.

Hill gained ordination in the Church of England, but he pursued an evangelical ministry. At the death of his father in 1783, he resolved to use his

---

[7] Rev. Jay, *Autobiography*, 16–17.
[8] Ibid., 18, 22–23.
[9] Ibid., 35–37, 41.

substantial inheritance to erect a meeting hall. Surrey Chapel was built south of the old City of London, in Southwark just over the River Thames in a region that was relatively undeveloped. Hill's fiery sermons attracted large audiences, but he occupied this pulpit only six months of the year with six months tended by substitute pastors called "supplies."

Hill was an old friend of Winter, who had often encouraged him in the early years of his ministry. When Hill heard a sermon delivered by Winter's protégé Billy Jay, he asked the young man to take a turn in Surrey Chapel. The result became the stuff of legend. On a Sunday in June 1788, Hill was absent from the chapel, and a supply was anticipated: "Quietly seated in a corner of the room is a rustic, curly-headed youth, seemingly still in his teens.... [As time for the service to begin arrives] the youth rises, and modestly addressing one of the elders, says, 'Had I not better go now into the pulpit?'" The church officials were dumbstruck, but they directed this lad to the pulpit. The congregation was stunned but soon "held in rapt attention" as Billy Jay delivered the sermon "with a quiet self-possession...a deep earnestness of spirit, and...unexpected maturity."[10]

At the end of this first assignment of eight weeks at Surrey Chapel, there was a great clamor to appoint this extraordinary young man as a regular supply. Hill reported, with regret,

> It is the peculiar request of Mr Winter, who has the care of Mr Jay, that his first visit should be but a short one...[to keep him] humble and made useful [for the future].... [I]t is very young days indeed with him; but the other day he was but a very poor boy, getting his bread by hewing of stones by the sweat of his brow.... Had he not been called to the ministry, he most probably would have spent his life in the most perfect obscurity. It will be our wisdom to hope for the best...to see if he can weather the dangers of prosperity.[11]

In July 1788, Billy Jay received a call to the ministry in Wiltshire at the village of Christian Malford, and he wrote to Hill, "[T]he dear country-people in Wiltshire...told me...that, like the rest of the ministers who went to London, I should soon be drunk with popularity, and forget and neglect them; but I hope my conduct will prove the reverse."[12] From Winter, he received

---

[10] Newth, 1–3.

[11] R. Hill to J. Webber, July 1788, in Allon, 250–51. .

[12] Rev. Jay to R. Hill, July 19, 1788, in Allon, 252–53.

this message: "My dear Billy...I bless myself in my heart, that you are out of London." In the following year, Winter wrote to his beloved student, "What a noise have you made in the world! How many eyes are upon you. How many hearts fear for you! How many envy you! ...These are your best days, make much of them...shew [show] that you can be popular without being proud."[13]

PREPARING THE WAY TO BATH

Billy Jay stayed at Christian Malford for a year and some months. In 1789 he was invited to assume the pulpit at Hope Chapel in the Hotwells near Bristol, the great port city in the southwest of England. In this region, warm springs had prompted the development of a spa in the late seventeenth century to compete with the attractions of Bath. Hope Chapel, named for Lady Henrietta Hope, a Scottish peeress committed to the Methodist cause, primarily served the dissolute upper classes.

Early in 1790 Billy Jay was called to Argyle Chapel in Bath, perhaps on the evidence that he had not lost his bearing among the fancy people at the Hotwells, as this report from 1845 proposed: "His [Billy Jay's] resistance to the temptations of London [at Surrey Chapel]...and his unshaken identity while preaching...at the Hot Wells, near Bristol, unaffected and unchanged by the whirlpool of fashion, and folly, and splendor that encircled him, convinced his friends, that through divine grace he would not be contaminated by the seductions, even of Bath worldliness and of Bath corruption." It was believed that Billy Jay's "dignified simplicity" could conquer "the dissipation of the giddy and gay throngs of 'the city famed for cures' [Bath]."[14]

In 1790 Billy Jay was ordained to serve the Independent congregation at Argyle Chapel. With this appointment in Bath, he accepted the call to be an annual supply to Surrey Chapel, a commitment which continued for almost fifty years. For thirty years, he preached in London for eight Sundays each year, subsequently reducing his load to six Sundays, then four, then three. For the architect Jay's whole life, his father preached in Surrey Chapel. It was the London home of the Reverend Jay, and when the Reverend Jay spoke there the place filled to overflowing. He achieved considerable notice in his home pulpit in Bath, but his prominence was the consequence of his annual appearances in London.

---

[13] Rev. Jay, *Memoirs of...Cornelius Winter*, 265, 267.

[14] "Rev. William Jay," *Methodist Quarterly Review*, Apr. 1845, 241.

In 1932, more than a century after Jay had left Savannah, his lost name and reputation were recovered by way of a fortuitous discovery. A book of 1842 by a visitor to Savannah included the reference to "an English architect, Mr. Jay—son of the celebrated divine of that name at Bath."[15] From the time of that discovery, the story of the architect Jay has been buoyed and burdened by conceptions and misconceptions about what it meant to be the son of a quite famous evangelical preacher in England.

By the time Jay took up his studies in London in 1808, he moved in a world in which his father was legendary, loved by many and reviled by some. The Reverend Jay was a leader in nonconformist circles in an age when the number of dissenters threatened to overcome the number of declared adherents to the Church of England; when laws still constrained dissenters in opportunities for education and employment; and when evangelicals led the campaigns for all manner of reforms, including the end to slavery, the humane treatment of prisoners, the granting of rights to women, universal literacy, and care for the needy.

The Reverend Jay enjoyed a unique place in the complicated world of religious nonconformity in England during this era. He was a self-proclaimed "moderate Dissenter."[16] Indeed, his ministry was something of an anomaly. He claimed as his predecessors the Puritans and the Independents, groups of Old Dissent that had emerged soon after the establishment of the Church of England in the early sixteenth century as a consequence of the marital misadventures of Henry VIII. However, he was a product of New Dissent, the evangelical revival of the eighteenth century born in attempts to reform the Church of England. But, unlike John Wesley and George Whitefield, who preached in the villages and in the fields tending to the poor and needy, the Reverend Jay took a pulpit in the fashionable spa town of Bath where his hearers were often people of wealth and station in society. And for a few weeks each year, he preached in London in a chapel popular with influential businessmen, politicians, writers, and artists.

There were other great ministers of the day, but none whose lives could match the legend of Billy Jay the Boy Preacher. He had been a Wiltshire lad

---

[15] Buckingham in Gamble, "Tracking Down a Will-O'-The Wisp," May 11, 1932.

[16] Rev. Jay, *Autobiography*, 446.

of fifteen, son of a stonemason and apprenticed to that trade, and nearly illiterate when he was chosen to train for the evangelical ministry. By the age of sixteen, he was preaching in the fields. By the age of nineteen, he was preaching in London to a congregation of two thousand members. By the age of twenty-two, he had been called to be the pastor of Argyle Chapel in Bath where he would stay for sixty-one years, nearly to the end of his days. His long ministry would always be colored by the wonder of his unpromising start in the quarries of Wiltshire.

CHAPTER 2

THE FAMILY AT PERCY PLACE

The family of the Reverend Jay resided at 4 Percy Place, Bath, in the northern reaches of the city, a region newly developed in the 1790s.[1] The home was a commodious townhouse with a fine garden, pleasantly situated near open woodlands above the River Avon. The Argyle Chapel was in easy reach at a mile southwest through the old town and across the river at the Pulteney Bridge. Here this family prospered, and many who knew the Reverend Jay made this observation: "His home was his greatest comfort…his rest, his peaceful dwelling place. He never found himself to be so comfortable, so happy anywhere, as in his own habitation at Percy Place."[2] He had been fortunate in his marriage and delighted with his children, although life would deal him some hard turns in the long illness of his wife and the deaths of a son and a daughter.

The William Jay who would become an architect was the second child of six (there were three boys and three girls). As the eldest son, he might have followed his father into the pulpit as his youngest brother attempted to do. But, like his father, he struck a new path. And like his father, his life was shaped in considerable measure by his own remarkable family history.

THE ELDEST SON AND NAMESAKE OF THE REVEREND WILLIAM JAY

Throughout his life, from his birth in Bath to his death at the age of forty-four on the island of Mauritius, the architect Jay was known to all as the eldest son of the Reverend Jay. The notice of his baptism says, "William son of William & Ann [Anne] Jay of the Parrish [*sic*] of Bathweck [Bathwick] was born Nov. the 16, 1792—Baptized April the 6, 1793 by the Rev'd Corne's [Cornelius] Winter."[3] This document establishes an important connection to

---

[1] Robbins, 64.

[2] Wallace, 69.

[3] "Baptism of William Jay," Apr. 6, 1793, Rev. W. Jay Archives, Bath Central Reference Library, Bath, England.

Georgia and portends the voyage Jay would take to America. He was baptized by the Reverend Cornelius Winter, his father's mentor, whose own labors as an evangelist had begun in Savannah in 1769–1770 as a companion to Whitefield and as a teacher to slaves. Winter was often in the company of his most famous student, and he took a great interest in the fortunes of this family. As evidence of his concern, there is this note in his last letter to the Reverend Jay written just a few days before his death in early 1808: "I am pleased at the good account you give of William."[4] This son was just then sixteen years old and preparing to take up his study of architecture in London.

When the Reverend Jay was in his seventies, he was persuaded to write an autobiography. Composed as letters to his children, this work was published in 1854, the year after his death at the age of eighty-four. In the account of his children, the Reverend Jay gave the longest passage to his eldest son. He said:

> My second child was a son, named after myself. From the turn of his mind, when he had fulfilled his schooling, he was apprenticed to an architect and surveyor in London, where, after his time had expired, he continued for awhile, and then went to Savannah in Georgia. There he was employed for a few years; when, leaving many proofs of his professional ability behind him, he returned to England. After several attempts to succeed at home, he went out, by the appointment of Lord Glenelg, on government service, to the Mauritius. There his taste and talents met with full encouragement, and his prospects were very promising; but he was cut off by a premature death.... My son, besides professional talent and cleverness, had a large share of wit and humour, qualities always dangerous and commonly injurious to the possessor. So it was, alas! here. His comic powers drew him into company, not the most friendly to youthful improvement. He was led into expense by his admirers and flatterers, and for awhile left the path in which he had been taught to go.[5]

This description fixed in the minds of many the notion of Jay as an intemperate young man, but there is no evidence to support that claim. The central point of his father's message was that this son had been "led into expense by his admirers and flatterers, and for a while left the path in which he

[4] Rev. Jay, *Memoirs of... Cornelius Winter*, 238–39.

[5] Rev. Jay, *Autobiography*, 94–95.

had been taught to go." Jay fell victim to debt, the scourge of many entrepreneurs and scores of architects of that era. For work he did in Savannah and Charleston and later in Cheltenham, he was sometimes at the mercy of clients who could not, or would not, cover his expenses. He found himself occasionally unable to meet his obligations to suppliers, builders, and craftsmen. In England in the early nineteenth century, there was hardly a greater moral failing than debt. That was the blemish on his character that caused his father to grieve.

Nothing remains of Jay's own voice to tell us about his private life, his family and friends, his habits and passions. By his hand, there are no personal letters or diaries. A few reports from others survive to say that he was a genial fellow whose friendship was valued. Cyrus recalled that his brother was "a man who, besides possessing great talents as an architect, was of a most amiable disposition."[6] Jay wrote at least three long articles for newspapers in Savannah, and from these we can see that he was bright, articulate, and ambitious, just as his father was.

JAY'S FATHER

From the time of his early acclaim as Billy Jay the Boy Preacher to some decades after his death, the Reverend Jay was profiled in print (magazines, journals, and books) and in images (paintings, drawings, engravings, and sculptures). As one good example, in January 1819 he was featured in the *European Magazine and London Review.* This report included a portrait engraved after a painting by William Etty, the subject of a later chapter. The text surveyed the pastor's accomplishments: his humble beginnings, his early prominence, the unique character of his preaching, his successes in Bath and London, his contributions as an author (by that date he had published thirteen books), and his happy home, which included a loving wife and "six children, all living, and likely to be his future credit and his age's comfort."[7]

JAY'S MOTHER

About Jay's mother, Anne Davies Jay, we learn much from the testimony of her husband. He said, "It was she…who contributed so much to give me

---

[6] C. Jay, *Recollections*, 206.

[7] "Rev. William Jay," *European Magazine and London Review*, 5-8..

that exalted idea of the female character which I have always entertained and expressed.... She calmed my brow when ruffled by disappointment and vexation; she encouraged me when depressed; she kept off a thousand cares, and left me free to attend to the voice of my calling."[8]

Anne was the eldest daughter of the Reverend Edward Davies. A native of North Wales, Davies trained for the ministry at Oxford University and was ordained in the Church of England. During a residence in London, he became a friend and ally of the Reverend Rowland Hill and came to be counted as an Evangelical Anglican. On the occasion of his first assignment to Surrey Chapel in 1788, Billy Jay the Boy Preacher was provided with a letter of introduction to the Reverend Davies written by Winter soliciting some "kindly notice" for his student.[9] At the Davies's home, Billy Jay was smitten by Anne, and they were married in January 1791.

It was a mixed marriage. Cyrus remembered, "My mother frequently attended divine service at the parish church of Bath...she being a member of the Church of England."[10] Of this union, the Reverend Jay observed, "I married the daughter of a clergyman, but there was no separation in our devotions, or differences in the training of our children. We united with each other much more as Christians, than Episcopalians and Dissenters; and never had we, in a long and happy union, one word of discord, or even dispute."[11]

By every account, the marriage was an excellent one, even in difficult times. By the early 1820s, after some thirty years of marriage, Anne began to suffer seizures. As the condition worsened, she was subject to aphasia, described by her husband, "Thus she spoke of a drop of bread and a bit of water; she called the black white, and the white black, the cold heat, and the heat cold." Of her illness, the Reverend Jay said, "I cannot for a moment forget what she has been, and what she has done.... She needs and she occupies much of my attention, but attention endears her the more."[12] Anne died in 1845 at the age of seventy-nine, succumbing to dementia in her last years.[13]

---

[8] Rev. Jay, *Autobiography*, 92.

[9] Ibid., 89.

[10] C. Jay, *Recollections*, 22.

[11] Rev. Jay, *Autobiography*, 417–18.

[12] Ibid., 100–01.

[13] In 1846 the Reverend Jay married Marianne Jane Head, a family friend. He longed for someone to share his remaining years, but Cyrus observed, "This strange

JAY'S SIBLINGS

Anne Jay Bolton was the first born and, according to her father, "one of those who are sanctified from the womb." In 1808 she met Robert Bolton, an American who came to the home of the Reverend Jay with letters of introduction from Winter and Robert Spear, a wealthy cotton merchant of Manchester.[14] Bolton was the great grandson of another Robert Bolton, an Englishman, a sometime successful merchant in Philadelphia who became a follower of George Whitefield. His son, a second Robert Bolton, settled in Savannah and became a merchant, the first postmaster to Savannah, and a friend to Winter in his efforts to teach black children. His son, a third Robert Bolton, acquired property and became a head of the cotton house of Robert and John Bolton. His son, the Robert Bolton who became the suitor of Anne Jay, went to England in 1808 hoping to pursue a call to preach for which he trained at a dissenting academy near London.

Robert and Anne were married in 1811. They would have thirteen children, five boys and eight girls (a fourteenth child, a girl, died in infancy). Robert began an itinerant ministry in the region of Bristol, a dozen miles northwest of Bath. In 1816, with two children and one on the way, Robert and Anne moved to Liverpool where he became director of a branch of the Savannah cotton house. Here the young couple lived in considerable style in the years 1816–1822, until a faltering economy and strikes in the textile mills of Manchester caused the loss of the family business.

In 1824 Robert was called to the pulpit of the Independent Chapel at Henley-on-Thames. In 1836 he moved his family to the United States to gain income and provide for the education of his sons, settling at Pelham in West Chester, New York. In 1850 Robert and Anne returned to England to attend to Anne's father in the last years of his life.

In the arc of the career of the architect Jay, there are important connections with Robert and Anne. William was close to Anne, perhaps because they were the oldest children of the Reverend Jay. And it is clear that William benefitted considerably from a relationship with Robert, first in making the journey to Savannah and later at times of trial in both of their lives.

Arabella Jay Ashton was the third child, recalled by her father as "the most

---

marriage...greatly detracted from the high respect and veneration which had hitherto been paid to Mr. Jay" (C. Jay, *Recollections*, 235, 238).

[14] Rev. Jay, *Autobiography*, 92, 96, 432–37.

devoted of children."[15] In 1821 she married William Garfit Ashton, a solicitor and clerk of the peace at Cambridge. They had no children, but they were both attentive to her father and her mother—Ashton served as executor of the Reverend Jay's estate.

Cyrus Jay was the fourth born. As a child, he may have had a boisterous character, because his early education was entrusted to a Quaker school—the Reverend Jay admired the Quakers and their methods of training youths to habits of "order, and self-control." Cyrus bloomed into quite a colorful figure after he settled in London as an attorney. The notice of his death at the age of seventy-five declared that he "had a large knowledge of public men and events for the last half-century," which he shared in "sonorous disputations and peculiar guffaws."[16] Many of these tales were collected in *The Law: What I Have Seen, What I Have Heard, and What I Have Known* (1868), his account of the adventures and misadventures of London lawyers.

Edward Jay, the fifth child, trained for the ministry at a dissenting academy north of London, but he was obliged to give up this plan when he was overtaken by a dread of speaking in public. He became a solicitor, settled in Bath, and married a daughter of a very wealthy owner of an iron ore mine in North Wales. After her death at the age of thirty-two, he took a second wife, and many years later they made their way to Lausanne, Switzerland. Edward died there at the age of seventy-five, remembered in his obituary as the "youngest son of the late Rev. W. Jay, of Bath."[17]

Statira Jay was the sixth child. Her father reported that she was "not endowed with those personal attractions which some children possess," yet she was the one upon whom he doted. She was "My dear Sweet Pea, Though the last blown, yet not the least loved of all my flowers."[18] Her sudden death from typhus fever in 1820 at the age of nineteen was the single event of loss from which her father never recovered.

LIFE AT PERCY PLACE

By the accounts of the Reverend Jay, his son Cyrus, and many others,

[15] Ibid., 95.

[16] Ibid., 96; "Death of Mr. Cyrus Jay," *Bath and Cheltenham Gazette*, Jan. 26, 1872.

[17] "Deaths [Edward Jay]," *Bath and Cheltenham Gazette*, July 9, 1873.

[18] Rev. Jay, *Autobiography*, 96, 494.

the home at Percy Place was happy and well ordered. The Reverend Jay planned his days and weeks so that they were balanced with work and pleasure. He rose each morning at five o'clock. With breakfast there was a "morning exercise," a family service with readings from the Bible and prayers. Then he took up the work of preparing his sermon for the coming Sunday. By afternoon there was time to receive visitors and to make calls on others. The day was concluded with an "evening exercise" for the family and a supper. His sermon was done by Friday, and work never intruded on Saturday, which was reserved for time with the children.

What did the Reverend Jay count of his life? Near the end of his labors, he recalled,

> Preaching has been the element of my heart and my head.... The seat of my residence [Bath] was, of all others, the place of my preference. My condition has been the happy medium of neither poverty nor riches. I had a most convenient habitation, with a large and lovely garden—a constant source of attraction, exercise, and improvement. I had a sufficient collection of books of all kinds. My wife was a gentlewoman, a saint, and a domestic goddess. My children were fair, and healthy, and dutiful. My friends were many, and cordial, and steady.[19]

ON BEING THE SON OF THE DISSIDENT DIVINE OF BATH

Surely the life of the architect Jay was colored by this powerful patrimony. His brother Cyrus gave this report to his father: "On several occasions [in London], when the conversation was running close, and many of the company were boasting largely of their rank and pedigree, I said: 'Gentlemen. I am the son of a Dissenting minister at Bath, of the name of William Jay.'... [T]here were generally some of the company who knew you well, and I was, in consequence of your being my father, frequently invited to their private apartments."[20] But, for William the advantage may not have been so clear. Because an architectural commission was often awarded for reasons other than the merits of the design, his father's position as a prominent and popular member of the dissenting clergy had the potential to bring unwanted attention to a project.

What did the Reverend Jay offer to his children? Thomas Wallace, a

[19] Ibid., 158–59.

[20] C. Jay, *Recollections,* 178.

native of Bath who had grown up in the Argyle Chapel, observed, "The character of Mr. Jay was marked by great *fondness for home*.... He remarked [to me] one day, 'I pity no men more,—and especially husbands and fathers—than those who...have no desire to remain in it [the home], or...who are always glad to get away.'...His domestic sensibilities were very lively and powerful. As a husband, none could be kinder, more considerate, more attached, more devoted. As a father, none could be more tender-hearted and faithful in his regards."[21]

[21] Wallace, 69–71, 112–17.

CHAPTER 3

CITY OF BATH: "THE PLACE OF MY PREFERENCE"

Jay's early years in Bath were the happy result of the decision his father had made to settle in this place. The Reverend Jay was trained in the dissenting academy of Cornelius Winter and schooled in itinerant preaching. He might have committed himself to a life in the roving ministry, a noble calling that took the faith into places where it was most needed. Or, given his early success as a boy preacher, he might have gained the pulpit of a large and influential chapel in London. But he gladly took an offer from an Independent congregation in Bath where he remained for sixty-one years. Looking back on his long life, he said, "The seat of my residence [Bath] was, of all others, the place of my preference."[1]

When the Reverend Jay accepted the call to the Argyle Chapel in 1791 and settled in Bath with his young bride, the city looked much as it does now. Set in the valley of the River Avon and framed by rolling hills and woodlands, Bath was fitted with broad avenues, pleasant parks, and handsome buildings of a congenial style and scale and made of a local honey-colored stone. To have been born and raised in Bath surely had meaning for the architect Jay. This was as beautiful a blend of nature and architecture as one could imagine.

Bath had not always been beautiful. In the early eighteenth century, it was a crowded and dirty medieval town contained within old walls and surrounded by large tracts of land held in private hands, much of it farmland. Around 1703 the city fathers began in earnest to exploit the natural springs by promoting a tourist industry, but the accommodations were remarkably unlovely. According to Oliver Goldsmith reporting in the 1760s, "The lodgings for visitants were paltry, though expensive; the dining-rooms and other chambers were floored with boards, coloured brown with soot and small-beer [cheap and dark], to hide the dirt.... The city was in itself mean and contemptible; no elegant buildings, no open streets, nor uniform squares!"[2] From

[1] Rev. Jay, *Autobiography*, 158.
[2] Goldsmith, 4:51.

this unhappy condition, a new Bath would grow all of a piece in the course of a few decades.

THE ORIGIN OF BEAUTIFUL BATH

Bath is a spa town of ancient origin, although how ancient has been a matter of some debate. This is the site of Britain's only natural thermal springs. The water has high concentrations of sodium, calcium, sulfate, and chloride, with temperatures ranging from 104 to 120 degrees Fahrenheit. There is evidence of settlement near the springs dating around 8000 B.C. and traces of Celtic tribes honoring a goddess named Sul or Sulis at this place around 2000 B.C. During their occupation of this territory in 43–367 A.D., the Romans constructed a large complex of baths (hot, warm, and cold) along with temples and recreational facilities, but these were abandoned when the Romans retreated. In the Saxon era (410–1066 A.D.), the location of Bath caused it to become an important political and religious site. A monastery was founded here in 781, and at the abbey in 973 Edgar the Peacemaker was crowned as the first king of England.

Over the years, the fortunes of Bath declined as political alliances changed, but the reputation of the springs grew as a place of healing. Then in the eighteenth century, Bath flourished for reasons other than "taking the waters." New fortunes were being made in industry and commerce, and the newly rich joined members of the old privileged classes in serious and deliberate pursuit of rest and recreation. Along with the promise of healing waters, Bath and other spa towns offered a variety of entertainment, such as theatrical performances, concerts, balls, spectacles of all sorts, and games, including gambling. Rural locations added to the appeal, as vacationers sought to escape noisy and dirty metropolitan areas, and travel into the countryside was made easier by improved roads and transport by rivers and canals.

In this era, Bath became the premier spa destination in England, and it was shaped by three men: Richard "Beau" Nash, who defined the social environment; Ralph Allen, who conceived a plan for the town; and John Wood, who rendered the plan and designed the buildings.

In 1703 Nash came to Bath to gamble. When he arrived, the town was a provincial backwater, an unattractive little place filled with people of rude manners. A genial fellow, he soon became the "master of ceremonies" of the spa. For nearly five decades, Nash held sway over the town with the full force of his two nicknames: "Beau," which described his dandy swagger and his preference for extravagant fashion, and "King of Bath," which acknowledged that it was he who set the rules for Bath society. He promoted a varied program of activities and established standards of dress and behavior. In all affairs, civility was required, the privilege of class was muted, and gossiping was banished. Bath was soon known as the most desirable place in all of England to enjoy one's leisure.

But, there were insufficient accommodations for the coming crowds. That matter was addressed by Allen, a resident of Bath who by 1720 had reformed the national postal system and gained a great fortune. Allen saw that the Avon Valley was a uniquely beautiful setting for grand houses and apartments that could be rented seasonally by visitors to Bath. Landowners were just then eager to turn their land into cash, and for construction there was an abundant supply of local stone. "Bath stone," golden or honey-colored, is an oolitic limestone made up of granular matter, so-called oolites or egg stones, tiny bits coated with lime and often containing the remains of marine life. It is a "freestone" and can be cut or squared in any direction. Allen bought two local quarries, reformed the way in which the stone was cut, with surfaces dressed smooth and profiles sharp to suit the new classical styles. Then, he engaged John Wood, later John Wood the Elder, to plan the new Bath and to design its central structures.

Wood gets the credit for the look of the city. It was he who had the vision to shape Bath to be compatible with the natural landscape, blending broad avenues and parks with Palladian classical structures built of the honey-colored stone. He designed accommodations that would both achieve a stately grandeur and meet the needs of a very diverse array of seasonal guests, in a city plan that included squares, promenades, and parks.

The son of a local builder, Wood was born in Bath. He had taken apprenticeships in the north of England and in London, but he was largely a self-trained architect gaining his knowledge from reading and experience. By the time he returned to Bath in 1727, he had learned the Palladian style, and he was determined to bring to the new Bath an echo of its own ancient heritage. According to John Summerson, "[Wood] knew the city had been Roman, and determined to re-endow it with Roman monuments, including a Forum, a Circus, and what he called an Imperial Gymnasium."[3] Wood hoped

[3] Summerson, *Architecture in Britain*, 361.

to build a forum, a place of assembly; a circus, an arena for sport and entertainment; and a gymnasium, an area for physical exercise.

Queen Square, Wood's first successful development, was a design that unified a number of private dwellings into one structure. Built in 1729–1736, three terraces (rows of houses) were joined to give the impression of a grand palace embracing a courtyard.

The North and South Parades, built from 1743, were two long ranks of row houses, each with a unifying facade and planned as the sides of a Royal Forum.

The Circus, constructed in 1754–1769, was designed by Wood but completed by his son John Wood the Younger. This circular structure, formed of three curved terraces, was inspired by the Roman Colosseum, the great amphitheater of antiquity.

The Royal Crescent, built in 1767–1775, was essentially a curved parade. Designed by Wood the Younger, this was the first great crescent in English architecture and the source for many crescents to follow. More than any of the Bath projects, this building, set into the contours of a hilly landscape, realized a harmony of architecture with nature.

LATER ARCHITECTS OF BATH

Wood the Elder's imprint on Bath was profound although he finished relatively few projects before his death at the age of fifty in 1754. His conception for the city was carried forward by his son, and the Woods were followed by a number of architects who valued being in a place that cared for its built environment. At least two of these men were well known to the Reverend Jay: Thomas Baldwin and Henry Edmund Goodridge.

Baldwin began work in Bath in 1774 and was made city surveyor in 1776 and city architect in 1780. Among his several commissions were the Guildhall (1775–1779) and the Old Pump Room (1783–1784). Baldwin was also responsible for the development of Bathwick, a region south of Bath on the far side of the River Avon and made accessible to the city by the building of Pulteney Bridge in 1773. Just over this bridge, in Bathwick, Baldwin designed the Argyle Buildings (1789) in Argyle Street, a row of shops and residences. A site in this development was secured by an Independent congregation, and Baldwin was paid a very modest sum to draw the plans for the Argyle Chapel constructed in 1789. The Reverend Jay would take the pulpit here in 1791.

Among the members of Argyle Chapel were several architects, including Henry Edmund Goodridge, son of a successful Bath builder. In 1821 Goodridge designed a renovation for the chapel, extending and elevating the front of the building and finishing it in a classical style. Later he worked in a variety of revival styles, including Romanesque, Gothic, and Renaissance. When the Reverend Jay retired from the pulpit in 1852, some of his followers built a chapel at Queen Square Place, named Percy Chapel to honor his years of residence at Percy Place. That structure in a Byzantine style was designed by Goodridge.

JAY'S BATH

For most of the eighteenth century, Bath prospered. Set in a picturesque countryside with gracious public parks, gardens, and promenades, there were the urban amenities of commodious dwellings, fine shops, cafes, and restaurants. Social events included theatrical performances, concerts, and dances. And, at subscription libraries, one could attend lectures and peruse newspapers, journals, books, maps, and prints.

Having grown up in such a place, why did Jay leave Bath? Why not apprentice to one of the several working architects of the city and establish a practice in this location where his father was prominent? A probable reason is that by the turn of the century, Georgian Bath was old-fashioned. According to this account written in 1864, "The feeling of the old *habitués* at the opening of the [nineteenth] century was that Bath was spoilt. It was overgrown, and cockneyfied, and the bloom of its prime was past."[4] Jay would make his way to busy, modern London.

[4] Earle, 233.

PART TWO

LONDON: TRAINING AND TRIALS

CHAPTER 4

BECOMING AN ARCHITECT

In late December 1817, Jay stepped off a ship from Liverpool, England, and walked into Savannah, Georgia. He was twenty-six years old, just at the beginning of his career. A few weeks later, in early February 1818, he made a proud announcement in a local newspaper of his credentials as a professional architect. Writing as "A Friend to the Fine Arts," he declared that he was not a "mechanical builder" who had learned a trade. He was an "architect," educated in the "science" and the "art" of architecture. He observed that this training equipped architects to render buildings of exceptional quality and durability *and* of such pleasing form and ornament to excite the emotions and lift the spirit.[1]

In Jay's opinion, the existing buildings in Savannah revealed a lack of understanding of the "true principles" of fine architecture, often resulting in "a huge pile of unconnected parts" with decoration in "tawdry profusion." The modern manner, which he identified as the "Grecian style," was based on recent studies of ancient Greek structures. Contemplating this "pure style," uncorrupted by the Romans and later builders, contemporary architects could design structures "uniting correctness with elegance, and permanence with grandeur." Jay promised to offer, "by the union of taste and knowledge," buildings for Savannah that would "attain magnificence" by "well directed" expense and careful economy.

There was nothing modest in this announcement. Jay revealed himself to be confident in his abilities, perhaps even a little arrogant, and eager to begin work. He surely knew that he was one of only a very few trained architects in the United States, and the only one in the South. He imagined that his skills would change the face of Savannah, and he expressed the "hope" that soon, throughout the country, "public attention will turn to those arts [sculpture and architecture] that raise a nation to eminence—and which so distinguished that seat of genius and liberty, Athens."

Because Jay was young and relatively inexperienced when he designed

---

[1] W. Jay, arch., attrib., A Friend to the Fine Arts, Feb. 19, 1818 (hereafter cited in text).

buildings of extraordinary quality and character in Savannah, later observers of his work found it difficult to account for his training. The truth is that there were many factors. First, there was his native gift for what he would come to understand as the "art" of architecture. By way of inheritance, he could count a grandfather who was a stonemason, a traditional role in the building trades. Then, he had grown up in Bath, an exceedingly beautiful planned urban center.

Evidence of Jay's ambition comes in his decision to pursue his studies in London. No doubt the city was well known to him, because his father spent several weeks each year in the pulpit of Surrey Chapel. And, by the beginning of the nineteenth century, Bath was done and dull; London was lively, and new architecture was the talk of the city. In this environment, Jay would forge a "professional" preparation by way of a long apprenticeship in the office of an architect/surveyor and by participating in programs of the Royal Academy. And he would gain much from his experiences in London, the most vibrant metropolis of the period.

REGENCY LONDON

Jay's London was shaped by George Augustus Frederick of Hanover, Prince of Wales, who assumed rule as regent for his father in 1811–1820 when the old king was indisposed as ill or mad or both.[2] The prince was the first of fifteen children born to King George III and Queen Charlotte. He was wholly lacking in his father's virtues of piety, marital constancy, frugality, and love of nature. However, the prince had excellent artistic sensibilities. He labored to make his surroundings rich in design and ornament as befitted monarchy in the greatest country of the age. He was a munificent patron of painting and sculpture, but of all of the arts he most loved architecture. In 1826 a contemporary remarked, "The King…never thinks of anything but building."[3]

The Regency as a political moment is dated 1811–1820. But 1783 marks the beginning of a Regency style. In that year, the Prince of Wales at the age of twenty-one was granted a separate residence and an annuity, both of which would turn out to be woefully inadequate for his needs. His several building

---

[2] George III (b. 1738) ruled from 1760 until his death in 1820. His reign was punctuated by seizures and incapacity, perhaps a consequence of porphyria, an inherited metabolic disease.

[3] Lady Elizabeth Shelley in Hibbert, 702.

projects define this style, dated from 1783 through the reigns of the prince as regent in 1811–1820 and as king (George IV) in 1820–1830. The style lingers into the rule of his brother William IV in 1830–1837.

Steven Parissien describes the Regency style as an expression of a particularly restive and dynamic era with many conflicting themes, including the opulence desired by the prince regent, the turbulence of many wars, and the social turmoil resulting from the clash of new wealth and dire poverty.[4] It was also an age of exploration and exploitation of far-flung places, such as India and Africa. Discoveries of ingenious technologies fueled the Industrial Revolution. And busy presses turned out astonishing numbers of books, journals, newspapers, pamphlets, and broadsheets conveying information and ideas to an increasingly literate population in all classes of society. It was an anxious and audacious age in which risks were taken in politics, commerce, personal conduct, and the arts.

In this raucous environment, George IV would be lampooned and vilified for the conduct of his personal life, including his extravagant spending on architecture. But, his enthusiasm for building changed the look of London. As one of his few admirers declared, "Public buildings are the most lasting and effective ornaments of a country.... [They] make a people love their native country."[5] Indeed, it was being proclaimed in some circles that architecture was the most necessary and the most ingenious of all of the arts. But there was no central authority to direct the education of architects or to compel the accomplishment of remarkable projects.

THE STATE OF ARCHITECTURE IN LONDON

When Jay arrived in London to begin his training, probably in 1808, the city was crowded and vibrant. England had become the world's center of industry, commerce, and banking; its capital city counted one million residents. And, as architecture was said to be the very emblem of nations, the feeble presentation of that art in London was a matter of very great concern. Not since the aftermath of the great fire in 1666 had there been so much construction in the city, including, as one critic lamented, "numerous monuments of bad taste which disfigure our metropolis and country."[6] A number of voices

---

[4] Parissien, 9.

[5] Elmes, *Metropolitan Improvements*, 3.

[6] Elmes, *Lectures on Architecture*, 3–4.

declared that the important work of architecture should be snatched from the hands of builders, masons, and carpenters, and entrusted to professional architects who were trained in all aspects of construction and design.

It did not go unnoticed that the French, with whom the English were continuing to wage wars, were dominant in all of the arts, especially in architecture. The French had settled on a plan for the training of architects in the mid-seventeenth century. The *Académie Royale d'Architecture*, founded in 1671 and controlled by the monarchy, provided a rigorous course of instruction and patronage for successful students. The result was that France, and most particularly Paris, began to fill up with beautiful buildings. By the time Jay arrived in London, a plan was evolving to improve the built environment in England. The scheme was based on more rigorous training for architects in both the "science" and the "art" of architecture.

The "science," or the mechanics of building, involved the knowledge of materials, the use of tools, and the understanding of measures. These matters had been conveyed for centuries in the method of apprenticeship in which a youth learned from the likes of a master mason by giving his labor in return for mastery of the craft. By the late eighteenth century in England, a new system had evolved in the form of "articled pupilage." By this means, a youth of fifteen or sixteen, having completed his liberal studies (a foundation schooling in history, literature, and mathematics), came into the office of a professional, paid a fee, and was tutored for a term of five or six years.

Jay learned the "science" of building in London during an articled pupilage with a practicing architect/surveyor, acquiring knowledge about the many matters involved in construction: gaining and dealing with clients, drawing plans, preparing estimates, crafting contracts, surveying sites, gathering materials, engaging the craftsmen needed to accomplish the project, and supervising the progress of the work. But, when he arrived in Savannah in late 1817, Jay identified himself as an "architect," a professional, not a mere builder. The difference between an architect and a builder was the mastery of the "art" of architecture. But how would a student learn this "art"? Art concerns matters of creativity and invention posited on knowledge of the history and theories of the art form revealed over the centuries. The French had understood that these subjects were in the domain of the academy.

THE ART OF ARCHITECTURE: THE ROYAL ACADEMY OF ARTS

The Royal Academy of Arts was founded in London in 1768 to train English painters, printmakers, sculptors, and architects, and to foster in the realm an increased appreciation of the arts. The academy sponsored annual exhibitions; programs in painting, sculpture, and architecture were led by professors who were expected to give an annual suite of lectures. Students in painting and sculpture had regular classes in drawing (anatomy and perspective) and ready access to studios and a library. By contrast, students in architecture generally spent their days learning on-the-job in positions of articled pupilage, limiting their use of academy facilities. However, what they did have were opportunities to show work in the annual exhibitions and to hear the lectures given by the academy's professor of architecture.

The Professor. In 1806, two years before Jay arrived to begin his studies in architecture, John Soane was appointed as professor of architecture at the Royal Academy. The son of a bricklayer, in 1768 Soane had begun his training as an apprentice to George Dance the Younger, one of London's leading architects. Then by the force of his own talent, ambition, and perseverance, he was admitted to study at the Royal Academy. In 1777 he won the academy's traveling prize, a scholarship to support three years of study abroad focused in Italy.

Soane had early success as the designer of great country homes, but he desired opportunities for public commissions in London and worked hard to get them. Finally, in 1788 he achieved what may have been the most lucrative appointment in the city, architect for the Bank of England. This was the government bank, an institution of enormous influence in this period. The bank was housed in a complex of buildings secured by fortress walls on a large site, and the demands of this great institution would occupy Soane for most of his working life. However, Soane came to be fixed on the sorry state of English architecture and the inadequate programs available for the training of young architects. In 1806 he sought and was awarded the professorship at the Royal Academy, assuming the responsibility to present an annual series of six lectures.[7]

Jay at the Royal Academy. So far no documents have been found to verify that Jay matriculated as a student at the Royal Academy although he would

[7] Darley, 169–71.

make that claim. There is good evidence that he participated in programs of the academy by exhibiting works in the annual exhibitions and by hearing Soane's lectures. From these experiences, Jay forged an academic training. He was an ambitious fellow, and he surely realized that an affiliation with the Royal Academy would bring not only useful knowledge but also additional cachet to his résumé.

Jay showed architectural renderings at the academy in five annual exhibitions in 1809–1817. During his student years, he presented "Design for a public library" (1809), "Design for a boat-house" (1810), and "Design for a Grecian casine" (1812). Subsequently he exhibited "Design for a boat-house" (1815) and "Church at Savannah" (1817).[8]

Notice that Jay heard Soane speak comes in a curious way. In 1814 a competition was held for a project in Liverpool, a building planned to accommodate social activities and entertainments. There were eight serious competitors and four finalists, of whom Jay seemed the certain winner. One of the finalists recorded the progress of the competition in a diary and made this note of the moment when it appeared that Jay's design would lose to another: "Nov. 11, 1814, W Jay objects to Aikins Elevation/ he says Soane always cautioned them in his Lectures against circular porticos."[9] This report confirms that Jay heard Soane and valued his teaching. But the real evidence is that Jay's own work bears the imprint of Soane's manner, suggesting that the professor's lectures were likely the most stimulating and provocative experiences of Jay's training in London.

When might Jay have attended Soane's lectures? From the time that he came to London in 1808 until late 1817 when he left for Savannah, Jay would have had the opportunity to hear all of the lectures Soane prepared, all of which were open to the public. Work and family obligations constrained Soane, so in the end he presented only twelve lectures, two courses of six delivered intermittently over eight years. The first four were given in 1810. In January 1812, he gave the last two lectures of the first course. This first series was repeated in 1813, and the second series was delivered in 1815. In 1817 he repeated the first series.[10]

---

[8] Graves, 4:238.

[9] Rickman, diary, Nov. 11, 1814, Thomas Rickman Collection, Royal Institute of British Architects Library, London (hereafter cited as RIBA).

[10] D. Watkin, intro., in Soane, 21.

In the *Annals of the Fine Arts* for January 1818, "W. Jay" was cited in a list of London architects, his address was given as "12, Gray's-inn-square," and the entry was marked with an asterisk identifying him as a student of the academy. This may have been by Jay's own report, however the editor of this journal made this claim: "The Lists of Artists, their professions and addresses, have been collected with considerable pains, from the catalogues of all the various exhibitions, from private information, and from every other possible source."[11] No matter his particular status at this institution, Jay knew the value of declaring his participation in programs of the Royal Academy.

"A Friend to the Fine Arts." There is compelling evidence in the character of his own designs that Jay had a particular regard for Soane's work and words. And in the newspaper article written just a few weeks after he arrived in Savannah, Jay, writing as "A Friend to the Fine Arts," made a number of observations that echo themes of Soane's lectures, including the following:

According to Jay, "In America, generally, and in this city [Savannah] *in particular—architecture has been considered rather as a trade than a science."* The assertion that architecture was not a trade but rather a science and an art, disciplines of the liberal arts, was a persistent theme of Soane's teaching. In fact, Soane asserted that architecture was superior to the sister arts. He declared, "[P]ainting and sculpture, with all the mighty and justly admired powers they possess, are arts chiefly of imitation, but architecture is an art purely of invention, and invention is the most painful and the most difficult exercise of the human mind."[12]

Once the character of this "most difficult art" was understood, Soane said, "great public and private works will no longer be entrusted to ignorant mechanics," among whom he included "bricklayers and paper-hangers." He warned, "He who is satisfied with heaping stone upon stone, may be a useful builder, and increase his fortune.... [B]ut such a man will never be an artist, he will not advance the interests or credit of the art, nor give it importance in public estimation. He will neither add to its powers to move the soul, or to speak to the feelings of mankind."[13]

According to Jay, "In considering the buildings of antiquity, and particularly

---

[11] Elmes, *Annals of the Fine Arts* (hereafter cited as *Annals*), Jan. 1818:586; Elmes, "Preface," *Annals,* July 1816:iv.

[12] Soane, Lecture VII:174

[13] Ibid., Lecture I:41; Lecture XI:255.

of Greece... [one finds] *perfect knowledge and perpetual remembrance of the true principles of their art... uniting correctness with elegance, and permanence with grandeur."* In his lectures, Soane offered his students the gathered knowledge of architectural history as it had come to him by the early nineteenth century, including reports of early accomplishments in India, China, Egypt, and Greece. He declared that all of these very diverse traditions added to the young architect's "stock of ideas." But he made it quite clear from his opening lecture that no development could rival that of the ancient Greeks. He said, "The Greeks...cultivated architecture so successfully that they left to succeeding ages only the humble task of imitating their works, works which will be ever admired but perhaps never be equalled."[14]

Soane asserted that central to Greek achievement was the invention of the three orders—Doric, Ionic, and Corinthian. He lamented the misguided attempts of the Romans to invent new orders, such as the Tuscan and the Composite; and he decried the "mania" in subsequent eras to concoct others. The three orders of ancient Greece formed the architect's "alphabet," having the ability "to express every quality that can be made sensible by architecture." He said, "The Doric and Ionic convey correct ideas of masculine strength and female gracefulness, and in the Corinthian we trace the highest degree of elegant decoration that architecture can produce. It is delicate, gay, and impressive."[15]

Soane argued for a respectful classicism, based on "pure" Greek forms and measures, but his own complex work often mixed elements of various styles. For Soane, invention was at the heart of fine architecture, declaring, "He that only copies or imitates will always be left behind."[16] His own work was so singular that it defies the conventional labels. Careful historians have been reduced to calling it "Soanean" or the "Soane style." Summerson offered this assessment: "The Soane style is one of the curiosities of European architecture.... [A]t maturity, there was not, anywhere in Europe, an architecture as unconstrained by classical loyalties, as free in the handling of proportion and as adventurous in structure and lighting."[17]

According to Jay, "I hope that 'now in the piping time of peace' [following the

---

[14] Ibid., Lecture I:30–33, 37.

[15] Ibid., Lecture III:63–65; Lecture II:44–45, 55.

[16] Ibid., Lecture XI:249.

[17] Summerson, *John Soane*, 1.

War of 1812] *the public attention will turn to those arts that raise a nation to eminence—and which so distinguished that seat of genius and liberty, Athens.*" Soane was consumed with the need to transform English cities, London in particular, so that they might reflect the achievements of a great nation. He lamented, "In the great metropolis of this mighty empire to whom Europe owes its choicest blessing, we in most cases can only contemplate a prodigious extent of buildings of various descriptions formed without any general plan of beauty and convenience, and with an almost total disregard to national grandeur."[18]

In Savannah, no doubt moved by the conviction of his father and his father's friends of the promise of America, Jay announced his desire to design buildings worthy of this new nation. And, for a very brief time in the American South, Jay would be supported in his goal by unique circumstances. As Soane had observed, "Give architecture patrons with intellect as well as wealth, let taste, and the mind of genius, and not necessity alone, direct our public and private works."[19] In America, Jay found a few stalwart patrons who had the vision and means to support his best creative work. He would be buffeted by critics and finally brought down by a failing economy. But the particular circumstances in Savannah, for little more than a moment in history, offered a young architect opportunities that few of his contemporaries would ever experience.

The Grecian Style. Jay was pledged to a particular contemporary style of architecture, a style proclaimed by Soane and exalted by his followers, among whom was the architectural critic James Elmes. Called the "Grecian style," this was a rendering of composition and ornament forged in the mid-eighteenth century in the gathered enthusiasms of English scholars, artists, and politicians. The lands of Greece had been held captive by the Ottoman Empire since the fall of the Byzantine Empire in 1453. Three centuries later, as Ottoman influence declined, adventuresome Englishmen began to make their way to Greece, a region still held by the Turks and fraught with discomforts and dangers for travelers. But the reward was the revelation of seeing original ancient Greek monuments. Prominent among these early visitors were a painter James Stuart and an amateur architect Nicholas Revett, who in 1751 were among the first Englishmen to visit ancient ruins in Greece.

---

[18] Soane, Lecture X:228.
[19] Ibid., Lecture XI:258.

What Stuart and Revett found was astonishing. They saw examples of an authentic style before it had been taken over and changed by the Romans. But they found fragile remains, survivors of years of occupation, war, and neglect. Their findings were revealed in careful measured drawings, published as *The Antiquities of Athens and Other Monuments of Greece* in four volumes, the first in 1762 and the last in 1816. These drawings became essential sources for architects prompting what one late nineteenth-century reviewer called "Grecian Gusto."[20]

This "Grecian" manner was promoted by Soane as the style best suited to be the emblem of modern Britain, representing as it did the authentic expression of classical antiquity. However, this new style had some difficulty taking hold, because it required careful study of the prototypes and diligence in applying newly revealed exacting standards. Before these discoveries, English architects and builders had embraced various free and decidedly impure renderings of the ancient classical style, often inventing their own interpretations or flourishes. According to Soane's method, architects were required to be respectful of pure Greek modes and measures, but the results could not be slavish copies. Fundamental to this new style was invention, the means by which the ancient style became modern.

One of the first essays to articulate the importance of the Greek model was written by Edmund Aikin, an associate of Elmes and the person to whom Jay would lose the contest for the design of a building in Liverpool in 1814. In 1810 Aikin published *An Essay on the Doric Order of Architecture*, representing the Doric, the oldest of the classical orders, as the most pure expression of the Greek style before it came to be corrupted by the Romans.

In numerous publications, Elmes lobbied for the Grecian style and called out those who violated this new canon. According to Elmes, a notable miscreant was John Nash, architect to the prince regent. He said of the designs of Nash, "[T]he whole, as wholes, are in general admirable...but alas, Sir, the detail, the parts, the alphabet, the orthography of our Art, in your hands is defective, is graceless...cumbrous and inelegant." He accused Nash of abandoning the pure Greek style and adopting the "spoliations of Roman barbarism." He reminded Nash that in Roman hands the Greek orders (Doric, Ionic, and Corinthian) were "mongrels...like children stolen by gipsies [*sic*], disfigured and misnamed." Elmes charged Nash with "a crime in the realms

[20] Cust, 81.

of Art, and a misdemeanour against good taste."[21]

Jay embraced this new Grecian style. He learned it from the lectures of Soane and from the writings of Elmes and Aikin. And he found this style also in the work of the architect/surveyor from whom he learned the "science" and the practice of architecture.

THE SCIENCE OF ARCHITECTURE: "AT MR. D. R. ROPER'S"

The Reverend Jay said about the professional training of his eldest son that he was "apprenticed to an architect and surveyor in London."[22] The first record of Jay in London is a report of his entry at the annual exhibition of the Royal Academy in 1809. He is listed as "Jay, W.—Architect, At Mr. D. R. Roper's, Stamford Street, Blackfriars." For the exhibition, he submitted a drawing, a "Design for a public library."[23]

Jay was articled to David Riddall Roper, whose office and work sites were located in the regions of Southwark and Lambeth on the south bank of the Thames in rapidly developing new suburbs of the city. Roper was an architect and a surveyor; while these occupations were very different, there were at that time no separate licensing requirements. There are records of his work in both fields, but he made his greatest contribution as a surveyor. This ancient occupation had grown in importance in the late eighteenth century. Rapid increases in population, industry, transportation, and wealth made it necessary to resolve boundaries and to address land and waterway management issues. A Surveyors' Club was founded in 1792 in London, drawing membership from the ranks of both surveyors and architects, and Roper was president of that club in 1813.[24]

Why was Roper chosen as Jay's mentor? This decision would have been made by the Reverend Jay. While not in the first rank of architects working at the time, Roper was a competent professional with a record of steady work, including several projects for nonconformists. It seems likely that he was a dissenter and a member of the congregation of the Reverend Rowland Hill at Surrey Chapel, which had a very large presence in the region of his practice and where the Reverend Jay occupied the pulpit for a term of several weeks

---

[21] Elmes, "A Letter to John Nash, Esq.," *Annals,* Jan. 1817:315–18, 322.
[22] Rev. Jay, *Autobiography*, 94.
[23] Graves, 4:238.
[24] Colvin, 705.

each year.

The Reverend Jay may have known Roper through Roper's association with Samuel Robinson, a prominent dissenter who gave generously to nonconformist causes. Robinson, an architect/surveyor, had an important role in directing the development of the London docks, an enterprise from which he gained a very large fortune. Roper trained in Robinson's office in 1790–1796. By 1811 Robinson and Roper were in partnership to conduct the property evaluations for the development of Regent Street in London, named for the prince regent and directed by Nash.[25] This project was perhaps the most remarkable example of town planning in a city that had never been well planned.

Jay probably came into Roper's office in 1808 when he was sixteen years old and left in 1814 when he was twenty-two. A usual term of articled pupilage was five or six years, during which the student participated in the work of the office and began to develop his own portfolio. Students often prepared drawings, learned how and where to source materials, and assisted with site supervision. And, while the focus was on learning the "science" or the mechanical aspects of the profession, clearly there would be opportunity to learn something of the "art" of architecture if the teacher placed value on matters of design. In this regard, Jay was fortunate. Roper must have prompted his students to exhibit at the Royal Academy as he had done.[26] And Roper worked in the Grecian style.

Roper conducted a successful practice, gaining public and private commissions. He was skilled in construction, and he was an able interpreter of the modern style. As a very good example of what Jay could learn from Roper, there is this structure:

Albion Building, Bridge Street and Ludgate Street, 1805. By the time Jay came into this office, Roper was known for at least one significant building in a busy commercial district. In 1805 he was appointed surveyor to the Albion Fire and Life Insurance Company, a relatively early enterprise in the growing industry of insurance, and he designed the company office building.[27] The structure occupied a corner of Ludgate and Fleet Streets, a busy region of stores, bookshops, and coffee shops. Given its location, the building was no-

[25] Graves, 4:238.

[26] Ibid.

[27] Causton, 383.

ticed. It was described as a "splendid specimen of domestic architecture" featuring "Grecian Doric porticos."[28] The company closed in 1827, and by the end of the century, Roper's building was gone.

ROPER'S PROJECTS DURING JAY'S APPRENTICESHIP

Of particular significance for Jay's story is the work pursued by Roper in 1808–1814, the years of Jay's term in this office. Roper's students would have been required to participate in various tasks for these projects.[29] Records survive for two of these commissions:

Brockwell Hall, Herne Hill, Lambeth, 1811–1813. An important project for the firm during Jay's term, this imposing Regency villa is located in the southwest London borough of Lambeth. This was the residence of John Blades, the premier glass manufacturer of the time and purveyor of cut glass to George III. The project offered a student abundant lessons about planning and constructing a house for a gentleman of wealth and influence, work of the sort Jay would take up in Savannah and Charleston.

Surrey Chapel Almshouses, 1811–1812. In 1814 Roper exhibited at the Royal Academy a drawing titled "Surrey Chapel Almshouses."[30] This project was commissioned by the Reverend Hill, and Jay may have been given a significant role because of the powerful relationship between Hill and his father. Only an engraving and this written description survive: "[I]n Gravel-lane, we meet with a charmingly picturesque set of alms-houses.... The building consists of three *corps de logis* [buildings], for the accommodation of twenty-four poor old women belonging to the congregation [of Surrey Chapel]...The whole edifice is in the modern Gothic style, and by its regularity presents a neat and interesting appearance."[31]

LATER BUILDINGS ATTRIBUTED TO ROPER

Three structures designed in the years following Jay's time in this office

---

[28] Elmes, *London and Its Environs*, 60; Elmes, *Topographical Dictionary of London*, 7.

[29] During Jay's time in Roper's office, he had at least two student colleagues: William Brooks (1787–1867) and Alfred Bower Clayton (1795–1855), both nonconformists.

[30] Graves, 6:361.

[31] Wilkes, 13:522.

account for much of what is remembered about Roper's work.

St. Mark's Church, Lambeth, 1822–1824. This building, which survives, was commended for its Grecian style as "a very handsome church of the Doric order."[32]

Walker's Shot Manufactory, Lambeth, 1826. On the south bank of the Thames, this structure was an engineering feat. The tapered round tower contained two levels from which molten lead was dropped to form small and large shot. Closed in 1949, the structure was demolished in 1962.

Haberdasher's Alms Houses, Hackney, 1827. This is the best surviving example of Roper's work, and it continues to be cited as a good example of the Grecian style. It was an original conception for the time, a remarkable departure from the norm. Almshouses were conventionally designed in medieval styles to reflect their origin in that era. For the Reverend Hill at Surrey Chapel in 1812, Roper had obliged with a Gothic confection.

THE SUM OF JAY'S STUDIES

When Jay arrived in London, there was no clear path for training in architecture. The method of articled pupilage had evolved from the apprenticeships of medieval guilds, and lectures in history and theory were offered at the Royal Academy. But these two experiences were not linked in meaningful ways. Noisy critics complained about this state of affairs. Only a small number of students matriculated in architecture at the academy, and few were awarded rank as members. And, unlike the comparable French institution, the Royal Academy had no means to direct important commissions to its members.

One critic who was unsparing in his criticism of the Royal Academy was Elmes. He proclaimed, "To call the Royal Academy an academy of Architecture is so absurd that I am convinced the academicians themselves, particularly those few who are architects, could not hear of such an epithet without a smile." At the close of a long list of the deficiencies of the institution, he concluded, "The Architecture students are indebted for their education to their private studies."[33] In this Jay was fortunate. In his private studies with Roper, he gained broad experience in the practice of architecture. At the Royal Academy, he participated in the only two programmatic elements said to be of

---

[32] Elmes, *Topographical Dictionary of London*, 292.

[33] Elmes, *Lectures on Architecture*, 396; Elmes, "Publications," *Annals*, July 1818:456–57.

benefit to architecture students, the lectures given by the professor of architecture and the annual exhibitions. By these means, Jay fitted himself with the necessary skills and habit of mind for the professional practice of architecture.

A REGENCY ARCHITECT

Jay is most often remembered as a Regency architect. The attribution is correct. Jay was trained in Regency London, and much of his work shows the hallmarks of what is called the "Regency style." Among the characteristics of that style are these:

The Regency style was British—not French, not Italian, not Greek. And it was modern. The Regency style of architecture was fostered by English political, social, and cultural institutions of the late eighteenth and early nineteenth centuries. This was a great age of British achievement and expansion of influence. While the American colonies had been lost in 1783, there were still valuable holdings in Canada and the West Indies; and the East India Company had come close to possessing India. The success of British industrialization was unmatched in the world, bringing new technologies and products and fast fortunes. By 1815 conquest of the French in the campaigns of the French Revolutionary War and the Napoleonic Wars brought recognition of British military superiority and dominance of the seas. These achievements and others prompted a rush of building in London and elsewhere in the country to fit the needs and aspirations of a powerful and prosperous empire.

The Regency style was eclectic, drawing on a great variety of sources. By the late eighteenth century, British architects had access to a rich heritage of classicizing modes, including the Neoclassic, Palladian, Adam, and Grecian styles. Also emerging in this period was an interest in the Gothick (Gothic), the style of the late Middle Ages claimed as a native invention, not French and not German. A fascination with Chinese ornament (*chinoiserie*) reemerged encouraged by the prince regent. Indian architectural styles and ornament appeared as British domination of India grew. Admiral Lord Nelson's victory over the French at the Battle of the Nile in 1798 popularized Egyptian motifs. Russian designs were celebrated as Napoleon retreated from Russia in 1812. Fashion provided evidence that the world was becoming small, and designs appropriated from distant times and places represented a kind of conquest by art, a way of showing who was dominant in this new era.

The Regency style proposed new conceptions of interior and exterior space and new relationships to nature. A goal of the Regency style was to capture a sense of being in a new and important age. Space is a potent symbol, and Regency architects were masters at defining volumes and vistas to convey significance. Approaches and entries were often animated by sweeping stairs. Interiors, even spaces of modest size, could be made to appear more extensive by joining adjacent rooms through great double doors. Rooms swelled as their shapes took the unexpected profiles of circles, ovals, and octagons. Ceilings were domed or vaulted, with light spilling dramatically from clerestory windows, lanterns, or oculi ("eyes") posed in the center of domes. House and garden became increasingly integrated, as large doors led out onto balconies or extended the space of drawing rooms into the surrounding landscape.

The Regency style was distinguished by new materials and techniques. The Industrial Revolution made possible a great variety of new materials and methods of construction. By the 1790s, load-bearing timber could be replaced by cast iron, offering the values of greater lightness of forms, variety in the shapes of elements, increased strength, less decay, and resistance to fire (or so it was believed). Cast iron balconies could be extended from the building mass, and stairs could stand free of load-bearing walls. An array of exterior wall dressings, such as stucco, disguised the brick masonry that was no longer in fashion. New inventions provided for domestic comfort and convenience in the use of steam heat, gas lighting, and (at last!) efficient flushing toilets. And steam made possible machines to weave textiles and to print fabrics and wallpapers for home interiors.

A Regency interior was intended to catch the eye—the goal was display. In the residences of the prince (then regent, then king), no expense was spared to achieve a rich display of elegant design and precious materials, with furnishings and ornament of great variety and in great profusion. In homes where the budget was less than princely, many of the same decorative effects were achieved through tricks of illusion. Areas of plain wood, such as doors, could be painted with graining to imitate more exotic and costly varieties. Classical columns fabricated of wood could be painted to resemble marble. Walls might be grained as wood, marbled, or hung with fabric or wallpaper. Interior and exterior ornaments were made efficiently and inexpensively in molded plaster, cast iron, or artificial stone (a product of cast and fired clay). In fact, the very concept of "interior decoration" had been introduced by Thomas Hope, whose book *Household Furniture and Interior Decoration* (1807) prompted the fashion of selecting rich and unique ensembles of furniture, objects, carpets, draperies, and wall coverings.

The Regency style in architecture is manifest in the projects commissioned by the prince, including these: in 1783–1826 the renovation of Carlton House, an unremarkable early eighteenth-century mansion on Pall Mall, granted to the prince as his first official residence (demolished in 1826); in 1785–1815 the construction of the Royal Pavilion in Brighthelmstone (later Brighton), on the southeast coast of England; and in 1811–1825 the development of Regent Street and Regent's Park, an audacious reform of a region of central London into a ceremonial avenue and a site for grand homes. The renovation begun in 1826 of Buckingham House, the former home of his parents, would result in Buckingham Palace, today a suitably grand official London residence of English kings and queens. Two years earlier, George IV set about to transform Windsor Castle, the residence of kings since the time of William the Conqueror in the eleventh century, from a motley group of buildings into a handsome and coherent rendering of a modern Gothic style.[34]

George IV retired to Windsor Castle in 1826 and died there in 1830 at the age of sixty-seven. Noting this event, the *Times* of London was unkind: "There never was an individual less regretted by his fellow-creatures than this deceased King....Nothing more remains to be said about George IV but to pay—as pay we must—for his profusion."[35] Seven years after the death of the king, this more generous assessment of his "profusion" was offered: "The nation owes an eternal debt of gratitude to George IV for the planning and effecting of Regent-street. The profusion which was natural to him was on that occasion more productive of solid good, than perhaps the wisest and most rigid economy would have been. Amid the dingy, dismal, uninspiring streets of London, the lavish splendour of what is indeed a Royal road, 'rose like an exhalation.'"[36]

EXPORTING THE REGENCY

There is no Regency style in American architecture, for the very good reason that American history harbors no regent and no yearning for monarchical splendor. This English style arrived on these shores, notably in the

[34] Hibbert, 697.

[35] Ibid., 783.

[36] "Alderman Wood's *Metropolitan Improvements*," *Mechanics' Magazine, Museum Register, Journal, and Gazette*, Mar. 18, 1837:468.

hands of Jay, at the very moment when many Americans were busy about the relatively new business of defining just what it meant to be Americans. So, in American architecture the Regency style is anomalous. It is lovely, but it is a foreign and rather exotic plant.

Jay was trained in the years of the Regency at its center in London. When he came to Savannah, he worked for men who by their business enterprises were still linked to the fortunes of British trade. Jay's buildings in Savannah met the desires of these patrons to sponsor public structures and to own homes of a unique presence and elegance. In Savannah these buildings came to be models of such refinement and ingenuity that they influenced much of what came after them. In many respects, Savannah is a Regency city, filled with old and new echoes of Jay's designs.

THE FATE OF THE GRECIAN STYLE

What was the fate of the Grecian style in English architecture? In 1854 a London reporter offered this assessment: "[T]he ultra-Grecism affected in the earlier part of the present century, when little else was required to gain credit for classical design than handing over to the stonemason the copy of a plate in Stuart's 'Athens,' has passed away."[37] By this time, a conventional view was that the Grecian style had been too constrained in its adherence to the pure original source. Few critics comprehended that, when marked by ingenuity as in Soane's hands or Jay's, the results of the Grecian style were extraordinary. Regrettably, most Grecian buildings in England were lost to "progress," their places taken by Victorian structures in a profusion of exuberant revival styles.

[37] "The Present State of Architecture," *Quarterly Review*, Sept. 1854:352.

CHAPTER 5

A PORTRAIT OF JAY AND THE RECORD OF A FRIENDSHIP

By way of the many profiles of Jay's very famous father, we do know something of the life of this eldest son. But, although dozens upon dozens of images of the Reverend Jay survive, it was not until very recently that we came to see Jay's face. There were reports here and there that Jay's portrait had been painted. In 1820 in Charleston, South Carolina, Jay commissioned his portrait in miniature by Charles Fraser. Two years earlier, at the age of thirty-six, Fraser gave up the practice of law to follow his passion to paint. Accomplished in the technique of rendering a likeness "in little" with watercolor on ivory, he kept an account book in which he recorded the names of his subjects and the amount paid for each work. The entries for 1820 include this notice: "Mr. Jay—$50."[1] But, this work has not been found.

Next there is this promise in the will of the Reverend Jay: "I give unto my grandson Ernest Jay the portrait of his father my late son William."[2] This image may have been the painting by Fraser, but had it been it was likely to be described as a miniature. In fact, the reference to this work comes in a list of several paintings of family members then hanging in the residence in Bath.

AN ARTIST AND A FRIEND

William Etty was a dear friend of Jay by Etty's own testimony. A painter who gained prominence in his lifetime, Etty left a full record of his life in copious correspondence. Among his letters, there are references to Jay revealing a close relationship during their studies in London and for a few years thereafter. These comments by Etty suggest some measure of Jay as a person and as a friend.

Etty was the son of Methodists, people of good, sturdy faith. Born in

---

[1] "Charles Fraser's Account Book" in Severens and Wyrick, 124.

[2] "Will of the Reverend William Jay of Bath," May 31, 1849, London Public Record Office, London.

York, he was the seventh of ten children, only five of whom survived infancy. His father was a miller and baker of modest means. When Etty was eleven years old, he was apprenticed to a printer. By 1805 a solicitous older brother and a wealthy uncle gave him the support he needed to go to London to pursue his goal to become a painter. He was by then eighteen years old, a late start on any career in that era, and the achievement of his success would come slow and hard. He entered the Royal Academy in 1806, and in 1807 he pursued a year of study with Thomas Lawrence, a great portrait painter of the age.

By 1809 Etty had inherited funds from his uncle allowing him to be financially independent. He took rooms in London and worked doggedly, learning his craft in the life drawing studios at the Royal Academy and preparing works for exhibition. In these early years, he often accepted commissions for portraits, the bread-and-butter work of many painters. But Etty's goal was history painting, then considered the most elevated of the subject categories, ranking first above landscape, portraiture, and still life. He would devote himself to classical and biblical subjects, in particular classical histories featuring the nude form.

Etty came to be known as the greatest English painter of nudes in the nineteenth century. His use of this subject was often criticized, a matter he found bewildering. He observed, "[M]y character has been much misunderstood by some...because I have preferred painting the unsophisticated human form divine, male and female [unclothed], in preference to the production of the loom [clothing].... I have been accused of being a shocking immoral man!"[3]

Etty and Jay came to London as students at about the same time. They may have met in the circles of artists, or they may have become acquainted in the community of religious dissenters. In London, Etty attended Surrey Chapel where, according to Jay's brother Cyrus, he "frequently heard Mr. Jay preach, and was one of his greatest admirers."[4] Etty was five years older than Jay, and apparently they were quite different in character. Jay was an affable fellow, and Etty was very reserved, described as a shy man "more at ease with one person at a time with whom he had learned to be intimate." A sober man,

[3] "Obituary—William Etty, Esq. R. A.," *Gentleman's Magazine*, Jan. 1850:98.
[4] C. Jay, *Recollections*, 102, 104.

he suffered only one addiction and that was to English tea with milk.[5]

By 1816 Etty resolved to tour the continent, with Paris as a pass-by and Rome as the goal. With the end of the Napoleonic Wars in 1815, it was again possible for English artists to accomplish the grand tour regarded by most as a necessary component of their education. At the beginning of his journey in early September, Etty confessed to a cousin that all was not well. He wrote, "I hope I shall like Italy better than Paris.... I wish my friend Jay could have come with me: I should have enjoyed the tour much more."[6]

Etty returned from this unhappy trip abroad by early 1817, and later in that same year Jay left for America. Etty labored on in London, and slowly he began to achieve recognition at the Royal Academy. In 1820 and 1821, his large history compositions drew attention and praise. In 1822 he again toured the continent, first to Paris, then Rome, and finally Venice. Venice pleased him most of all because he felt a kinship with the works of the great Venetian Renaissance masters Titian, Tintoretto, and Veronese. His affinity for this place and this art was rewarded by his election to an honorary membership in the academy at Venice. By early 1824, he was back home in England and finally the recipient of awards that many thought were long overdue. In that year, he was made an associate of the Royal Academy, and four years later he was promoted to the rank of academician.

It is certain that there was communication between Etty and Jay in 1817–1818, as Jay was constructing a theater in Savannah. Paintings by Etty were commissioned as part of the ornament for the interior. The opening of the theater in December 1818 with the display of Etty's work may have occasioned his nomination for honorary membership in the South Carolina Academy of Fine Arts in 1821–1822. In a letter to his brother, Etty recalled that "Charleston, America, gave me the first Diploma; Venice the second."[7]

Several references to Jay in Etty's letters offer evidence of a close friendship that began and flourished during their student years in London, with Etty's observation that Jay became "essential" to his "happiness."[8] That affection, joined to the record of Etty's work for the Jay family, argued for the

---

[5] Robinson, 119; Farr, 23.

[6] Gilchrist, 1:64–65.

[7] Ibid., 163.

[8] Etty to his brother Walter, Jan. 30, 1823, William Etty Collection, Manuscript Collections, British Library, London (hereafter BLMC).

prospect that he painted a portrait of this dear friend, probably in 1817 in the months before Jay left for America.

ETTY'S PORTRAITS OF JAYS AND BOLTONS

Before Etty gained prominence as a member of the Royal Academy, he painted at least four portraits of members of the Jay family: the Reverend Jay; Anne Jay Bolton, the preacher's first child posed with her two oldest children; Anne's husband, Robert Bolton; and Arabella Jay, the preacher's third child and second daughter. Etty's biographer Dennis Farr was a great admirer of these early portraits of the Jays and the Boltons, taking these as evidence that "Etty's artistic powers were now increasing steadily, certainly in portraiture."[9]

Portrait of the Reverend Jay, 1817. From the time of his beginnings as Billy Jay the Boy Preacher to the end of his life as the Dissident Divine of Bath, the Reverend Jay had his portrait drawn and painted many times. Often these images were engraved and sold in bookshops to his many admirers. Of all of these portraits, none is more accomplished or better known than one painted by Etty in 1817, identified as an image of the Reverend Jay in his forty-eighth year.

Bolton family records report, "Etty, the artist, then rising into reputation, was a guest for some weeks in Mr. Bolton's house in Liverpool, painting family portraits. His likeness of Mr. Jay, placed in the Royal Academy Exhibition of the year, and engraved twice, was painted at this time."[10] Etty's first biographer, Alexander Gilchrist, observed that this likeness had caused the Reverend Jay to erupt in poetry, which was sent to the artist and "carefully preserved by the flattered painter." Titled "Lines Written on Seeing My Portrait by Mr. Etty, Designed for Mr. and Mrs. Bolton, At Liverpool. Sept. 13, 1817," the verse begins, "Etty, 'tis done! The very man breathes now;/ I feel the likeness, and my friends avow."[11]

According to Cyrus, "Etty always considered this portrait as one of his best productions in that line." The work was exhibited at the Royal Academy in 1818, and Cyrus recalled that the painting was in the possession of Robert Bolton at the time of the death of the Reverend Jay in 1853. But, it is now

---

[9] Farr, 25.

[10] R. Bolton, *Genealogical...Account of the Family of Bolton*, 155.

[11] Gilchrist, 1:77; Rev. Jay, *Autobiography,* 1855 ed., 2:220–21.

lost, known only in painted and engraved copies.[12]

Portraits of Robert Bolton and Anne Jay Bolton, 1817. According to Bolton records, "some family pictures, by Etty, of the Royal Academy of England" hung in Pelham Priory, the Bolton home in West Chester, New York, after 1837. These included a portrait of Robert Bolton and one of his wife, Anne, with the two eldest children. This work was accomplished while Etty was a guest of the Boltons during a period of prosperity for the family when Robert was directing the affairs of the Liverpool branch of the Savannah cotton house in 1816–1820.[13]

Likely the portraits of Robert and Anne were done in 1817, near the date of the portrait of the Reverend Jay. Etty's image of Robert includes a distant view to a ship at sea, a reference to his occupation engaging ships for the transport of cotton from Savannah to the mills in the region of Liverpool and Manchester. Anne is shown with her first two children, Robert and Anne, ages three and two in 1817. These two portraits remained at Pelham Priory after Robert and Anne returned to England in 1850. Subsequently they passed from family hands to the New York Historical Society, and in 1975 they were granted on long-term loan to the Telfair Academy to be displayed at the Richardson-Owens-Thomas House.[14]

Portrait of Arabella Jay, c. 1817. Cyrus described the image of Arabella as "exquisitely beautiful," noting that it had been praised by Lawrence, the master of portraiture with whom Etty had studied.[15] The size and style of this work is unlike the other family portraits. It is small in format; the figure is animated, even coquettish; and the style is painterly and coloristic in the manner of Lawrence. But, although different in character, it is likely that the image of Arabella was done at the same time as the others in 1817 when this middle daughter was twenty-two years old. In his will, the Reverend Jay conveyed the portrait of Arabella to her. As she had no children, the painting

---

[12] C. Jay, *Recollections*, 98; Graves, 3:65. Etty's portrait of the Reverend Jay, painted in 1817, was engraved by James Thomson for the *European Magazine* (Jan. 1819) and by W. [William] Holl for the frontispiece of the reverend's autobiography (1854).

[13] R. Bolton, *History of the County of Westchester*, 1:555; R. Bolton, *History of the Several Towns...of Westchester*, 2:91; R. Bolton, *Genealogical...Account of the Family of Bolton*, 155.

[14] Zimmerman, "The Boltons Return to Savannah," *SMN*, Mar. 23, 1975.

[15] C. Jay, *Recollections*, 98–99.

remained in the line of her husband's family until 1956 when a great-great-niece bequeathed it to the National Gallery, London.[16] It is now in the collection of the Tate Gallery, London.

A PORTRAIT OF A GENTLEMAN, PERHAPS THE ARCHITECT WILLIAM JAY

When the portrait of Arabella was exhibited at the Royal Academy in 1819, it was joined by a work titled *Portrait of a Gentleman.* A painting known by that title had been for many years in the collection of the York Art Gallery. Attributed to Etty and dated 1818–1820, its provenance was unknown. Farr said of this work, "The painting is of exceptionally fine quality, and if by Etty, probably dates from about 1818–1820. The sitter bears some resemblance to the Rev. Robert Bolton, and may be another member of that family."[17]

In 1950 James V. McDonough mused on the possibility of the existence of a portrait of Jay by Etty. In 1983 Hanna H. Lerski was the first to propose the York Art Gallery's *Portrait of a Gentleman* as an image of Jay. In 1985 this portrait was identified as Jay and published in *Architecture, Men, Women and Money in America 1600–1860* by Roger G. Kennedy, who took this image to be that of the architect and evidence of Etty's affection for his friend. Finally, in 2011 the curators of a survey of Etty's work at the York Art Gallery affirmed the claims that this painting is by Etty and that it does depict the architect Jay.[18]

This attribution confirms this evidence: By the testimony of the Reverend Jay, we know that a portrait of his eldest son was made. Next, there is ample evidence of a close relationship with Etty, who in 1817 painted four portraits of members of Jay's family. The painting titled *Portrait of a Gentleman* was shown at the Royal Academy in 1819 in the company of the depiction of Arabella. A plausible date for this work is 1817, the same year in which Etty painted the other family portraits.

The subject is a young man in Regency garb, fashionably done up with a coat of broad lapels, a vest, and an elaborate cravat tied at the neck. The hair is cut short, combed forward and tousled, with long sideburns, in the style of

---

[16] Farr, 171.

[17] Graves, 3:65; Farr, 25.

[18] McDonough, 119; Lerski, 28; R. G. Kennedy, 164–65; Burnage, Hallett, and Turner, 12 fig. 7.

the period. The features resemble those of the Reverend Jay in the engraved versions of the lost Etty portrait—a prominent nose, low arching eyebrows, and a good solid jaw. This is a good-looking fellow, intelligent and spirited, who might be in his mid-twenties.

In 1817 Jay was twenty-five years old. He had endeavored to establish his career in England but without much success. Later that year, he would depart for America. Perhaps Etty placed the portraits of Arabella and William together on exhibition at the Royal Academy in 1819 for these reasons: The painting of Arabella had drawn comment as an example of his accomplishment in the art of portraiture, and the image of her older brother William was a reminder of an absence borne with difficulty by his family and by his dear friend the artist.

CHAPTER 6

"MEET ME AT THE PLUM-CAKE": JAY'S ALBION CHAPEL

In 1816 Jay saw the completion of the Albion Chapel in London, the only one of his designs to be constructed before he left for Savannah, Georgia. In 1827 this building was designated a praiseworthy "metropolitan improvement" in a city that had been busy about the business of making improvements. Soon this handsome domed structure, known fondly as "the Plum-cake," became a landmark in the district of Moorfields, a newly developed area at the northern boundary of the old City of London.[1]

This was the home of a congregation of Presbyterians known as Seceders, affiliated with the United Associate Synod of Scotland. This group had broken with the Church of Scotland in 1740 over the issue of the appointment of ministers. Because it was a renegade assembly and because members held many beliefs in common with English dissenters, the Seceders were often allied with other nonconformists. The Albion Chapel was frequently the site of meetings of Independents/Congregationalists, Baptists, and Methodists when they gathered in London for denominational conventions or when representatives of these groups came together to promote shared interests, such as the abolition of slavery and the promotion of foreign missions.

Although it was made for a sect of Scottish Seceders, it seems clear that Jay gained this commission with the support of his father. At the opening of the building in November 1816, the Reverend Jay preached the evening sermon in the Albion Chapel.[2] His appearance at the opening of any chapel guaranteed a large assembly and a substantial donation toward the debt incurred by the project. In this case, the Reverend Jay may have urged the appointment of his son in promise for his appearance at the opening, as he would do later for a project in Cheltenham.

This chapel was built for the ministry of the Reverend Alexander

[1] Elmes, *Metropolitan Improvements*, 170; "Volunteer Reminiscences," *Table Book*, June 1827:56.

[2] "The Late Rev. Alex. Fletcher, D.D.," *Mother's Magazine*, Nov. 1860:245.

Fletcher. Fletcher had come to London from Scotland in 1811 as a young man to take up the ministry of a very small meeting house near London Bridge. His success was quick and remarkable. Members of the congregation pledged support for a new building, as they were obliged to do since nonconforming groups received no state funds. Land was acquired in the new development district of Moorfields, Jay was engaged as the architect, the foundation stone was laid in November 1815, and the building was raised at a cost near £10,000.[3]

THE DESIGN OF A DISSIDENT CHAPEL

The Albion Chapel was charming in its simple but pleasing form, but it was remarkable in the history of religious architecture. Jay was working with a building type that had not been well defined, and he brought to this problem uncommon intelligence and creativity. This was a structure made for a nonconforming sect, shaped by the events of the eighteenth-century evangelical revival that had brought hundreds and then thousands to these ministries. It was not a church, not in name nor in design.

Among the several strictures that set nonconforming groups apart from the Established Church was the naming of these places of worship. They were called meeting houses, or simply meetings, or chapels. They did not take their names from the panoply of saints, but rather from locations, such as streets, or from neutral labels, as in this case. "Albion" is a word of Latin origin, from "alb" (mountain) or "albus" (white), used from ancient times to refer to England. Another tradition links the word to Gaelic, in which "Albany" (hilly land) is the name of Scotland, an apt reference for this chapel.

As for the design, early in their history nonconforming groups had met in rooms in private homes. When the Methodist revivals came in the mid-eighteenth century, the crush of numbers resulted in meetings in the out-of-doors. There were no houses or halls large enough to contain the gathered crowds, sometimes recorded in numbers near fifty thousand. When structures were raised, they had the simple requirements of a space with seating to accommodate the congregation, focused to a pulpit from which the gospel was preached. In the matter of style, nonconformists were firm believers in the

[3] Goodfellow, 225.

Protestant critiques of the Roman Church. They opposed all pomp and ceremony and ostentatious ornament. Meeting houses had no use for spaces for procession and performance of a liturgy; embellishment with sculpture, painting, and stained glass was an abomination.

In the wake of the success of the evangelical revival, there was a rush to build nonconformist chapels in the late eighteenth and early nineteenth centuries. But given their very simple requirements and the generally very parsimonious budgets for construction, professional architects were rarely employed. Most often the structure was sketched by the minister or a member of the congregation and raised by an obliging builder. The architect-designed chapel was rare.

As inspiration for Jay, there were at least two notable examples of accommodations for dissenters in London. Not far north of the Albion Chapel were George Whitefield's Tabernacle built in 1756 and John Wesley's Chapel built in 1777. Both were large rectangular buildings with interiors of simple form, with seating on a ground floor and in galleries above, oriented to a pulpit. Jay knew these structures, because they were iconic among dissenters and well familiar to the Reverend Jay. In terms of function, these were the precedents for Jay's design, but it was left to him to forge a uniquely satisfying solution to the problem of how to design a modern meeting house. To his experience of these plain spaces, he brought an understanding of the significance of architecture and the history of that art conveyed in the lectures of John Soane at the Royal Academy.

In *Metropolitan Improvements; Or, London in the Nineteenth Century* (1827), Elmes commented on Jay's building, and the structure was portrayed in a steel engraving by Thomas Hosmer Shepherd. Elmes observed, "Albion Chapel, Moorfields, is a neat and unaffected building, with a pretty little diastyle portico in antis [recessed] of the Ionic order, designed by a young architect of the name of Jay. The roof gives it somewhat the air of a theatre, but it possesses a character of original thinking in its design that is highly pleasing."[4] Several images of the domed chapel survive, and these confirm Elmes's assessment that this was "a neat and unaffected building" and rather like a theater.

The theater reference is apt. Jay would later design two theaters, one

[4] Elmes, *Metropolitan Improvements*, 170.

constructed in Savannah in 1818 and one only proposed for Augusta, Georgia, in 1822. And he would claim the design of a third, the "New English Opera" in London. In 1815 plans were announced to build an English opera house in the Strand, and it is likely that Jay made a proposal for that project, which he did not win, just as he was designing the Albion Chapel. To resolve a plan for a nonconformist chapel, a scheme for a theater offered useful solutions. These were common considerations: accommodate a large audience (in this chapel, room for one thousand people), draw the focus to a single area (here, a pulpit), supply appropriate sources of light, and provide for easy and safe entry and exit of the space.

At the exterior, the Albion Chapel gave the appearance of a large, one-story structure of oblong form, rendered in brick, with a central hall topped by a dome. Fronting Finsbury Pavement, the portico was a pedimented Greek temple front with engaged piers flanking free-standing Ionic columns. The entry was raised, approached by steps, and recessed. At each side of the entry, the wall was animated by a tall, blind, round-headed arch. On London Wall Street, there was a side entrance to the vestibule. On this flank of the building, there were three tall, blind, round-headed arches pierced in their upper portions by windows. The opposite side of the building was likely identical, but early depictions of the chapel show that a neighboring building came to abut that wall.

Some views of the structure suggest that the portico was little used because an iron gate closed across this entry. It would seem that, by habit or convenience, entry to the building was gained through the side door of the vestibule located on London Wall Street, perhaps because the fronting street was a broad and busy passway. The building was surmounted by an entablature and an attic with a horseshoe-shaped superstructure, behind which was posed a dome over the meeting space. At the center of the dome was an oculus ("eye") topped by a very low lantern, which admitted light from the center of the roof into the room. The dome was pierced at its base by twelve half-round windows, allowing light to spill under the dome.

Little is known of the interior. The entry led into a rectangular vestibule, and from this chamber one moved into the open meeting room or upstairs to the gallery. This was a congregational space fitted to accommodate at least one thousand people with focus to a pulpit. An early observer wrote, "The interior is very plain, without the least attempt at ornament; the plan is in the form of a horseshoe, the end enclosed with a wall. The whole building is surrounded with a gallery, sustained on Ionic columns."[5] The raised horseshoe form of the attic story suggests that the meeting room was shaped rather like an amphitheater, curved at its rear and flat at the front of the room behind the pulpit. The dome probably rested on pendentives (wedge-shaped elements) at the corners of the front of the hall and then rose from the curve of the horseshoe at the rear.

The dome was a happy solution for covering the hall, both aesthetically and acoustically. This feature may have been suggested by Surrey Chapel, just over the River Thames in Southwark. For Jay's whole life, his father preached in Surrey Chapel for four weeks each summer—it was the London home of the Reverend Jay. When it was built in 1783, it was the largest nonconformist meeting hall in the city, accommodating two thousand people. When the Reverend Jay spoke here, the place filled to overflowing.

Surrey Chapel, located on what was then called Great Surrey Street, was designed and built by the Reverend Rowland Hill. It was an octagon, constructed of brick, covered by a segmented dome, and topped by a prominent lantern that directed strong light down into the well of the space and to the region of the pulpit. Windows ringed the lower and upper galleries, and seating was arranged at both levels. The pulpit was placed somewhat off center, with a great organ behind to accompany the spirited singing featured at evangelical gatherings. The virtue of the plan was that, in this very large assembly hall, all attending were not far from the pulpit. No doubt Jay knew Surrey Chapel well, particularly during his student years in London; his friend the painter William Etty came here. In this setting, Jay could appreciate the ability of a domed space to bring a sense of intimacy to a large gathering.

Jay's chapel was, as Elmes said, full of "a character of original thinking."[6] It was a refined design in the Grecian style, spare in its decoration, and attentive to the needs of a nonconformist assembly. It was expressed in simple shapes, clear volumes, and tasteful ornament, rather like the best of Jay's work to come.

---

[5] Allen, *History and Antiquities of London*, 3:419.

[6] Elmes, *Metropolitan Improvements*, 170.

THE NEIGHBORHOOD

The Albion Chapel was remarkable as a building design, and it was important in another aspect. This was among the first public buildings to be constructed in an urban development project in the district of Moorfields. The plan for this region had been conceived in the late eighteenth century by George Dance the Younger, who served as surveyor for London from 1768 until his death in 1825. It would take several years for Dance's scheme to be realized. This area had a long history as a soggy landscape, with moors (Moor Fields, later Moorfields) and marshes or fens (Fensbury, later Finsbury). By the early sixteenth century, attempts had been made to drain this area, and for a time this was the location of a large public park. In the late seventeenth century, the region just to the north of the old London Wall was occupied by Bethlehem Hospital, the asylum for the mentally ill known as "Bedlam."

For this project, Dance was inspired by the work of the John Woods Elder and Younger in Bath. On the site of old Finsbury Manor, he proposed a circus, a large oval park that came to be called Finsbury Circus. On its northern perimeter was the London Institution, the city's first public library, a much-praised structure begun in 1815 and completed in 1819. At the south of this park, the old Bethlehem Hospital was pulled down, and the Albion Chapel rose on that site. In an unusual confluence of talent, these two prominent buildings were designed by students of David Riddall Roper, William Brooks at the London Institution and Jay at the Albion Chapel.

THE LATER LIFE OF THE ALBION CHAPEL

The Albion Chapel served a group of Seceders for half a century. A noteworthy moment in the life of this place came in 1840 with the ordination of David Livingstone, a Scot just then beginning his service in Africa under the auspices of the London Missionary Society. By 1850 the ministry at the Albion Chapel began to falter, and in 1866 the congregation was disbanded. In 1879 the structure was demolished and replaced by an office complex.

Dance's plan for the reclamation of Moorfields was a great success. Shortly after the construction of the Albion Chapel, this became a very fashionable neighborhood. Wealthy professionals were drawn to this area of fine new homes proximate to the center of London and within reach of a magnificent park. Doctors and surgeons moved their practices to this region. A cluster of nonconforming places of worship appeared here, because these were not generally allowed within the precincts of the old City of London. So, here to join the Albion Chapel came a Unitarian chapel, a Welsh Baptist chapel, a Jewish synagogue, and St. Mary's Catholic Chapel, all built in the 1820s. None of these early nineteenth-century buildings remain.

CHAPTER 7

THE LESSONS OF LOSING: WELLINGTON ROOMS AND NEW ENGLISH OPERA HOUSE

In April 1822, Jay was in Augusta, Georgia, presenting his proposal for a new theater. By then he had few prospects in Savannah and Charleston, South Carolina, and he was looking for opportunities elsewhere. Augusta held promise for him. The town had been founded in 1736 by James Edward Oglethorpe just three years after the establishment of Savannah. Located at the navigable head of the Savannah River, this place had grown prosperous through trade, first tobacco then cotton.

Jay was received with some enthusiasm. The *Augusta Chronicle and Georgia Gazette* reported,

> Mr. Jay, the celebrated architect, is now in our town, on his way to Washington City [Washington, D.C.]; and we fondly hope that the inhabitants of this place, will give him an opportunity of erecting in it some monument of taste worthy of himself, and corresponding with the rising importance of Augusta. He built the Church in Moorsfield [*sic*], the New English Opera, in the Strand, London, and the Wellington Rooms, Pleasant Square, Liverpool; but is better known to most of us, on account of those elegant structures he has reared in Savannah.[1]

There was in this newspaper announcement a large dose of hyperbole. Of course, Jay did build "the Church in Moorsfield," the Albion Chapel in Moorfields, London (1815–1816). But he did not build "the New English Opera, in the Strand, London" (1815–1816) or "the Wellington Rooms, Pleasant Hill, Liverpool" (1814–1815). Both of these were competitions that Jay entered but did not win. In both cases, he learned the hard lesson that the practice of architecture was often more about politics than about art.

Why would Jay have made the claim that he built the Wellington Rooms and the New English Opera House? Surely a goal was to enhance his résumé while he was bidding for work in Augusta, and he may have guessed that in

[1] "Mr. Jay, the celebrated architect…," Apr. 22, 1822.

Georgia he could get by with these white lies. Besides, it is likely that the drawings for these projects were in his portfolio, available for viewing should anyone ask.

By the early nineteenth century in England, a conception of the professional architect was taking hold. In previous eras, a builder was chosen based on personal relationships or the testimony of friends. In this new age, when a project was announced, architects responded by submitting drawings. And, it was presumed that a selection would be made based on the merits of the design.

In these circumstances, architects expected to build their practices by winning competitions. Some won many, and some won few. For Jay at the beginning of his career, we have the records of one win (the Albion Chapel) and two losses (the Wellington Rooms and the New English Opera House). Given the report in the Augusta newspaper in 1822, the particulars of which were surely supplied by Jay, it is likely that these three competitions accounted for the sum of his efforts to establish a practice in England following his articled pupilage. It was not a promising beginning. As his friend William Etty said of the start of their careers, "Business disappointed both of us."[2] These early disappointments certainly contributed to Jay's decision to abandon his native land to make the long journey across the Atlantic.

THE WELLINGTON ROOMS IN LIVERPOOL

An account of the competition for the design of the Wellington Rooms in Liverpool survives in the diary of Thomas Rickman, one of seven architects to submit proposals for this project. From this record, we gain a sense of how contests proceeded, and we learn why some battles were won and some were lost.

Rickman began his report on January 21, 1814, with the news that the search for a site was underway.[3] This project was typical for the era. These were assembly rooms (a ballroom, a card room, and a supper room) to be built by public subscription for the various amusements of members of a very prosperous merchant class in Liverpool. The city had grown rich fast in the late eighteenth century. It was the chief port of entry for trade with Ireland, the West Indies, and the United States. In particular, cotton came to Liverpool

---

[2] Gilchrist, 1:64–65.

[3] T. Rickman, diary, Jan. 21, 1814, RIBA (hereafter cited in text).

from the American South and made its way to the mill towns of Lancashire where textiles were produced to be shipped out to world markets. Liverpool merchants were clever and industrious workers, and they were serious about their recreation according to this report of 1832: "The whole [of the Wellington Rooms] are appropriated to the amusements of the upper classes of society, as subscription balls, assemblies, and occasionally fancy-dress balls. These amusements are no where greater favourites than in Liverpool, where successful enterprise furnishes the means of splendour, and the disposition to display."[4]

On February 12, Rickman noted in his diary that he planned to propose "a Doric Front as there is none in the Town," evidence of the appetite in Liverpool for the Grecian style just then being promoted in London as the modern mode. Some months later, other competition drawings began to appear. On September 30, Rickman wrote, "W Jay has sent in a Perspective View of his Rooms full of false drawing & false shading/ indeed I am surprised how a man of such poor execution should set up for an Architect for his Compositions are worse than his Execution in many respects."

In 1814 Jay was just twenty-two years of age, at least seven years younger than any of the other competitors. All were more experienced than he, and some had a hometown advantage. There is no evidence that Jay was prompted to enter this contest by friends of his father, although that is possible. Robert Spear of nearby Manchester, an influential merchant in the cotton trade, was a close family friend. And, Robert Bolton, an heir to a Savannah cotton house, had married Jay's sister Anne in 1811 although Robert and Anne did not move to Liverpool until 1816.

Rickman's comments about Jay's composition and drawing skills can be attributed to meanness. This was, after all, a competition. And Rickman, who had been established in Liverpool for at least seven years, had an early expectation that he would take the prize. He was quick to criticize each submission as it arrived. By October 8, Rickman seemed confident that he would prevail, but just two days later came a hint that Jay's plan had captured some advantage. This did not please Rickman, who now doubted that his entry would be accepted because "Jay's plan can be executed cheaper/ however the convenience of his bears no comparison with mine."

More proposals arrived, and the competition became more intense.

---

[4] Allen, *Lancashire Illustrated*, 106.

Rickman reported on November 2, "[S]ome very fine things are come in. [Joseph Michael] Gandy very fine but far too expensive. [George or Joseph] Gwilt the same & both not good elevations/ [Robert] Lugar good & cheaper but too tame & flat." But, next came trouble.

THE SPOILER: EDMUND AIKIN

On November 3, the game changed. Rickman wrote, "We have today from Edm[un]d Aikin a Plan & Elevation so very superior that I think there is no doubt of its Execution. I have rough estimated it & think it may be done for very little more than they can spare. The Elevation is all from [James] Stuart & has more of Classical Composition in it than any I have seen." Now Jay was sunk.

Aikin was a trained architect, but he did not have a record of building. However, in 1810 he published *An Essay on the Doric Order of Architecture*, which had helped to propel the Grecian style to prominence. And, in Liverpool he had the support of William Roscoe. Roscoe was a successful author, best known for a prodigious study of Lorenzo de' Medici published in 1796. Often called the "Lorenzo of Liverpool," Roscoe was a connoisseur of art and literature, a founding member and patron of Liverpool's library, art museum, art academy, and botanic garden. He was a friend of Aikin's father, also a noted author—and he had promised to secure the commission for the Wellington Rooms for Aikin.[5]

In very short order, Aikin won the day. Rickman wrote on November 5, "The Wellington Com[mittee] met today & have approved Aikin." Jay must have been surprised, even stunned. It was a bitter loss, probably the first of his professional life. He did not take the disappointment well and hurled a criticism of Aikin's design. Rickman recorded on November 11, "W Jay objects to Aikins Elevation/ he says Soane always cautioned them in his Lectures against circular porticos as I suppose not keeping the Weather out/ but I do not think that a good objection here as no one is obliged at any time to stand in it for shelter."

Jay's comment is odd and grudging, and his meaning is not clear. Nothing appears in the transcriptions of Soane's lectures that speaks to the hazards of circular porticos. And, just a few years later, Jay would use a circular portico

[5] Aikin, 103.

as the central feature of perhaps the most beautiful house he built in Savannah, the Bulloch House. But here he was angry. He had come close to winning this commission, and now it was clear that he had lost. The project was awarded to Aikin, and the work began on January 21, 1815.

THE AFTERMATH

The building was a grand success. Opened in 1816, it was early in a long line of Grecian monuments in Liverpool. And it was well suited to its purposes, as described here in 1823: "This [is an] extensive suit of assembly-rooms...at the upper end of Mount Pleasant. The front, which is of stone, is in the Grecian style of architecture." However, Jay's critique of the portico was vindicated. Not many years after the opening of the building, the lovely open porch was walled up, occasioning this comment in 1832: "The circular portico in front was originally open...[but] was found practically inconvenient. In consequence, the spaces between the beautiful Corinthian columns have been closed up by a dead stone wall, and a door has been placed in front, the dimensions and appearance of which would be much more appropriate to a house of correction."[6] The building survived, one of only a very few from the Grecian moment in English architecture to have done so. Jay had made a good showing in this competition, but the cards were stacked against him. He lacked experience, but more significantly he lacked a Mr. Roscoe.

THE NEW ENGLISH OPERA HOUSE IN LONDON

Despite his claim that he designed a London theater, "the New English Opera, in the Strand, London," Jay was not the architect for this building, and there is no ready evidence that he entered the competition. However, based on his claim in Augusta, it seems likely that he did submit a design for this structure in 1815. When the commission was awarded, the project involved two of his closest friends with whom he might have collaborated on a proposal. Then, there is this: Why did Jay make the long and difficult journey to Georgia if his only commitment there was the completion of a house for Richard Richardson, a business associate and brother-in-law of Jay's brother-in-law Robert Bolton? The success of the residence he had designed for Richardson may have prompted some quick commissions for other private homes,

---

[6] Kaye, 167; Allen, *Lancashire Illustrated*, 106.

but Jay wished to make his mark in the design of public buildings. Savannah had been preparing for some years to build a theater. If Jay had drawn a proposal for a London theater, he did not journey to Savannah to look for work. Work was waiting for him.

A proposal and set of drawings for the New English Opera House could have been adapted easily and quickly to the needs of Savannah. In developing a plan for a London project, Jay would have surveyed the concerns of modern theaters: the preferred arrangement for the stage and seating, the prevailing fashion of interior ornament, new methods and materials of construction, and where supplies could be secured. That preparation would go a long way to explain why Jay gained the commission for a theater in Savannah less than four months after his arrival in late 1817 and how he accomplished such a complex assignment in seven months.

THE CONTEST

In London, a program to foster "native talent" in opera and musical theater began in the late eighteenth century. Opera was popular in London, but most of it was imported from the continent, particularly from Italy. A persistent lament at the time was that England dominated in many endeavors but lagged in the arts. A venue for English performers of opera had been founded in London by Samuel Arnold, organist and composer to George III. Arnold located his program in the old Lyceum Theatre in the Strand, a building of 1765 that had housed various sorts of entertainment.[7] Around 1794 he rebuilt a portion of that structure. But he was unsuccessful in gaining a license for his musical theater because the owners of the "winter theaters" of Drury Lane and Covent Garden wished to limit their competition.

By 1809 his son Samuel James Arnold had taken over his father's enterprise, and the younger Arnold did secure a license for a "summer theater" to operate as "an English opera house," a place where "native talent" could flourish.[8] At the close of the season in September 1815, the younger Arnold announced that plans were in place to raise a new building on the site of the old

[7] Buildings at this site were known variously as Theatre Royal, Lyceum; Theatre Royal, English Opera House; English Opera House; Royal Lyceum Theatre (D. Howard, 144).

[8] Britton and Pugin, 1:274–76.

Lyceum as "an entirely new, airy and commodious theatre." Construction began immediately, and the new theater was opened to the public on June 15, 1816.[9]

A LIKELY COLLABORATION

In 1815 Jay had established an office in London, taken up the work of the Albion Chapel, and suffered the loss of the contest for the Wellington Rooms in Liverpool. He was certainly eager for work, but what is the evidence that he entered the competition for the New English Opera House in London? First, there is his later claim that he had built this building, and then there are notices that two of his very close friends were chosen for this project. A plausible conclusion is that Jay advanced a proposal as principal architect with two associates whose talents were directed to supporting roles. Jay lost, but his two collaborators prevailed.

Jay's friends who participated in this project were Albinus Martin, trained as an architect and civil engineer, and the painter William Etty. Many years later, Martin wrote to Etty, remembering with fondness their student days, the "old times," of "Billy Jay, dirty gingerbread, the one glass of excellent Sherry, and endless number of cups of no less excellent tea." Clearly these three were close friends. There is ample evidence of Jay's relationship with Etty, and their friendship would be sustained through the time Jay worked in the American South. In 1815 Etty was still a student at the Royal Academy, seven years distant from the attention that would ultimately propel him to a measure of fame. Martin and Jay may have attempted an early professional relationship because a list of artists working in London in 1817 shows that both of these men established offices at Gray's Inn Square, London.[10]

A collaboration of Jay, Martin, and Etty seems probable. All three were young, relatively inexperienced, and hungry for work. None of them had any record of accomplishment in theatrical design and ornament, but each one could bring unique talents to this project. It seems likely that they submitted a proposal in 1815 for the design of the New English Opera House with Jay as lead architect, Martin as civil engineer, and Etty as interior decorator. When the results of the competition were announced, Samuel Beazley was

[9] Nicholson, 256; A. E. Wilson, 34–35; "New English Opera-House," *New Monthly Magazine and Universal Register*, July 1, 1816:542.

[10] Gilchrist, 2:278–79; Elmes, "List of Artists," *Annals*, Jan. 1818:586.

named as the principal architect. Martin was appointed as "second architect," and he was charged with "accommodation and convenience, facility of ingress and egress, and security against every accident." Etty was selected to provide ornaments for the "first circle of boxes," classical scenes "illustrating the history of music."[11]

Martin had trained first as an architect and subsequently as a civil engineer. In 1815 he must have been at the beginning of his career, as Jay was. The elements of the building design credited to him included the plans for entry and exit, circulation, and safety. Likely it was he who devised an ingenious arrangement of areas of seating linked to separate entries. This traffic plan was in response to a growing concern for safety in crowded theaters, to allow speedy exit in the event of disturbances, such as the occasional riot or the regrettably frequent fires. Martin also proposed fireproofing measures, such as the use of cast iron columns as supports on the interior and an elaborate water delivery system intended to suppress fire. Martin probably planned another remarkable element of this structure, as "The ceiling is unusually light; it is composed of a series of arches, springing from slender columns."[12]

Etty painted a series of classical images to decorate the first circle of boxes. At the opening, one reviewer called Etty's contribution "elegant" and "beautiful."[13] Because the New English Opera House was dedicated to music, Etty's paintings conveyed the history of that art, featuring Apollo, among whose several responsibilities were music and song, and the Muses, the very origin of the word "music." In technique, Etty's scenes must have been *basso relievo* (paintings in imitation of low relief sculpture), painted *en grisaille* (in monochrome, usually gray or brown), very like what he would accomplish for his friend Jay just a few years later for the theater in Savannah.

Arnold the younger, the proprietor of this theater, had a taste for the opulent. In the old Lyceum, he had undertaken a renovation in 1812 in "an ostentatiously elegant style…[the boxes] painted with vermilion border edged

---

[11] "Incidents," *New Monthly Magazine and Universal Register*, Feb. 1, 1816:74; "New English Opera-House," *New Monthly Magazine and Universal Register*, July 1, 1816:542.

[12] Ibid.

[13] "New English Opera-House," *New Monthly Magazine and Universal Register*, July 1, 1816:542.

with gold."[14] The ornament of the new theater was composed of these elements: "The auditory [auditorium] is richly decorated with composition ornaments and scrolls, in burnished and oiled gold. The prevailing colour is salmon, and the interior and backs of the boxes are lined with crimson moreen [wool appearing to be watered silk]; the seats, cushions, &c. are dark green."[15] This ensemble of ornament—good Regency motifs and colors, and Etty's cycle of classical paintings—comes very close to the description of the interior of Jay's Savannah Theater built just two years later.

THE WINNER: THE UNFAIR ADVANTAGE OF AN INSIDER

Plans for a new building at this site on the Strand were announced in September 1815, and the theater opened in June 1816.[16] The competition must have been executed very quickly. Samuel Beazley was selected, a trained architect and an amateur playwright. This was his first commission for a theater, perhaps his first for a building of any sort. When he began this project, he was twenty-nine years old and recently returned from adventures in the Peninsular War. He had written his first play at the age of twelve. His first professional production occurred at the old Lyceum Theatre in 1811, when he was twenty-five, and subsequently he would write over one hundred pieces for the theater.[17]

If Jay participated in this competition, it was, as in Liverpool, not an entirely fair fight. In the theatrical world, Beazley was an insider. Jay, the son of a prominent evangelical preacher—evangelicals were known to abhor the theater—must have been counted as an outsider. Beazley was known at the Lyceum, and there was one particular element of the design that may have caused him to win and Jay to lose.

For this new construction, an existing theater was demolished to retain the site which fronted the Strand. This is the path from Trafalgar Square to Fleet Street, and in Jay's time it was the center of London nightlife and the location of several theaters. But, this site was awkwardly shaped and crowded

[14] Chandler and Gilmartin, 209.
[15] Britton and Pugin, 1:278.
[16] Nicholson, 256–59; A. E. Wilson, 34–35.
[17] "Obituary — Samuel Beazley, Esq.," *Gentleman's Magazine*, Dec. 1851:660.

by nearby structures. Beazley exploited this unusual configuration by designing the ground plan of the building in the shape of "an antique lyre."[18] The symbolism of the lyre, an ancient harp and an emblem of Apollo, signaled the dedication of this building to musical theater.

The form of the lyre was fitted to a site with a narrow frontage. As the lyre swelled from its base, the shape provided for an expansive auditorium. As the neck of the harp was pinched, the sides of the house were drawn closer to the stage. Reviewers often praised the ingenious form of this building and its ability to make a relatively large house, seating at least two thousand, appear to be somewhat more intimate. A few years later at his theater in Savannah, Jay would defend his own properly Greek semicircular plan.

The precautions against fire notwithstanding, the New English Opera House burned to the ground in 1830. It was much lamented. One reviewer said, "We were accustomed to consider the late English Opera House as the best constructed Theatre in London." Arnold wasted no time in rebuilding, and a new theater opened in July 1834. Beazley was again the architect, but with no collaborators this time. By then he was known as the premier theater architect of the time.[19]

LOSSES AND GAINS

For Jay, the loss of the commission for the New English Opera House must have been a bitter defeat. And a familiar one. Again the award of a contract had gone to someone with an unfair home advantage, very like his experience in Liverpool. Still, these two unhappy experiences may well have helped to shape Jay's future. These two contests surely increased Jay's professional skills and added impressive drawings to his portfolio. The experience of proposing a design for a London theater may have been the event that prompted Jay's journey to Savannah. And the assembly hall in Liverpool might have proved useful in the plan for an art academy in Charleston, a building with the same requirements for assembly and display.

---

[18] "New English Opera-House," *New Monthly Magazine and Universal Register*, July 1, 1816:542.

[19] "English Opera House," *Mirror of Literature, Amusement, and Instruction*, Feb. 20, 1830:136. In 1904 the theater was rebuilt, leaving only Beazley's grand Corinthian portico of 1834. That structure was restored in 1996.

PART THREE

JAY IN SAVANNAH, GEORGIA

CHAPTER 8

"MR. JAY HAS GONE TO AMERICA"

In October 1819, this notice appeared in a London journal of the arts: "Mr. Jay has gone to America, to superintend some public buildings of his own designs."[1] By this date, Jay had been in Savannah for almost two years. The announcement of his venture may have been postponed until he was ready to declare that he was in the United States tending to the important business of raising important buildings. The report was brief, but it solves a mystery about why Jay would undertake such a journey.

The legend has persisted that he came to oversee the completion of a house he had designed for Richard Richardson, a Savannah merchant and shipper who was the brother-in-law and business associate of Robert Bolton, the husband of Jay's sister Anne. That would appear to be a flimsy reason to undertake an arduous passage across an unpleasant ocean. Now it seems that Jay had larger prospects in offer if not in hand. His report to the editor of the London journal was that he had secured significant work in Savannah. These were public, not private, projects—and they were several.

JAY'S PROFESSIONAL PROSPECTS IN 1817

Jay arrived in Savannah at the close of 1817. From the evidence of his work before that date, it appears that his decision to leave England had not been taken quickly or carelessly. By 1814 Jay had left the office of David Riddall Roper to establish his own practice in London. The first project for which he applied, unsuccessfully, was the Wellington Rooms in Liverpool in 1814. In 1815 he may have submitted a proposal for the English Opera House in London, which he did not win. The Albion Chapel, London, which he did design, was completed in November 1816. This record suggests that by early 1816 Jay may have come to the unhappy conclusion that his prospects for work in England were not good.

He certainly knew the sad stories of young English architects who had

---

[1] Elmes, "Notice of Works in Hand...Foreign and Domestic," *Annals*, Oct. 1819:487.

been unable to launch professional careers. The habit of hiring a properly trained architect had not yet taken hold in either England or the United States. An architect directed all aspects of design and construction and exacted a percentage of the costs in exchange for his labors. Often the work could be done more cheaply by builders or tradesmen. By the middle of the nineteenth century, the role of architects would be more firmly established. So, in his timing to begin a professional career, Jay was unlucky.

In these early attempts to secure work, Jay surely learned the important lesson that success in his field of endeavor often depended less on one's skills than on personal connections. His two losses had been awarded to individuals with community attachments, and his win was certainly a nod to his famous father. So, where might he find ready clients? A very good possibility was Savannah, Georgia, in the American South. Jay was well familiar with Savannah. As a lad, he had heard the stories told by Cornelius Winter, who knew the early history of the place. And, in 1811 his eldest sister had married the son of a prominent merchant of Savannah who knew the promise of the place.

AMERICA AS A CAREER OPTION

First would come the difficult decision to leave England and make his way to America. In this era, there were a number of books and articles addressing this very question: Could an Englishman, wanting opportunities in the homeland but finding none, achieve success in the United States? In 1819–1820 William Faux, an English farmer, traveled across Maryland, Virginia, the Carolinas, Kentucky, Pennsylvania, Ohio, and Indiana. His advice was this: "To my countrymen disposed to emigrate, but who can, by encreased [*sic*] exertion, keep their unequalled comforts and honour unimpaired, I would say…'*Stay where you are*; for neither America, nor the world have any thing to offer you in exchange!' But to those of *decreasing* means…I would say, '*Haste away*; you have no other refuge from poverty, which, in England, is crime, punishable with neglect, and contempt everlasting!'"[2]

GEORGIA: A "REFUGE FROM POVERTY"

Georgia, the last of the English colonies in North America, had been established for just this very reason, to offer opportunities for remunerative

[2] Faux, 329–30.

labor to men of talent and energy. Founded in 1733, the Georgia settlement had not yet reached the century mark when Jay arrived. Of the thirteen colonies, this last one was an adventure quite unlike the others. To begin, it had come quite late—all of the other English colonies of North America had been established in the seventeenth century. And, unlike the earlier settlements, the primary motive was philanthropy rather than profit. This altogether worthy plan had been formed as a response to an investigation of the condition of London jails. The study had been led by James Edward Oglethorpe, a remarkable fellow who abandoned a brief but distinguished military career to take up a family seat in Parliament in 1722 where he soon began to support various humanitarian causes. In the jails, Oglethorpe found that debtors, often incarcerated for the want of even very small sums, were imprisoned in the company of convicts and felons and in circumstances rife with disease. Further, the number of debtors was large and growing. Oglethorpe concluded that opportunities for work and wages might be found in a new colony in North America.

A proposal to rescue debtors ultimately gave way to something rather more practical and more promising. The colony would be settled not by declared debtors but by tradesmen wanting work, whose skills could contribute to the formation of a successful and independent community. The project was directed by a group of trustees who selected the participants. Passage to Georgia was provided, as were modest grants of land, and provisions of food, articles of clothing, and tools. These settlers were expected to clear the land, raise a town, and undertake certain agricultural efforts for profit in the English market—early hopes rested on the production of silk and wine.

Then came the usual political tactic of enhancing the proposal to assure its success. To the worthy goal of providing employment to men who lacked opportunities in England was added an even more compelling reason for establishing a thirteenth colony. Charles Town (called Charleston by 1783) and the rich plantations of South Carolina faced threats from Spaniards in Florida and from the restless populations of enslaved Africans and disenfranchised Indians. This new colony of Georgia would, the trustees promised, provide a buffer for all of the northern colonies. That pledge changed somewhat the nature of the settlement. A town would be made so that it could be secured against attacks, and it would be populated by men fit and willing to take up arms.

These goals, to provide work and to protect the southern border, were announced in the opening lines of the charter for the colony issued by George II, "Whereas we are credibly informed, that many of our poor subjects are, through misfortune and want of employment, reduced to great necessity...[in America] they might not only gain a comfortable subsistence for themselves and families, but also strengthen our colonies and increase the trade, navigation, and wealth of these our realms." Of threats to the existing colonies, particularly South Carolina, which had been "ravaged by Indian enemies" with "great numbers of the English inhabitants miserably massacred," the king observed, "[W]e think it highly becoming our crown and royal dignity to protect all our loving subjects."[3]

With joined initiatives of philanthropy, commerce, and military preparedness, the proposal for this thirteenth colony met success. Oglethorpe accompanied the first group of settlers and directed the beginning of the enterprise. Trained and practiced in military operations, he saw to the construction of several fortifications, recruited a force of Highland Scots for the coming battles, and in 1742 successfully thwarted Spain's claim against British holdings in this region.

The other goals of the settlement proved to be difficult to achieve. First there was an uncongenial climate as the summers were hot and sultry and bred disease. Then there were a number of pesky rules established by the founding trustees. Hoping to advance good, honest labor in the most moral environment, the trustees limited the size of estates and rights of inheritance to exclude the amassing of great fortunes. And, desiring that the holders of the land be those who worked the land, slavery was banned.[4] Labor was to be earnest and sober, so there were restrictions on the consumption of spiritous liquor, such as rum; however, "strong beer" was allowed, as were Madeira and other wines.

The rules failed on several fronts, and the population of the colony declined drastically, succumbing to the twin curses of despair and disease. First there was insufficient labor to build an infrastructure to support the colony. The limits on land holding and rights of inheritance diminished incentives to work the land profitably. The productions of silk and wine were unsuccessful,

---

[3] "Charter of the [Georgia] Colony" (1732) in Candler, *Colonial Records of the State of Georgia*, 1:11–12.

[4] "An Act for rendering the Colony of Georgia more Defencible [*sic*]" (1734), ibid., 1:49–52.

because neither the imported silkworms nor the imported grapevine stock adapted to Georgia's climate and indigenous insects and diseases. And, in Georgia's heat, sobriety was often undesirable. The settlers pressed their complaints, and by 1752 control of the colony was passed from the trustees to a royal governor. Limits were lifted on the size of estates, the rights of inheritance were expanded, and the prohibition of hard liquor was removed.

With the passing of trustee leadership, surely the most treacherous act of all was the decision to allow slavery in 1751. The neighboring colony of South Carolina had grown rich on the backs of Africans, and now Georgians with large holdings of land and enslaved labor began to realize great fortunes. Large plantations were formed to support the culture of rice, indigo, then cotton, the money crops that would make the region rich. By 1793 Eli Whitney, employed as a tutor at a plantation near Savannah, had perfected the cotton gin (engine). This device separated the seeds from cotton, making it possible to increase production and profits. Cotton became king, and the port city of Savannah took its place as one of the most important markets in the country. By 1815, with the end of the War of 1812, Savannah seemed nearly to burst with promise for the future.

SAVANNAH: A PLACE BUSY AND BEAUTIFUL

At Jay's arrival in late 1817, the city had probably changed very little from this account by John Melish, a Scot who came to Savannah on business in 1806:

> Savannah is situated...on a high sandy bank, or bluff on the south side of the Savannah river, 17 miles from the sea. The city is laid out on an elegant plan, and is about a mile in length from east to west, and about a quarter of a mile in breadth. It consists of 30 streets, 16 squares, and 6 lanes [alleys], containing about 1000 houses, and 5500 inhabitants; of whom about 2500 are slaves. The public buildings are a court-house, jail, academy, bank-office, and five places for public worship. There has lately been built a very handsome exchange, with a spire and observatory, from whence vessels may be seen out to sea 10 or 12 miles. The situation of Savannah is favourable both for health and commerce.... The streets are broad and airy, and the city...frequently enjoys a sea breeze, which is cool and refreshing

> in the summer season.[5]

Melish also commented on the commerce of Savannah:

> The trade of the city is considerable, and employs 13 regular ships to Britain; 15 packet brigs and schooners to New York; two or three to Philadelphia, Baltimore and Boston; two or three sloops to Charleston; and four or five vessels to the West Indies.... Cotton and rice are the staple commodities of the state; and Savannah being the only shipping port in it, is, of course, the general mart for the disposal of these articles. The sea-island cotton of this state is reckoned superior to any in America.[6]

A report from January 1818, on the morning of Jay's arrival, noted some changes in the intervening dozen years, such as a larger population and more substantial construction in brick and stone—there had been a disastrous fire in 1796. Unchanged were the sand pathways and the effective (if unattractive) means of disposing of unwanted waste:

> Savannah is improving in buildings, good brick and stone houses occupying the place of wood: its form is a parallelogram; the streets running at right angles, and open squares being left alternately, tend to its improvement both in health and appearance.... Walking in the town is rendered exceedingly uncomfortable by the sand, which is from three to six inches deep, becomes very hot by the sun, and is driven by every little breeze. The only favourable opportunity for walking is after rain. Here are also great numbers of turkey buzzards, which the law protects, on account of their fondness for putrid flesh, thereby removing what in this hot climate would very much increase the insalubrity. The population of Savannah does not exceed eight thousand, and a great portion of these are coloured, slave and free.[7]

By 1817 Savannah was the southernmost outpost of commerce and culture on the eastern seaboard. The city was well known for her "elegant plan" and "open squares"; however, this plan had not originally aspired to elegance. In laying out the settlement in 1733, Oglethorpe had security on his mind. He put in place four wards (districts), each one with a central square, flanked at the north and south by private residences and at the east and west by public

---

[5] Melish, 36–37.
[6] Ibid.
[7] Harris, 69–70.

buildings (administrative, religious, and commercial). The scheme, the origin of which is disputed, provided handily for the ready containment and defense of the settlers and their possessions in the event of an attack. The plan was particularly ingenious because of its capacity to be multiplied. There were four to begin. By the time Oglethorpe returned to England in 1743, six wards with central squares had been laid out. By the time Jay arrived in late 1817, there were sixteen wards, and their squares had become the centers of neighborhoods, valued green spaces long before city planners began to realize the importance of green.[8]

CONTEMPLATING A MOVE TO SAVANNAH

While the stories of Georgia told by his father's teacher Cornelius Winter may have helped to paint a picture of the place, the impetus for Jay's move to Savannah surely came from Robert Bolton, the husband of his older sister Anne, and from Richard Richardson, Bolton's business partner and brother-in-law. By 1816 Robert and Anne and their rapidly expanding family had moved to Liverpool where Robert took up the work of directing the English branch of the Savannah cotton house established by his father.

Bolton had grown up in Savannah as the eldest son of one of the most prosperous merchants in town, so he knew the recent history of the place. Established in the family business in Liverpool, he received regular reports of Savannah's new-found prosperity. His partner Richardson had come to Savannah from Bermuda as a young man in 1804. He soon gained success in business and prominence in civic affairs, including a share of the Bolton firm and marriage to a daughter of the family. Richardson had firsthand knowledge of the extraordinary fortunes of the city that had come in the aftermath of the War of 1812, and he surely knew the prospects for an able architect. His hand rested on at least two projects, his own desire for a fine home and the need for a building to house the bank of which he had been named president in early 1817. Further, Richardson served on a committee to raise a new church, and he was involved in the planning for a new theater. He was prominent in social and business circles, so he could speculate on the

[8] Oglethorpe's plan had been extended to twenty-four wards and squares by 1851. Of these, four squares (Franklin, Ellis, Liberty, and Elbert) were lost to development in the twentieth century, but two squares were recovered (Franklin in the 1970s and Ellis in 2010).

number of houses that might be designed for his affluent friends and associates, particularly those among the recently rich.

Given Jay's struggle to gain commissions in England, the reports of Savannah's prosperity must have seemed very promising. Here was a wealthy corner of the world, where there were old and new family ties, and it was at that moment without the services of a trained architect. Opportunities were abundant, and it would seem that there was no competition—and competition had recently disappointed Jay.

THE JOURNEY TO SAVANNAH AND SETTLING IN

In Liverpool, Jay boarded the ship *Dawn*, and he arrived in Savannah on December 30, 1817, one of sixteen passengers. He claimed at his arrival "two trunks, one bag, one parcel portfolio, three paper parcels, and bedding."[9] Drawings are an architect's stock-in-trade, so it is likely that the "parcel portfolio" contained the plans for the Richardson House then underway in Savannah and the Albion Chapel recently completed in London, as well as the Wellington Rooms in Liverpool and the New English Opera House in London, both failed submissions to design competitions. Other drawings might have included a variety of plans and sketches dating from his student years, including the renderings exhibited at the Royal Academy. His portfolio could show potential clients his creative and technical abilities.

It seems that Jay took up residence with the family of Richardson, whose new home was just then in progress on Oglethorpe Square. For the census of 1820, Richardson claimed as occupants of his house two "free white males" between the ages of sixteen and twenty-six. One of these was noted as a "foreigner not naturalized."[10] Surely this was Jay. In 1820 Jay was twenty-seven years old, and he was a foreign national, an Englishman.

As Jay took up his work, he endeavored to become part of the social network of Savannah. His name appears on the rosters of two prominent organizations of the time, the Savannah Lodge of Freemasons and the Georgia Hussars. The record of his membership in the Masonic Order is brief, noting

---

[9] "Ship Dawn from Liverpool, England, December 30, 1817," U.S. Custom Service, Baggage Entries at Savannah, GA (1817), National Archives, Washington, D.C. (cited hereafter as USCS/BE).

[10] 1820 Census, Georgia, Chatham County, Richard Richardson and household, U.S. Census of Population and Housing, Census Bureau, Suitland, MD.

only that he was initiated in 1819 and withdrew the following year.[11] Also in 1819, Jay joined the Georgia Hussars. At this time, just four years after the end of the War of 1812, there was a reasonable certainty that peace had settled in, yet all able men, including resident foreign nationals, were required to join a military unit and be prepared to serve should the occasion arise. The most prestigious of these groups was the Hussars, which traced its origin to the Rangers founded by Oglethorpe in 1736. Jay's only burden of membership was to outfit himself in the splendid uniform of the regiment. The record shows only that he was admitted to active duty in 1819.[12]

These associations would have brought Jay into contact with the men who became his clients. For the most part, these were businessmen, such as factors, merchants, and shippers. And these were men with important roles in the conduct of regional affairs, members of the two prominent churches of the town (Christ Church, an Episcopalian assembly, and the Independent Presbyterian Church), and directors of various charities. Jay's work would require that he gain the attention of men of mark in Savannah.

"BY THE UNION OF TASTE AND KNOWLEDGE"

On February 10, 1818, a Savannah newspaper carried a very forthright assessment of architecture in the city. The author is unknown, identified only as "A Friend to the Fine Arts," but the writer was certainly Jay. Having resided in this city for little more than a month, here he declared his credentials as a professional architect, his opinion of the existing buildings, and what he hoped to accomplish in Savannah.[13] It was an audacious and lengthy statement, framed by quotations from Shakespeare. Featured were the central tenets of the teaching of John Soane: that architecture is a science and an art, based on standards and rules established by the ancient Greeks, and that beautiful architecture has the capacity to express the character and the morality of a nation. The lofty tone and strong opinions expressed in this article would not win friends for Jay among Savannah's community of builders or their clients. But, this was an announcement by an ambitious young professional directed to the equally ambitious citizens of the city who would come to be his

---

[11] *Ancient Documents of the Grand Lodge of Georgia*, 1818–1820, docs. 38, 39.

[12] Duncan, 175.

[13] W. Jay, arch., attrib., A Friend to the Fine Arts, Feb. 10, 1818 (hereafter cited in text).

patrons.

Jay opened his report in the company of Shakespeare, as the means to claim the significance of architecture in public life: "When we mean to build, we first survey the plot..." (Lord Bardolph, *Henry IV, Part 2, Act I, scene 3*). Jay's motive in this article was to inform the good people of Savannah that architecture was both a science ("a mechanical art") and an art "among the liberal arts." He lamented the state of the profession in this country, saying, "In America, generally, and in this city in particular—architecture has been considered rather as a trade than a science...and it has perhaps been imagined that...the accomplished architect has little advantage over the mechanical builder."

At this date, Jay could claim correctly to be the only professionally trained architect in Savannah and only one of a very few then working in the United States. He declared as the value of hiring a professional, "[I]t is only by the union of taste and knowledge, that economy can produce simplicity, or expense, be well directed to attain magnificence." The model for excellence was to be found in the buildings of the ancient Greeks, in "the true principles of their art...uniting correctness with elegance, and permanence with grandeur," and in the expressive language of the three orders, "the strong [Doric]—the elegant [Ionic]—and the rich [Corinthian]."

Jay was not sparing in his criticism of buildings in Savannah, saying,

> It must be allowed in viewing the buildings in this city—that the principles and rules laid down by the ancients have been little attended to, and that the consequence is—they present a huge pile of unconnected parts—or collection of extravagant decorations—which spread over every part leaving the eye no repose among the tawdry profusion.

At the end of this long report, Jay's closing was conciliatory: "But I cease to censure—and hope that 'now in the piping time of peace' the public attention will turn to those arts that raise a nation to eminence—and which so distinguished that seat of genius and liberty, Athens." Here again his literary companion was Shakespeare, the phrase "now in the piping time of peace" taken from the opening lines of *King Richard III* and used here to welcome a new era of peace and prosperity following the end of the War of 1812.[14]

SAVANNAH LABORS

In less than five years, Jay accomplished a remarkable number of projects in Savannah. At least one early bid failed when he did not gain the commission for the Independent Presbyterian Church, the story of which is told in a later chapter. But in very short order, he was at work on a theater and several fine homes.

One particular record casts a light on Jay's activities in 1819, perhaps his busiest year. In the early years of the nineteenth century, city officials became fixed on sustaining Oglethorpe's unique town plan and on improving the general appearance of the place. Considerable attention was given to surveying and recording lots, maintaining the public squares, and clearing the roadways. A committee on streets and lanes received reports from the city surveyor and conveyed matters of concern to the city council. At the beginning of each meeting, the docket of information relayed the names of offenders, the character of their offenses, and the fines levied. These accounts were subsequently published in the minutes of the city council.

In these reports, Jay's name appeared eight times in 1819. He was seldom the only offender—sometimes the list was short (two or three persons), sometimes the list was long (four or more). Among the entries are these:

> Monday, February 2—Wm. Jay, obstructing street at Mr. Scarborough's [*sic*], Fined fifteen dollars and costs; Same offence at Mr. Telfair's, Same decision./ Monday, May 31—Wm. Jay, for obstructing the street at Habersham's house, Fined thirty dollars and costs./ Monday, June 14—William Jay, obstructing street & not keeping sufficient lights at Mr. H. Kimball's lot, Fined thirty dollars and costs; Same offence at Mr. Telfair's house, 10 nights, Same decision.[15]

The record shows that Jay found an abundance of work in Savannah. His accomplishments included several private residences, a theater, a school for indigent children, a custom house, a bank, and perhaps a hotel. He had come

---

[14] Shakespeare, *King Richard III,* from the opening lines spoken by Richard, Duke of Gloucester (later King Richard III), which begin, "Now is the winter of our discontent..." (I.1).

[15] Savannah City Council Minutes, "Docket of Information," 1819, Savannah Municipal Archives, Savannah, GA (cited hereafter as SMA).

to Savannah at just the right moment. While the colony had experienced a bumpy beginning, by the time of Jay's arrival in late 1817, the city was prosperous. Cotton had spawned an industry of wealthy planters, factors (agents who managed sales), merchants, and shippers. Jay's ambition and talents matched perfectly the needs of a number of Savannah entrepreneurs, men who were eager to build grand houses and to ornament the city with fine public buildings worthy of its growing importance. He satisfied those desires and made works of tasteful opulence that came to define the now ubiquitous expression "Savannah style."

AN EPILOGUE: JAY IN SAVANNAH, LOST AND FOUND

In spite of the imprint that Jay made on Savannah, after he left in 1822 it was as if he had disappeared into a mist. In 1927 the *Savannah Press* carried this woeful headline: "Is Jay a Myth?—No Record of Him Extant." All to no avail, the author of this article had consulted a reference specialist at the Savannah Public Library; a researcher at the Georgia Historical Society; Thomas Gamble, a well-known local amateur historian; and Fiske Kimball, the dean of American architectural historians. The remorseful conclusion of this report was, "Just whether there ever was a Jay seems to be coming doubtful."[16]

Not one to leave a question about Savannah's history unanswered, the aforementioned Gamble wrote to the librarian of the British Museum in London. This sad news came back, reported in yet another headline of the *Savannah Press*: "Jay's Reputation as 'Famous Architect' Gets Another Jolt—Authorities in England Say They Never Heard of This Builder."[17] Undaunted, Gamble set about to solve this problem. Here and there the name "Jay" survived, but the tales about him differed wildly. Jay was an unknown architect, or he was very famous. He was an amateur or a builder or he was a trained professional. He was English, probably from London, but perhaps from the West Indies. He was young when he began his work here, perhaps as young as twenty—or he was older, even considerably older.

In 1932 Gamble announced that his hunt for the elusive architect had ended when a friend told him of a book recording an Englishman's visit to

[16] "Is Jay a Myth?" Dec. 8, 1927.

[17] Gamble, "Jay's Reputation as 'Famous Architect' Gets Another Jolt," Mar. 3, 1928.

the Southern states in 1840. The author had observed in Savannah "a few mansions, built by an English architect, Mr. Jay—son of the celebrated divine of that name at Bath—which are of beautiful architecture, of sumptuous interior, and combine as much of elegance and luxury as are to be found in any private dwellings in the country."[18] From that reference, Gamble came upon the flood of writings by and about Jay's father. He soon learned that the Reverend Jay's eldest child had married a Bolton of Savannah. The result was "Romance of Wm. Jay, Savannah Architect; His Genius Is Reflected in Buildings Here," the headline for Gamble's long account in a Savannah newspaper in May 1932.[19]

There were a number of omissions in Gamble's report: little notice of Jay's training in London; no reference to his first commission, the Albion Chapel; no mention of his activities in South Carolina, or of his work back in England at Cheltenham or later in Mauritius. But, perhaps most regrettably, Jay would now be known by the words of the Reverend Jay, who had written that his son had "left the path in which he had been taught to go."[20] Gamble took this lament of the Reverend Jay and forged the legend that Savannah, in her famously genial way, had caused this namesake of a quite famous preacher to fall into vats of Chatham Artillery Punch, with the result that the architect had left town broke, broken, and drunk.

Gamble wrote, "Small though Savannah was, it had its temptations. It had its full share of noble women and righteous men, but, to tell the truth, it was a rather hard drinking town, with a large number who loved the gaming table and the theater and horse racing and all other available sports." Jay was, according to Gamble, "free from the restraints of an austere and religious home in Bath" and victim to "the forgivable follies of youth."[21] For the record, Jay was plagued by debt throughout his career as were many architects of the period, but there is no evidence that he succumbed to strong brews. The account of his work in Savannah and elsewhere suggests that he always labored hard and long and sober. And, there is ample testimony that austerity did not characterize the person or the home of the Reverend Jay.

---

[18] Gamble, "Tracking Down a Will-o'-the Wisp," May 11, 1932. Gamble cites Buckingham, 1:120.

[19] Gamble, "Romance of Wm. Jay, Savannah Architect," May 8, 1932.

[20] Rev. Jay, *Autobiography*, 95.

[21] Gamble, "Romance of Wm. Jay, Savannah Architect," May 8, 1932.

CHAPTER 9

THE CONSEQUENTIAL MATTER OF SLAVERY

In Savannah, Jay designed buildings for men of substantial wealth who gained their fortunes directly or indirectly by the labor of black men and women brought from Africa. Much of the work to raise these structures came from the toil of these enslaved persons. What could these circumstances have meant to Jay? Quite a lot, as it happens. From his father and his father's friends, Jay knew the unhappy history of Britain's participation in the slave trade and the efforts that had been made to end this sordid enterprise. His father counted among his dearest friends three leaders of the abolition movement: the Reverend John Newton, William Wilberforce, and Hannah More. And his own mentor, Cornelius Winter, had started his journey of Christian service as a teacher to Africans in Savannah, a mission prompted by the great evangelist George Whitefield.

On some matters, even theological issues, the Reverend Jay was known to moderate his views to raise a larger tent for his flock. But, on the subject of slavery his indignation was full blown. His friends and associates were abolitionists, and he shared their fury. The cause was the great passion of English evangelicals. In 1808, the year in which Jay left home for study in London, his father declared, "Torn from their native country—oppressed by merciless exactions—treated like beasts that perish—fed and valued only for the purposes of labor and drudgery.... Who can but lament that our country should so long have 'Traded in the persons of men.'"[1]

The case for abolition was argued in Parliament, led by William Wilberforce, who had been urged on by the Reverend John Newton. Wilberforce was aided by a handful of close companions, one of whom was Hannah More. These three were good and loyal friends of the Reverend Jay although these relationships existed under something of a cloud. Newton, Wilberforce, and More were all prominent members of the Church of England, yet all were evangelicals who shared a commitment to social reform. All three were drawn

[1] Rev. Jay, *Memoirs of... Cornelius Winter*, 99–100. The phrase "Traded in the persons of men," derives from Ezekiel 27:13.

to the Reverend Jay because of the character and temper of his gospel message, his engaging style in the pulpit, and his gracious and gentle demeanor. For Wilberforce and More, the association with the Reverend Jay was sometimes problematic. But Newton, an ordained priest of the Established Church, was well known for his evangelical proclivities, and his advanced age placed him beyond the reach of those who would criticize him for cavorting with a nonconformist.

THE REVEREND JOHN NEWTON: "BLIND, BUT NOW I SEE"

In 1788, soon after Billy Jay the Boy Preacher first appeared at Surrey Chapel in London, he came to the attention of the Reverend John Newton. By then a beloved older figure among Evangelical Anglicans, Newton often counseled younger ministers. The Reverend Jay recalled that Newton came to him after one of his sermons at Surrey Chapel, saying, "I am concerned for your safety and welfare," warning of "the snares and dangers" of the adulation the young preacher was experiencing.[2] From that time, during his regular summer supply to Surrey Chapel, the Reverend Jay often joined a group at Newton's home for breakfast where matters of faith and social concern were addressed.

Newton's history was well known. The son of the master of a merchant ship, he went to sea as a youth and ultimately was caught up in the slave trade, first as crew and later as the captain of a slave ship. This was Newton's own report of this time in his life: "Disagreeable I had long found it; but I think I should have quitted it sooner, had I considered it as I now do, to be unlawful and wrong.... What I did I did ignorantly."[3] By 1754 poor health had obliged him to abandon the occupations of the sea, and in Liverpool he was drawn to Methodist revivals. He was ordained in the Church of England in 1764, but he took the path of an evangelical faith. A feature of his service was the composition of many hymns, one of which was "Amazing Grace." The first lines capture the early dissolute years of his life and the weight of regret that he carried with him to his grave: "Amazing grace! (how sweet the sound!) / That sav'd a wretch like me! / I once was lost, but now am found; Was blind, but now I see."[4]

---

[2] Rev. Jay, *Autobiography*, 270.

[3] Newton, "Thoughts upon the African Slave Trade," 6:521.

[4] Newton, Cowper, and Montgomery, 58–59.

Newton had kept journals during his years at sea, and these included accounts of the slave trade. In 1788 he wrote a summary of his experiences titled "Thoughts upon the African Slave Trade," presented as testimony to Parliament.[5] Three years earlier, Newton had persuaded William Wilberforce to remain in politics to advance programs of social reform, and it would be Wilberforce who led the campaign in Parliament to end slavery in all British holdings.

WILLIAM WILBERFORCE: THE "FEELING, FEARLESS, PERSEVERING" OPPONENT OF SLAVERY

The Reverend Jay met Wilberforce soon after his appointment to Argyle Chapel in Bath in 1790. Wilberforce was by then a member of the House of Commons representing the large district of Yorkshire, distinguished as a brilliant orator and well known as an evangelical reformer. Over the years, Wilberforce gave his attention to a great number of worthy causes, including education for poor children, prison reform, prevention of cruelty to animals, the promotion of Christian missions in India, the free distribution of Bibles and "little books" or tracts to teach moral values, and many other initiatives. But no cause took up more of his energy than that of abolition.

Wilberforce and his wife often retired to Bath, in part to restore his fragile health. From their first meeting, Wilberforce and the Reverend Jay had a cordial relationship and often met for tea or supper. However, the statesman may have heard the pastor preach only a few times to avoid questions about his loyalty to the Church of England.

In 1832 the Reverend Jay dedicated to Wilberforce *Evening Exercises for the Closet*, which would come to be the most popular of his numerous published works. Thousands of copies were sold, many of them to an especially appreciative audience in North America. In the very long dedication, the Reverend Jay observed that his friendship with Wilberforce had endured for forty years, and that he saw in this great statesman "the feeling, fearless, persevering, and successful opponent of a traffic [slavery] 'that is a reproach to any people.'"[6] To which Wilberforce, then ill and near death, replied, "I feel honoured as well as gratified by the proof of your esteem and regard for me.... It

---

[5] Newton, "Thoughts upon the African Slave Trade," 6:517–46.

[6] Rev. Jay, *Evening Exercises for the Closet*, 1:iii, xi. "Righteousness exalteth a nation: but sin is a reproach to any people" (Prov 14:34), here the sin of slavery.

gives me unaffected pleasure to reflect that my name will thus be permanently associated with yours." Years earlier, he had reported to a friend of the Reverend Jay, "Dear Jay, I love Jay!"[7]

Through all of the years that the Reverend Jay shared this friendship, Wilberforce was consumed nearly to exhaustion by pressing the case of abolition in Parliament. His first speech proposing an end to the slave trade was made in the House of Commons in 1789. The progress of the debate was slow, but finally in 1809 Parliament passed the Abolition of the Slave Trade Act, banning the trade on British ships. In 1833, on the eve of Wilberforce's death, the Abolition of Slavery Act freed enslaved persons in all British territories.

HANNAH MORE: A POWERFUL PEN

Friend to Newton, Wilberforce, and the Reverend Jay, Hannah More was one of the most influential women of the day. Born near Bristol, More was one of five daughters of a schoolmaster. Her intelligence, wit, and facility with words prompted her to write, and she began as a playwright, achieving success with works produced on the London stage. By the mid-1780s, she had withdrawn from London society and abandoned the theater, which she had come to view as immoral. She returned to live in her home district of Somerset where she wrote poems and essays on the need for the reform of morals.

Like Wilberforce, More was an Anglican with evangelical sympathies. Perhaps because she was a woman and more vulnerable to attack, her association with the Reverend Jay got More into some fierce trouble, including a public humiliation for the grave offense of once having taken communion at Argyle Chapel. Still, she suffered through this affair and continued to have an affectionate relationship with the Reverend Jay and members of his family.[8]

In 1787 More met the Reverend Newton, and he and Wilberforce encouraged her to work for the cause of abolition. With Wilberforce, she joined a group meeting at a home in Clapham, then a suburb of London. Most members were Evangelical Anglicans. They came to be known derisively as the "Saints," then years later as the Clapham Sect. In this group were individ-

---

[7] Rev. Jay, *Autobiography*, 309, 206.

[8] Thompson, 200–201; Rev. Jay, *Autobiography*, 328–46; C. Jay, *Recollections*, 18.

uals who had spent years researching the issues and the consequences of slavery. Their plan was to bring the matter of abolition forcefully before members of the public in a great variety of forms. They distributed broadsheets and pamphlets featuring slave narratives, other testimonies, documentary evidence, stories, and poems. As indignation became widespread, petitions were presented to Parliament where the case for abolition was framed in speeches by Wilberforce.

More's facility in writing and her commitment to this cause made her a particularly valuable member of the group. Among her several contributions to this effort was "The Slave Trade: A Poem," written in 1788 and distributed just at the moment when the campaign was being launched in Parliament. This very long poem includes these lines:

> Was it decreed, fair Freedom! at thy birth,
> That thou shouldst ne'er irradiate all the earth?...
> Perish th' illiberal thought which would debase
> The native genius of the sable race!...
> Does then the immortal principle within
> Change with the casual colour of a skin?...
> What strange offence, what aggravated sin?
> They stand convicted—of a darker skin?...
> They are still men, and men should still be free.[9]

This became an important document in the campaign to draw public attention to the abomination of slavery.

THE SINGULAR STORY OF SLAVERY IN GEORGIA

Jay knew the history of Georgia because it was connected in important ways to his own family. Reports of slavery in the American South had come from Cornelius Winter, the Reverend Jay's mentor. And, Hannah More was a likely source for an accounting of the unique circumstances of the birth of the thirteenth colony in 1733.

As Jay was contemplating his journey to Georgia in 1817, the former colony was still young, still shy of the century mark. But the story of the founding of Georgia had become mythic, and at the center of this enterprise

[9] More, 405, 407, 409.

was James Edward Oglethorpe. One of his intimates in the last years of his life was Hannah More, a noted opponent of slavery. In 1784 she wrote to her sister, "I have got a new admirer, and we flirt together prodigiously; it is the famous General Oglethorpe, perhaps the most remarkable man of his time."[10]

More and Oglethorpe shared a commitment to reforms of English society. When they met she was just beginning her foray into evangelicalism, and Oglethorpe had been an evangelical in spirit if not in name long before the Methodists began to preach in the fields. Soon after his entry to Parliament in 1722, Oglethorpe took up several campaigns against injustice. He advertised the plight of debtors and railed against the foul conditions and corrupt administration of London's jails. He spoke against the practice of impressment or the taking of young men for service in the navy by force. A fierce campaigner against the deleterious effects of spiritous or distilled beverages, he advocated a high tax on consumption of gin to promote the use of fermented beverage, such as beer or wine. And, he was an early subscriber to the Society for the Propagation of the Gospel in Foreign Parts, an effort by the Church of England begun in 1710 to extend the Christian faith into the colonies of North America.

From More, the Reverend Jay and his family could hear of the establishment of the colony of Georgia. It had been a unique initiative prompted by philanthropy and sometimes called the greatest adventure of the age. And, in this enterprise, there was no more remarkable feature than the ban on slavery.

It is impossible to know precisely what occasioned this stand against slavery. While there was a growing resistance to the odious trade in England in the 1730s, no influential politicians or churchmen spoke against the practice. Betty Wood suggests several reasons for the ban: One aim of the Georgia project was to provide work for white laborers from England, and the presence of enslaved blacks seemed to be at odds with that goal. Also, there was a growing perception that slavery in South Carolina had fostered a privileged and dissolute class of white plantation owners, something the Georgia founders hoped to avoid. And, there was apprehension about the growing numbers of enslaved Africans in South Carolina and the threat they might pose to the safety and well-being of British colonists.[11]

The ban on slavery in Georgia instituted by law in 1735 lasted no more

[10] Roberts, 1:316–17.

[11] Wood, "James Edward Oglethorpe, Race, and Slavery" 66–79.

than a few years before it was assailed. Georgia settlers complained that, without slaves, they could not produce sufficient goods for competitive markets, and South Carolina planters agitated for an end to the ban so that they might extend their operations into Georgia. In 1752 the poor progress of the colony brought about the end of trustee rule, but, even as they were transferring responsibility to a royal governor, the trustees expressed no outrage about the institution of slavery and sought in their final moments only to constrain certain of its effects. According to Wood, among the final instructions of the trustees was the directive that masters should see to "the spiritual welfare of their slaves." She observes, "Blacks were forbidden to work on Sundays, and their owners were obliged to see that they attended 'at some time on the Lords Day for Instruction in the Christian Religion.'"[12] There was no assertion that slavery was abhorrent and should be prohibited.

Late in his life, Oglethorpe claimed,

> My friends and I [as trustees] settled the colony of Georgia.... We determined not to suffer slavery there; but the slave-merchants, and their adherents, occasioned us not only much trouble, but at last got the then government to favour them. We would not suffer slavery (which is against the Gospel as well as the fundamental law of England) to be authorised under our authority; we refused, as trustees, to make a law permitting such a horrid crime.[13]

No matter the truth of this history, the adventure of Georgia and the ban on slavery made of Oglethorpe an iconic figure in his own lifetime.

THE PLEAS OF JOHN WESLEY

The Reverend Jay was not a Methodist, but he had been drawn as a boy to evangelical service by a Methodist. He knew the legends of the founders John Wesley and George Whitefield and their roles in the early years of the colony of Georgia. In 1789 he met Wesley and heard him preach.[14]

Wesley arrived in Georgia in early 1736, just three years after the founding of the colony. He had been recruited by Oglethorpe as a missionary for

---

[12] Wood, *Slavery in Colonial Georgia*, 85.
[13] Hoare, 157.
[14] Rev. Jay, *Autobiography*, 414.

the Society for the Propagation of the Gospel in Foreign Parts to seek conversions of Indians and to serve as rector of Christ Church. As he set about his labors, he met resistance. The colonists, who pursued a comfortably feeble faith, did not welcome his more rigorous and methodical practices, and the natives ignored his entreaties to join the ranks of Christians. Disappointed in both efforts and soon caught in a dispute with the family of a young woman whom he had once courted, in 1738 he left Savannah quickly and returned to England.

This would be Wesley's only trip to North America, and in his brief stay he did not see the arrival of sanctioned slavery in Georgia. But he did form opinions of the practice in the neighboring colony of South Carolina, which he termed "the horrid trade."[15] Throughout his life, Wesley was a strong opponent of slavery, yet he did not press for abolition in his own ministry. Perhaps he realized, as others had, that this battle could be won only in the arena of politics. The last letter he wrote, just six days before he died in 1791, was addressed to Wilberforce. In it he predicted the daunting effort that remained. He said, "I see not how you can go through your glorious enterprise in opposing that execrable villainy, which is the scandal of religion, of England, and of human nature. Unless God has raised you up for this very thing, you will be worn out by the opposition of men and devils. But, 'if God be for you, who can be against you?'"[16]

THE ACCOMMODATIONS OF GEORGE WHITEFIELD

A clue to how Jay would understand the matter of slavery in the American South comes in the close ties his father had to the ministry of George Whitefield. Whitefield died the year after the birth of Billy Jay. But, decades later the Reverend Jay would proudly claim, "I am a kind of grandson of Mr. Whitefield. He begat Winter, and Winter begat me."[17] It was not an idle boast. Throughout his long career, the Reverend Jay was frequently compared to Whitefield in the character of his message and his preaching style. It was often remarked that, as Whitefield had been the voice of the first wave of evangelism in the eighteenth century, the Reverend Jay was the great declaimer of the gospel for a new age.

---

[15] Wesley, "Thoughts Upon Slavery," 6:291.

[16] Lelièvre, 240. The quotation derives from Romans 8:31.

[17] Wakeley, 294–95.

Whitefield came to Georgia in 1738 as a successor to John Wesley. He found in North America fertile ground for his ministry where Wesley had not. But Whitefield's role in the history of slavery in the American South is complicated. A truth is that this man, the greatest evangelist of the age, professed to abhor slavery but came to advocate for the repeal of the ban in Georgia and came to own slaves. But, as in most reports of the past, there are several shades of the truth.

Whitefield made seven trips to North America. On his first journey in 1738, he was appointed rector of Christ Church in Savannah, a position he held intermittently for two years. He came with the intention to establish an orphan house in Savannah, and that plan very quickly became the center of his life's work. His sermons—to tens of thousands in England, Scotland, Ireland, and North America—inevitably closed with pleas for funds for the orphan house in Georgia.

During his early tours of this country, Whitefield witnessed slavery in the Carolinas. He abhorred "the vile treatment of the slaves,"[18] but he did not speak against the practice of owning slaves. Indeed, most members of the Anglican clergy did not for fear they might offend wealthy and influential constituents involved in the trade. However, from the beginning of his ministry, Whitefield was concerned less with the conditions of life on earth than with the saving of souls. The motive of his preaching was revealed early in 1739 when he spoke to crowds of coal miners in Kingswood Hill, a district near Bristol in Southwest England. An early biographer of the evangelist reported, "The colliers [coal miners] were numerous and utterly uncultivated. They had no place of worship. Few ventured to walk even in their neighbourhood, and, when provoked, they were the terror of Bristol."[19] Whitefield met these men in the out-of-doors because no church would allow this filthy and foul-smelling hoard to enter and no church or hall could contain them, as they came first by the few hundreds and then by the ten thousands.

In his ministry to the coal miners of Kingswood Hill, Whitefield perceived that he could not change the grim circumstances of these lives on earth, but he could save these souls. So it was with enslaved persons in the American South. Whitefield had seen slaves who were worked to exhaustion, starved, and brutalized; he knew of slaves who had been killed. He reasoned that all

---

[18] Whitefield, 4:37.

[19] Philip, 103.

of this suffering might come to good if this misery would, in his words, "dispose their minds to accept the redemption wrought out for them by the death and obedience of Jesus Christ."[20] His remedy for the villainy of slavery was to educate enslaved Africans so that they might read the Bible and find their way to Christ.

Whitefield had been warned about the hardships prevailing in the new colony of Georgia. But when he arrived he found matters more desperate than he had imagined. The building of the town and the planting of various crops had not gone well. Many settlers had succumbed to disease in the hot climate, and the growing number of homeless children posed the urgency for an orphan house. At a site just a few miles south of Savannah, he founded Bethesda, the "house of mercy," where the children would be cared for and provided with a course of Christian instruction.

In 1747, four years before the ban on slavery was lifted, Whitefield wrote to a benefactor of the orphan house. Lamenting "that despised place called Georgia," he observed that the colony could not survive "without the use of slaves." For his own beloved orphanage, he gladly received gifts of money and land and slaves. This was his determined opinion: "[H]ot countries cannot be cultivated without negroes. What a flourishing country might Georgia have been, had the use of them been permitted years ago?" He concluded,

> [T]hough it is true, that they [slaves] are brought in a wrong way from their own country, and it is a trade not to be approved of, yet as it will be carried on whether we will or not; I should think myself highly favoured if I could purchase a good number of them, in order to make their lives comfortable, and lay a foundation for breeding up their posterity in the nurture and admonition of the Lord.[21]

Clearly, Whitefield deplored the enterprise of slaving, yet in a great leap of his faith he took this abomination as an odd blessing. In his view, these black men and women who had been lost in the dark lands of Africa were now entrusted to the Christian world. He could not change the convention of slavery as it existed in his time, but he believed that he could bring comfort, save souls, and prepare for a future free of this villainy.

---

[20] Whitefield, 4:40.

[21] Ibid., 2:90, 404–405.

CORNELIUS WINTER: CAST OFF TO "SINK OR SWIM"

On Whitefield's last journey to North America in 1769—he died while on this tour, in Newburyport, Massachusetts, where he is buried—he brought with him Cornelius Winter, a promising young candidate for the ministry. Winter's charge was to settle in Savannah to teach the enslaved Africans to read in preparation for the establishment of a black church. He came in the company of Whitefield, but his service had been requested by a coterie of businessmen who had inherited from Oglethorpe and Whitefield certain notions of Christian obligation to the slaves.

In Savannah, Winter was met by James Habersham, a London businessman who had accompanied Whitefield in 1738 to help the evangelist manage his affairs in Georgia. When Winter met him, Habersham was a leader in the community and had prospered as a rice planter and a commercial shipper. Winter recalled the ominous greeting: "Mr. Habersham met me at the door, embraced me in his arms, saying, 'I will be your friend if nobody else will.... I will stand by you, you shall instruct my negroes, whoever else refuses you.'" As Whitefield left to begin his tour of the North, his parting words to Winter were, "Now I cast you off, sink or swim."[22]

Winter's stay in Savannah was difficult. He was supported by Habersham and by Robert Bolton, Habersham's brother-in-law. Those two and a few others of "no inconsiderable property" supported the mission to educate the enslaved persons, with the prospect of establishing "a church of Africans."[23] But, his work was thwarted by the planters who vigorously opposed the goals of this enterprise. By the year's end, it was agreed that Winter should return to England to gain ordination in the Church of England. Then, with this greater mantle of authority, he would return to Savannah to continue his work.

In England in 1770, his application was denied by church officials, in spite of pleas from his sponsors in Savannah and from Benjamin Franklin, Whitefield's old friend, who was just then in London serving as the colonial agent for Georgia. Distrust of Whitefield's evangelizing had grown in the Established Church, and now that he was dead his young associates, such as Winter, were cut adrift. Reeling from this rejection, Winter set a new course

---

[22] Rev. Jay, *Memoirs of... Cornelius Winter*, 92–93, 102.

[23] Ibid., 140–41.

for his life. He took up his religious work as a nonconformist, ultimately establishing an academy to train youths for dissenting ministries, an effort that resulted in the discovery and nurture of Billy Jay the Boy Preacher. And, although the mission to Savannah had been hard and disappointing, Winter always remembered America with affection.

JAY IN THE LANDSCAPE OF SLAVERY

When Jay arrived in Savannah in late 1817, he confronted the circumstances of slavery. Georgia was not the place Oglethorpe had hoped it would be, but it was a place born of good intentions. Through his father and his father's friends, Jay knew the labors of the English abolitionists, and he knew the history of Georgia. Among his Savannah clients were the descendants of Winter's old allies. These men did not stand against slavery. Indeed, all of them owned black men and women, but they had inherited from Whitefield certain convictions of responsibility. They supported the education of slaves, prohibited by convention if not by law. And they encouraged the growth of the black church in Savannah, which flourished in this place as it did not in South Carolina.

At the beginning and at the end of his career as an architect, Jay made his way in slave-owning societies. He spent the last two years of his life working as an assistant to the surveyor general in the civil service of Mauritius, an English possession taken from the French in 1810. In the very long list of his responsibilities, he was charged with overseeing the emancipation of black slaves who had toiled as government laborers, providing for their transition to a condition of apprenticeship. He reported only that the burden of this duty was immense.[24]

We do not know how he responded to the culture of slavery in the American South, but the matter may have weighed in his decision not to return to the U.S. after he left in 1822. No doubt he discussed his continuing prospects

[24] W. Jay to J. A. Lloyd, Jan. 13, 1837, National Archives of Mauritius, Surveyor General's Department Collection (1836–1837), Coromandel, Mauritius (hereafter cited as NAM/SGD). Enslaved Africans were brought to Mauritius by the Dutch in the seventeenth century with the establishment of sugar plantations. They became an integral part of plantation culture during the rule of the French in 1715–1810. The British took the island in 1810, and in 1833 the Emancipation Act freed the slaves.

in the South with his brother-in-law Robert Bolton, who was just then concluding business affairs in New York City and preparing to return to England to take up his call to preach. From his father, Bolton had inherited slaves and a share of the family enterprise of shipping cotton brought from the fields by slaves. He had also inherited—from his great-grandfather, grandfather, and father—Whitefield's mandate to care for the souls of enslaved people.

Bolton's son later described three reasons for his father's commitment to the ministry. The earliest was his recognition as a child of his mother's desire that he become a preacher. The second, also a childhood memory, was the attention of Andrew Cox Marshall, "the family coachman…not only a respectable, but a religious person," a black man who saw in this child an inclination for pastoral service. The third was his own remembrance of the support that his grandfather had given to Winter in the effort to educate the Africans.[25]

During his appointment at the Independent Chapel at Henley-on-Thames in 1824–1836, Bolton came to be known for his commitment to enslaved Africans and to African missions. George H. Peters believed that Bolton's "missionary enthusiasm" had been formed by the resolve of his grandfather and father to follow the teachings of Whitefield and Winter to "uplift the slave."[26] During these years in Henley, Bolton joined the Reverend Jay to become active in the affairs of the London Missionary Society. A close friend was John Philip, a Scot who served as superintendent of the society's South African operations and who insisted on the participation of natives in the management of mission programs.

For Bolton, there seems never to have been a moment when he considered returning to Savannah to live, not at the beginning of his married life or later in 1836 when he moved his family to the U.S. to see to the education of his sons. In Savannah, his roots were deep, and he surely regarded this place with affection. But he must have determined that he could not take his wife and children to live in a slave-owning town, remembering from his own experiences that being in such an environment required accommodations of

---

[25] R. Bolton, *Genealogical…Account of the Family of Bolton*, 128, 143–44, 147–48. Andrew Cox Marshall led the First African Baptist Church in Savannah in 1812–1856. The church had been founded in 1777 and often enjoyed support from city officials.

[26] G. H. Peters, 82–86.

mind and spirit.

What had Jay come to conclude about the presence of enslaved persons in Georgia and South Carolina? Perhaps for a time he was sustained by Bolton's commitment to Whitefield's mission of compassion. Or, perhaps Jay simply carried with him the hardy optimism of his father. Both were spirited men, men of good will, generous with their belief in others even when that trust failed them. As his life was coming to a close, the Reverend Jay announced, "I do not believe that in this earth misery preponderates over good. I have a better opinion of mankind than I had when I began my public life.... The state of the world *has* been improved and *is* improving. Who justifies slavery now? What noble efforts have been made to break every yoke, and to let the oppressed go free!"[27]

[27] Rev. Jay, *Autobiography*, 159.

CHAPTER 10

"A CHURCH, NOW ERECTING AT SAVANNAH, IN AMERICA"

In later years, one of the several stories told about Jay was that he was the architect of the Independent Presbyterian Church in Savannah. It stood to reason. This church was generally considered to be the most beautiful structure in the city. At the dedication of this building in May 1819, it was declared, "For grandeur of design, and neatness of execution, we presume, this church is not surpassed by any in the United States."[1] Soon notice came from near and far, including these: "an elegant building of stone," "one of the most splendid buildings in the city," and "truly magnificent...probably not surpassed in the country." This church was so lovely and so loved that, when the building burned in 1889, the quick decision was to replace it with an exact copy.[2]

In 1914, in a survey of early American churches, Aymar Embury II named this church in Savannah as one of only four in the South worth comment. He credited the design to "an English architect named Jay, although this is not certain." He praised the spire as "one of the best designed of all the old church spires." He concluded, "The church is the most famous in Georgia and very properly so, since it is quite the handsomest in the city, and one of which any community might well be proud."[3] And the community was proud. In 1918 Savannah historian Thomas Gamble declared that this lovely edifice was the work of "an English architect named Jay," who had "excellent training and good taste" and had built some of the city's "most beautiful residences and public buildings," including "the Independent Church."[4]

Jay may have presumed that he would be named the architect for this structure. The last work he exhibited at the Royal Academy in London was

---

[1] "New Church," *Columbian Museum and Savannah Daily Gazette*, May 10, 1819.

[2] Kayser, 37; Barber and Howe, 1:742; Parsons, 23; Calhoun, 243.

[3] Embury, 145–46.

[4] Gamble, "Savannah Theater, One of the First in America," Nov. 17, 1918.

titled "Sketch of a church, now erecting at Savannah, in America."[5] Shown in 1817, the drawing must have been prepared in 1816, the year in which the Savannah project was initiated. But Jay did not prevail. Documents survive to tell us when and how the search for an architect was conducted, and who was chosen. Still, these questions linger: Why was Jay identified with this church long after he had abandoned Savannah? And what might account for the fact that his proposal for this commission failed?

THE SEARCH FOR AN ARCHITECT

Records of the Independent Presbyterian Church reveal that the decision to build a new church was first addressed in early 1816. On January 27, the committee of repairs reported to church trustees that the present building on St. James Square (or St. James's Square, later Telfair Square) was in "a decayed Condition" and recommended the construction of a new edifice "of Brick & Stone on an enlarged plan." A meeting of the pew holders ensued, and the project was approved. By February 6, the committee charged with selecting a site had designated as the "most Central &...most eligible Scite [*sic*], the five Lotts [*sic*] fronting on Bull & South Broad Street [later Oglethorpe Avenue]." On April 22, at a meeting of the pew holders, a committee was named "to have a new church erected, to purchase the Lotts, to purchase materials, to procure a plan to be decided on by said Committee & the Trustees."[6] The building committee had seven members and two had ties to Jay, John Bolton and Richard Richardson.

John Bolton, born in Maryland, was a young first cousin of Robert Bolton, the head of a prominent cotton house in Savannah. As a child, John was sent to Savannah to be raised by Robert, and in 1802 he married Robert's oldest child Sarah (Sarah's brother Robert would marry Jay's sister Anne in 1811). John was taken into the family business as a partner, and for many years he was active in the affairs of the Independent Presbyterian Church.[7]

Richard Richardson, a native of Bermuda, was also a partner in the Bolton cotton house. In 1811 he married the elder Robert Bolton's third daughter

---

[5] Royal Academy of Arts, *Exhibition* [1817], Entry #891.

[6] Independent Presbyterian Church, Savannah, Minutes, Jan. 29–Apr. 22, 1816, Independent Presbyterian Church Archives, Stuart A. Rose Manuscript, Archives, and Rare Book Library, Emory University, Atlanta, GA (hereafter IPC).

[7] R. Bolton, *Genealogical...Account of the Family of Bolton*, 114, 139.

Frances. Directing the shipping business for the cotton house took Richardson frequently to Liverpool, where the English branch of the family firm was managed by the younger Robert Bolton in 1816–1822. Here Richardson met Jay, and by early 1816 he had engaged the young architect to design a home for his growing family on Oglethorpe Square in Savannah.

By April 1816, when the search for an architect began, Jay was eager for work. He had lost competitions for the Wellington Rooms in Liverpool and the new English Opera House in London, and work at the Albion Chapel in London was well advanced and would be completed by the end of that year. He was close to his sister Anne and her husband, Robert. At their home in Liverpool, he would meet Richardson, and a guest of the Boltons in mid-1817 was the Reverend Henry Kollock, minister of the Independent Presbyterian Church. Having served that church for six years, Kollock had been granted a sabbatical to travel in Europe, perhaps knowing that it was wise to be away at the time of a construction project.[8] But, by the time Kollock arrived in Liverpool for his stay with the Boltons, the commission for the church in Savannah had been awarded to someone other than Jay.

If anyone had an inside track in this search for a designer of the new Independent Presbyterian Church, Jay did. He might have presumed that this project would come his way. He was a well-trained professional, and in this contest he could claim some important associations with the enterprise. Two members of the building committee were relatives by marriage, and there were other significant familial attachments to Savannah, to this church in particular, and to the larger community of Presbyterians. The Independent Presbyterian Church traced an impetus for its founding back to the ministry of George Whitefield,[9] which was often linked to the labors of the Reverend Jay. Further, Jay's father enjoyed close ties to Presbyterian communities throughout Great Britain, and Jay had just built a prominent meeting house for a Presbyterian Seceder group in London, the Albion Chapel.

However, church records show that the members of the building committee immediately began to correspond with "the principal architects in Philadelphia, New York, and Boston." There is no mention of interest in an English architect. By late 1816, a selection had been made. It was to be John

[8] Ibid., 152; Calhoun, 94.
[9] Calhoun, 5–15, 25–35.

Holden Greene, who had recently designed and built the First Congregational Church of Providence, Rhode Island. He arrived in Savannah on January 2, 1817, to begin his work and to consult with members of the committee. The cornerstone for the building was laid on January 13.[10]

THE DESIGN

As the members of the building committee looked to the North, the report of a handsome new building raised in 1814–1816 by Greene in Providence must have caught their attention fairly quickly. The world of churches and churchmen in the United States in the early nineteenth century was fairly small. Major Protestant organizations (including Presbyterian, Congregational/Independent, and Baptist) often collaborated in various initiatives. While acknowledging their differences, they readily embraced the shared principles of a Calvinistic and evangelical faith. The fact that the Presbyterians of Savannah found a church design that suited them in a plan nearly identical to a recently erected Congregational church in Rhode Island is not at all surprising. The proposal met all of their theological, liturgical, and aesthetic requirements.

Pursuing contacts in the North would have been easy. Many Savannahians made regular forays to that region, particularly in the unseasonable Southern summers. The Reverend Kollock was a native of New Providence, New Jersey. Having trained at the College of New Jersey (later Princeton), he began his work there. After he accepted the call to Savannah in 1806, he adopted the habit of long tours of the North to escape the "insalubrious" climate of coastal Georgia in late summer and early autumn.[11] Likely Kollock and members of his Savannah congregation knew about, perhaps even visited, Greene's church.

THE SOURCE OF THE DESIGN

The composition of the Independent Presbyterian Church is a variant, albeit a most lovely version, of the most common church design in early American architecture. The pattern had been invented in 1720–1726 by James Gibbs, a Scottish architect trained in Rome. For St. Martin-in-the-

---

[10] Ibid., 92–93.

[11] Sprague, 4:268.

Fields at Trafalgar Square, Gibbs took the form of a Greek temple with a pedimented and colonnaded portico, and he perched a steeple on top of this porch. Because he distributed his designs by publishing pattern books, including *A Book of Architecture* (1728) and *Rules for Drawing the Several Parts of Architecture* (1732), St. Martin-in-the-Fields became the most frequently used model for churches in the colonies.

From John Soane at the Royal Academy, Jay would have heard a critique of Gibbs and the church at Trafalgar Square. Soane judged Gibbs to be an architect of "no fixed principles" who "mistook confusion for variety." For Soane, St. Martin-in-the-Fields was an architectural abomination, and he warned his students of the faults of this design. First, he found this composition to be "a patchwork of different ages," a pedimented classical Greek temple front topped by a Gothic spire. Then, there was the problem of the spire. Fundamentally Soane disliked spires, but he conceded that spires and towers had come to be regarded as "necessary appendages to places of worship." When these elements rose "out of the ground," they were tolerable. However, when they sat "upon the tops of roofs, as at the church of St. Martin in the Fields," they were unbearable.[12]

CONSEQUENCES FOR JAY AND SAVANNAH

In April 1816, the building committee of the Independent Presbyterian Church issued certain specifications for the new structure, including design elements and measurements. The building was to seat 1,000 in the lower pews and 350 in the galleries. The materials were to be of brick and stone, although "the whole to be rough cast [covered with coarse-textured plaster or cement] to appear like stone." There was to be an elevated steeple "but without a spire and calculated for a Bell and clock, to be at the East end of the building." A portico should be "so planned that it may be adopted or not, circular or Elliptical." The ceiling was to be "a very flat or Elliptical arch to span the whole building and depressed at the ends." They desired "a Venetian window at the west and behind the pulpit" and windows "large and suitable to a warm climate."[13]

The design guidelines offered considerable latitude. If Jay had received them, he could have met these requirements easily, but his solution would

[12] Soane, Lecture IX:200, Lecture IV:102, Lecture VI:142.

[13] Independent Presbyterian Church, Minutes, Savannah, Apr. 1816, IPC.

have been in his own way ingenious. Jay's proposal for the Independent Presbyterian Church in Savannah is lost, but it is an easy guess that it resembled Greene's plan only in the very broad particulars. It is likely that Jay shared Soane's contempt for the composition of St. Martin-in-the-Fields.

Some have seen this affair as a missed opportunity for Savannah. The city might have gained yet another important structure by Jay. It is odd that, in spite of his obvious potential as a designer of religious structures, particularly of the nonconformist variety, Jay built no church in the city. But, this much is certain: Now after two centuries, it is impossible to imagine Savannah without this church designed by Greene, located in the very heart of the city, on the southwest corner of Bull Street and Oglethorpe Avenue.

CHAPTER 11

JAY'S SAVANNAH HOUSES: "THE FAVORED JEWELS OF A DIADEM"

In Savannah, Jay is most often remembered for four private residences. Three of these survive: the Telfair House as the oldest art museum in the South, the Scarbrough House as a museum of Savannah's maritime past, and the Richardson-Owens-Thomas House as a house museum property of the Telfair Academy. The fourth, the Bulloch-Habersham House, was demolished in 1916 in the name of "progress," an act still recalled and lamented as an object lesson in municipal malfeasance. From the time these structures appeared in 1818–1820, they were often noticed, as here in 1834 by the Irish actor Tyrone Power: "With this little city [Savannah] I was exceedingly pleased.... [There are] several very ambitious-looking dwellings, built by a European architect for wealthy merchants during the palmy days of trade; these are of stone or some composition, showily designed, and very large."[1]

In 1897 three of these houses were celebrated in long articles in a Savannah newspaper—the Telfair mansion had been converted to an art museum in 1883–1885. One of these accounts included the following comment on Jay's four houses, expressing sentiments that have prevailed in this city for over a century:

> There are a few old houses in Savannah which have been spared throughout a century, with all their historic worth and grandeur of architectural design, to adorn the city here and there like the favored jewels of a diadem...[These] are, strange to say all the creations of one and the same architect, Mr. Jay...[structures of] dignity, grace and beauty...monuments to the "golden, olden glory of the days gone by."[2]

The stories of each of these four houses will be told separately. Each one is a testimony to Jay's talent and an object lesson in historic preservation. Only

---

[1] Power, 2:117–18.

[2] "An Historic Old House," *SMN*, May 16, 1897. The quotation is from "The Days Gone By" (1882), a poem by James Whitcomb Riley.

the Richardson-Owens-Thomas House survives in something close to the original condition. The Scarbrough and Telfair Houses come to us much altered because they were adapted to new uses. The Bulloch-Habersham House endured with relatively little alteration for almost a century until it was demolished in 1916 to make way for a city auditorium. The sequence of these projects is not altogether clear, but this is the usual report:

The first was certainly the Richardson House because it was underway before Jay arrived and because the design was the most impetuous, charming but a little over-dressed and a little old-fashioned. The Scarbrough House is usually claimed to be next, begun in 1818 and rushed to completion by May 1819 to accommodate the visit of President James Monroe. Stylistically it is a clear departure from the playfulness of the Richardson House, spare in its exterior ornament and sober in its rendering of the Doric order.

The Telfair House would seem to be next, because it resembles the Scarbrough House in many ways, although it was configured to meet the needs of a very different sort of client. For the purpose of this narrative, the Telfair residence will appear third even though it is dated to 1819. The Bulloch House begun in 1818 is reserved for last, because it was quite unlike the other three. In this structure, there was such a remarkable display of creativity that we regret all the more Jay's quick departure from Savannah and the demolition of this house at the beginning of the twentieth century.

Since Jay was only twenty-six years old when he arrived in Savannah and he had completed only one commission, the Albion Chapel in London, these Savannah houses reflected his native ingenuity and his training in London rather than lessons learned in the course of previous accomplishments. It is a measure of Jay's gift that, in spite of his inexperience and in less than five years, he made these four great houses and gave each one a very distinct character. Still, all four shared a number of features, including the general character of the sites, the plans, the methods and materials of construction, and the elements of ornament.

THE SITES

Nothing enhances the appearance of fine architecture more than a commodious setting, and Jay could not have been more fortunate in this regard. Savannah has a remarkable town plan. The place had been laid out by Oglethorpe, a founding trustee of the colony of Georgia and in 1733 the leader of the first group of settlers. On a high bluff of the Savannah River, Oglethorpe arranged the town in wards or districts, each one providing for public and private needs and for defense in the event of invasion by hostile forces. The source of this plan is uncertain, and a number of influences for it have been proposed. There are resemblances to ancient military encampments, British work towns of the seventeenth century, and the fashionable London squares built following the great fire of 1666. But, in its particulars the Savannah plan was unique.

The module of the plan was the ward. The shape of the ward was rectangular, usually square. At the center of each one was a square called a "Market Place" in an early document.[3] Originally these central areas were open patches of sand and mud, very unlike the parks they were to become by the early nineteenth century.

Along each side of the central square was a street, and a street intersected (but did not penetrate) the midpoint of each side of the square. This arrangement resulted in eight regions of development. North and south of the square in four sectors (northwest, northeast, southeast, and southwest) were four tythings (or tithings, referring to "tenth parts"). Each tything had ten lots in two ranks. Five of the lots faced the square and five sat behind, the two ranks separated by a passway or alley, known locally as a lane. Each tything lot measured sixty feet in frontage by ninety feet in depth, and these lots were granted to the colonists for their private dwellings.

At the west and east of the square were eight trustee lots, two linked in each one of the four sectors. The measurements of these lots varied by the size of each square, but often they conformed to the size of a tything lot (sixty feet by ninety feet). Of the two trustee lots in each region, one had frontage on the square and the second sat at the rear of the first. These lots were granted to the trustees of the colony and planned as sites for public buildings. Often these lots were joined, resulting in sixty-foot frontage on the square and 180 feet in depth. Over time, several of these joined trustee lots came to be sites of grand residences.

Three of Jay's houses (the Richardson, Telfair, and Bulloch Houses) occupied sites on squares that consolidated two trustee lots, giving them unusual prominence in the city. These sites each measured sixty feet in frontage on the square and 180 feet in depth, having streets on all four sides. In each case,

---

[3] Reps, 187.

Jay set the residence to face the square. The structure was built forward on the lot, allowing for a shallow front garden. Behind the house was a high-walled courtyard, providing for service areas and perhaps a kitchen garden. At the far end of the property was a carriage house that incorporated slave quarters. The fourth house, the Scarbrough House, was built in a new and fashionable district formed at the western perimeter of the city, on a somewhat more ample lot having ninety feet frontage and 195 feet in depth.

THE PLANS AND ELEVATIONS

These Savannah houses reflected a building type then fashionable in England and later called "the Regency villa." In Jay's interpretation of this style, the footprint of each structure was a square, filling most of the sixty feet allowed by the lot size, and the elevation was a square mass. A high basement included kitchen and laundry areas; a first story had public rooms and areas for family gathering, such as parlors and a dining room; and a second story contained bedchambers. Set on the property with a small garden forecourt, at three of these houses (the Richardson, Scarbrough, and Telfair houses) a one-story colonnaded portico was the central feature. The porch was accessed by double stairs, one flight at each side. This motif was changed at the Bulloch House to a circular porch and stairs. At the Richardson and Bulloch houses, the main entry was set back in an exedra or niche.

The number of windows in each structure was limited, providing for substantial masonry walls. For structural integrity, windows at the second story surmounted those of the first story. These openings were recessed into the wall, often set in blind arches or blind rectangles, called reveals, to emphasize the mass of the building. With the exception of the Richardson House, the ornament of the exteriors was spare, with walls animated only by the horizontals of cornices and string courses and the verticals of set-back corners.

At the Richardson, Telfair, and Bulloch houses, the entry opened to a vestibule and revealed a central-hall plan with rooms arranged to the right and left. Just beyond the vestibule was a grand stairway leading to the second level. Usually this entry hall was surmounted by a skylight, and the second floor had large windows centered at each end to promote ventilation. At the Scarbrough House, entry was through a large open atrium, with spiral stairs to the second story set at the far side of this space.

The central hall and the adjoining rooms were conformed as single or multiple cubical spaces, resulting in high ceilings. Curved or polygonal elements provided elements of surprise. These included curved end walls of some interior rooms, rear walls that resulted in projecting bays, and shaped rooms such an octagonal study at the Telfair House and a circular parlor at the Bulloch House.

THE MATERIALS AND METHODS

Aspects of Jay's work reveal his dependence on local conventions, including certain materials and methods of construction unique to the coastal region. More remarkable is the use of a number of imported products, some of which may have made their first appearance in American architecture in these Savannah houses. In particular are elements cited by John Summerson as hallmarks of the Regency style: stucco, artificial stone, and ornamental cast iron.[4]

The extent to which Jay relied on imported goods is exemplified by a bill of lading for cargo on a ship from London in 1818 consigned to "R. R." (Richard Richardson) and "W. J." (William Jay), which cited these materials and merchandise:

> 300 casks Roman Cement, painters colors (160 kegs paint, 50 jugs of oil, 10 casks of oil), 8 cases copper, 5 casks painters colors (white lead in oil), 24,500 bricks, 5 cases lamps figures &c., 2 cases child's chaises, 2 cases kitchen ranges, 37 cases of household furniture [marked for "R. R."]; 36 cases stone, 2 cases paintings, 1 case paper watercolors, 4 packages containing gig [to raise nap on fabric] complete with chaise harnesses &c., 1 case locks &c., 1 cask colors, 1 case paint brushes [marked for "W. J."].[5]

The builders or contractors were white men, often from the Northeast, who had come to Savannah in search of work. Likely much of the labor was rendered by black men. Some of these were freedmen who had achieved the status of skilled workers, such as masons or carpenters; some were enslaved persons, perhaps plantation slaves who were hired out for labor during times when they did not work the fields.

Jay used a variety of materials:

---

[4] Summerson, *Architecture in Britain*, 438.

[5] "Entry of Merchandise imported by R. Richardson, Ship Cora from London," Nov. 9, 1818, U.S. Custom Service, Inward Foreign Cargo Manifests, Savannah, GA (1817–1819), National Archives, Washington, D.C. (hereafter USCS/IFC).

Ballast bricks and stone. Early residents of Savannah had built with wood, which was abundant in the region. A disastrous fire in 1796 provoked conversations about the need to use nonflammable products in construction, but brick and stone were not readily available. By 1819 bricks were being manufactured near Savannah, but records suggest that most of the brick and stone for Jay's projects were brought as ballast on ships from England.

Bermuda stone. Bermuda stone is a type of coquina or fossilized limestone. A primary material for construction in Bermuda, it had been transported for use in the coastal regions of the American South in the colonial era. This material was surely introduced to Jay by his first client Richard Richardson, a shipper and a native of Bermuda.

Tabby. Jay would not have known tabby (a composite of lime, sand, and crushed oyster shells mixed with water) before his arrival in Georgia. The material was formed into molds for structural elements, such as foundations and walls. Its origins are uncertain (perhaps Africa or Spain), but it had been used in the region of Florida at least since the late sixteenth century and later in South Carolina and Georgia. Tabby was also widely used in Bermuda and would have been known to Richardson. Its advantages were that the components were readily available, the product was familiar to local craftsmen, and the result was a very durable material.

Slate roofing. Twenty years after his work in Savannah, Jay found himself in the British civil service on the island of Mauritius in the Indian Ocean, occupied with plans for a new central market in the capital city of Port Louis. Among his recommendations for this project was to use slate for the roofs of the bazaar. In a report to his supervisor, Jay wrote, "I have the honor to state that I was the first to introduce these [French slates] in Savannah in Georgia...and I feel quite assured that if good slates are used here and well laid on it will be one of the most useful and ornamental introductions this island ever enjoyed."[6]

Plumbing. At least one of Jay's houses, the Richardson House, was fitted with cisterns to hold rain water to accommodate two flushing toilets, various sinks and bathtubs, and a shower. Lead pipes conveyed the water collected from the roof into attic cisterns, allowing the water to flow by gravity. Brick

[6] W. Jay to J. A. Lloyd, Jan. 21, 1837, National Archives of Mauritius, Public Record Office and Colonial Office Correspondence Collections (1835–1845), Coromandel, Mauritius (hereafter NAM/PRO-CO).

drains and ceramic sewer pipes carried waste from the house.[7] Such a system may have been unique in this country at this time. Still rare in England, plumbing appeared in only the finest homes of the era, particularly in urban settings such as London. While most of the components were imported from England, the plan for plumbing at the Richardson House may be credited to Richardson. For geologic reasons, plumbing systems had an early history in Bermuda. Generally, plumbing in American houses did not appear until the mid-nineteenth century in populous areas with the construction of public waterworks and sewer systems.

EXTERIOR FINISHES AND ORNAMENT

The exteriors of Jay's Savannah houses featured a variety of English products of the era, including stucco, artificial stone ornament, and elements of cast iron:

Stucco. A modern feature of Jay's Savannah buildings was their skin of stucco applied over brick. A versatile material, stucco was sometimes smooth, sometimes textured with sand, and sometimes scored to resemble stone blocks. It could be tinted with pigment or painted with wash colors to imitate the appearance of various types of stone. In England brick had declined in popularity by the mid-eighteenth century, and stone became the preferred material. But in busy-building Regency London, quantities of stone were limited, and costs were high. An economical solution was to hide bricks under stucco.

Stucco was not a new product. It was a formulation akin to cements made from lime, sand, and gravel, which had a history reaching back at least 7,000 years. By the 1770s, stucco had become fashionable in England in the hands of Robert Adam, a popular architect who rendered a very refined and elegant version of the Neoclassical style. By 1814 John Nash, the architect favored by the prince regent, was well known for his use of this material, earning him this rebuke: "Augustus at Rome was for building renown'd,/ And o' marble he left what of brick he had found;/ But is not our Nash, too, a very great master?—/ He finds us all brick and he leaves us all plaster."[8]

The finishing material Nash used was a product known as "Parker's stucco" or "Parker's Roman cement." In 1796 James Parker, an Englishman,

---

[7] Matero and Studenroth, 103–109.

[8] "Architectural Improvements in London," *Quarterly* Review, June 1826:193.

was granted a patent for a new quick-drying product that could be applied to unsightly brick walls and scored to resemble ashlar (dressed stone). By 1810 Parker's patent had expired, and the market quickly offered forty-some products of similar character.[9]

The means by which Jay achieved the modern surfaces of his Savannah residences is documented in a report he sent to François Didier Petit de Villers, a local merchant, at the time of the work on the Scarbrough House. Jay wrote, "I hope you will always avail yourself of any information I can give and I shall be extremely happy in procuring you any quantity of cement your friend may require. I go to England early this summer but should it be wanted before I will send for it. I can procure it much more reasonable than any one else." To this note, Jay appended the following explanation:

> Roman cement is used either on Stone—wood or brick.... I have never yet accurately ascertained how much feet one barrel would cover—but I find that Mr. Scarbroughs [sic] House—which is 60 feet square, & 36 high, has taken 85 Barrels—and is sufficiently strong.... The calculation of expence [*sic*] I make, is that, it will cost materials and labor 1 dollar and a half a square yard.... The cemented walls are generally painted over with water or oil colours; & when painted in oil, sand is frequently dashed upon, before the paint is dry, which gives it the appearance of hewn-stone building.[10]

The stucco Jay used in Savannah has been determined to be a natural cement of the sort patented by Parker. This was a formulation not then in use in this country, so it was certainly imported.

Coade stone ornament. The porticos of all four of these houses were distinguished by classical columns and capitals of refined proportions and details. Often admired, the capitals appeared to be products of the art of stone carving. In 1917 Fiske Kimball issued a report to the Archaeological Institute of America with the sad news that "the beautiful Bulloch house in Savannah...[was] demolished by the municipality and its delicate Greek capitals were thrown into the stone crusher in spite of efforts to save it."[11]

---

[9] Summerson, *Architecture in Britain*, 438–39.

[10] W. Jay to Petit de Villers, n.d. [early 1819], Keith M. Read Collection, University of Georgia Library, Athens, GA.

[11] S. F. Kimball, "Report of the Committee on Colonial and National Art in North America," *Bulletin of the Archaeological Institute of America*, Dec. 1917, 64.

Jay's capitals were castings of a ceramic material fabricated to imitate stone, but less costly and more durable. Stone has the unhappy characteristic of responding to weather, deteriorating over time in conditions of damp and cold. In England, where damp and cold are common, experiments with an artificial stone made of terra cotta ("baked earth" or fired clay), which would resist the effects of weathering, had been made as early as the 1720s. By the end of the eighteenth century, this product was successful and exceedingly popular.

The principal purveyor of this material was the Coade Artificial Stone Manufactory in Lambeth, on the south bank of the River Thames in London. In 1769 Eleanor Coade, a single woman who took the title of "Mrs." commonly extended to unmarried businesswomen, opened a factory to make products of artificial stone. The process involved mixing fired and unfired clay with flint, sand, and ground glass; then setting this material in plaster molds and firing it at a very high temperature. The result was a superior stoneware impervious to moisture.[12]

Through the period of the Regency, Coade stone was a great success. A number of the greatest architects of the day commissioned unique ornaments for public buildings and private residences, and Mrs. Coade filled these requests with the designs of well-known sculptors and painters. But most Coade products were made in quantity and sold at a cost very much below what would be required for carved stone. These castings were listed in an extensive catalog and displayed at a factory showroom.

Although there were other purveyors of artificial stone, it seems likely that Jay secured his materials from Coade. He may have known members of the Coade family. They were prominent dissenters, and the factory was in the region of David Riddall Roper's office where Jay took his training. One wonders if, when he returned to England in 1822, Jay rushed to acquire a copy of a Coade stone bust of his father, advertised in March of that year: "REV. WM. JAY, OF BATH./ At Coade's Ornamental Stone and Scagliola Marble Works, Narrow-wall Lambeth, the Friends and admirers of this celebrated Character can be furnished with finely executed Life-size Busts of him, which having been made from an Impression of his face, present a likeness strikingly

[12] Van Lemmen, 8–9.

correct. Price Three Guineas each."[13]

Cast-iron architectural ornament. Summerson named cast iron as one of the characteristic elements of Regency architecture. First used in the construction of bridges, by 1796 it was employed in the structure of mills where fire-resistance was desired. In fact, early cast iron was not fire resistant—it buckled in the heat of fire and cracked when firefighters doused it with water. But, because the material was malleable, with the capacity to be cast in all manner of shapes and patterns, it soon became popular for a great variety of ornamental elements, such as decorative railings and balusters and for components of construction, such as columns and window units.[14]

There are handsome cast iron elements at all of Jay's Savannah houses, and these are among the earliest examples of ornamental cast iron used in this country. On the exterior of Jay's houses, the decorative flourishes of cast iron often contrast with the spare mass of these structures. Of these elements, the most remarkable is the south balcony of the Richardson House, known as "the Lafayette balcony," a story saved for a later chapter. There is also beautiful ironwork at the south porch of the Scarbrough House, and the Telfair House has fine shallow balconies at the two windows flanking the portico. The gates and fencing at the Bulloch House, sold at the time the house was demolished in 1916, were judged to be among the most valuable elements of the property. All of these products were certainly imported from England, perhaps from the region of Liverpool where cast iron was manufactured in abundance and variety and where Jay spent several weeks in 1814 pursuing the commission for the Wellington Rooms.

INTERIOR FINISHES AND ORNAMENT

Inside Jay's houses, walls were generally free of applied ornament, broken only by the sculptural elements of niches or alcoves. Doors set in curved walls were made to conform to those curves. Moldings framing doors and windows were deep and richly carved. The base molding was tall with a bold profile, a pattern derived from the base of an Ionic column. Surfaces were painted in the rich and nuanced colors of the Regency, often featuring schemes of various reds and greens. Some surfaces were painted in *faux bois* ("false wood") in

---

[13] "Rev. Wm. Jay, of Bath, At Coade's Ornamental Stone and Scagliola Marble Works," 19.

[14] Summerson, *Architecture in Britain*, 438.

imitation of the distinctive grains of exotic woods, such as red oak. Selective details were rendered in gilt, such as column capitals or elements of stairway balusters. Doors and moldings were painted in a cream color.

Ceilings were animated by stucco patterns of Greek ornament, such as the Greek key, or occasionally painted with *trompe l'oeil* ("fool the eye") sky scenes. Cornice ornament or crown molding was formed of various Greek patterns or shapes cast in plaster and standing in relief against a painted cove. Floors were of "heart pine" (or "heartpine"), wood taken from the heart or center of an old growth tree having no knots, a material which was dense, strong, and resistant to disease and decay. These floors were covered with fine carpets, rugs, painted floor cloths, or straw mats. Windows were fitted with Venetian blinds, and some were elaborately draped in the Regency manner. Some windows held colored glass, such as the amber glass in the Richardson dining room.

Some products Jay imported from England:

Stock plaster ornament. One of the efficiencies of building in this era in England was the availability of stock plaster or composite ornaments to trim interiors. Before this time, large projects had required battalions of carvers working in wood, stone, and plaster. But, with the building boom of the late eighteenth and early nineteenth centuries, there were too few competent carvers to meet the needs of the industry. No matter, a Regency villa could be decorated with elegant trim and with relative ease and efficiency by the use of stock patterns reproduced by molds. The effect was fine, and the cost was much reduced.

Among the patterns used prominently were motifs from ancient Greek temples and monuments. Employed in the ancient world as potent symbols, they were now chosen for aesthetic reasons. An architect's gift was in knowing where and when to use what shapes and in what combinations. Part of Jay's skill was his ability to employ this vocabulary of ornament to make each of his rooms "speak," each with a different voice and to a different effect.

In the repertoire of familiar motifs, Jay favored *Meander patterns*, named for the winding River Meander in Turkey, decorative borders formed of a continuous line shaped into repeated motifs, such as the rectangles of the Greek key or the running spirals of the Vitruvian wave; the *laurel wreath*, a circle formed of the broad leaves of the bay laurel; and the *anthemion*, resembling a flower, variously associated with the honeysuckle, the blossom of an acanthus plant, the lotus, or a palmette having fan-like fronds. Of these elements, Jay most favored the anthemion. Likely of Egyptian origin, the Greek anthemion appeared first in the Ionic style of the late fifth century B.C. During the Regency, this figure was an emblem of elegance and refinement.

Faux finishes and a distinctive color palette. Another mark of high style in the Regency was the use of *faux* (false) finishes, such as bronzing, marbleizing, and wood graining. For example, the less expensive material of cast iron could be bronzed by painting it green or brown in imitation of patinated or weathered bronze. Columns made more cheaply and quickly in wood could be marbleized, painted with the distinctive colors and veins of marble. Trim or panels of unremarkable wood or plaster surfaces could be grained, painted to resemble exotic woods. Often these treatments were economies, but occasionally fashion determined that a *faux* finish could more effectively render the aspect of sumptuousness desired during this period.

The color palette for the style was remarkable in the range and character of the colors used. Dining rooms were often painted in a saturated red, while hallways and other chambers were treated with nuanced colors in a dull-lustre finish, including French gray (a gray tinted with bits of blue and red); greens in sage, pea, sea, and olive; apricot; peach; yellow fawn (a light yellow tinted with brown); and buff.[15]

Imported fixtures and furnishings. Jay's Savannah houses were equipped with many imported elements such as light fixtures and fireplace mantels. He was familiar with the accoutrements of the modern Regency style, he knew the suppliers from his time and training in London, and his first patron in Savannah, Richard Richardson, was a prominent shipper. These goods from England could come to him readily and frequently.

Of particular note were the carved mantelpieces in Jay's houses. Quality in material and manufacture differed according to the prominence of the room in the house, so fine mantels were located in the public rooms and simpler ones in the bedchambers above. In all of Jay's surviving houses, there is no more elegant chamber than the parlor of the Richardson-Owens-Thomas House, and centered on the east wall in the room is a handsome white marble mantelpiece. This mantel is original to the house and dated to around 1819. At each side of the opening is a female figure clothed in the classical manner with diaphanous drapery and standing on a plinth in an arched recess. This

[15] Matero and Studenroth, 110.

mantel has been credited to Richard Westmacott, a prominent sculptor of the day. It is probable that it was a product of Westmacott's studio, a busy enterprise in which a number of assistants produced high quality ornament for the building trades.[16]

A PRECEDENT FOR THE SAVANNAH HOUSES

There is no evidence that Jay designed a private residence before he planned the Richardson House in 1816. Yet, all of his Savannah houses are remarkably sophisticated renderings of the plan and ornament of a Regency villa. How might he have gained experience with this style? As a student and young professional in London in 1808–1817, Jay would have seen the proliferation of this building type. Regency villas were fine and well-appointed houses, smaller versions of grand country estates, often built in suburban areas such as the outskirts of London. The occupants were the newly rich, the beneficiaries of the Industrial Revolution and the expanding empire in which fortunes, often large and quick, were made through the production and trade of goods.

During Jay's articled pupilage, his mentor, Roper, designed and built a house on Herne Hill, south of the old City of London and now in the London Borough of Lambeth. Brockwell Hall was built for John Blades, a self-made man of very considerable accomplishment and wealth, rather like some of Jay's patrons in Savannah. Blades produced chandeliers, candelabra, and other glass ornaments in opulent designs, and in 1789 he was appointed "Cut Glass Manufacturer to His Majesty, George III." His suburban estate survives as the center of Brockwell Park, one of the great parks of London. It is frequently cited as a good example of a Regency villa in the Grecian style.

THE VERY GOOD ADVICE OF JOHN SOANE

Jay's apprenticeship with Roper did afford him good practical experience, but an important teacher was John Soane, whose lectures he may have heard at the Royal Academy and whose opinions about the art of architecture he valued. In the course of a very short stay in Savannah, Jay came to express himself in a remarkably mature and facile style, suggesting that the voice he was hearing in his head was that of Soane.

---

[16] Lerski, 74, 325 n. 32; M. G. Sullivan, 1356-66.

Soane taught the preeminence of systems of proportion and ornament of ancient Greek architecture. From these guiding principles, he deduced that the plan of a domestic building should be based on the figure of the square, with volumes of spaces based on the cube. However, he warned, "It has been said by foreigners (and perhaps with too much truth), that the architecture of England is in general so very deficient in variety that it seems as if all our architects had but one mind and manner."[17] An answer to that criticism was to promote the addition of other shapes in house plans, such as circles, ellipses, and various polygons. Jay's square houses were enlivened by shaped rooms (octagons and circles) and rooms with curved ends.

Soane declared that "solidity" was "essential" to architecture. He said,

> The solidity of a building depends on the goodness of the materials and their application, the sufficiency of the foundations and the walls raised upon them, all of which must be made regularly decreasing in thickness as they advance in height, and raised truly perpendicular in every part. All the openings of every kind must be placed exactly one above the other, so that in every part solid may rest upon solid and void be seen over void.[18]

Accordingly, Jay built sturdy houses. His compositions were distinguished for the restraint with which he pierced the wall and for the careful arrangements of solid over solid, void over void.

Soane defined beauty in this way: "[A]n edifice...must be perfect in its symmetry and uniformity.... In a word, an edifice can only be considered beautiful when all its parts are in exact proportion, well balanced and combined together with proper quantities of light and shadow, richness and repose."[19] For Jay, classical symmetry was a controlling principle. The placement of a window echoed another window, even when the second was blind, and a door echoed another door, even when the second led nowhere. And, Soane warned, "[T]he young architect is too often led astray, thinking that a profusion of ornaments always increases the beauty of a building. This is a mistake: it is in simplicity that all real decoration is to be found."[20] Characteristic of Jay's designs are balance and restraint, hallmarks of the ancient Greek style as they had been described by Soane.

---

[17] Soane, Lecture XI:249.

[18] Ibid., Lecture VII:165–66.

[19] Ibid.

[20] Ibid., Lecture XI:240.

THE CLIENTS

Little is known of Jay's relationship with his clients, yet this matter is central in forming the character and style of a private residence. This much can be surmised: Richard Richardson, William Scarbrough, Alexander Telfair, and Archibald Stobo Bulloch were young, ambitious, and prosperous—although for three of them wealth was fleeting. These four houses expressed the accomplishments and aspirations of these men and the women with whom they shared their lives. Each design was remarkable and singular, but what these men shared was trust in the taste and skills of a young English architect trained in the modern style of Regency London.

Above, Billy Jay the Boy Preacher, at nineteen years old; middle, the home of William Jay, the stone mason; below, Fonthill Abbey, the Gothic Revival mansion built for William Beckford.

Anne Jay Bolton and her two eldest children
as painted by William Etty in 1817.

Engraving of the Reverend Jay, the Dissident Divine of Bath, based on the painting by William Etty done in 1817.

The Prince Regent.

Brighton Pavilion.

Wellington Rooms, Liverpool
Edmund Aikin, architect.

Almshouses, Hackney, London
David Riddall Roper, architect.

Jay's Albion Chapel, Moorfields, London.

Billy Jay's meeting hall at Christian Malford, Wiltshire.

Independent Presbyterian Church, Savannah, 1817
John Holden Greene, architect (photographed in 1893).

Hannah More.

Robert Bolton, husband of Anne Jay Bolton.

Above, Rev. Cornelius Winter; middle, Rev. John Wesley; below Rev. George Whitefield.

Above left, set-back corner; above right, window with deep reveal and apron panel; below, Coade stone balusters.

Above, Coade stone capital, Corinthian of the Choragic Monument of Lysicrates, Athens; below, Coade stone capital, Ionic of the Propylaea, Acropolis, Athens.

Above, front porch; below, builder's inscription
of construction dates behind the entry stairs.

Above, front porch; below, ironwork detail on the south porch.

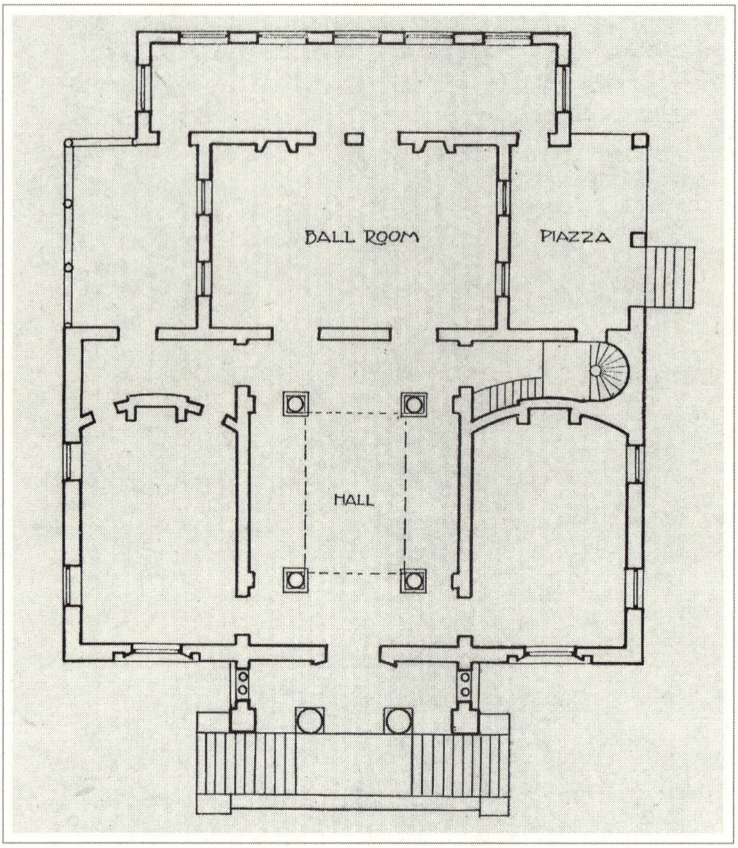

Plan for the main floor.

Eaton Hall, Cheshire, country seat of Lord Grosvenor
was often compared by traveling Savannahians to Jay's Scarbrough House.

President James Monroe,
a resident of the Scarbrough House in 1819.

The *Savannah*, a ship fitted for sail and steam power.

Children of the West Broad Street School, Scarbrough House, ca. 1940.

CHAPTER 12

RICHARDSON-OWENS-THOMAS HOUSE: A "DELIGHTFUL HOME"

The house designed for Richard Richardson may have been Jay's first plan for a private residence. It was the first of his projects in Savannah, the opportunity for him to reveal his skills to prospective clients. In fact, this house is quite different in character from the other residences, an exuberant design rather more like a "show piece" than Jay's later more sober compositions. Planned in 1816, construction began in November of that year, thirteen months before Jay arrived in Savannah.

This house is the only one of Jay's Savannah projects to survive virtually intact. While Richardson's time here was brief, the house soon came into the hands of George Welshman Owens, an appreciative owner who understood its special character. Owens tended to its needs with minimal alterations and obliged his heirs to do the same. Occupied by members of the Owens family from 1830 until 1951, it was bequeathed to the Telfair Academy of Arts and Sciences on the condition that this home be preserved as a house museum. It was a gift gladly received. In its very long history as a private residence, this place had come to be appreciated in Savannah as a uniquely beautiful building and a "delightful home,"[1] a true ornament of the city.

The Richardson-Owens-Thomas House was the subject of a long profile in the *Savannah Morning News* in 1897, praised as the only one of the Savannah residences designed by Jay that had survived as a family home. By that date, the Scarbrough House had been fitted as a school for black children, the Telfair House had been transformed into an art museum, and it may have been known that the Bulloch-Habersham House would soon pass into other hands with its future uncertain. The author of this article observed that the Richardson-Owens-Thomas House was a reminder of a proud and prosperous past, writing, "[T]he exterior of the house bears that commanding aspect now which its distinguished creator [the architect "Mr. Jay"] seems to have

---

[1] C. R. A. [Agnew], "In Memoriam—James Gray Thomas, M.D.," *American Practitioner, A Monthly Journal of Medicine and Surgery*, Mar. 1885, 185–86.

caught from the grandeur of the times when he drew the plans for its construction."[2]

A TOUR OF THE HOUSE

The long survival of this extraordinary building has been a matter of pride to Savannahians, a delight for visitors to the city, and a subject of interest to architectural historians. It is an ingenious design, combining motifs from several different styles, and it is somewhat whimsical, reflecting the playfulness of a young architect and the enthusiasm of an obliging client.

As at the other Savannah houses by Jay, the spirit of the building is suggested by the classical order featured at the entry. The Scarbrough House is a solemn and stately Doric, and the Telfair is a patrician Corinthian. Here the theme is Ionic—feminine, graceful, lyrical. At the portico, the volutes or scrolls of the Ionic capital are echoed in the curves of the stairs, the profiles of the floor and the roof of the porch, and the play of arches above the windows of the second story. The double curved stairway is a composition often and aptly called "welcoming arms." The portico bows out gently, topped by a serpentine entablature, drawing the visitor onto a porch where there is the further surprise that the entry to the house is set back in a great niche. Standing in this hollow at the front double doors, you have already come into the space of this home.

Compared to Jay's later works, the facade is fussy, even a little old-fashioned. Here there is a five-bay front; the three-bay fronts of the later houses were more modern. The corner quoins of the first story are leftover from Georgian ornament, but they disappear at the second story and are replaced by another Georgian convention of end pilasters, here Doric. The roof of a very low pitch is concealed by a parapet or wall, giving the illusion of a fashionably flat roof. The parapet is punctuated by the march of a charming motif, a recessed rectangle with corners of concave curves, each rectangle posed above a rank of windows on all of the faces of the building. Above that engaging portico, an arched window (actually French doors) echoes the niche below and is set beneath the shape of a pediment, which is fixed at its ends by more Doric pilasters. The rectangular windows of the second story are recessed in arched reveals—more curves, as grace notes.

[2] "An Historic Old House," *SMN*, May 16, 1897.

The same elements—a center pediment, quoins, pilasters, and arched reveals—appear on the south flank of the house. Originally the rear of the structure was distinguished by two polygonal projections rising for only one story with an open porch stretched between them. In his only substantial renovation of the building, Owens added rooms at the rear by extending these polygons to two stories and enclosing the space between them above the open porch.

Entering this house from the front porch, one steps into an elegant though shallow formal vestibule. Just beyond this space, and flanking a magnificent stairway, are two grand Corinthian columns, fluted and with gilded capitals. These two columns mark the first rise of the stairway that fills the center hall, a style appropriately called "imperial stairs." Prominent stairs were the centerpieces of three of Jay's Savannah houses (here and at the Telfair and Bulloch-Habersham Houses), but this is the only one that survives. Great center stairways were passing from fashion in the early nineteenth century because they gave too ready access to the private rooms above. But their formal presentation must have pleased some of Jay's Savannah clients, who relished the symbolism of descending such a splendid cascade of steps.

In this house, the adventure of ascending these stairs promised another surprise. The journey up comes in two stages, first halfway to a landing and then up a divided return to the second story. On the second floor appears an arched cantilevered walkway across the stairwell, connecting to rooms at the back of the house. This feature has the appearance of a bridge. It is a delightfully odd invention, so curious that some have doubted that this was original to the house, but careful studies have shown that it was.[3] And while it may be odd, it is efficient, allowing access to the back rooms and leaving the central space open to permit the circulation of air in a climate where circulating air is very often much desired.

There is sometimes a quarrel about what name should be given to the style of this structure. "Regency" is the right choice to describe its aspect of "showiness" and the delights and surprises that are met at every turn. For example, the ceiling of the parlor, the first room to the right of the vestibule, is elegant trickery. This square room is topped by a shallow dome. To fool the eye into believing that a rectangle can be covered by a dome, the ceiling is supported at four corners by spandrels, triangular segments here appearing as

---

[3] Matero and Studenroth, 90–91.

fans of gathered cloth.

Across the vestibule is the dining room where there are several ingenious elements. A shallow niche on the north wall provides space for a richly carved Regency console, the only piece of furniture remaining from the Richardson era. Above the console is a high narrow window with amber glass behind a Greek key screen, causing a golden light to spill into this space. At the east end of this room are curved walls with fitted curved doors topped by demilune (half-moon) windows. The cornice of this room is enlivened by a popular classical motif often used by Jay, a row of anthemia (stylized lotus or honeysuckle blossoms) drawn together with swags, standing free against a painted background, catching light on their surfaces, and casting deep shadows behind.

Also on the main floor was a bedroom suite on the south just beyond the parlor, which included a dressing room and—among the true wonders of this house—chambers for a fully functioning bathtub and toilet. And on the north just beyond the dining room, a family or common room. The second floor was configured with bedrooms and a library. The basement contained the kitchens and pantries, including space for the storage of blocks of ice. Here also were a laundry room, a bathing area with tubs and a shower, and a large cistern where rainwater collected by gutters and pipes from the roof were stored.

Located on two joined trustee lots at the northeast corner of Oglethorpe Square, the main house was built forward on the site, facing the square and with a small front garden. Behind the house was an ample courtyard closed from the streets by high walls of tabby, likely a work space for the home—a well and privies were here, and perhaps a kitchen garden. The carriage house at the rear of the lot included quarters for the slaves.

THE CLIENT: RICHARD RICHARDSON

This house was built for Richard Richardson, a Savannah merchant, shipper, and banker. And just as we look for the hand of a gifted and ambitious young architect in the design of this house, it is right to search for evidence of the man for whom it was built. Commissioned residences are collaborations between clients and architects, usually unequal partnerships in which the client prevails. There is no reason to imagine that Jay's Savannah houses were exceptions to this rule, and perhaps the house that reveals the heaviest hand of the client is this one. After all, it was designed in England for a plot of land in the American South. Jay had never seen Savannah. He was entirely dependent on Richardson for the description of the site, its measurements, its topography, the conditions of the climate, and the availability of materials and of skilled and unskilled labor. In an age when gentlemen of means often designed their own houses, Richardson was surely very involved in this project. In part, this would be true because Jay was young; so far as is known this was his first attempt at the design of a residence. In part, this was true because Jay was absent for the first year of the construction of this house, leaving the important initial phases of building to the watchful eye of Richardson.

Richardson was born in Bermuda in 1785, the son of one Robert Richardson. He found his way to Savannah by 1804 at the age of nineteen, just when he might be setting the course for his life.[4] Though little is known of Richardson before this date, his was likely the story of many young men from Bermuda in those years. In fact, when the history of this house was recounted in the 1897 newspaper article, what was remembered about Richardson was that he was from Bermuda, as if that signified something important about his character and meant something for the style of his house on Oglethorpe Square.[5]

Bermudians were well known in the American South in the early nineteenth century. These seven islands—or more than one hundred if you count the array of outcroppings of porous limestone formed during the era of glacial advance and retreat—were not settled until the English claimed them in 1609 as part of the sometimes unsuccessful efforts to establish a colony in Virginia. The small land mass (only about twenty square miles) could hardly accommodate the number of English families who settled there. Sons were sent to England to study, and by the several hundreds these sons emigrated to the American South where their seafaring skills were much valued.

By the early eighteenth century, Bermudians were second to none in their mastery of the maritime industries. Of the native cedar, they built the Bermuda sloop, a fore-and-aft rigged sailing vessel made for speed and maneuverability, with a deep hull capable of carrying a large cargo. Through the eighteenth century, these ships commanded much of the trade between the American South and the West Indies (the islands of the Caribbean). In 1850

---

[4] R. Bolton, *Genealogical...Account of the Family of Bolton*, 139.

[5] "An Historic Old House," *SMN*, May 16, 1897.

Charles Dickens told the history of the islands in this way: "[E]very Bermudian, being born within a mile of the water, was bred amphibious.... [T]he whole population was occupied in building, or rigging, or manning, or loading, vessels of some kind.... White or black, they were all sailors and seafaring to a man, almost to a woman."[6]

Little is known of Richardson before he arrived in Savannah, but Jay's brother Cyrus had these memories of Richardson's brother:

> [He] was one of the largest merchants in Bermuda, and when in England—for he was very partial to his mother-country—spent a considerable portion of his time at the London Coffee-house, Ludgate Hill. He was a great grower and importer of arrowroot, which at that time was almost universally displayed in the shop-windows as Richardson's arrowroot. He was rich and fond of company, and frequently invited myself and young Cooper [Henry Cooper, a colorful London lawyer] to dine with him; the dinners and wine were first-rate.[7]

In Savannah, Richardson prospered. In 1808, at the age of twenty-three, he entered into partnership with Robert and John Bolton, prominent cotton factors (agents) and shippers in regular commerce with England. In December 1811, this association was further cemented when Richardson married Frances Lewis Bolton, the third daughter of Robert (the founder of the factorage) and Sarah Bolton.[8] Frances was the sister of Jay's brother-in-law Robert Bolton. When Robert married Anne Jay in May 1811 in Bath, Richardson may have attended the ceremony. On that occasion, he would have met Anne's brother William, who was nineteen years old and three years into his training in London.

Richardson became a man of many occupations: merchant, seaman, attorney, banker, and broker for goods and real estate. He was quick to establish a place in the community. He joined the Georgia Militia and soon came to serve on a variety of boards, including the building committees for the Independent Presbyterian Church and the Savannah Theater. He was often a contributor to charitable organizations, but, in the confounded universe of his day, Richardson owned and sold slaves, and he provided for the purchase of

---

[6] C. Dickens, "The Good Governor," *Household Words*, Aug. 31, 1850, 547–48.

[7] C. Jay, *The Law*, 339–40.

[8] "Partnership," *Republican and Savannah Evening Ledger*, Jan. 30, 1808; R. Bolton, *Genealogical...Account of the Family of Bolton*, 139–41.

some to reunite families. He was well known as the guardian and trustee for Andrew Cox Marshall, to whom he advanced money to buy his freedom and assume the leadership of the First African Baptist Church in Savannah, a ministry Marshall pursued from 1812 until his death in 1856.[9]

BUILDING A HOUSE ON OGLETHORPE SQUARE

By early 1816, Richardson had made the decision to build a home in Savannah to accommodate his growing family (there were three children by that date) and to proclaim his status in the city. In March 1816, he secured Trust Lot X in Anson Ward on Oglethorpe Square, a location as much a symbol of his success as his house would be. The site for Richardson's house was composed of two trustee lots that had been joined, resulting in a single lot sixty feet wide as it faced the square by 180 feet deep, bounded on all four sides by streets. In 1756 these lots had been granted by George II to the two men who had surveyed the original colony. Subsequently these two properties were sold and joined, changing hands several times before this land was acquired by Richardson.[10]

Richardson might have designed his own home or hired a local builder capable of drafting a plan. There were no professional architects in the city or for that matter in the whole of the South, and there were only a very few in the Northeast. But, Richardson and his wife must have heard often of the accomplishments of Jay from Robert and Anne Bolton. While there is no evidence that Jay had previously designed a house, when Robert settled in Liverpool in 1816 in a fine residence at No. 8 Great George Street, he "greatly enlarged" his home to accommodate a very substantial collection of books.[11] Jay may have contributed in some measure to that project.

In the usual telling of this tale, sometime between March and November 1816, Jay was persuaded to design a house for Richardson. Then, after the house had been in construction for a year, he journeyed to Savannah to direct the completion of this project. More likely, the plan for the Richardson House was drawn by mid-1816 with no prospect that the architect would travel to Georgia. Richardson assumed oversight of the work. Then, by late 1817 Jay

---

[9] Sprague, 6:255–56.

[10] R. Richardson, "Anson Ward, Trust Lot 'X,' 1816," Chatham County Records Office, Deed Books (1818–1823), Savannah, GA (hereafter cited as CCRO).

[11] R. Bolton, *Genealogical...Account of the Family of Bolton*, 152.

determined that he was ready to leave England after having failed to establish a practice in London. By that date, news of the success of the remarkable house being built on Oglethorpe Square and the promise of other commissions—a theater, a bank, perhaps other residences—was enough to encourage Jay to pack his bags for the long and bumpy ride across the Atlantic.

BERMUDA CONNECTIONS

The 1897 newspaper account of Richardson's house included these curious observations:

> The palatial residence which Mr. Richardson had caused to be built was, it is said, a reproduction of the government house of the Bermudas. Mr. Jay, the architect from England having had much to do with the government work there. Mr. Richardson himself was born in Bermuda, which fact serves to corroborate the statement that the mansion he directed to be built should have been after the pattern of the government house there.

Of course, Jay had nothing at all to do with Bermuda, nor was he as declared elsewhere in this same article "one of the most noted architects of England."[12] But, the connection of Richardson and Bermuda could explain much of the character of this house.

The report that Richardson's "palatial residence" was a copy of the government house in Bermuda is difficult to assess. In 1897, the year of the Savannah newspaper account, Bermuda's Government House was well known as quite a grand edifice, but it had been built only a few years before in 1892. That building had replaced Mount Langdon (built in 1815), an unremarkable structure bearing no resemblance at all to the house on Oglethorpe Square. Of more significance was the fact that the homes of prosperous Bermuda families were well built, with elements of fine English architecture, which by the late eighteenth century included the fashionable flourishes of classical styles.

In England, Richardson and Jay could have collected ideas for the plan and ornament of this new house from the abundant examples of Regency villas. But some features suggest particular Richardson connections. At the portico are "welcoming arms" stairs, which graced fine homes in Bermuda in the eighteenth century. One of the classical motifs on the interior, on the sides

[12] "An Historic Old House," *SMN*, May 16, 1897.

(the stringers) of the very grand central staircase, is an ancient pattern called the "Vitruvian scroll," a figure resembling a stylized wave, an apt symbol in the home of a prosperous shipper. Further, some elements of Richardson's house reflect methods of construction on Bermuda. In particular are the materials of "Bermuda stone," cement, and tabby. And, these islands may be the source of the elaborate plumbing system, now recognized as one of the most remarkable features of the Richardson House.

Life in Bermuda was shaped by its curious limestone, a coquina known as "Bermuda stone." Coquina is a porous and soft limestone composed of bits of shells and corals, easily quarried because it is soft and can be cut with a saw, then hardening when it is exposed to the atmosphere. Early Bermuda houses were made of wood, but the native cedar did not stand well against the strong winds and hurricanes. Further, as the ship building industry grew, the cedar was protected for that use. The coquina, which was abundant, became the material of necessity and preference. Large blocks were cut for walls, and more dense varieties of the stone were hand cut for roof slates. Coquina had to be joined by mortars and protected by coats of a cement such as stucco or plaster. So, Bermuda had an early industry in the development of efficient mortars and cements, including a material not unlike the tabby used early in the coastal regions of Georgia that incorporated oyster shells. Various recipes for mortars, made of coquina (limestone) burned in kilns and turned into quicklime, were developed to accommodate the needs of construction.[13]

Bermuda stone came to be well known as a construction material in North America. In the eighteenth century, it was carried as ship's ballast to coastal regions where stone was desired but not readily available. Surely Jay had no experience with this material, but Richardson would have known Bermuda stone well, including how to secure it and how to direct its use. In Richardson's house, Bermuda stone is used at the second story, set on the heavier materials of rubble and tabby in the cellar and at the first story.

A usual conclusion has been that the advanced plumbing of the Richardson House came from modern developments in England, but it is more likely that this amenity was drawn from Richardson's early life experience. The porous Bermuda stone is permeated by sea water, so there is no source of fresh water on these islands other than a few shallow basins that collect rainwater. From the earliest settlement there, methods were devised to capture rainwater

[13] A. Short, 19-26.

for use in homes. By the eighteenth century, fine houses were fitted with roof gutters and pipes to catch and direct rainwater to large cisterns for storage. This system at the Richardson House is often cited as an early use of plumbing in North America, and likely it was modeled on Bermudian technology to gather and use rainwater.

THE TRIBULATIONS OF CONSTRUCTION IN SAVANNAH

There is a record of the construction dates of this house written in cement under the steps at the portico. The builder John Retan must have sensed that this was a project of special note and wished to record his contribution here. The scrawl in cement reads, "John Retan/ Began Nov[ember] AD 1816, Finished Jun[e] AD 1819."

There is evidence that construction materials arrived from Liverpool and London in shipments consigned to Richardson. An early record of this transport of goods comes in October 1817 and includes "23,400 bricks, 37 tons slate, 124 drain pipes, 300 flooring tiles, 2 bales carpeting." At least thirteen subsequent manifests dated through December 1819 record materials as diverse as roofing slates, flagstones, copper and copper nails, "composition stone" (Coade stone ornaments), balusters (of artificial stone), cast iron columns, glass, glass knobs, Roman Cement (stucco), "painters colors," paint brushes, stained glass, boards and railings for a staircase, and a marble hearth.[14]

Before Jay arrived on December 30, 1817, his house for Richardson had already achieved a kind of notoriety that seemed to divide the city right in two, a harbinger of what would come of Jay in Savannah. There would be those who admired Jay's work and were glad for his skills and his ability to portray a high standard of taste in this city. Then there were those who must have thought that Jay's houses were pretentious, even ostentatious, a little too "showy" for the New Republic. If imitation is sincere flattery, Jay won in the end, because Savannah's streets later filled with houses having hints of Jay about them. But, the battle that began before he arrived certainly did portend some of the difficulties he would encounter in his very short tenure in this place.

The beginning of a contentious affair is recorded in the minutes of the

[14] "Entry of Merchandise imported by R. Richardson…[to the] Port of Savannah," Oct. 3, 1817–Dec. 23, 1819, USCS/IFC.

city council in mid-December 1817. For some weeks, Richardson had been fined—first five dollars and costs and thereafter one dollar and costs—for "obstructing the Street with lumber, rubbish &c. & having no lamp." Three months later, the plot thickened with this report, "Whereas information has been given to the City Council that there are many encroachments recently made in this city, Be it resolved that the Street and Lane Committee do ascertain where all encroachments have taken place within the limits of the City."[15]

At issue were two grave matters: first, the dangerous and unhealthy deposit of construction materials and refuse in the streets and lanes of the city; and second, the taking of public land by private persons whose projects extended beyond surveyed lot lines. These concerns persisted in the deliberations of city council until early November 1818 when a culprit was named in the minutes, as "Resolved that the Street and Lane Committee proceed to examine the enchroachment [*sic*] made by Richard Richardson on the Public Square and Street in Anson Ward." Quick came the reply that Richardson's construction did encroach "four feet on State Street, four feet on President Street and twenty feet on the public Square which is known by the name of Oglethorpe Square." That being determined, a directive was issued that Richardson should remove these violations within ten days.[16]

It seems that Richardson appealed this order and won a stay. But, by early February 1819, the issue was met by city council with new resolve, as, "[T]he Squares and Streets of the City of Savannah are public property, and...no compromise can be made or compensation received by Council for permitting the said encroachments to continue." Richardson was given twenty days to "remove the obstruction he has made on Oglethorpe Square," or he would answer to a special committee.[17] One of the members of that committee was Isaiah Davenport, a carpenter and builder from Rhode Island who had come to Savannah in 1808 where he found work and served as a city alderman in 1818–1822.

In 1812 Davenport purchased a lot in Columbia Ward, on Columbia Square just one block east of Oglethorpe Square. Here in 1820–1822, he raised a house for his family, a structure intended to advertise his skills as a

[15] Savannah City Council Minutes, Dec. 15, 1817, and Mar. 23, 1818, SMA.
[16] Ibid., Nov. 2, 16, 1818.
[17] Ibid., Feb. 2, 1819.

builder. To understand why Davenport's vote always came against Richardson and Jay in the affair of the encroachments, all one needs to do is to make the quick walk between these two buildings. To take in the details of the spare Federal style of the Davenport House and the opulent Regency style of the Richardson House is to see the street-side battle of two prevailing architectural traditions, one of them resolutely American and the other certainly English.

By late February 1819, the matter had spilled onto the pages of two competing local newspapers. The editor of the *Savannah Republican* accused some members of city council of allowing encroachments on city squares, an infringement of "the rights of the people" and "an abominable outrage."[18] A correspondent for the *Columbian Museum and Savannah Daily Gazette*, who identified himself as "Fair Play," conceded that a majority of city council members opposed any encroachments on city squares and streets. However, he believed that Richardson's petition deserved a careful review.[19]

When the dust settled, the truth emerged. Richardson's violation of Oglethorpe Square consisted of the protrusion of an edge of the entry steps and their railings and an encroachment of palisading (fencing) well within what had previously been tolerated in the city. In other words, there had been a great lot of noise about pretty much nothing at all. As a response to the public outrage, the city council called upon the city surveyor to make a report of other encroachments in the city. He found that there were at least sixteen, most of them properties of some of Savannah's leading citizens and all of them violations which had heretofore gone unremarked. Consequently, a new ordinance was passed declaring very precise allowances for steps and railings. Given these new rules, just two days after Richardson had been ordered to remove the offending elements, he was permitted by city council to replace them.[20]

THE RICHARDSON RESIDENCY

By mid-1819, the house had been completed, furnished, and occupied by Richardson, his wife, and children. A list of the contents of the house pre-

[18] [Richardson House encroachments], *Savannah Republican*, Feb. 22, 1819.
[19] "Fair Play," *Columbian Museum and Savannah Daily Gazette*, Feb. 25, 1819.
[20] "An Alderman," *Georgian*, March 13, 1819.

pared for a sale in 1822 confirms that most of the furnishings had been purchased in England.[21] And, while only the dining room console table survives, that list and the results of later surveys of the building reveal that the interior was appointed in fine Regency style. There were fashionable *faux* finishes, including marbleizing on columns and wood graining on doors and some trim; elaborate window treatments; and fine imported carpets. It was surely the most modern and the most sumptuous residence in the South, perhaps in the whole of the country. But regrettably, Richardson and his family would occupy their splendid new home for only three years.

An economic calamity arose now remembered as the Panic of 1819. Banks failed, and loans and mortgages were recalled, causing huge numbers of bankruptcies and foreclosures. Richardson was caught in these events. In an awful irony, he was snared by the policies of the Bank of the United States, the very bank he served as president of the Savannah branch in 1817–1821.

This federal bank had been re-established in Savannah in January 1817, and Richardson was elected president in February.[22] Beginning in 1819, in an attempt to quell speculation and to establish greater control over excessive loads of debt, the Bank of the U.S. called in loans and required state banks to act accordingly, causing borrowers to crumble in heaps. As president of the Savannah branch, Richardson was obliged to execute these directives, but it must have been exceedingly difficult. His own load of debt was enormous. Then in January 1820 came a great fire that ruined much of the town and decimated the business district. Richardson's new house on Oglethorpe Square was spared from the flames, but his business and investment property losses were significant.

In April 1821, Richardson resigned as president of the Savannah branch of the Bank of the U.S. In June came the announcement that he had been named director of the Planter's Bank of Georgia, a prominent state bank where the policies of the Bank of the U.S. were much reviled. But by July of the following year, he had left the Planter's Bank.[23]

Within three short years, Richardson was financially ruined. However,

---

[21] Matero and Studenroth, 161–65.

[22] C. Anderson, "Second Bank of the United States, Savannah Branch," *Georgia Numismatic Association Journal*, Autumn 2006, 3, 6.

[23] [U.S. Bank directors], *Savannah Republican*, June 13, 1821; [R. Richardson at Planter's Bank], *Georgian*, July 27, 1822.

personal tragedies must have broken his spirit. In summer 1819, his second-born son, John, died at the age of three. Then a crushing blow came in June 1822 with the death of his wife, Frances. In October he sold the house on Oglethorpe Square to his partner Durham T. Hall and left Savannah for New Orleans, another location popular with Bermudians. He was looking for a new beginning, but tragedy followed him there—his daughter Rebecca died in October of that year. In late May 1823, he affirmed before a notary public in New Orleans that his partnership with the Boltons and Hall "has been recently dissolved by the mutual consent of the partners." Once again, he took up the enterprise of merchant shipping. He conducted business for another eleven years until his death at sea as he was returning from Le Havre, France, to New Orleans in 1833.[24]

AFTERMATHS

By 1824 the house on Oglethorpe Square had been taken by the Bank of the U.S. In that year, the building was leased to Mrs. Mary Maxwell, a widow who ran some of Savannah's finest rooming houses. Because she catered to important and wealthy visitors to the city, it was her good fortune that into her hands came two Jay houses, the Richardson House and the Bulloch House, two of the most luxurious properties in Savannah.

In 1830 the house was purchased from the bank by George Welshman Owens. Owens was a Savannah native, his father having arrived here from North Wales shortly after the Revolutionary War. At the age of twenty-eight, he inherited from his father a plantation on St. Catherine's Island, a sea island fifty miles south of Savannah, and eighty-seven slaves. Trained as a lawyer in England, Owens soon prospered. He became a planter as his father had been, ultimately owning five large plantations. He was a solicitor and a politician, serving as mayor of Savannah in 1832–1833 and as a member of the U.S. Congress (1835–1839). A banker and investor, he was among the early leaders of Savannah to prompt the development of canal and rail systems to the interior of the state.

The house was sold by the Savannah Branch of the Bank of the U.S. for

---

[24] R. Richardson, "Declaration in the City of New Orleans of Richard Richardson, of the Parish of St. Bernard," May 29, 1823, Chatham County Superior Court, Court Records (1818–1823), Savannah, GA (hereafter CCSC); R. Bolton, *Genealogical...Account of the Family of Bolton*, 139–40.

$10,000. This would be the home of Owens and his wife, Sarah Wallace, whom he had married in 1815, and their four sons and four daughters. As testimony to Owens's goal to preserve this residence, subsequent studies of the fabric of the building revealed that during his time here very few structural alterations were made. There were cosmetic changes because in 1830 the taste for the flamboyant Regency style was waning.

In the next generation, the family home on Oglethorpe Square was inherited by Margaret Wallace Owens, the youngest daughter. She and her husband, James Gray Thomas, a physician, had one son and four daughters, but only two of the daughters survived to adulthood and neither married. By 1917 the house had come into the possession of the surviving daughter, Margaret Gray Thomas, known as Meta. As family resources had grown lean, first the carriage house and later the second story of the residence were altered to accommodate rental apartments. But, the family pledge to preserve this house was sustained, allowing these changes to be later restored to the original plan and ornament.[25]

"THE OWENS-THOMAS MUSEUM"

Margaret Gray Thomas died in December 1951 at the age of eighty, the sole survivor of the family that had owned the Richardson House for 121 years. By the provision of her will, the structure was left to the Telfair Academy "for the use of the public as a memorial to my grandfather, George W. Owens, and my father, James G. Thomas, to be called the Owens-Thomas Museum."[26] She wished to honor her grandfather's commitment to preserve this house and her father's contributions to the practice of medicine in Georgia (he had been instrumental in establishing a state board of health).

This was an important and generous gift, with the perilous proviso that there was no grant of money to support the project. But, in spite of this tremendous obstacle, remembering the valuable structures in Savannah already lost to "progress," agreements were reached so that the opportunity to preserve this house would not be lost. From the city, there was an initial commitment of operating funds, though it was a small amount with an unpredictable future.[27]

[25] Matero and Studenroth, 169–75.
[26] Godley, Hawes, and Gignilliat, 5.
[27] Ibid., 13.

In 1954 the former residence was opened as a house museum, a property of the Telfair Academy. In 1965 a careful study of the building was made by J. Everett Fauber Jr., an architect who specialized in historic preservation and was associated with the restoration of Colonial Williamsburg. He declared this structure to be "the finest example of English Regency architecture in this country."[28] In 1976–1977 the house was designated a National Historic Landmark and listed on the National Register of Historic Places.

In 1993 a study of the carriage house was undertaken to gain an understanding of life "at the back of the house" in the early nineteenth century. This building had originally contained slave quarters in the north half, and these rooms were recovered, including a large field of blue paint on the ceiling known in local legend as "haint" blue, a barrier to malevolent spirits.[29] This structure has come to be recognized as perhaps the best survival of a residence of urban slaves in the South.

From the time of its opening in October 1954 as a house museum, the Richardson-Owens-Thomas House has garnered all sorts of accolades. It has been identified by the American Institute of Architects as "one of the outstandingly beautiful examples of old American architecture" and cited in various books and magazine articles as "Savannah's most beautiful house," a "most perfect example of the architecture of the old South," and "one of the purest of this [the Regency] style in America."[30]

An authoritative voice in this chorus was that of the architectural historian Talbot Hamlin. When Hamlin visited Savannah in 1954, he offered the opinion that this would come to be "one of the most distinguished house museums in the country."[31] And, as Hamlin predicted, visitors to the Richardson-Owens-Thomas House soon learn that in this place there is very much to see. At every turn, there is some ingenious detail of construction or ornament: curved walls with curved doors; odd symmetries such as a real door balanced by a fake one or glazed windows matched with blind ones; unexpected appearances of colored glass; and *faux bois* where real wood might be. And, as perhaps the greatest curiosity of all, here is an elegant example of the

---

[28] Fauber, n.p.; K. Haeberle, "Detective Probes Museum," *Savannah Evening Press,* July 18, 1965.

[29] M. Shuter, "The Beauty Out Back," *SMN*, Nov. 4, 1995.

[30] Godley, Hawes, and Gignilliat, 5–7.

[31] "Hamlin Lauds Owens-Thomas Restoration," *SMN*, Oct. 24, 1954.

English Regency style quite at home in the sultry American South.

THE LEGEND OF THE LAFAYETTE BALCONY

The most storied architectural feature of the Richardson-Owens-Thomas House is the south veranda. It is cast iron, perhaps from one of the fabricators Jay came to know in Liverpool in 1814 when he was working hard to gain the acceptance of his design for the Wellington Rooms. Attached iron balconies and conservatories had grown popular in England in the early years of the nineteenth century. This one is a rather flamboyant version of the type. The balcony sits high on its supports of acanthus leaves, the preferred classical foliage, with a canopy topped by antefixes of anthemia. Delivered in pieces, it was assembled at this site. Grooves in the columns suggest that it was once fitted with retracting shades. This porch opens from the bedroom located on the main floor, and there is evidence here on the south flank of the building that a second and surely identical balcony was planned for access from the front parlor. Legend has it that this twin fixture was ordered from England and lost at sea.

Unscientific surveys tell us that this veranda is the most loved and most often photographed architectural element in all of Savannah, a city brimming with photogenic building details. This balcony deserves to be famous beyond Savannah because this may well be the first significant use of cast iron as architectural ornament in this country.

In Savannah, this side porch is known as "the Lafayette balcony" and recalls a momentous event in the history of the city. In March 1825, the city welcomed the Marquis de Lafayette, who would come to be called "the hero of two nations" to acknowledge his contributions to both the American Revolution and the French Revolution. In Savannah, he received the finest accommodations the city could provide. At the Richardson House, then an elegant rooming house, he was lodged in the main floor bedchamber, which opened to the magnificent cast iron veranda fronting on President Street. And a legend would persist that Lafayette spoke to the citizens of Savannah from this balcony.

As a young military officer, Lafayette became captivated by the talk of "the rights of man" and the struggles of revolutionary forces in America against the British. By 1777 he made his way to this country and soon became a member of the staff of George Washington, commander-in-chief of the

Continental Army. His devotion to Washington (for whom he would name his own son George Washington Lafayette), his commitment to the cause of this war, and his ingenuity in plotting the course of several critical military engagements led to his near deification in the hearts and minds of Americans.

Following his return to France in 1781, Lafayette became involved in the several misadventures of the French Revolution, attempting but rarely succeeding in the pursuit of rational discourse. Not always loved in his own country, in America he was celebrated. In 1782 he returned to visit all of the states with the exception of Georgia. The grand tour in which Savannah participated came in 1824, at the invitation of President James Monroe to mark the fiftieth anniversary of events leading to the birth of the nation. This tour began from Washington City (District of Columbia) in February 1824 and ended in September 1825, including stops in all of the existing twenty-four states, with Savannah being the southernmost location. A report of this tour, by Lafayette's secretary Auguste Levasseur, cited the fine accommodations in Savannah in an "elegant mansion" and observed that the kindness of Georgians had brought Lafayette "almost to tears."[32]

[32] "General Lafayette," *Niles Weekly Register*, Apr. 9, 1825, 85; Levasseur, 2:58–67.

CHAPTER 13

SCARBROUGH HOUSE: "SIGHTLY IN THE EYES OF MAN AND CREDITABLE TO THE CITY"

The house that Jay designed for William Scarbrough, local merchant and entrepreneur, was likely the first commission for a private home gained after the architect arrived in Savannah. While each of the houses Jay built in this city would come to have a unique architectural character and a particular role in the history of this place, none would rival the distinction of the Scarbrough House. Built for the most ambitious of his clients, the building was perhaps Jay's most successful composition, although the competition for this award is fierce. It met every requirement for a house that was designed to be an emblem of Savannah's prosperity and a stage for Savannah's society. This structure would come to play such a prominent role in the life of this city that, in 1878, when it was given over to the public trust for a school for black children, the donor specified that the building should be maintained so that it would be "sightly in the eyes of man and creditable to the city."[1]

SEARCHING FOR JAY AT THE SCARBROUGH HOUSE

It takes some effort to see what President James Monroe saw when he resided here in May 1819 during an official visit to Savannah. And it is impossible to know just precisely what Jay had planned for this project when work began in early 1818 since it was rushed to completion to accommodate Monroe. If some elements of the original design were unrealized, they likely remained so—Scarbrough succumbed to bankruptcy very soon after his fine house was visited by the president of the United States. The sad truth is that evidence of Jay's hand in this project is somewhat elusive.

It was an ingenious design, a fine representation of the Grecian style. According to an 1897 newspaper report of the history of this structure, written when some Savannahians who had known the building in its youth were still

---

[1] "Scarborough [*sic*] Mansion Held in Trust by School Board," *Savannah Evening Press*, Feb. 27, 1946.

alive, it was "the most palatial of all residences in the town."[2] From the street, it had a commanding presence, more so in 1819 than now. It once sat higher on its basement foundation—over nearly two centuries, earth fill has swallowed several inches at the front of the building. It was once located at a stately distance from the street, but the forecourt was diminished by the expansion of a busy roadway. It had begun life in a district of handsome houses, but, soon after the conflagration of the Civil War, all of the fine homes in this quarter save this one were lost.

The facade is a relatively simple composition keyed to the Doric order, the first of the classical orders and the one most spare in ornament, most weighty in form, and most powerful in effect. From a distance, the house is seen as a substantial rectangular mass, a shape emphasized by the play of light and shadow at the set-back corners and at the deep moldings marking the top of each floor. Characteristic of a Regency villa, the roof is a shallow hip design surrounded by a parapet wall at the edge, giving the illusion of a flat roof.

The windows are classical shapes, round-headed at the first story and rectangular at the second. They are large but relatively few in number to emphasize the mass of the wall and to protect the inhabitants from the summer sun. The tall round-headed windows of the first story are set in recessed arches and rest on simple panels carrying the uncomplicated pattern of the Greek key or meander. As a complement to the arched windows, at the second story above the portico, there is a great half-round or Diocletian window, echoed by the same shape carved into the base of the porch.

The main entry, at the east, announces the theme of the house: the Doric order, certain evidence that this is an important place. Here this is an early, sturdy version of the style, almost Archaic (the Greek style of the seventh and sixth centuries B.C.). The columns are unfluted and somewhat squat, carrying the heavy load of a tall entablature, the weight of which seems to flatten each column's head (the capital) and make the neck (the echinus) narrow. The entablature carries a Doric frieze made of triglyphs (the three grooves that evoke the origin of the style in the crossbeams of wood structures) and metopes (the intervening spaces usually containing sculptures but empty here).

At least two features of the front of this building are uncongenial additions, the balusters of the porch and an entry for carriages at the north. The curious march of balusters supporting a stone rail and posed in front of the

---

[2] "Where Revelry Reigned," *SMN*, May 23, 1897 (hereafter cited in text).

columns was added during the occupation of the school. The composition is unlike that at the Richardson-Owens-Thomas, Telfair, and Bulloch-Habersham Houses where the columns of the portico are seen in full and stately profile, allowing the element of a column to be comprehended as the module or unit of measure for the larger scheme of the structure. And the carriage entry just to the north of the house, called the Water Gate, is a feature of uncertain date that was reconstructed in the 1970s in a style entirely lacking in the grace of Jay's designs.

In 1819 a step through the fine Doric portico of the Scarbrough House to the interior revealed swelling spaces that only waited for an evening's celebration. In fact, this was less a home for the Scarbroughs and their several children than a very grand setting for the next splendid banquet and ball. A guest came first into a magnificent two-story entry hall or atrium rimmed by a balcony at the second level. The Doric columns supporting this balcony are different than those of the portico. These are Classical (the style of the fifth century B.C.), more slender and fluted with grooves to catch the light and emphasize their handsome shape.

In other Jay houses, the entry hall was filled with a great formal stairway, "imperial stairs" made for the parade down from the private rooms above to greet one's guests. Quarrels persist about whether stairs of this sort were centered in the atrium of the Scarbrough House. However, there are reasons to believe that this space was open, with spiral stairways tucked in at the two western corners, one at the right for the residents and a smaller and less conspicuous one at the left for the servants. In part this evidence comes from the remembrances of those who knew the building before it was much altered. In the 1897 newspaper article, there is the claim that a "great hall in the center [led] from the front door to a cross hall, which in turn formerly led to the winding stairway on the right."

The 1897 account described the effect of standing in the entry hall:

> In old days there was an arcade on each floor of the house, the same size all the way to the roof, and directly above these arcades on the roof was a beautiful sky-light, or dome upon which there was an enchanting painting by an artist of degree [or accomplishment—perhaps a work by William Etty]. The painting represented nothing but the heavens, and gave the effect to the upturned eye below of the natural sky. The stranger...was almost invariably deceived by this painting and thought when looking overhead he was seeing the skies naked and bare to the eye, until upon close

inspection he realized the mistake.

This description underscores the conception of this space as an atrium, like an ancient Roman courtyard, a place for gathering and open to the sky. It was quite simply, as Frederick D. Nichols announced after his review of the building in the 1950s, "one of the grandest spacial compositions in American domestic architecture."[3]

This entry hall is unique among Jay's Savannah houses. Another singular feature here is the fact that this first floor plan is perfectly symmetrical. At the north and south sides of the atrium were two parlors, each one a simple room made elegant by ample height, by the curvature of the end or western wall which featured a fireplace, and by the dressing of deeply carved moldings. From the atrium, one entered a great hall or ballroom that extended across the width of the house and spilled onto verandas at the north and south sides. A second story provided living quarters, including bedrooms. What was in this basement is uncertain, but the evidence of the Richardson-Owens-Thomas and Telfair Houses suggests that the kitchen and service areas were here.

In sum, the Scarbrough House was a grand structure, elegant in its proportions and likely fine in its ornament and furnishings although all trace of those is lost. It had been planned as a magnificent setting for lavish parties. Indeed, this house was the location for at least two of the most grand events in Savannah's history: the reception of President Monroe in 1819 and a "fancy ball" in 1837. There is no building in Savannah with a more storied past, from its conception to its present as a museum of the city's maritime past.

THE CONSTRUCTION OF THE "CASTLE"

In 1803 William Scarbrough acquired two lots in an area then called the Village of St. Gall, near the Savannah River and just west of the original town settlement, a "garden district" planned as the site of a number of elegant homes. The region came to be known as Court End, a fitting location for a house Scarbrough would name the Castle, a fine residence for the "Merchant Prince" and his "Countess," titles earned by Scarbrough and his wife. Scarbrough was born in North Carolina, the son of a shipbuilder and merchant. He was educated in England and trained in the arts of commerce. In 1799, at

[3] Nichols, 40.

the age of twenty-two, he settled in Savannah and prospered as a shipper. In 1805 he married Julia Bernard, also from North Carolina, a beauty known for her wit and social ambition. From this union, there were two sons and three daughters who survived to adulthood.[4]

Soon after Jay's arrival in late 1817, he was commissioned by Scarbrough to build a residence at this site fronting West Broad Street (later Martin Luther King Jr. Boulevard). The design of this house had the very particular goal of serving the social ambitions of Scarbrough and his wife at a time when Savannah rewarded ambition. A hint of what they desired in this new home is provided in the correspondence of a contemporary, a woman from Massachusetts, who in 1787 had been obliged to settle in Washington, Georgia, a rugged and desolate place nearly 200 miles northwest of Savannah near Indian territory. By 1818 she had come to know the delights of Savannah. Writing to her son, she said,

> We have been so much in a constant flutter among the butterflys of Savannah, that I begin to feel like one myself.... The ladies in Savannah...overload us with civilities, and draw us into parties which they justly think will excite our astonishment.... Mrs. Scarborough [*sic*] lately sent out cards of invitation to five hundred persons. Three hundred attended. Every room in a large house was newly furnished for the occasion, the beds etc sent out; refreshments handed round from garret to cellar through the night to guests, who were mostly standing and 'delightfully squeezed to death.' How delightful![5]

Construction of this structure began sometime in 1818. By April 1819, the work was hurried to prepare for the visit of Monroe. As quite the grandest residence in town, Scarbrough's house had been selected to accommodate the president. In early May, Scarbrough wrote to his wife, then detained in New York, that their new home "seems to bring to the Recollection of all who have lately visited it—the House of Lord Grosvenour in the neighborhood of Chester & Liverpool."[6]

In later studies of the Scarbrough House, this comment provoked much

---

[4] R. Davis, "Biographical sketch [W. Scarbrough]," 1980, 2, Virginia and John Duncan Collection, Savannah, GA (hereafter cited as VJD).

[5] M. A. Boggs, 6–17, 49–50.

[6] W. Scarbrough to J. Scarbrough, May 6, 1819, William Scarbrough Collection, Georgia Archives, Morrow, GA (hereafter cited as GAM).

interest. First, it was seen to be very presumptuous that a Savannah merchant would compare his residence with that of Lord Grosvenor, then the 2nd Earl Robert Grosvenor. Next, it was unclear which of the several homes of Lord Grosvenor occasioned this comparison. This reference would have been easily comprehended in 1819 by the several Savannahians who traveled abroad frequently. The mansion to which they referred was the new and very fashionable home of Lord Grosvenor at Eaton Hall, the country seat of this venerable family, near the city of Chester in Cheshire about thirty miles south of Liverpool. This was the second structure on this site, constructed in 1804–1812. A review in 1819 observed that this spectacular mansion was "built entirely of white stone, in the florid Gothic style of Architecture...fitted up in the first style of splendour and elegance...[and made at] an enormous expense."[7] This building survived into the 1870s, when it was replaced by a larger structure in a ponderous and less delightful version of the Gothic style.

In the early nineteenth century, visitors from America made the passage to Liverpool—there were regular runs from New York and Savannah. Many began their tours of England in the region of Chester, and Eaton Hall was, according to a recent report, "the Yankee visitor's first exposure to ducal splendor."[8] While in every detail of Gothic ornament it was different from Jay's design for the Scarbrough House, traveling Savannahians must have been struck by the shared presumptions of high style and extravagant display.

THE VISIT OF PRESIDENT MONROE

Soon after his inauguration in March 1817, Monroe set out on a tour of northern states and territories; two years later, in March 1819, he began a tour of the South. Monroe made these visits to gain an understanding of the new nation's readiness for war, remembering that the lack of preparedness for the War of 1812 had resulted in three long years of combat and the near destruction of Washington City.

Notice of a presidential visit to Savannah, scheduled for May 8–13, came to city council in early March 1819, and it was resolved "that Council will take every measure in their power to entertain the President in a manner suitable to his office and his eminent virtues." By March 10, a committee had been established to determine what manner of celebrations should be devised for

[7] "Eaton Hall," *Gentleman's Magazine,* Nov. 1819, 393.
[8] Lockwood, 41.

the visit and who should be included in these. In the same report, the question of housing the president was asked and answered, "That Council ought to provide a well furnished house for the residence of the President and his suite, there to be entertained during his stay...[and] that William Scarbrough Esquire has politely offered his new and elegant house at the West end of the town for the reception and residence of the President and which your Committee have accepted with thanks."[9]

The decision was not met with universal acclaim. A newspaper reporter dubbed "Republican" complained that the use of "the house of a private person" would have the effect of limiting access to the president by "all the citizens of the place." Unmoved by this concern, the committee charged with making these arrangements published an expression of thanks to Scarbrough "for having patriotically offered the use of his dwelling house for the accomodation [*sic*] of the President and suite during their stay in this city."[10]

In his letter to his wife, written just two days before the arrival of the president, Scarbrough said,

> Our House is quite in readiness for him. It is most tastefully & elegantly decorated & furnished.... The president must be pleased with Savannah;—as in the whole Course of his extended Tour, he may be rec[eive]d at a more costly & splendid Rate; but no where with such pure & genuine Taste;—& Jay will begin to attain the preeminence which low Jealousy & perverted Judgment would not before award him.[11]

This comment reveals that Jay, in just seventeen months, had come to be buffeted by "low Jealousy & perverted Judgment." No doubt it had been a poor public relations plan for Jay to declare, in a newspaper article soon after his arrival, that he had found architecture in the city to be of inferior quality, requiring the exercise of his own refined taste and excellent training to remedy the existing situation. That announcement surely did not win him friends and supporters in the building trades or among citizens with less exalted expectations of architecture.

Also at this auspicious occasion of a presidential visit, there was yet another display of Jay's taste and talent. The city council awarded Jay a contract

---

[9] Savannah City Council Minutes, Mar.8, 10, 1819, SMA.

[10] "Republican," *Savannah Republican,* Mar. 11, 1819; "Town Meeting," *Savannah Republican,* Mar. 17, 1819.

[11] W. Scarbrough to J. Scarbrough, May 6, 1819, GAM.

to design a temporary structure for a dinner and ball to celebrate the president's last night in Savannah. Raised in Johnson Square, this temporary building was a tour de force of elegance, display, and illusion—all hallmarks of the Regency.

According to one report,

> Although the exterior of this building was unpolished, the interior was truly magnificent, and beautiful. The ceiling consisted of a single Flag of immense size. The walls were lined with crimson, set off with fluted pilasters, made of muslin, which, by candle light might be mistaken for fine marble or alabaster. The hall was brilliantly lighted with large chandeliers and lustres [candle holders with cut-glass pendants], a variety of flags, with different devices, projected from the walls. The supper-room was lined entirely with flags, obtained from vessels in port: they were fancifully arranged, and produced a most pleasing effect on the heart as well as the eye.[12]

This was the art of stagecraft, a temporary structure of the sort Jay might have seen in London where the prince regent was fond of giving elaborate parties for which the number of invited guests far exceeded the space in his homes.

THE *SAVANNAH*

In offering his new house for a presidential visit, Scarbrough no doubt saw a potential business opportunity. He wished to reveal to the president of the United States a sailing ship equipped with a steam engine and ready for a transatlantic crossing. In early 1818, Scarbrough directed the incorporation of the Savannah Steam Ship Company, gathering shareholders and investing heavily in the venture. A sailing packet—a relatively small, trim vessel then under construction in New York—was selected and fitted with an auxiliary steam engine. Ingenious paddle wheels were designed to retract when the ship was under sail, and the smokestack swiveled according to the wind, directing smoke and sparks away from the sails. A news report declared that this vessel was planned to become "a regular trader between this city [Savannah] and Liverpool, principally for the accommodation of passengers," observing that

[12] "President's Ball," *Daily Georgian*, May 14, 1819.

the ship was exceedingly beautiful and a model of ingenious engineering.[13]

The ship arrived in Savannah in time to convey the president from South Carolina into Georgia. According to later testimony by an officer of the ship,

> The President was greatly pleased with the vessel, and stated to Mr. Scarbrough, that, upon the arrival of the *Savannah* from her cruise across the Atlantic, (which was then about to be made,) he desired the vessel to be brought to Washington, and he thought there would be no doubt the government would purchase her and employ her for a cruiser upon the coast of Cuba, &c.[14]

The ship left Savannah on May 26, 1819, and delighted crowds of crowned and uncrowned heads met her first at Liverpool, then at ports in Denmark, Sweden, and Russia. She returned to Savannah on November 30. The *Savannah* earned her place in history as the first ship equipped with steam to cross the Atlantic, although later naysayers argued that she was a hybrid of sail and steam and that most of the passage was conducted under sail. The Atlantic crossing was a singular achievement—but it was a failed business venture.

When Scarbrough wrote to his wife in May 1819, he expressed some anxiety about the outcome of his investment in the *Savannah*. In this letter, he cajoled his wife, "I hope you will not allow any foolish Apprehensions to prevent your going across with me; for in my Mind she is, if any Thing safer than any other Kind of vessel."[15] But Julia did not go, nor did William. The ship was populated only by the crew. When no buyer could be found to sponsor ocean crossings, the *Savannah* was sold and her engine removed to take up life as a sailing packet operating between New York and Savannah. On November 5, 1821, she ran aground at Long Island, New York, and met her ruin.

BANKRUPTCY AND THE FATE OF THE HOUSE

By May 1819, when the *Savannah* embarked on her grand passage, Scarbrough was already caught in the snares of the Panic of 1819. Banks recalled loans, and for those whose debts were deep, bankruptcy was inevitable. Sadly,

---

[13] [The steamship *Savannah*], *Savannah Republican*, Sept. 3, 1818.

[14] Mallory, 2:35–36.

[15] W. Scarbrough to J. Scarbrough, May 6, 1819, GAM.

Scarbrough was one of that number. Then, in January 1820 a great fire in Savannah destroyed many commercial properties and inventories as well as private homes. The Scarbrough House escaped the fire, but other of Scarbrough's holdings were lost.

From June 1819 through November 1820, Scarbrough scrambled to meet the demands of his creditors, selling both business and personal assets. A court notice of September 13, 1820, reported that he was in jail for debt, "insolvent, but willing to surrender all his estate for the benefit of his creditors as the law directs." By late November came this notice, "For Sale ON ACCOMMODATING TERMS. That extensive and commodious DWELLING HOUSE & LOTS on West-Broad St. At present in the occupation of Wm. Scarbrough."[16] To the great relief and benefit of Scarbrough and his family, the house and its contents were purchased by Savannah cotton factor Robert Isaac, who had married Scarbrough's sister Lucy. Isaac granted the family continued use of the home and its provisions.

Among the many to whom Scarbrough became indebted was Jay. The cost of the Scarbrough House was near $75,000. A debt to Jay recorded on November 1, 1819, claimed that Scarbrough owed the architect $17,484, in addition to damages of $100. By April 29, 1820, a judgment was rendered for payment to Jay in the amount of $8,742.[17] This was a sad ending to a remarkable collaboration between a gifted architect and an enthusiastic patron.

By mid-1822, Jay was gone, on his way back to England. Scarbrough, "a bankrupt," would never again be allowed to hold property in his name, but by June 1822 he was back at work directing a saw mill in Darien, Georgia. Praised for his enterprise and his integrity, he continued in various businesses and sought a number of patents for inventions to improve the operation of steam engines.[18] None of these efforts returned to him the great fortune he had once achieved. When he died in 1838, he was still a resident of the home that had been designed for him by Jay and still concerned for the maintenance of this extraordinary structure.

---

[16] "Inferior Court, Chatham County Chambers, September 13, 1820 [Petition of W. Scarbrough]," *Daily Georgian,* Nov. 1, 1820; [W. Scarbrough, sale of property], *Daily Georgian*, Nov. 22, 1820.

[17] "William Jay vs. William Scarborough [*sic*]," 1819, U.S. Circuit Court for the Southern District of Georgia, Eastern Division (Savannah), National Archives at Atlanta, Morrow, GA.

[18] R. Davis, "Biographical sketch [W. Scarbrough]," 1980, 5, VJD.

CARING FOR THE "CASTLE"

By 1835 the house had fallen into a poor condition, and Scarbrough was away much of the time at work in Darien. Anxious about the state of the house and about his wife and two sons in the home, Scarbrough invited Godfrey Barnsley, his son-in-law, to bring his talents and his money to the project. In April 1835, he wrote to Barnsley, "I have learnt with much Satisfaction from Mrs. S. of your willingness again to take up your Quarters at the Castle as we call it—It is now, & for some time has been, in a state of great dilapidation, which of course in any climate, let alone in this, would every day become greater, unless by some prevention, the means for which are not at our command." Scarbrough offered Barnsley and his family rent-free occupancy of the house for a term of five years in exchange for a restoration of the house.[19]

Born in England to a cotton mill owner, Barnsley came to Savannah in 1824, at the age of nineteen, where he made a great success in the cotton trade. In 1828 he married Julia Henriettta Scarbrough, the second of the three daughters of William and Julia, and they would have six children who survived to adulthood.

As he revealed at the Scarbrough House and in later projects, Barnsley was an interested gentleman architect of considerable taste and discernment. He made a number of alterations to the mansion when it came into his care, but there is no evidence that he changed Jay's original design in any uncongenial way. Barnsley was a great admirer of his father-in-law, and he knew the pride Scarbrough took in this once-elegant house. Over the next few years with his ample resources, Barnsley directed a number of projects. He added or enclosed a gallery at the rear or west end of the house just beyond the ballroom. He completed some finishes, such as elements of ironwork. The grounds were further planned and developed, including the addition of a cast-iron fence across the front of the property and tall brick walls at the rear and sides.[20]

The Barnsleys continued to live in the Scarbrough House until 1843, when Charlotte De Bernier Scarbrough Taylor, the eldest child of William and Julia, contested ownership of the place. By then Barnsley had resolved to

---

[19] R. Davis, "Scarbrough Family House 1818–1850," 1978, 11, VJD.
[20] S. Johnson, 7–8.

move his family to property he had acquired in northwest Georgia in the foothills of the Blue Ridge Mountains, in Cherokee lands taken by the state of Georgia in 1831. There he designed and built the Woodlands, an estate which included a mansion in the style of an Italian villa with extensive gardens.[21]

In 1850 Charlotte, by an appeal to the U.S. Supreme Court, was awarded possession of the property. In that same year, she sold the house and grounds to Mrs. Margaret O'Byrne, the recent widow of Dominick O'Byrne, a prosperous lumber merchant. Mrs. O'Byrne lived here with her three sons, one a lawyer and two following in their father's trade. To accommodate this matriarch, her adult sons and their families, the house was expanded in 1851 with the addition of a third floor.[22]

After a residence of fifteen years, the exit of this family from the house was hasty. In January 1865, during the occupation of the city by Federal troops, a fire of unknown origin exploded a well-supplied Confederate arsenal. In the subsequent conflagration, the region of Court End was ravaged. The wonder is that the Scarbrough House was spared. However, there is little wonder that the O'Byrnes left that evening and never returned.[23] For the next five years, the house was occupied and tended only by a few servants.

THE WEST BROAD STREET SCHOOL

By a deed recorded in January 1870, the O'Byrnes granted the house to the Catholic bishop of Savannah.[24] Various plans for the structure were considered, but none were realized. In 1876 the property was sold to generate funds to help pay for the new Cathedral of St. John the Baptist. By 1878 the once very grand house had become derelict, a crumbling wreck in a neighborhood that was no longer lovely. The story of the Scarbrough House might have ended here, with the demolition of the building to make way for something new. But, to the rescue came George Wymberley Jones DeRenne.[25] He was a descendant of Noble Jones, one of the founders of Georgia and the

[21] R. Davis, "Scarbrough Family House 1818–1850," 1978, 11, VJD; Coker, 29–32, 91.

[22] B. Howard, 8:183–209; Milner, "Historic William Scarbrough House," n.p.

[23] A. Gunderson, "Scarbrough House," *Savannah News Press*, Sept.21, 1969.

[24] G. B. Smith, "Chain of Title of the Scarbrough House," c. 1970, VJD.

[25] Born George Frederick Tilghman Jones, he changed his name legally to George Wymberley Jones DeRenne in 1866.

developer of Wormsloe Plantation, ten miles southeast of Savannah. DeRenne, a gentleman of considerable accomplishment, was an historian and bibliophile who had assembled an extraordinary collection of books on Georgia history.

DeRenne's plan for thc Scarbrough House was announced in April 1878. His purchase of this property was first conveyed to trustees, who prepared a transfer of the deed to the Board of Education for a purpose defined by DeRenne. The project would serve "the people called of African descent [who] came among us not of their own motion nor for their own gain...[and who] by their sudden emancipation...have been left helpless save for their labor." DeRenne declared,

> [T]he name of the premises shall be the West Broad Street School; that the said property shall be used for the education of colored of African [descent] exclusively...that the instruction given in the said school shall be confined to the reading and writing of English, arithmetic, and geography...that the buildings of all kinds on the said property shall always be kept in such repair that they may be not only useful for the purpose for which they are devoted but sightly in the eyes of men and creditable to the city.[26]

Renovations were necessary to make the house and grounds ready for the school. Walls surrounding the property were repaired, and the grounds were prepared for a playground with dirt and cinders. A wide plain stairway was set in the atrium to accommodate the coming and going of children. For security, some windows were closed over, and interior ornament was removed or covered by paint.[27]

The West Broad Street School operated for nearly nine decades. It was closed in 1962, the condition of the building having been assessed as beyond repair for its continuing use. Later critics and historians would worry about this chapter in the history of the Scarbrough House, but in many respects it was a brilliant plan. The occupation of this building by this school preserved the structure for a later time when improved methods of historic preservation could address the restoration of this once-elegant residence. And, the beneficiaries of this school were the hundreds upon hundreds of black children who

---

[26] "Scarborough [*sic*] Mansion Held in Trust by School Board," *Savannah Evening Press*, Feb. 27, 1946.

[27] S. Johnson, 9.

were cared for in this place.

TENDING TO "A BEAUTIFUL LADY"

In 1934–1936 the Scarbrough House was included in the Historic American Buildings Survey. The state of the building was assessed as "Present Condition: Not good."[28] A civic interest in the preservation of the house can be dated to DeRenne's resolution in 1878 to save the structure by directing its use as a school, to hold the building in trust for the future. Renewed concern for this place emerged in the 1940s primarily through the efforts of Walter C. Hartridge Jr., a local lawyer. In 1948 a newspaper article titled "West Broad School Suited for Shrine, Not Education," cited Hartridge's devotion to the old mansion. For years he campaigned to bring attention to the plight of this house. In 1956 he declared, "Of all Jay's splendid designs, this is in many respects the most notable." In 1962 in an article titled "A Beautiful Lady," Hartridge mused, "On one of Savannah's busiest streets a silent lady stands haunted by 144 years of memories.... [B]ehind her facade—wrinkled a bit with age and in need of fresh makeup—beats the heart of a beautiful lady."[29]

In 1965 the dilapidated structure was returned to the heirs of DeRenne, and by 1968, in a sequence of sales, transfers, and gifts, the property came into the custody of the Historic Savannah Foundation. Plans for restoration of the building were begun. The work ahead was enormous, and it would be costly. The first initiative was to restore the main floor "to its original condition...in the style of the Regency period." The two upper floors (Jay's second floor and the third floor added in 1851) were expected to house offices for nonprofit organizations. But the first order of business was to stabilize the structure. It had been vacant since 1965, and rain was coming through the roof.[30]

In 1972–1976 a second restoration proceeded. Crumbling exterior walls were stripped down to brick and re-stuccoed. On the interior, doors and baseboards had survived in good condition, but little else had. Abused interior

[28] "Scarborough [*sic*] House, Savannah, Georgia," 1936, Historic American Buildings Survey, Library of Congress, Washington, DC (hereafter cited as HABS).

[29] G. Ables, "West Broad School Suited for Shrine," *SMN*, Aug. 1, 1948; Hartridge, "Magnificent Home," Apr. 20, 1956; Hartridge and Palmer, "A Beautiful Lady," Aug. 19, 1962.

[30] A. Gunderson, "Scarbrough House," *Savannah News Press*, Sept. 21, 1969.

walls were stripped and re-plastered, and damaged wood floors were replaced. The fine fireplace mantels had been lost or inadvertently destroyed, and the ornamental trim elements were now just a matter of conjecture. As the project advanced, all exterior and interior surfaces were refurbished with as much fidelity to original forms and materials as possible, and ornament was introduced in modest measure based on elements in other Jay houses.[31]

This labor included these particularly complicated tasks: the removal of the third floor added in 1851, the replacement of the roof, the restoration of the ceiling of the atrium, and the elimination of the large stairway added to accommodate the students of the West Broad Street School. Some solutions led to disputed results. The roof was fitted with a lantern with clerestory windows although none of the other Savannah houses by Jay had been topped by a lantern. The institutional stairway built in the atrium was removed, but quarrels ensued about what might have existed here. Many were convinced that the house had been equipped with "imperial stairs" of the sort found at the Richardson-Owens-Thomas and Telfair Houses. However, as previously noted, gathered evidence showed that a spiral staircase had existed at the northwest corner of the atrium, and at the southwest corner was a more modest stairway, perhaps as access for servants.[32] For want of agreement, the space was left open—as it surely was intended to be.

THE SHIPS OF THE SEA MUSEUM

For two decades, the Scarbrough House was in the custody of the Historic Savannah Foundation, but the costs of maintaining the structure plagued the organization. In 1990 the house was deeded to the Telfair Academy of Arts and Sciences, making the Telfair custodian of all three surviving Jay residences: the Richardson-Owens-Thomas, Telfair, and Scarbrough houses. But, once again the burden of maintenance proved to be too much, and after just four years the Telfair relinquished ownership.

The future of the mansion was again in peril. Happily, in 1994 the house came into the hands of Mills B. Lane IV. His plan was to use the structure as a new home for a museum of Savannah's maritime past founded in 1966 by his father. To prepare for this new role, a third restoration of the Scarbrough house began in 1996. In this phase of work, the lantern added in the 1970s

[31] Milner, "Specifications: Restoration, William Scarbrough House," A.1.

[32] W. Parker, interview with J. Duncan and V. White, Nov. 23, 1987, VJD.

was removed, and the roof was transformed to a shallow hip roof with a central dome and skylight. The dispute about a stairway in the atrium continued, but again the decision was to leave the space open. To provide for efficient entry into the Ships of the Sea Museum, a new portico was designed at the rear of the house; and, at the back of the property, an existing garden was enlarged and enhanced. The "indomitable Scarbrough House," as Lane described it, was granted new life as a museum of Savannah's maritime history.[33]

FINDING JAY AND THE GRECIAN STYLE AT THE SCARBROUGH HOUSE

Having sponsored the work of the third restoration of this house in 1996, Lane observed, "Perhaps the pursuit of absolute authenticity is an illusory and misguided goal and an impossible one in this instance."[34] Still, even when we account for the years of change and loss, the art of this structure prevails in the expression of simple volumes, the restrained ornament of the exterior, and the elegant symmetry of the interior plan. It is, as most of Jay's work, rather like a piece of fine sculpture, offering us heightened experiences of spaces and surfaces.

The Scarbrough House is perhaps Jay's most elegant rendering of the Grecian style of the Regency, keyed to the Doric order. Oddly, through much of its long history, this structure has been claimed to be one of the earliest examples of the Greek Revival style in American architecture. Grecian or Greek Revival? In 1898 William Rotch Ware explained this confusion better than later scholars. He observed that a "revived interest in Grecian forms seems to have been felt earlier in the South than at the North." He described the Southern interest in ancient Greek architecture as a "disease…of rather a mild type," prompted by the travel abroad of wealthy Southerners who saw and admired "the newest fashion in architecture" in Regency England. By contrast, Ware said, Northerners copied the ancient Greek style from literary sources with results that were "bookishly pure" but suffered from a "pedantic stiffness."[35]

The style that would come to bear the label of Greek Revival was documented by Talbot Hamlin in *Greek Revival Architecture in America* (1944). In

[33] Lane, *Mr. Scarbrough's House*, n.p.

[34] Lane, *Architecture of the Old South: Georgia*, 121.

[35] Ware, "The Greek Revival and Some Other Things" in Ware, Part 12:107.

the foreword to this book, Leopold Arnaud, then dean of the school of architecture at Columbia University, declared that this Greek style was "peculiarly American" born of "a conscious separation from Europe and a fierce will to be American."[36] Hamlin asserted that this American development was prompted by two factors: "One was negative—hatred of England. One was positive—idealization of the classic world [Greece and Rome]." He observed that, after the War of 1812, "a new urge to a national life, a national art, was growing irresistibly." And he concluded that, by the late 1820s, inspired by the ideals of both the ancient and the modern Greeks, the Greek Revival emerged as the first great national style of architecture in America.[37]

For obvious reasons, Jay's efforts in the American South had nothing at all to do with what would become the Greek Revival in this country. However, the emergence of that style and its nationalistic assertions would come to complicate both Jay's tenure in this country and subsequent evaluations of his work.

A CODA: "THE FANCY BALL"

In March 1837, the Scarbrough House realized its destiny as the setting for a magnificent party. It became the site of an extravagant event memorialized in *The Fancy Ball: A Sketch* (1837), a long poem by Henry Bowen Anthony, one of the guests. Sparing no expense, Barnsley and his wife invited two hundred members of Savannah's "best" families to a celebration at the "Castle."

The event featured the usual music, dancing, and fine food and drink. But it also involved two types of spectacle then popular in Europe but not yet prominent in the United States, a "fancy ball" and *tableaux vivants*. Both of these forms of entertainment were costume pieces. For a fancy ball, each guest came in elaborate dress representing a character from history, legend, literature, or some exotic locale. For the *tableaux vivants* ("living pictures"), actors chosen from among those invited were costumed and posed in a large frame to portray familiar scenes taken from history or literature as they had been represented in popular paintings or prints.

[36] L. Arnaud, foreword to Hamlin, *Greek Revival Architecture*, xv–xvii.

[37] Hamlin, *Greek Revival Architecture*, 3–4, 36.

Memories of "The Fancy Ball" lingered long in Savannah. In a town where parties are fine and frequent, none can claim to equal that evening in 1837 in the Scarbrough House. It was, in the words of Anthony, a "brilliant sight/ When wit and beauty held their festal night."[38]

[38] Anthony, 3.

CHAPTER 14

TELFAIR HOUSE: "THE SAME SHALL BE PRESERVED"

The Telfair House is important in the histories of Savannah and Jay for several reasons. It was once the home of a family descended from a great patriot, politician, and three-time Georgia governor. It was the only private house designed by Jay to be occupied for several decades by the family for whom it was built. And it might have been the only Jay house in this city to survive without alterations were it not for circumstances that caused it, happily or unhappily, to endure a substantial renovation in the 1880s. What is left is something quite wonderful: the Telfair Academy, the first art museum in the South. But less wonderful is the truth that much of Jay's original design has been lost, in spite of the specific provision in the last will and testament of Mary Telfair that "no part of the lot or improvements shall ever be sold, alienated or encumbered, but the same shall be preserved."[1]

What is known of the origin of this house is this: Sometime after Jay's arrival in Savannah, he was engaged by Alexander Telfair to build a house on St. James's Square (later Telfair Square). As the work proceeded in 1819, Jay was fined for leaving construction materials at this site, the violations recorded on February 2, June 14, and October 18.[2] No document has been found to confirm Jay's appointment to this project, and for many years there was some reluctance to assign this design to him. A survey of Georgia landmarks in 1940 identified this structure as a "stuccoed brick building, believed to have been designed by William Jay."[3] But, this is a Jay house, resembling in many aspects the residences he designed for Richard Richardson and William Scarbrough.

---

[1] M. Telfair, 107.

[2] Savannah City Council Minutes, Feb. 2, June 14, Oct. 18, 1819, SMA.

[3] Georgia Writers' Project of the W.P.A, 139.

THE TELFAIRS

This was a house for a very important family. The patriarch was Edward Telfair, a Scot who had emigrated in 1758 at the age of twenty-three. He soon settled in Savannah where he accumulated substantial wealth as a landowner, planter, and merchant. In 1774 he married Sarah Gibbons, a member of a venerable Georgia family. In a match not unusual for the time, he was almost forty, and she was a mere sixteen. From this union came four sons and three daughters who lived to adulthood.

In 1818 at the age of twenty-nine, Alexander, the fourth-born, became the sole surviving son, and it was he who commissioned this house designed by Jay. Edward, the namesake, had died in 1797 in his late teens; Josiah, a planter, had died in 1817; and Thomas, a planter and a promising politician, had married in 1809 but died in 1818 at thirty-two, leaving a widow and three very young daughters. Alexander was left to manage the family estate, which included the holdings of his father and two brothers. And he was left to care for his widowed mother, the widow and children of his brother Thomas, and his three sisters (Mary, the eldest daughter, unmarried; Sarah, widowed in 1816; and Margaret, unmarried until 1842).

Why did Alexander commission this house? He was prominent in Savannah society, a landowner possessing several plantations and a ship owner involved in international trade. He was active in a number of organizations and philanthropic ventures, often serving as an officer of these groups. Among his several civic commitments was membership on the committee to sponsor the building of a new theater in Savannah, a project for which Jay had been retained. In this context, Alexander may have recognized the unique opportunity of having this well-trained and gifted architect design a home for his family. His financial resources were certainly equal to the demands of Jay's methods. And, a commodious dwelling would accommodate his own busy life in commerce and public service and provide for his mother and three sisters (two unmarried and one recently widowed).

Alexander's mother died in 1827, and he died five years later at the age of forty-three. Custody of the Telfair estate passed to Mary, the oldest surviving child of Edward and Sarah Telfair. She lived to the age of eighty-four, and, for want of any male heirs in the next generation, Mary was the last of this family to carry the Telfair name.[4] Ultimately, it would fall to her to provide for the distribution of the accumulated wealth and properties of this family, including the family home designed by Jay in which she lived for over half a century.

After Alexander's death, his three sisters continued to live in this house, Sarah for another dozen years, and Mary and Margaret for another four decades. The goings and comings of the Telfair women were remarked by many. John Wallace, son of the British vice-consul for Georgia, wrote to his mother in 1814, "The Pumpkin faced Telfairs were here [Augusta, Georgia] a few days since. They cut so many high flourishes, I could not refrain from comparing them to some of the country wenches I have seen in their Sunday gowns."[5] These were, in his view, plain women who put on airs.

In 1934 William Harden, a lawyer and officer of the federal district court, offered several comments about the Telfair women. Because he was born in 1844, Harden remembered only Mary and Margaret—Margaret had married in 1842, but she and her husband William Brown Hodgson continued to live in the Telfair House. In a long list of "recollections" about Mary and Margaret, he observed that they were "rather inseparable companions," carrying themselves with "an air of self importance" and "aloofness." They venerated "the name Telfair" and held a view of the family's elevated status because it was "one of the colonial families of Savannah" of Telfair and Gibbons "blood." He remembered, "[W]hen Miss [Mary] Telfair and Mrs. [Margaret Telfair] Hodgson rode around town in their carriage, they wore an air as if inviting people to behold them as the most important people in town." They associated with only a "small select group of socially elite" and entertained "with dinners in their home." They were, he said, "unattractive looking," "dried up old women," always dressed "very plainly." And he reported that they had the "reputation of being very close about spending money."[6]

Of Mary Telfair, Harden said that he did "not believe she ever had a chance to marry," and there was the rumor that Mary was loath to take a name

---

[4] C. Johnson, 410–11.

[5] Hartridge, *Letters of Robert Mackay to His Wife*, 313 n. 9.

[6] D. Floyd, interview with Mr. Wm. Harden, Feb. 20, 1934, M. H. and D. B. Floyd Collection, Georgia Historical Society, Savannah, GA (hereafter cited as GHS).

other than that of Telfair.[7] Of Margaret's marriage to Hodgson, there is an account by Sidney George Fisher, a denizen of Philadelphia, an occasional gentleman farmer, and a sometime lawyer whose diaries were filled with acerbic observations of the passing scene. He wrote, "[Philadelphia] December 12, 1847...a dinner at Mr. Atherton's [a prominent Philadelphia lawyer whose wife was from the South] on Thursday given to Mr. and Mrs. Hodgson & Miss Telfair from Savannah, whom the Athertons met last summer at Saratoga. Hodgson is a well educated man, who has spent nearly all of his life in the East, where he was a dragoman [someone familiar with Middle Eastern language and culture]. He married Miss Telfair two or three years ago, she an old maid very plain, he, comparatively a young man & well looking, she very rich, he very poor, the old story."[8]

There are other tales of the Telfair sisters, but generally they confirm these matters: Mary and Margaret were devoted to their brother Alexander. Before and after his death, the sisters kept their own counsel, were keenly aware of the Telfair mantle, and cultivated an elevated station in Savannah society. They enjoyed relationships with only a certain elite of the town and entertained their very select associates at sedate dinners in their home.

Jay's design for the family home bears the imprint of Alexander and his sisters in the functional aspects of the plan and in the ornamentation of the structure. And, in the particular case of this house, there is at least as much symbolism in the site as there is in the character of the building.

TRUST LOT "N" OF HEATHCOTE WARD

The plot that would come to be occupied by the Telfair House was known as Trust Lot "N" of Heathcote Ward, and it had quite a colorful history. This ward was one of the original six set in place by Oglethorpe. It had been named for George Heathcote, an influential founding trustee of the colony. At the center of Heathcote Ward was St. James's Square, named for a speculative land development in London. Established in 1684, this London square was planned for the construction of exclusive homes facing a central garden, rather like what would come to be the character of most of the squares in Savannah.

In 1756 Trust Lot "N" of Heathcote Ward was granted by the crown to

---

[7] Ibid.

[8] Fisher, 1:203.

the trustees of the colony to build "a fit and commodious dwelling house for present and future governors in Savannah."[9] The house raised here was first occupied by Henry Ellis, the second royal governor of Georgia. The next resident was James Wright, the third and last of the royal governors. In January 1776, Wright was taken prisoner in this house by one of the Liberty Boys in an audacious act of revolution. Among the membership of the Liberty Boys was Edward Telfair, and in 1818 his political commitment was honored by his sole surviving son in the acquisition of this site for the family home.

The land was cleared in November 1818. Notice of work here appears in the records of city council for February through October 1819. In April and November 1819, shipments of brick from Charleston were delivered to Telfair, and likely other materials came in consignments from England to Jay by way of Richard Richardson. By 1820 tax records show that the value of the property had increased substantially, suggesting that the new house had been completed by that time.[10]

DESIGNING A HOUSE FOR THE TELFAIRS

As in the case of the Scarbrough House, much of Jay's design for the Telfair House was obscured by later changes. In the late 1880s, Mary Telfair bequeathed the family home and its contents to the Georgia Historical Society to serve as a "Library and Academy of Arts and Sciences." And, although she had clearly stated her wish that nothing be substantially changed, much was.

Fortunately, as the building was being studied for its new role as an art museum, Detlef Lienau, the New York architect charged with the work, made careful drawings of the original plan and elevation.[11] Next, because this was a project aimed to serve the public good, local newspapers chronicled the work as it was progressing, taking care to observe what changes were being made.

---

[9] Walker, 172–73.

[10] "Buildings for Sale," *Columbian Museum and Savannah Daily Gazette*, Nov. 25, 1818; Savannah City Council Minutes, "Docket of Information," Feb. 2, June 14, Oct. 18, 1819, SMA; "Ship News: Port of Savannah—Arrived," *Columbian Museum and Savannah Daily Gazette*, Apr. 22, Nov.1, 1819; A. Telfair, "121 Barnard Street, Trust Lot 'N,' Heathcote Ward," 1820, CCRO.

[11] D. Lienau, "Plans of the Telfair Mansion," c. 1883, Avery Architectural Library, Detlef Lienau Collection, Columbia University, NY.

Finally, in the 1930s and 40s, Dolores Boisfeuillet Floyd, a Savannah historian, gathered observations of the original condition of the Telfair House from citizens who had known the home and who remembered the conditions of Mary Telfair's gift.

According to Floyd, "The premises bequeathed by Miss Telfair presented an entirely different external appearance from that which is familiar today." She reported,

> The mansion consisted of a two story brick house, plastered over, situated upon the eastern portion of the lot; a carriage-house with servants quarters above it, also of brick, upon the extreme western end of the lot; an old-fashioned garden between the two structures.... [T]here was a two story wooden porch across the rear of the house overlooking the garden.... [T]he whole [was] surrounded by a high brick wall.[12]

The original structure was a Regency villa, two stories set on a high basement, a mass almost square in its proportions with an apparently flat roof. The exterior was stucco over brick, spare of ornament but with corner setbacks, deeply recessed windows, and a string course marking the separation of the two upper stories. The windows were rectangular, taller at the first level and fitted with headers and sills. At the two windows flanking the porch were shallow iron balconies, the geometry of the ironwork featuring the Greek key motif, a pattern evoking restraint rather than exuberance.

In the center of the three-bay front, the portico had four great columns of the Corinthian order, the third mode invented by the Greeks but the one favored by the Romans. Here, unsurprisingly, Jay used the Corinthian of a proper Greek heritage, that of the Choragic Monument of Lysicrates (c. 334 B.C.), rather than one of the many debased versions of the style propagated by the Romans. These capitals, beautifully complex, were casts made of a composite material, likely Coade stone imported from London. As at the Richardson and Scarbrough Houses, the porch was approached by double stairs. And, like the Scarbrough House, the center of the facade was emphasized by a Diocletian or great half-round window at the second story and echoed by a half-round recessed area below the porch.

The interior was a center hall plan. The entry hall featured an octagonal

---

[12] D. Floyd, "Georgia Historical Society's Ward: Telfair Academy of Arts and Sciences," n.d., M. H. and D. B. Floyd Collection, GHS.

skylight, and the space led quickly to a grand double stairway to the second level. At the main floor, there were rooms with unusual shapes—one an octagon, one an oval, others terminating in semi-circular ends. The base, door, and window moldings were broad and deeply carved.

Features of the plan show that it was drawn to suit this particular family. On the main floor were the public rooms. Just inside the entry on the left was a library, octagonal in shape. This room would come to be known to the family as the "oak room," named for the painted treatment of the wall in *faux bois* ("false wood"). The library was the domain of Alexander, who as head of the family had numerous and varied responsibilities. The affairs of the women (his mother and three sisters) were centered in the other rooms on this main floor. Just beyond the library on the left was the dining room of generous and graceful proportions, terminating at the west end in one of Jay's lovely curved walls. To the right of the entry hall was a double parlor fitted with pocket doors to divide the space and accommodate large or small groups. Both the east and west ends of this large room were curved, so it took the shape of an oval.

On the second story, there were six bedrooms. Access to this floor was gained by an imposing double stairway that rose in the entry hall and paused at a landing to continue in a single flight of stairs. As at the Richardson House, a basement held the kitchen and laundry; and a courtyard surrounded by a high wall was located between the main house and the carriage house. In the carriage house were living quarters for the black men and women who were the house slaves, or "servants" in Mary Telfair's parlance.

This was not, as was the Scarbrough House, a place arranged for grand entertainments. This was a family home where visitors came to call and where guests might be welcomed for extended stays. And, it is likely that this place was not "showy," a word that Mary used often to describe the ostentatious display of which she did not approve. This was, by the announcement of the Corinthian entry, an important and sober place, suggesting that the Telfairs were persons of significance and substance in this community.

IN THE MATTER OF ORNAMENT

Very little is known of the nature of Jay's collaboration with his Savannah clients. We can only guess what he proposed to them and what constraints they may have imposed on his designs. For the Telfairs, we do know something about the character of Alexander, his mother, and his sisters. We have hints of the rhythm of their lives, and we can see how the original plan of the dwelling suited the needs of this family. However, in the matter of interior decoration, much is conjecture. Many elements of the original ornament of the house were lost when the building was renovated in the 1880s to create spaces and surfaces congenial to the display of art.

Two particular elements of the interior do survive. These are the two marble mantelpieces in the double parlor just to the right of the entry, and they are curious in the context of Jay's work. For the ornament of his Savannah houses, it was Jay's usual habit to acquire the most sophisticated materials available, usually from the English markets. As one good example, the marble mantelpiece of the front parlor in the Richardson-Owens-Thomas House is classical in style and subject and is credited to the studio of a well-known sculptor who was a member of the Royal Academy in London.

The two mantelpieces in the double parlor of the Telfair House are the work of John Frazee, an American artist who would come to be declared "the first sculptor of American birth and parentage." These two works in Savannah date from very early in his professional life, before he gained access to academic training. According to Lydia Hyman, in 1818 Frazee had just emerged from his apprenticeship with stonecutters who were his first teachers. He set up shop in New York City as a carver of monuments and mantelpieces, work he pursued until the mid-1820s. The subjects of the Telfair mantelpieces are pastoral scenes, one inscribed "The Shepherd Boy" and the other a rendering of "The Peaceable Kingdom." In both compositions, the figures are anatomically improbable and set in awkward landscapes, revealing, according to Hyman, "a somewhat clumsy classical style…[and a] lack of sophistication in design and execution."[13]

The choice of these mantels for a Jay house suggests the heavy hand of a client, perhaps the Telfair women who often spent the summer season in the Northeast where they might have become aware of the work of a native artisan. The provincial style may have appealed to these women by way of contrast to the high style and flourishes of the Regency. Or, as good Presbyterian women, they may have been drawn to the subject matter. Both themes, Christ as the Good Shepherd and the Peaceable Kingdom, were prominent in Early

[13] Shedd, 260; Hyman, 53–54.

Christian and later Protestant iconography.[14] And, with a reputation for some parsimony, the Telfair women may have acquired these mantelpieces at a very considerable savings when compared to the cost of a refined carving in the academic style from London.

MARY TELFAIR'S "HOME"

This was a beloved family home. Testimony survives in letters from Mary Telfair written over seven decades to Mary Few, a friend whom Mary Telfair had known from childhood.[15] In this correspondence are expressions of great spirit and intimacy, revealing what Mary Telfair thought about the world and her place in it, including a number of references to "home," the house on St. James's Square. These letters do not speak of the architectural plan or ornament of the house, but they tell of the lives lived here. These observations help to explain why, at the end of her life, Mary Telfair directed that "no part of the building shall ever be occupied as a private residence or rented out for money."[16] This was to be, for all time, the house in which the Telfairs of Savannah had lived.

Both Mary Telfair and her friend Mary Few spent their lives in their family homes consigned quite happily to the state of "single blessedness," as Mary Telfair, borrowing from Shakespeare, described their status as unmarried women.[17] She said often, "Home is the centre of attraction to me and I never wish even for a day to leave it." The house on St. James's Square became her center. For many years, the Telfair sisters enjoyed summers in the North, often in Newport, Rhode Island, in the era of vacation cottages before Newport came to be populated by preposterous mansions. In 1839 Sarah and Margaret expressed their desire to build a cottage in Newport, but Mary opposed the plan. She wrote to Mary Few, "[T]he cottage will end in talk if it rests upon my decision. Milton said *one* tongue was enough for a woman & I think one *Home* enough for a woman."[18]

---

[14] The motif of Christ the Good Shepherd has its origin in John 10:1-21; the Peaceable Kingdom takes its imagery from Isaiah 11:6-8.

[15] Mary Few was the daughter of William Few, a friend and associate of Edward Telfair. The Fews moved from Georgia to New York in 1799.

[16] M. Telfair, 107.

[17] Shakespeare, *A Midsummer Night's Dream*, I.1, Theseus to Hermia.

[18] Wood, *Mary Telfair to Mary Few*, 102, 194.

This was the place that Mary came to know as the seat of her family, the residence she occupied from the age of twenty-eight until she died at the age of eighty-four, the home made for this family by her brother Alexander. Mary, the oldest of the sisters and likely the dominant voice, abhorred pretension and "show" in all matters—in manners, ceremony, dress, and ornament. She announced, "[N]o one admires true elegance more than I do, but true elegance consists in simplicity and freedom from ostentation & parade."[19]

The center of this home was the library, the "oak room." This was Alexander's domain until his death in 1832. In later years, according to Mary, it was here that she and her sisters passed the hours reading books, writing and reading letters, and tending to needlework. In one very specific reference to this room, Mary Telfair reported to Mary Few that the arrival of a letter "of charming length" had the result "to illuminate the dark walls of our oak room, which candles & lamps fail to enliven."[20]

MARY TELFAIR AND THE REVEREND WILLIAM JAY OF BATH

What Mary knew of Jay is unknown. In none of her letters is there mention of the young English architect, although it seems certain that she met him in Savannah as work was progressing on what would come to be her beloved home. But she did know and admire the writings of the Reverend Jay, and she visited him in Bath at least once. In Mary's view, the Reverend Jay "realized more than other living Divines my beau ideal of a Christian Minister."[21]

In 1840 Mary entertained in her home Jay's sister and brother-in-law, Anne and Robert Bolton—they had moved from England to America in 1836 and settled in the following year in Pelham, New York. Mary was delighted with their company. She wrote to Mary Few, "[The Boltons are] so pious, so intellectual—so fresh and natural in their feelings (to those who appreciate character above all things).... I wish such could oftener cross my dreary path of life. Every year, I may say every day, I feel less disposed to listen to chatters."[22]

During the first of four tours of Europe, Mary met the Reverend Jay. In

---

[19] Ibid., 230.

[20] Ibid., 197.

[21] M. Telfair to M. Few, [1841], #170, William Few Collection, GAM.

[22] Ibid., Feb. 9 [c. 1840], #209, GAM.

July 1842, she was in Bath, writing to Mary Few,

> We arrived in Bath this morning and this afternoon I went to see Mr. Jay with my letter of introduction [surely prepared by Robert Bolton]—The servant at the door of the sweet little manse with its flower garden in front took it up & returned to say he was at home and would be glad to see us—We sat an hour with him and I was charmed with his conversations, his countenance, & his manner—He talks in the most unstudied style and you never forget for a moment his sacred calling—for he looks & talks like a Minister of the Gospel.[23]

Might they have discussed his son William, then dead for five years? Or her brother Alexander, for whom Jay had designed the house on St. James's Square, then dead for ten years? That seems likely, but no record survives of those topics.

"A LIBRARY AND ACADEMY OF ARTS AND SCIENCES"

In 1832 at the death of Alexander, Mary became custodian of the Telfair legacy. Her father had died in 1807, her mother in 1827. She outlived all of her brothers and sisters, and, from the marriages of her siblings, no sons survived. She was the last to carry the Telfair name. In 1875, on the day before her death, she signed her will, which provided for the dispersal of the Telfair fortune and the perpetuation of the Telfair name.

It is often said that Mary's principal goal in directing her inheritance to various charities was to proclaim the family name. That surely weighed in her decisions, but Mary was a participant in the nineteenth-century evangelical tradition in which philanthropy played an important role. Her bequests were carefully devised to extend benefits to a wide range of worthy causes.[24] In her letters to Mary Few, she spoke often of the burden of wealth. In her view, "The poor generally speaking are happier than the rich." She was persuaded that "the only people who ought to have wealth are those who dispense it judiciously."[25]

Mary had a conviction of the rightness of charity, and she was a great

---

[23] Wood, *Mary Telfair to Mary Few*, 225.

[24] Among several gifts, Mary Telfair provided for the establishment of a "Library and Academy of Arts and Sciences," a hospital for indigent women, and grants of land to the Union Society and the Widows Society.

[25] Wood, *Mary Telfair to Mary Few*, 204, 291–92.

believer in the salutary effects of education in the realms of the practical, intellectual, and moral. It would come as no surprise to those who knew her well that her primary bequest was the grant of the family home, its furnishings, and income to establish a "Library and Academy of Arts and Sciences." She entrusted the project to the men of the Georgia Historical Society, and item fourteen of her will stated the conditions for this award, including a number of provisions regarding the house:

> I hereby give, devise and bequeath to the Georgia Historical Society and its successors, all that lot or parcel of land, with the buildings and improvements thereon, fronting on St. James Square...having been for many years past the residence of my family, together with all my books, papers, documents, pictures, statuary and works of art, or having relation to art or science and all the furniture of every description in the dwelling house and on the premises...to keep and preserve the same as a public edifice, for a Library and Academy of Arts and Sciences, in which the books, pictures, and works of art herein bequeathed, and such others as may be purchased out of the income, rents and profits of the bequest hereinafter made for that purpose, shall be permanently kept and cared for, to be open for the use of the public.[26]

One condition of the gift was

> that the Georgia Historical Society shall cause to be placed and kept over and against the front porch, or entrance to the main building on said lot, a marble slab or tablet, on which shall be cut or engraved the following words, to-wit: TELFAIR ACADEMY OF ARTS AND SCIENCES, the word "Telfair" being in larger letters and occupying a separate line above the other words.

All other changes to the structure were prohibited. Even restoration was restricted: "[W]henever the walls of the building shall require renovating by paint or otherwise, the present color and design shall be adhered to as far as practicable."[27]

Mary Telfair called for the establishment of a "Library and Academy of Arts and Sciences," not an art museum. Her passions were reading and nature. She loved books and read voraciously—she often spoke of finding a life in

[26] M. Telfair, 106–107.
[27] Ibid.

books. She also loved travel, the chief pleasure of which was the discovery of thrilling landscapes. In her early years, there were the summer journeys to the northeastern United States where she found places of more varied terrain than the flat lands of the Georgia lowcountry. In 1841 at the age of fifty, Mary embarked on the first of four trips to Europe. The landscapes of Europe delighted her, particularly when these were ornamented by the picturesque remains of castles and churches.

There is no evidence that Mary Telfair pursued with any passion or plan the acquisition of works of art although her will makes clear that the family home contained some "pictures, statuary, and works of art." Her appreciation of art was conventional for the time, a preference for verisimilitude, technical virtuosity, and the portrayal of exquisite sentiment. Of a marble sculpture in a private collection in Baltimore, Mary said, "Nothing that I have ever seen from the pencil or the chisel can compare with it. The shroud is perfect—so transparent that the knees were seen through it. I felt disposed to say, *this cannot be marble*." The sculptor was Horatio Greenough, an American artist. The work was *Medora* (1832), the depiction of a dead heroine from Lord Byron's *The Corsair* (1814), a lengthy poem with which Mary was certainly familiar.[28]

An "academy" would suit her. Mary valued education, and, in her letters to Mary Few, she offered several accounts of nieces and nephews whom she hoped to take into her charge to form their character through proper training and instruction. In conceiving of her bequest, she probably had no particular curriculum in mind. More likely she thought of the establishment of a library and museum rather like the American Academy of Arts and Sciences chartered in 1780 in Boston, the mission of which was "To cultivate every art and science which may tend to advance the interest, honour, dignity, and happiness of a free, independent, and virtuous people."[29]

Mary Telfair's desire for a "Library and Academy of Arts and Sciences" seems to have survived for at least six years after the will was read. In 1881, Charles Colcock Jones Jr. addressed the Georgia Historical Society. Jones was simply beside himself in contemplating the promise of Mary Telfair's gift. He

---

[28] M. Telfair to M. Few, Nov. 15 [1837], #165, William Few Collection, GAM. This sculpture, made for Robert Gilmor Jr., a wealthy Baltimore merchant, is now in the Baltimore Museum of Art.

[29] American Academy of Arts and Sciences, 11:79.

said,

> It is the misfortune of this new country that we are, in large degree, ignorant of true art and almost totally wanting in everything which savors of antiquity. Our vulnerable monuments are but the works of yesterday.... [W]e lack music, we lack art-galleries, we lack public libraries, we lack gymnasia, we lack free temples of learning.... [This academy] will prove a magnet in our midst around which will concentre all that is beautiful, instructive, and refining. Let us have a care that we admit nothing within its walls...which does not possess genuine value and serve aptly to illustrate some department of knowledge.... Above all, let this Academy illustrate Georgia, her archaeology, her mineralogy, her flora, her fauna, and exhibit everything which may tend in Art and Science to interpret her past, glorify her present, and minister to the grandeur of her future.[30]

It is possible that, upon hearing the full thunder of Jones's oration in 1881, the good men of the Georgia Historical Society were prompted to reconsider what could truly come of all of this. They were just then contemplating the prospect of the old Telfair home, worn down by six decades of occupation, filled with an odd lot of paintings and sculptures, burdened with books, and heaped with specimens of organic and mineral remains. A report in 1893 looked back at the beginning of the project and offered this confession:

> It would scarcely be possible to exaggerate the feeling of helplessness and uncertainty that was in the hearts and minds of every member of the Board of Managers of the Georgia Historical Society when, as the representatives of the Society, in spring 1883 they were first called to assume the responsibilities of the Telfair trust.... On the one side an old family mansion...and on the other side a party of gentlemen without artistic knowledge or experience, who were expected to create from the means at their disposal an Academy of Arts and Sciences.[31]

There had been further complications. Soon after the death of Mary Telfair in June 1875, her will was challenged by two groups of heirs, each of whom had been provided for—but in terms insufficient to their desires. The

[30] Jones, *Anniversary Address*, 34–36.
[31] Telfair Academy Board of Managers, 4.

disputes made their way through the Georgia courts, and the contest was finally resolved in the U.S. Supreme Court in October 1882.[32] The legacy did not come to the Georgia Historical Society until May 1883.

PLAN TWO: "A MUSEUM OF FINE ARTS"

Initially, there was a period of "much uncertainty and some vacillation," including some "narrow escapes." These circumstances were described in a 1907 report by Alexander Rudolf Lawton, then president of the Georgia Historical Society. According to Lawton, the trustees had come to understand that the charge to establish and maintain "an expensive library of arts and sciences, a scientific museum, an elaborate art school, and a museum of fine arts...[was] far too ambitious and comprehensive for the funds at their disposal." They resolved to establish "a museum of art, with incidental teaching." Next, the trustees determined that no one of their number, indeed no one in Savannah, was sufficiently skilled to advance this plan.[33]

One name came forward as someone who could lead this project: Carl Ludwig Brandt. Born near Hamburg, Germany, in a region then part of Denmark, he was the son and grandson of eminent physicians. Brandt studied art in the great galleries of Europe and emigrated to the United States in 1852 to become very successful painting portraits of the very wealthy. In 1870 he established his studio in Hastings-on-Hudson, New York, a region frequented by residents of Savannah. In 1871 he was commissioned by Margaret Telfair Hodgson to paint the portrait of her husband; the painting was destined for the new home of the Georgia Historical Society.[34]

When the appointment of a founding director for an art museum was being contemplated, Brandt was the first choice. According to Lawton's 1917 report, both Savannah and Brandt were calculated to gain in this enterprise: "[Brandt] possessed wonderful energy, ingenuity, and versatility. He had been successful in life, and was willing to devote his time and energies to the Academy for small compensation, correctly believing that it would be his monument."[35] Brandt began work in August 1883. His scheme was grandiose. He conceived of a museum that would expose Savannahians to the very best of

[32] Otto, 17:174–91.
[33] Lawton, 17–18.
[34] C. Johnson, 362–63.
[35] Lawton, 18.

the fine arts by presenting them with evidence of the great and enduring classical tradition in painting and sculpture. And, with no apologies to the lingering spirit of Mary Telfair, Brandt advanced full throttle a plan to alter the old family home to make it a proper museum of art.

Brandt had very clear ideas about what changes in the old house were required, and he quickly secured the services of Detlef Lienau, a prominent New York architect. Lienau was born in the same region of northern Germany as Brandt. He studied architecture in Munich and Paris, settling in New York City in 1848 to begin a long and successful practice focused on private residences. In 1873 he was engaged by Margaret Telfair Hodgson to design the new home of the Georgia Historical Society as a memorial to her husband.[36]

The progress of the work on the old Telfair mansion was followed with interest in Savannah's newspapers. It was, after all, a project in the public interest, and anticipation of its opening was keen. In these accounts, care was taken to observe how the wishes of Mary Telfair were being followed in regard to the preservation of her beloved home. In February 1884 came this announcement: "Under the terms of the will of Miss Telfair the Board of Managers are required to limit the improvements so as not to essentially change the architectural features of the original structure. Hence, though several necessary improvements have been made in the building, they are not of such a character as will change its general appearance." And the reporter noted reassuringly, "All the improvements have a substantial look, and everything savoring of gaudiness will be assiduously avoided in the colors and fixtures."[37]

In all of these early reports, there was an anxious effort to declare that changes had been few, tasteful, and necessary. In truth, there were significant changes on the exterior and in the interior. The height of the parapet was increased to extend the attic story. The front hall was opened up by removing the original stairway near the entry and moving the stairs to the far end of the hall. The original octagonal skylight was replaced by a large rectangular light.

---

[36] Kramer, 277, 281. Lienau's work in Savannah included designs for Hodgson Hall (1873–1876) and the Telfair Hospital for Indigent Females (1883), alterations for the Telfair Academy of Arts and Sciences (1885–1886), plans for the remodeling of the Wayne-Gordon House (1886), and a consultation on the remodeling of the Andrew Low House (c. 1886).

[37] "Miss Telfair's Request," *SMN*, Feb. 24, 1884.

The old double parlor had been relieved of its center doors to function as an open sculpture gallery. Several windows at both levels were closed up to control light and provide more wall area for the display of art. The "oak room" was retained as an office space, and the dining room was left largely intact as a Telfair memorial room displaying family furniture and a collection of portraits. By 1884 the trustees had authorized further changes to the property including the addition of a large annex to the rear of the mansion comprising a sculpture gallery below and an elegant octagonal picture gallery above lighted by a skylight. And, in the place of the old carriage house, a residence was built for the director, and two art studios were provided for instruction.

There were two important final touches to the renovation, one of which had been dictated by Mary Telfair. The front of the mansion was emblazoned, as she had requested, with a prominent notice above the entry: TELFAIR (in very large letters), ACADEMY OF ARTS AND SCIENCES. Brandt added, as a signboard of sorts, a line of five carved figures standing at various states of attention in front of the building, five fine fellows who were understood to be the greatest artists in history.

In the center is Phidias, the master sculptor of the Greek Classical age, whose colossal statue of Athena had been housed in the Parthenon—a small image of this Athena was once held in the outstretched hand of the Telfair Phidias, but she went missing many years ago. To the right and left of Phidias are his most revered successors, the great artists of the High Renaissance, the sculptor Michelangelo and the painter Raphael. And flanking these figures, at the right and the left, are the masters of the Baroque, the painters Rembrandt and Rubens.

The idea to pose these fellows in front of the new museum in Savannah had come to Brandt during one of his trips to Europe to gather art. In Vienna in late 1883, he saw the new construction of the Ringstrasse, the circular road enclosing the central area of the city. One of the grand new buildings on this street was the Künstlerhaus, built for an association of artists as an exhibition hall. Planned to stand at the entry to this hall were four statues of artists, including Rubens carved by the Viennese sculptor Victor Oskar Tilgner. Pleased by this effect, Brandt commissioned Tilgner to produce five figures for Savannah to be carved of Marzano stone, a hard limestone from Marzano (later Marean) in Istria (later Croatia).[38]

[38] Van Nimmen, 64–73.

So what would Mary Telfair, who despised "show," have made of the several substantial alterations to the old family home, the enormous new galleries attached to the western end of the house, and the gathering of the five stone interlopers now posed on her front lawn? An easy guess is that she would not have been charmed by these changes to her beloved home. However, Mary would have been pleased by the action of city council in July 1883 to change "the name of St. James square to Telfair place."[39]

"THE ART CENTRE OF THE SOUTH"

As work on the facility progressed, Brandt busied himself with the collection of materials that would represent to the citizens of Savannah the finest in art through the ages. It was a daunting task. This was to be a museum made quite from nothing—Brandt was quite unimpressed by the "art" gathered by the Telfairs. Supplied with $20,000 from the trustees, Brandt made four trips to Europe, visiting Amsterdam, Munich, Vienna, Venice, Florence, Rome, Naples, Berlin, Hamburg, Düsseldorf, Cologne, Paris, London, and Liverpool.[40] Plaster casts of ancient sculptures were commissioned from the European museums where these antiquities were held. Photographs served to reveal paintings by the masters of the Renaissance and the Baroque. Contemporary art was represented by originals purchased at exhibitions of the great European art academies.

In February 1885, the Telfair Academy of Arts and Sciences was ready for a "temporary opening."[41] By this time, the foundation was being dug behind the old mansion for the annex to include a "cast room" at the lower level and a "picture gallery" above, work that was completed in 1886. In January 1888, *Harper's New Monthly Magazine* featured a profile of Savannah. The author was Isaac Wheeler Avery, who declared that the new Telfair Academy of Arts and Sciences "properly managed, developed, and utilized, must make Savannah the art centre of the South."[42]

The men and women of Savannah were delighted by this remarkable addition to the city. The art collection flourished, first in the hands of Brandt,

---

[39] "Telfair Square," *SMN*, July 19, 1883.

[40] Telfair Academy Board of Managers, 5; C. Johnson, "Mary Telfair's Legacy" in McCullough, 14–15.

[41] "The Telfair Academy…Temporary Opening," *SMN*, Feb. 1, 1885.

[42] Avery, 271.

whose choices had been fine examples of the academic tradition of the late nineteenth century. After Brandt's death in 1905, the Telfair gained the service of Gari (Julius Garibaldi) Melchers, a well-known American painter in the modernist tradition and friend of many painters of the day. Drawn to Savannah because his wife was a native of the city, he served as consultant to the museum and directed the purchase of important works of early modernism, including examples of American Impressionism and the Ashcan School, paintings for which the museum is still well known. By the end of Melchers's tenure in 1916, the Telfair had established itself as a first-rate museum in this country.[43]

RECOVERING JAY AT THE TELFAIR

By the middle years of the twentieth century, regret was emerging about what Brandt and Lienau had done to the work of Jay. In truth, it is fortunate that Jay had fallen into the hands of Lienau. Ellen W. Kramer observes that the character of Lienau's style was quite congenial to that of Jay: "[T]he emphasis in Lienau's work was generally on the precisely defined, closed, regular contour, on a relatively smooth wall surface, on symmetry, order, and restraint....His was a rational, classical approach."[44] If elements of Jay's work were lost, a classical spirit endured.

In 1941 there was a call to "relocate" the statues still standing prominently in front of Mary Telfair's house. The complaints were that the sculptures were "machine-made," "made of sandstone," and "turned out in quantity"—all quite untrue. However, it was true that these fellows somewhat obstructed the view of Jay's facade.[45] Consideration of the matter was given, but the statues remained.

In 1980 Alexander V. J. Gaudieri, director of the museum, launched a "march through the Telfair," which a local newspaper reported as "sort of like Sherman marching through Georgia."[46] Gaudieri reasoned that the old mansion designed by Jay was one of the treasures of the museum, and he and members of his staff began to consider how to recover lost elements of Jay's

---

[43] McCullough, 49–66.

[44] Kramer, 258.

[45] "Telfair Academy Fifty Years Ago," *SMN*, June 20, 1941.

[46] T. Brown, "Telfair: Restoration Goes On," *Savannah News-Press*, Jan. 9, 1983.

design. Two important projects were the careful restorations of the dining room and the "oak room."

THE "OAK ROOM": "THE MOST IMPORTANT ROOM IN AMERICA"

Likely the renovation most pleasing to the hovering spirit of Mary Telfair was the work that was undertaken in 1981 to restore the octagonal room Mary had known as the "oak room." According to the drawing made by Lienau, the footprint of the room was unchanged. Here was a fine octagon, reflecting the Regency's affection for unusual and often polygonal spaces. It was known that, at Brandt's behest, Lienau had stripped most of the walls of their original finishes during his renovation of the building, but it was determined that bookcases had been built into four niches at some date before the 1880s. When the original wall treatment was discovered behind these bookcases, a museum staff member declared, "It was plaster, which had been painted to look like wood grain. When we found it, it just knocked your socks off."[47]

Further study of the room revealed that all of the walls and the woodwork were painted in *faux bois*. The original surfaces of the niches were restored, then a painter trained in "graining" was employed to finish the room in *faux bois* panels. Aside from the unique and lovely effect of this treatment, the significance of this discovery was that, while the process was popular in the early nineteenth century, few examples of this method have survived.[48]

The consultant for work on the "oak room" was Berry B. Tracy, former curator-in-charge of the American wing of the Metropolitan Museum of Art. So stunning were the results of this project that Berry declared this to be "the most important room in America."[49] According to another expert who participated in this work, here was evidence of "the presence of high style English Regency design on American soil in the early 19th century."[50] Now, as a result of this exemplary project in restoration, there may be no better place in Savannah to contemplate Jay's taste and ingenuity than in the "oak room" of the Telfair Academy.

---

[47] D. Kendall, "Restoring Telfair," *SMN*, May 1, 1986.

[48] Matero, 34–38.

[49] T. Brown, "Telfair: Restoration Goes On," *Savannah News-Press*, Jan. 9, 1983.

[50] Matero, 37.

CHAPTER 15

BULLOCH-HABERSHAM HOUSE: "A PRETENTIOUS PIECE OF WORK"

The house that Jay built in 1818–1819 on Orleans Square for Archibald Stobo Bulloch, and later occupied by various Habershams, gained attention in and beyond Savannah for two important reasons. First, it was a remarkably beautiful building, perhaps Jay's most ingenious design during his short stay in this country. The house was described in 1902, not unkindly, as "a pretentious piece of work," and in the following year by the same writer as "[p]erhaps the most refined, elaborate, and carefully planned" residence in the "Greek Revival" style in America.[1] And then, just short of its centennial, it was gone. Not even allowed to molder to an honorable decay, the Bulloch-Habersham House was destroyed, pieces of it sold at auction for pitiable sums or hauled away as refuse, to make way for a city auditorium.

The willful destruction of the Bulloch-Habersham House was one of the worst cases of metropolitan malfeasance to be documented in an era when the preservation movement was just beginning to gain attention. Some of the most significant voices of the age were heard to express their outrage at the event. It is not unusual for old buildings to be cleared away for something new. But, in the particular case of the Bulloch-Habersham House, what is unusual is the regret with which the destruction of this structure is still remembered. Gone now for a century, it is still prominent on those sad lists of lost treasures in the short history of American architecture.

In the sequence of Jay's designs for Savannah houses, the Bulloch House is usually named last—not in chronology but in conception. It was a singular composition. Descriptions of it survive in late nineteenth- and early twentieth-century accounts. From these reports, it is possible to reconstruct this house, to gain a sense of what it meant to see this structure from the street and to walk through the front door.[2]

---

[1] Horton, "Savannah and Parts of the Far South," 97; Horton, "Classic Houses of the South," 389.

[2] See Harvey for a proposed reconstruction of the Bulloch-Habersham House..

"A DESIRE TO INSPECT THE ANCIENT HOME"

In early 1916, two decades before Savannah instituted a popular tour of historic homes, the doors of the Bulloch-Habersham House were opened to the public. Having determined that the old mansion would be demolished, the mayor consented to four days of open house because, as a newspaper reported, "Many persons have been heard to express a desire to inspect the ancient home, famous for its architecture and historic associations."[3]

One of the several remarkable features of this structure was its site, a new square laid out in 1815. Through the eighteenth century, the boundaries of the city had been West Broad Street (later Martin Luther King Jr. Boulevard), East Broad Street, and South Broad Street (later Oglethorpe Avenue). In the aftermath of the War of 1812, there were prospects for a prosperous future, and city officials celebrated by establishing two new southern wards in 1815. The squares of these wards were named for battles of the recent war, and the wards were named for the commanders of these battles. Chippewa Square, named for the Battle of Chippawa [*sic*] (1814), was in Brown Ward, named for Jacob Jennings Brown. It was located on Bull Street, the central north-south route through the city and in 1818 the site of Jay's Savannah Theater. Just to the west of this square was Orleans Square, named for the Battle of New Orleans (1815), in Jackson Ward, named for Andrew Jackson. Orleans Square was immediately a site for grand homes, at least three of which were planned by Jay. But the one with the most magnificent setting was the Bulloch House, occupying two joined trust lots in the southwest sector of the square.

Like the other Jay houses, the Bulloch House was a block, almost a square. It was sited comfortably in a prominent location on this new and particularly commodious square. But, in almost every other way, this composition was unique. Here, on the exterior and on the interior, there was a play of circles and squares.

On the exterior, the pitch of the roof was not hidden as it had been at the other houses, perhaps to allow the peak to echo the outline of the half cone that surmounted the porch at the entry. The portico took the form of a round temple, half embedded in the structure, carving out an exedra or niche, and half-revealed as a temple with Greek Corinthian columns in the style of

---

[3] "Opening the Habersham Home," *Savannah Evening Press*, Jan. 27, 1916.

the Choragic Monument of Lysicrates (a structure near the Acropolis of Athens showing the first use of the Corinthian order on the exterior of a building). This porch was set high on a platform of two ranks of stairs with a terrace or pause between them. This entry was such a handsome composition that it gained special mention in an early survey of American domestic architecture by Fiske Kimball.[4]

Upon entering this house, it became clear that the round volume of the porch was a hallmark of the design. Throughout the building, there were rooms that terminated in half-round walls, a rhythm culminating in one fully round room. But the greatest surprise of all was the stairway to the second floor. Posed in full view as one entered the house, it stood as a kind of intricate sculpture in the space of the central hall. A circle of six monumental Greek Corinthian columns contained a spiral stairway of cast iron. It was a remarkable invention. One can imagine the adventure of descending those stairs—the delight of children, the ceremony of adults, and the apprehension of the elderly. For the deceased, there was a special problem according to one account of the memories of a child set down decades later:

> In the middle of the Habersham house ["the old Habersham house on Orleans Square"] was an octagonal hall, surrounded by columns from which rose a circular stairway of wrought iron [it was cast iron]. One of my elders once said to me, in a low tone, "They could never get a corpse down those stairs. The dead had to be *let down*." When you think of it I suppose that is a drawback in the home, as all of us will be the dead some day.[5]

This fanciful stairway was set forward in the long center hall that gave access to all of the rooms on the main floor. At the left was a dining room and at the right a double parlor extending the length of the house and divided by a screen of columns. At the back of the house and to the left, beyond the dining room, was a round room with semicircular niches and covered by a dome, perhaps originally a breakfast room. To the right of this room, at the end of the center hall, was a study sharing with all of the rooms at the back of the house a view to a rear garden. It was a plan, according to Frederick D. Nichols, that exemplified Jay's "daring experiments."[6]

---

[4] Kimball, 222–23.

[5] Lovell, 32.

[6] Nichols, 40–41.

The Bulloch House would come to be known for its rich and ingenious ornament, each room different from the next. Nichols often cited Jay's skill at embellishing interiors. Of the small circular room on the first floor, he said, "Here, a moulded architrave was surmounted with a unique and daring anthemion band, above which was incised a fret [meander or Greek key pattern] with lines converging in a centerpiece consisting of the fret around a handsome acanthus motif."[7] The fireplace mantels in this house were of such fine character that a condition of the sale of the house to the city was that these be withheld from the contract to be sold separately.[8]

The design of the exterior was deceptively simple. The two stories of the structure were separated by a string course or raised band, and the corners were set back. By contrast, the pattern of fenestration was exquisite and complex. The windows at both levels were rectangular and set in reveals, taller below and shorter above. At the first level, the windows were of a unique design, tripartite with a broad central light and narrow side lights, separated by cast-iron columns in the Ionic style and surmounted by a frieze of glass rondeles or rounds. Finally, as a grace note to remind us of the play of circles and squares, a small window in the gable above the portico was a good round Roman arch, the mullions or dividers of which were the pointed or broken arches of the Gothic.

ARCHIBALD STOBO BULLOCH, WHO "BUILT THE BEAUTIFUL AND CLASSIC HOUSE"

This house so admired by Nichols and others came to be named for two of the most important families in Georgia, the Bullochs and the Habershams. The Bulloch who commissioned this house lived here for only a very short time, perhaps for little more than two years. The residence of Habershams was so long (1834–1898) that, for most of the history of this structure, it would be known as the Habersham House. Both families deserve credit in this account, a Bulloch in the origin of the house and several Habershams in the long stewardship of it.

The first owner was Archibald Stobo Bulloch, a member of a clan that might be called the first family of Georgia. The patriarch was Archibald

---

[7] Ibid.

[8] "Delay in Start on Auditorium Work," *Saturday Evening Press,* Oct. 6, 1915; "Habersham House Is Now the City's," *Saturday Evening Press,* Nov. 1, 1915.

Bulloch, born and educated in Charleston, South Carolina, a grandson of the Reverend Archibald Stobo, a Scot who had established Presbyterianism in the lowcountry. In 1764, at the age of thirty-four, Archibald Bulloch moved to Savannah and immediately became involved in events preparing for the revolution. His contributions to the cause led to his appointment in 1775 as the first president of the provincial congress of Georgia. In the following year, he was elected the first president and commander-in-chief of Georgia; his tenure, however, was brief—he died eight months later at the age of forty-seven. A century after his death, he was recalled as instrumental "in shaping the political destinies of Georgia."[9]

Archibald Stobo Bulloch was the second of three sons (there was one daughter) of this quite famous father, and in 1818 it seemed that a grand home on Orleans Square would suit his accomplishments. He had gained a quick fortune by speculating in real estate and participating in various business ventures, including work as a cotton factor. With William Scarbrough, Richard Richardson, and others, he had invested in what promised to be the very lucrative enterprise of the Savannah Steamship Company. He achieved a number of political appointments, among them a judgeship and a term as a city alderman. Most significantly, he gained the appointment as collector of customs for the port of Savannah, a position he held from 1810 to 1822. This was a presidential appointment, assigned to the Treasury Department with the responsibility to collect tariffs for the federal government, an influential position in local and national affairs.

An early biographer remembered Bulloch for one particular achievement, observing, "He had built the beautiful and classic house, afterward owned by Robert Habersham, Esq."[10] The house designed by Jay for Bulloch was as grand a home as Savannah had seen to that date, sophisticated in its conception of spaces and elegant in its ornamental details. And, by the evidence of some surviving records, it may have been furnished in an extravagant style. Inventory and shipping records show that Bulloch took possession of a number of crates of furniture by Charles-Honoré Lannuier. Lannuier had been born in France in 1779 and trained there during the difficult years of revolutions and wars. To establish a shop in a more congenial market, he moved to New York City in 1802. He was an *ébéniste*, or master furniture

[9] Jones, *Biographical Sketches*, 14, 27.

[10] Bulloch, *History...of the Families of Bulloch and Stobo*, 23.

maker, expert in the use of fine woods, inlay, and gilt-bronze, and in the rendering of decorative figural and architectural motifs. His work was refined and costly, gaining him clients among the very wealthy.

The matter of how Bulloch's home might have come to be furnished with pieces by Lannuier is not clear. In September 1819, Lannuier was ill and intending to give up his business. He posted an ad offering to sell his remaining work at greatly reduced prices. He died in mid-October, and an inventory of his estate included the notice that a quantity of furniture had been sent to "A. S. Bulloch" in Savannah. Indeed, on October 5, 1819, ten cases of furniture arrived at the port of Savannah for "A.S.B." from "Honoré Lannuier."[11]

One possibility is that Bulloch acquired these pieces for use in his new mansion, perhaps guided in his choices by Jay. Or, he may have bought this merchandise on speculation, expecting to sell some or all to his colleagues in Savannah, men like him who were awash in fast money. If furniture by Lannuier ever made its way into the house on Orleans Square, it did not stay there long. Very soon after Bulloch unfurled the rugs in his new home, his world came quite apart. In the fragile economic climate of 1818–1822, his extensive real estate holdings were subject to devaluation and foreclosure. The money he invested in the Savannah Steamship Company was lost on that failed venture. Not only had his personal finances come to ruin, but he had spent government monies in the construction of a new custom house, a structure designed and built by Jay and destroyed in the great fire of 1820.

Surviving records tell some of this sad tale. Flush with funds, Bulloch bought the land on which this house would be built in March 1818. Four years later, in March 1822, he sold this property to relieve his debts.[12] In the matter of the construction of the new custom house, it appears that he was sued for costs by Jay, and there is evidence that in early 1824 Bulloch was imprisoned briefly and charged with misuse of federal funds by the government of the United States, a sad story told in a later chapter.

From enormously promising circumstances and the prospect of residence in what was perhaps the most elegantly appointed house in Savannah, Bulloch suffered a complete financial collapse and humiliation of circumstances. His

[11] Kenny, Bretter, and Leben, 59, 61, 135–37.

[12] "Indenture between M. McAllister and A. S. Bulloch," Mar. 21, 1818, CCRO; "Indenture between A. and S. Bulloch and J. Morel and D. Leion," Mar. 12, 1822, CCRO.

1858 obituary reported quite simply, "We regret to have to announce the death of Mr. Archibald S. Bulloch, an old and respected citizen, who died yesterday morning at an advanced age. Mr. B. was at one time collector of the Port of Savannah, but for a number of years past has lived in retirement."[13]

THE HABERSHAMS

By 1822 the house was leased to Mrs. Mary Maxwell, who ran a number of quality rooming houses in Savannah, including two Jay houses (the Richardson House and the Bulloch House). Ownership was transferred in 1825 and 1831, but in 1834 came the next owner of consequence in the person of Robert Habersham.[14] Robert was descended from James Habersham, a London merchant who had come to Savannah in 1738 to aid George Whitefield in his mission to care for orphan children in the Georgia colony. James became successful in business, establishing the first regular transatlantic commercial shipping from Savannah to England, and in politics, becoming acting governor of the colony of Georgia in 1771–1773. Of his three sons, two served with distinction in the Continental Army and gained appointments by President George Washington, Joseph as postmaster general of the United States and John as port collector for Savannah.

Robert Habersham, who came to occupy the Bulloch House, was the grandson of James and the son of Joseph. He was the sixth child of ten and the fourth son. He must have shown a particular aptitude for business, joining his father in a very successful factorage and merchandising business in Savannah. When his father retired from this enterprise in 1811, Robert became the sole proprietor when he was twenty-eight years old. The firm bought and sold a great variety of goods, arranging for transport on ships owned by the company or leased from others. Robert also represented real estate transactions, and over the years he accumulated vast properties, including several plantations in the region. His business successes were matched by numerous civic responsibilities and philanthropic commitments.

Habersham's many accomplishments were conspicuous, so he was a worthy resident of the house constructed by Jay on Orleans Square. A newspaper article in 1897 reported that he lived in this house from the time he purchased it in 1834 "until his death" in 1870. He married three times (his first two

[13] "Death of An Old Citizen," *SMN*, Mar. 9, 1858

[14] "The Habersham Homestead," *SMN*, May 9, 1897 (hereafter cited in text).

wives died in childbirth), fathering several children, three of whom are known to have resided in this house. William Neyle Habersham, the only son of the second marriage, was seventeen when his father acquired this house, and he resided here until he was married in 1840. William Neyle's tenure in the Bulloch-Habersham House occasioned this legend about its construction:

> The story goes that when Mr. [Archibald Stobo] Bulloch undertook the building of this notable dwelling he made a contract by which he was to pay for it on a basis of so much per brick that went into its construction.... Mr. William Neyle Habersham, while residing there, sought to dig a wine cellar through one of the basement walls. The laborers dug several days through a solid brick and mortar wall, and finally the undertaking was abandoned, when it was discovered that the wall was fifteen feet thick of solid brick.[15]

A subsequent resident of the Bulloch-Habersham House was John Rae Habersham, the eldest son of Robert's third marriage. Having worked in the New York office of the family business, he returned to Savannah at the time of his father's death and occupied this house from about 1879 until his own demise in 1896. Surviving him at the home was his sister Maria Elliott Habersham White, the widow of the Reverend Rufus White who had been rector of St. John's Protestant Episcopal Church in Savannah. She survived her brother by only two years and was the last of the Habershams to occupy this place.

New owners took on the challenges of this historic property, once the most elegantly appointed residence in Savannah but now eight decades old and in urgent need of repair. In 1903 Carleton Champion was reported to have "done much to restore it." In 1905 the property was acquired by the widow of a physician with four young children, who occupied the residence for nine years. Then, in late 1914, she announced her willingness to sell the house to the city for $13,500, a transaction concluded in early November 1915.[16]

---

[15] Ibid.

[16] Horton, "Classic Houses of the South," 389; "Historic Mansion Sold," *SMN*, Feb. 20, 1905; "Habersham House Is Now the City's," *Savannah Evening Pres,* Nov. 1, 1913.

NOTICING "A QUAINT AND PICTURESQUE OLD SAVANNAH MANSION"

The Bulloch-Habersham House was acquired by the city of Savannah, along with some adjacent properties, and slated for demolition to make way for a new municipal auditorium. Given the long history of this fine old mansion, this event was met by some astonishment. The house had been admired and discussed in and beyond Savannah for years.

In *Historic and Picturesque Savannah* (1889), Adelaide Wilson named "the Habersham mansion...by the eminent architect Jay" as unequaled "in beauty of design...substance and solidity." In a prescient note, the goal of Wilson's book was "to picture [with text and images] and preserve its [Savannah's] historic buildings and monuments before they have yielded to the work of time, and gone the way of all—brick and mortar!"[17] The phrase "gone the way of all brick and mortar," an echo of "gone the way of the flesh," conveyed a sense of inevitability that all buildings would crumble and decay.

Eight years later, in 1897, a local newspaper printed a long appreciation of this house, titled "The Habersham Homestead, A Quaint and Picturesque Old Savannah Mansion." This report affirmed that the spirit of historic preservation was stirring in Savannah in the last decade of the nineteenth century, giving as one example "the old Habersham house": "It stands today much the same as it stood in the early days of the nineteenth century, majestic, picturesque and beautiful.... In this busy day and time some people say they have not the time for sober reflection on things that are past.... But, fortunately in the city of Savannah, the number of such people is small."[18]

An early admirer of the Bulloch-Habersham House was Mrs. Thaddeus E. Horton, who also wrote under the names of Corinne Horton and C. R. S. (Corinne Ruth Stocker) Horton. She was a writer, not an architect or a specialist on architecture, and she was a Southerner, a native of South Carolina who for a time had been society editor of the *Atlanta Journal.* With those qualifications, she contributed articles on Southern topics to a variety of magazines. But, she gained particular recognition for her writing on Southern architecture that appeared in *"The Georgian Period," Being Measured Drawings of Colonial Work*, a series of twelve portfolios published in 1898–1902. This venture was one of the first attempts to record the beginnings of American

[17] A. Wilson, 146; C. H. S. [Charles H. Strong], preface to A. Wilson, vi.
[18] "The Habersham Homestead," *SMN*, May 9, 1897.

architecture, capturing in text and images (drawings and photographs) important examples of early buildings, some endangered and some already lost.

Only the last three portfolios of *"The Georgian Period"* considered the South, and most of that work was accomplished by Horton, who provided both text and photographs. Her review of Savannah came in the last volume in 1902, and here she had little to say of the Bulloch-Habersham House other than to observe that it was a remarkable design, quite out of the ordinary. However, the structure was illustrated generously with three photographs, a drawing of the ground plan, and a sketch of that remarkable spiral stairway. In the following year, in *House Beautiful*, Horton described the stairway as "the feature of the house…seen from every chamber of the first floor."[19]

In 1907 the Bulloch-Habersham House was profiled in the pages of *Architectural Record*. For a survey of architecture in the "Far South," the assignment came to Alabama native John Robie Kennedy Jr., an architect in Washington, D.C. Kennedy focused on Savannah, a city that seemed to please him immensely. He declared, "No town or city in the United States can be said to blend more perfectly the old and the new than Savannah.… [T]he people of Savannah as a rule have retained their refinement and taste in architecture as they have in other things, and it is the same taste and refinement that characterized their ancestors." He identified and gave particular notice to the houses designed by Jay, observing, "The four houses in Savannah which attract one most are those built by the English architect Jay." And, for the Bulloch-Habersham House, he had very high praise: "Here Jay, the fashionable architect of the day, seems to have excelled himself; the semi-circular portico and the spiral stairway in the front hall are the most interesting parts of the building." He recorded the ominous presence of a For Sale sign, noting, "For the future one can only hope that its occupant will appreciate its charms and will honor its traditions."[20]

In what may be the last accounting of this grand old house still standing, Lucian Lamar Knight featured the Bulloch-Habersham House in his 1914 survey of Georgia's landmarks. He declared, "One of the stateliest of the lingering land-marks of Savannah is Habersham House.… This quaint old

---

[19] Horton, "Savannah and Parts of the Far South," 93–94, 97, pl. 9; Horton, "Classic Houses of the South," 389–90.

[20] J. R. Kennedy Jr., "Georgian and Greek Revival Work in the Far South," 215, 220.

monument of the ante-bellum South possesses a charm of interest both for the relic hunter and for the lover of art.... [It] is a lordly mansion, suggesting the opulent days of the old regime."[21]

THE IGNOMINIOUS DEMISE OF THE BULLOCH-HABERSHAM HOUSE

In 1915, in a somewhat bewildering act of civic munificence, the city council of Savannah purchased the property on Orleans Square with the announced intention of clearing the lot to raise a city auditorium. The imminent demise of the Bulloch-Habersham House received notice from near and far.

First came this report in December 1915 in a local newspaper: "The Colonial beauties of the old Habersham home on Barnard street will, soon after Dec. 10, vanish under the hands of contractors, to make way for the city auditorium, which will rise in its place."[22] The article was tinged with regret, but real fury erupted in the same newspaper ten days later with the visit of a prominent critic of American art. Sadakichi Hartmann, born in Japan of a German father and Japanese mother, was raised in affluent circumstances in Hamburg, Germany. By 1882, as a very young man, he had landed in America and attached himself to the arts, particularly to the avant garde styles of Symbolism and Impressionism, offering his opinions in essays and lectures. By the time Hartmann arrived in Savannah in 1915, he was at the peak of his influence. He came with a very large voice, and he said,

> Is the South dead aristocratically? ... Have you not men here who are public spirited enough to realize what a great asset Savannah is losing [in] the destruction of the buildings that were erected in a bygone period? The Habersham house is wonderful. It is over one hundred years old [it was ninety-six years old], and yet it is artistically as beautiful to-day as it was the day it was erected.[23]

The destruction of the Bulloch-Habersham House on Orleans Square was not a quick or easy event. First came expressions of surprise, then murmurs of regret. From December 16, 1915, and on for several weeks, bits and pieces of the old house were offered at auction, including the "mahogany front

[21] Knight, 1:392–94.

[22] "Habersham House to be Razed Soon," *SMN*, Dec. 5, 1915.

[23] "Says Savannah is Losing Big Asset," *SMN*, Dec. 15, 1915.

door, storm doors and four handsome chandeliers," and the iron fence surrounding the property. Among the beautiful old carved mantelpieces, one was reported to be sold to Mrs. Douglas Robinson, sister of former President Theodore Roosevelt, because it was assumed that the mantels had been installed by "a direct ancestor of the Roosevelt family"[24]—the president's mother was a Bulloch. On January 27, 1916, the mayor was petitioned to open the old house "for the benefit of those who would like to see its historical interior." The request was granted, and four days were scheduled for a public viewing, rather like a wake. A final auction of fixtures occurred on February 9 with most items "sold for trifling figures." At last, on September 16, 1916, came the announcement, "On Monday the wrecking crew will start to raze the Habersham house."[25]

In 1917 the report of the demise of the Bulloch-Habersham House reached a concerned national audience. Fiske Kimball issued the following report to the Archaeological Institute of America:

> In the preservation of monuments of historic and artistic importance, the destruction or modification of which has been threatened during the year, the Committee [on Colonial and National Art in North America] has been able to intervene with some effect.... [Concerning] activity in behalf of the beautiful Bulloch house in Savannah...[the] house was demolished by the municipality and its delicate Greek capitals were thrown into the stone crusher in spite of efforts to save it.[26]

Also in 1917, Julian Leonard Street published a book of his travels in the South. A chapter titled "Beautiful Savannah" conveyed his love of the city and its inventory of fine old houses. But now Street had cause to lament the loss of one of them. He said,

---

[24] "At Auction; Contents of 'The Habersham Home,'" *SMN*, Dec. 12, 1915; "Sell Historic Fence," *Savannah Evening Press*, Dec. 17, 1915; "Habersham Mantel Sold," *SMN*, Dec. 30, 1915.

[25] "Opening the Habersham House," *Savannah Evening Press*, Jan. 27, 1916; "Habersham Home to be Open Four Days," *SMN*, Jan. 28, 1916; "Sale...Drew Big Crowd," *Savannah Evening Press*, Feb. 9, 1916; "Progress Being Made on City Auditorium," *SMN*, Sept. 16, 1916.

[26] S. F. Kimball, "Report of the Committee on Colonial and National Art in North America," *Bulletin of the Archaeological Institute of America*, Dec. 1917, 64.

> A sad thing was happening in Savannah when we were there. The Habersham house, one of the loveliest old mansions of the city, was being torn down to make room for a municipal auditorium.... The old house itself was built by Archibald Bulloch, a progenitor of that Miss 'Mittie' Bulloch who later became Mrs. Theodore Roosevelt, Sr., mother of the President. It was designed by an English architect named Jay.... To tear down such a house was sacrilege.[27]

Street's distress in this matter was surely provoked by the connection of this old house with President Roosevelt. The author had struck up a great friendship with the president in 1915, after Roosevelt had served his two terms (1901–1909) and retired from the presidency, if not from continuing to meddle in politics. Martha "Mittie" Bulloch Roosevelt, the president's mother and the paternal grandmother of First Lady Eleanor Roosevelt, was the daughter of James Stephens Bulloch, whose father was the brother of Archibald Stobo Bulloch, who had commissioned Jay to design this house.

In 1919 Savannah was profiled for *Harper's Magazine* by William Dean Howells, editor of the *Atlantic Monthly* who came to be known as the dean of American letters. For this project, he came in the company of his son John Mead Howells, a trained architect who provided line drawings as illustrations. Of the "many lovely old mansions in the heart of the city," the elder Howells had this to say: "These very characteristic and memorable mansions can still be counted by scores, but every now and then one of these disappears through natural causes, as well as through that effect of bad taste which asserts itself everywhere, or from some real or imaginary public demand. Only last year one [the Bulloch-Habersham House] was pulled down to free a site for an Auditorium."[28]

A dozen years later, John Mead Howells compiled a book of photographs of early American buildings that had been distinguished by fine design and were now lost or very much changed. He included three Savannah buildings by Jay: the Savannah Branch of the Bank of the United States, the Scarbrough House, and the Bulloch-Habersham House. In an introduction to Howells's volume, Kimball praised this effort "to realize the depth of our artistic and historic loss through the destruction of old buildings by war, by fire, by revolutions of taste, and by the ruthless march of urban 'improvement.'" In

[27] Street, 558–61.

[28] W. D. Howells, "Savannah Twice Visited," 323–24.

these pages, sounding a clarion call for the preservation movement, the Bulloch-Habersham House had a very particular place of honor. It was shown twice. A full view of the exterior was included in the photo essay, and a detail of the portico served as the frontispiece to Howells's book.[29]

THE AWFUL END

This remark by Caroline Couper Stiles Lovell, in the account of her childhood in Savannah in the 1860s and 1870s, is a neat summary of the regret felt by many: "The Habersham house is no more. Being one of the handsomest and most unique houses in the city, the Savannahians never rested until it was torn down and a modern auditorium erected in its place."[30] But, nothing conveys the sense of loss of this remarkable structure quite like this report of a sale in February 1916: "Before a large crowd the fixtures of the old Habersham home, one of Savannah's oldest and most beautiful landmarks, were sold this morning... [T]he iron fence...[sold for] $100. The two sets of gates...[sold for] $50 each.... The ten ornamental posts [columns]...[sold for] $1.50 each. The beautiful French cut glass chandelier in the hall...sold for $25."[31]

At this site rose a new municipal auditorium. A fine building for the moment, it was designed by Henrik Wallin, a Swede who had trained in France and Italy, settling in Savannah where he built a number of public and private buildings. Then, in 1971, the municipal auditorium met its demise, to be replaced by a new civic center, an unremarkable edifice in an ersatz Roman style, a reminder to many of what the city had lost in 1916.

---

[29] Kimball, intro. to J. M. Howells, n.p.; J. M. Howells, frontispiece, pl. 54..
[30] Lovell, 32.
[31] "Sale...Drew Big Crowd," *Savannah Evening Press*, Feb. 9, 1916.

CHAPTER 16

OTHER SAVANNAH HOUSES

In Savannah, Jay is most often remembered for the four remarkable houses whose stories have been told. There is evidence that he designed other residences, and, by the mid-twentieth century, as his work came to be better understood and more generously appreciated, an eagerness grew to find more Jay houses in Savannah. Consequently, a number of structures, surviving and lost, have been attributed to him. Many of these claims can be easily dismissed, because dates of construction do not correspond to Jay's time in Savannah or because elements of style are unlike his known work. But there are a few attributions to Jay that are sustained by documents, stylistic features, or persuasive legend.

THE WAYNE-GORDON HOUSE: "QUITE IN THE JAY TRADITION"

This is a very important house in Savannah. It was built for a native of the city who became a member of the U.S. Supreme Court and served that institution for the extraordinary term of thirty-two years. This house was later occupied by a local lawyer and entrepreneur who saw to the construction of what would be for a time the longest railway in the country. But, neither of these accomplished fellows are of any particular interest to the thousands of girls and young women who come to Savannah each year to see this house in which Juliette Gordon Low, founder of the Girl Scouts of the United States of America, was born.

Because this fine house has such significance for local, regional, and national histories, who designed this structure is a matter of considerable interest. The architect is unknown. There is a persistent claim that this is a Jay house, but no documents have been found to support that assertion. However, there are several reasons to imagine that Jay might have had a hand in this project.

JAMES MOORE WAYNE: A LIKELY PATRON

The house was built for James Moore Wayne, a young lawyer who had been elected mayor of Savannah in September 1817 at the age of twenty-seven. Jay arrived in December of that year. Very soon the young and ambitious Wayne would have become familiar with the work of the young and ambitious Jay. As Jay set about to design remarkable houses for some of Savannah's most notable citizens, evidence of his labor was often before the mayor and city council. First, there was the long quarrel about the encroachment on public property of the Richardson House, and on several occasions Jay was fined for leaving construction debris in the streets. Wayne was, along with other city officials, a subscriber to Jay's theater, which opened in December 1818. And, in early 1819, Jay was before city council with his plan for a temporary pavilion to house a dinner and ball to honor President James Monroe in May of that year. Wayne, as mayor, greeted the president, served as his host on tours of the city, and escorted him to his official residence in Jay's Scarbrough House and to festivities at Jay's pavilion.

At the very moment when Jay was busy with several projects in the city, Wayne was preparing to build a proper home for his young family. In 1813 he had married Mary Johnson Campbell, the stepdaughter of the Reverend Henry Kollock, the minister of the Independent Presbyterian Church. Following their marriage, the Waynes lived with the Kollocks, and in quick succession came three children. Planning for his own house in 1817, Wayne secured the property at the northeast corner of Bull Street and South Broad Street (later Oglethorpe Avenue). The site was surveyed and the foundation laid for a residence in mid-1819.[1]

In 1943 Wayne's biographer, Alexander A. Lawrence, guessed—and it could be only a guess—that Jay was Wayne's architect. Lawrence said, "Handsome new residences were going up around the city.... Among the houses designed by William Jay, the talented young English architect, was that of the Waynes." Lawrence asserted that the Wayne House was "a monument to Jay's artistry," noting that a "competent critic" had found this structure to be "one of his [Jay's] 'interesting and effective' designs though 'more modest' than the others." The "critic" here was Walter Charlton Hartridge Jr., the Savannah

---

[1] "Wayne-Gordon House, Savannah, Georgia," 1937, HABS.

historian who would do so much to rescue the Scarbrough House.[2]

A "modest" design by Jay would seem to be an oxymoron. But, in 1818 Wayne's financial resources were somewhat lean although his prospects were promising. His father, Richard C. Wayne, had settled in Savannah in 1788, having been asked not so politely to leave Charleston because of his support for the royal cause during the Revolutionary War. In Georgia he acquired land, business interests, political opportunities, and thirteen children—James was twelfth in birth order.

James Moore Wayne entered the College of New Jersey (later Princeton) at the age of fourteen and was graduated in 1808. Sadly, that year brought the death of his father and an inheritance burdened by debt. Needing to assure his own future, he took up the study of law. In late 1811, Wayne opened a law practice in Savannah that garnered success if not great wealth. As Lawrence observed, "No fortunes were accumulated at the Bar [in Savannah in those years] but the profession earned fair returns for the diligent and opened the door to public office."[3] Wayne was elected to the Georgia House of Representatives in 1815–1816. In 1817 he became mayor of Savannah, but he served for only two terms, resigning in summer 1819 to return to the practice of law.

Although Wayne's potential for earning was increasing, in 1817 he was not awash in funds. He was prepared to build a house, but he may not have been prepared to turn the project over to the likes of Jay, who accomplished his best work when money was abundant. According to family accounts, the wood and plaster ornament for the interior was selected by Wayne's wife, possibly as a cost-saving measure. Work on this residence continued long after Jay left the country in 1822. In 1826 Wayne advertised the house for rent, and the property was sold in 1831, perhaps still unfinished.[4]

Many efforts have been made to link Jay to this place. In 1937 a report of the Historic American Buildings Survey noted that the building was "Attributed to William Jay." In 1952 the house was featured on a tour of fine Savannah homes, and a newspaper article declared, "[The house] is said to have been built from designs of William Jay.... The carved door and window

[2] Lawrence, 23–24, 24 n. 6.

[3] Ibid., 16.

[4] "Wayne Gordon House" at www.juliettegordonlowbirthplace.org; "Gordon House Has Place in History," *Savannah Evening Press*, Mar. 12, 1952.

trim, the very heavy baseboard, and rounded ends to some of the rooms are all favorite patterns of the architect Jay."[5]

In 1950 James V. McDonough concluded that the Wayne House could be credited to Jay based on its resemblance to the Telfair House, suggesting that certain "discrepancies" in style occurred because the structure had not been completed until long after Jay had returned to England. But, in 1957 Frederick D. Nichols found this attribution troublesome. He conceded that there were resemblances to the Telfair House. It was almost identical in plan, having a center hall with rooms disposed at each side, each terminating in curved walls. But he observed that the Wayne House lacked the ingenuity of the Telfair's octagonal library and the original monumental stair placed forward in the center hall. In Nichols's view, the plan of the Wayne House was too conventional, lacking evidence of Jay's inventiveness and sophistication. He concluded, "It seems certain that Jay left drawings of this house which were executed by a builder unwilling to embark on the daring forms of the architect."[6]

Like other Jay houses, this is a Regency villa, a box of two stories over a raised basement. (The third story was added in 1886, designed by Detlef Lienau, the New York architect who was just then directing the conversion of the Telfair House for its new role as an art museum.) The structure is brick, clad with stucco and scored to resemble dressed stone masonry. The symmetrical facade has a central raised colonnaded portico. The interior arrangement is a central hall plan, and the end rooms at each side of the hall terminate in curves.

One possibility is that Jay, seeking to enhance his opportunities in the city, obliged the mayor by providing him with a basic plan for this house. Beyond the bones of this building, there is little compelling evidence of Jay's hand. On the main floor, the stairway is pressed ignominiously to the rear of the central hall. The rooms at each side of the stairs do terminate in curves, but other spaces are conventional. Carved wood and plaster ornaments include some elements that remind us of Jay. There are corner blocks at the top of doors and windows with classical faces similar to elements used at the Bulloch House, and there is an anthemion cornice in the drawing room. But,

---

[5] "Wayne-Gordon House, Savannah, Georgia," 1937, HABS; "Gordon House Has Place in History," *Savannah Evening Press*, Mar, 12, 1952.

[6] McDonough, 69–71; Nichols, 41.

these details lack the sculptural quality of Jay's work.

In 1819, just as work on this building was commencing, Wayne began a new law practice, and he was appointed judge for a newly formed Court of Common Pleas. However, tragedy struck the family when the Reverend Kollock died in late December of that year at the age of forty-one, probably of heart failure. Likely the Waynes continued to live with Kollock's widow until their house was ready for occupancy. Then, just a few years later, politics called Wayne away from Savannah, first to the Superior Court of Georgia and in 1829–1834 to the U.S. House of Representatives. Then, in January 1835, his life changed in many ways when he was nominated by President Andrew Jackson to the U.S. Supreme Court.

THE GORDONS

In 1831 Wayne sold this house to William Washington Gordon, and it would soon come to be known as the "Gordon House." However, this was not really the passing of property from one family to another. The Waynes and the Gordons were bound together by both familial and professional ties.[7]

William Washington Gordon was born on a family plantation seventy miles southwest of Savannah. A graduate of West Point, he resigned his military commission to read for the law in Savannah as an apprentice to Wayne. Here he met Wayne's niece, Sarah Anderson Stites, whom he married in 1826. By 1830 the first of seven children was born (three would die in infancy), and it was time to settle into a family home.

Admitted to the bar in 1820, Gordon served as mayor in 1834–1836. Soon he was named president of the Central Railroad and Banking Company of Georgia (later the Central of Georgia Railroad) to direct the construction of a railroad from Savannah to the interior of the state. Planned as the longest railroad in the world when it was conceived, the project was complicated by the enormous costs of construction, negotiations for rights-of-way, disputes with labor, and mortality in the hot and humid seasons of disease. It was an effort to which Gordon quite literally gave his life in 1842 at the age of forty-six in the year before the work was completed. His accomplishment saved the economy of Georgia, but at his death his family left Savannah in despair. The house on South Broad Street was closed. His widow took the children to New

[7] Nicoll, 38, 44–46.

Jersey to be educated in Northern schools as their father had wished. She did not return until the early 1850s, and then she was confronted with a house in rather desperate need of repair and refurbishment.

The restoration of the Gordon House was taken up by William Washington Gordon II. This son "Willie," a graduate of Yale University, returned to Savannah for work as a cotton factor and commission merchant. In 1857 he married Eleanor "Nelly" Lytle Kinzie, a Chicago native and granddaughter of John Kinzie, a colorful frontiersman declared by some to be the founder of Chicago. In the house on South Broad Street, Willie and Nelly raised six children, two sons and four daughters. The second child, born in this house on Halloween night in 1860, was Juliette "Daisy" Magill Kinzie Gordon, who would come to be the first Girl Scout.

In 1886 Willie engaged Lienau to design the additions of a third floor and a piazza or porch at the east end of the structure, and Nelly directed a redecoration of the interior in the fashion of the times. Most of the work was completed by December of that year to accommodate events surrounding Daisy's marriage to William Mackay Low, the charming but indolent son of Andrew Low, a Scot who had made a great success in Savannah as a cotton factor. Daisy's wealthy but worthless and philandering husband had the grace to expire in 1905, freeing her to found the Girl Scouts of the U.S.A. in 1912.

"THE BIRTHPLACE"

The Gordon House remained in family hands through another generation, but by 1950 the structure was thirteen decades old. Difficult and expensive to maintain, it faced the prospect of demolition. Just at a moment when parts of old Savannah were being abandoned, this house was rescued by the Girl Scouts of the U.S.A. (GSUSA). Purchased in 1953, the plan was to restore the structure as "The Birthplace," a memorial to Juliette Gordon Low, who had founded the organization.

A central figure in this initiative was Anne Hyde Choate, Juliette's goddaughter and a child upon whom Juliette, with no children of her own, lavished attention. Anne's mother had shared with Daisy the experience of "the Charbs," a boarding school in New York City run by the Mesdemoiselles Charbonnier of Paris, a sturdy institution with instruction in French and a dress code that mandated "a simple and tasteful costume" in black for all of the days of the week.[8]

By 1915 Anne had been recruited by her godmother for involvement in the GSUSA. In 1920–1922 she served as the second president of the organization when Juliette retired to take her place as "Founder." Long after Juliette died of breast cancer in 1927, Anne continued to serve on the national board, frequently leading various initiatives of the organization. But the one campaign most dear to her was the drive to purchase and restore "The Birthplace" in Savannah to honor her beloved godmother.

The GSUSA purchased the building from the Gordon family in 1953. After the first of several restorations, it was opened to the public in 1956 as a house museum to tell the story of Juliette Gordon Low.[9] The residence has been restored to portray the character of the home in the 1880s after the extensive renovations prompted by Juliette's parents. But, at its core, this is a Regency structure. There are hints here of Jay's hand, even though the truth of his involvement with this house may never be known.

THE ROBERT HABERSHAM HOUSE ON ORLEANS SQUARE

There are at least two good reasons for believing that Jay designed a home for Robert Habersham on the northeast corner of Barnard and Hull Streets. One is a drawing signed "William Jay, Architect" and labeled as the "South Elevation [of a house for] Robt. Habersham, Esqr., Savannah, Windows or Doors Down to the Floor." The second is this report in the minutes of city council for May 31, 1819: "Wm. Jay, for obstructing the street at Habersham's house, Fined thirty dollars and costs."[10]

The patron was the same Robert Habersham who in 1834 purchased and occupied the home designed by Jay for Archibald Stobo Bulloch. Habersham's history and his relationship with the Bulloch House have already been described. Before he came to occupy that residence, just across Orleans Square was a dwelling designed for him by Jay, probably in 1819. This house

---

[8] "Female Schools and Colleges," *National Quarterly Review,* Sept. 1873, 360.

[9] This was the second house museum to be established in Savannah. The Owens-Thomas House, a property of the Telfair Academy, opened to the public in 1954.

[10] "William Jay, Architect [signed]," "No. 5. South Elevation [of a house for] Robt. Habersham, Esqr., Savannah, Windows or Doors Down to the Floor," pen, ink drawing, n.d. [paper watermark: J BUDGEN 1814], VJD; Savannah City Council Minutes, "Docket of Information," May 31, 1819, SMA.

is long lost, but the drawing, old maps, and some grainy photographs suggest what the structure must have looked like. At the northeast corner of Barnard Street (running north-south) and Hull Street (east-west), the house faced west on Barnard with its south flank on Hull.[11] The south veranda overlooked Orleans Square, a clever design since it offered the occupants of this house a view of the pleasant square at the center of Jackson Ward.

This house was sited on one tything lot, although Habersham also owned the adjacent lot on Hull Street. The house was compact, nearly a square, two stories above a raised basement, with two semi-circular projections at the rear. (A third story was added at some later date.) At the entry on Barnard Street, a one-story unpedimented portico with columns stood between two tall round-headed windows set in arched reveals. On the south flank facing the square was a long masonry veranda, the flat roof of which was supported by piers, rather than the doubled columns proposed by Jay in his drawing.

Tax records for the property show that the lot had been "improved" by 1820, suggesting that the house was completed by that date. This appears to have been Habersham's residence until he purchased the Bulloch House in 1834. The structure designed for Bulloch had come to be recognized as a place "so elegant and princely, it might almost be called a palace," and it was very commodiously sited on a trustee block on the west side of Orleans Square.[12] The opulence of the Bulloch House must have pleased Habersham and persuaded him to move from the nearby residence that had been constructed for him.

Period maps show that the house at Barnard and Hull survived through the late 1880s. In 1890 the property was sold, and by 1898 these two lots were populated by joined town homes.[13] By 1916 much of Orleans Square had fallen victim to the incursions of a municipal auditorium and a burgeoning commercial district. In the end, both the first Robert Habersham House and the Bulloch-Habersham House were lost to "progress."

---

[11] The house occupied Lot 15, although records show that Habersham also owned the adjacent Lot 14, located at the rear of the house on Hull Street (Jackson Ward, "Sale of Lots 14 and 15 by I. and D. Minis to R. Habersham," 1818, Savannah Ward Books, CCRO).

[12] B. Lock, "Tax Records for Robert Habersham," 1983, VJD; Burke, 32.

[13] B. Lock, "Tax Records for Robert Habersham," 1983, VJD.

THE HAZEN KIMBALL HOUSE ON ORLEANS SQUARE

There is some evidence that in June 1819 Jay was busy with the construction of a home for Hazen Kimball on a site just across Barnard Street from the Robert Habersham House on Orleans Square. Minutes of city council for June 14, 1819, reported, "William Jay, for obstructing Street & not keep[in]g sufficient lights at Mr. H. Kimballs Lot, Fined thirty dollars & Costs."[14] Kimball was born in New Hampshire and made his way as a young man to Savannah where he achieved great success as a shipper and merchant, becoming prominent in civic and cultural affairs. A city alderman, an officer in the Chamber of Commerce with William Scarbrough, a member of the Independent Presbyterian Church with Richard Richardson, and with Alexander Telfair a subscriber to the Savannah Theater, Kimball must have been just the sort of fellow to be drawn to the work of Jay.[15]

Two adjoining tything lots located on Orleans Square in the northwest quadrant of Jackson Ward were purchased by Kimball in August 1817.[16] By that date, construction had begun on the Richardson House, and Jay would arrive from England in December. There is the possibility that Kimball acquired these lots expecting to engage the young architect. From May 1818 through April 1819, at least eight shipments came to Kimball from various ports in the Northeast of large quantities of building materials. These included bricks, pine boards, and casks of lime (for stucco), destined it would seem for a significant construction project.[17]

According to the city council minutes, Jay was at work at this site in mid-June 1819. A month later Kimball was dead, remembered in this notice posted in a local newspaper:

> DIED—In this city, on Friday, 16th inst. [July 16, 1819], Mr. Hazen Kimball, aged 52 years. He was a native of Concord, New-Hampshire, and for many years past a respectable inhabitant of this place. In the death of this gentleman, our city has lost one of its brightest ornaments, the mercantile

---

[14] Savannah City Council Minutes, "Docket of Information," June 14, 1819, SMA.

[15] Harden, *A History of Savannah and South Georgia*, 1:294, 386.

[16] B. Lock, "Jay at the Hazen Kimball Lot," 1983, VJD.

[17] Shipments to H. Kimball, May 1818–Apr. 1819, U.S. Custom Service, Inward Coastwise Manifests, Savannah, GA (1819), National Archives, Washington, D.C.

community, one of its most respectable and efficient members, and society in general, a firm and undeviating partizan [*sic*] in the cause of integrity and virtue. Active and enterprising in the pursuits of commerce, he soon realized an extensive fortune, without ever stooping to meanness, or practising any of those arts, which have sometimes sullied the character of those who were ambitious for wealth.[18]

In May 1822 the property was sold by the administrators of Kimball's estate as unimproved lots, suggesting that the work had been abandoned.[19] In his brief time in the United States, Jay suffered a number of disappointments. This was surely one of those events. By all accounts, Kimball would have been a worthy steward of a house by Jay.

REID SERVANTS'S QUARTERS AND CARRIAGE HOUSE

Perhaps the most unusual structure to be linked with Jay is this one. This was a service building located at 118 East State Street at the rear of the property, planned to house slaves and the family carriage behind a grand residence. The lot had been purchased in 1829 by John Hope Reid, a Scot who had settled in Savannah, married well, and prospered as a cotton merchant and shipper.[20]

In 1936 the Historic American Buildings Survey reported that Reid "anticipated erecting a mansion in the Adams [Adam] style and materials but because of the loss of a year's rice crop, changed his plans and built instead a small simple double frame house on the front of the lot." All that remained of the proposal to construct an elegant residence was the service building at the back of the lot. This structure survived, but it was described as "dilapidated" in 1936.[21] It was demolished after 1940.

Preserved in various images, this building is sometimes identified as possibly by Jay. It was a remarkable design for such an unimportant structure, and stylistically it does evoke Jay's Doric at the Scarbrough House. But, there are

---

[18] [Death of Hazen Kimball], *Columbian Museum and Savannah Daily Gazette*, July 20, 1819.

[19] B. Lock, "Jay at the Hazen Kimball Lot," 1983, VJD.

[20] "Reid Servants and Carriage House, Savannah, Georgia," 1936, HABS; Candler and Evans, 3:173.

[21] "Reid Servants and Carriage House, Savannah, Georgia," 1936, HABS.

several arguments against attaching Jay to this place. If the property was acquired by Reid in 1829, this construction took place well after Jay had left Savannah. In the matter of style, the forms were heavy. Piers took the place of columns, and a number of the arches were segmental rather than fully round, pressing weight against their supports rather than springing from them. Even the materials were dark and rustic, composed as they were of "brick faced with cut and dressed red sand stone."[22] In sum, there was little evidence here of Jay's sophistication and grace.

A guidebook of 1940 reported, "The carriage house is often used as a subject by local and visiting artists." The charm of this site is conveyed by an early postcard, probably from the late nineteenth century. This rare postcard is titled "Colonial Quarters of Old Reid Mansion, State St. Built 1775, Savannah Ga." The image has about it the aspect of a period painting, romantic figures in dappled light posed in the yard of a structure worn by time and nearly swallowed up by leafy trees and shrubs.[23]

Local legend holds that Jay designed this building, a conclusion buoyed by what Thomas Gamble called in 1932 the "Romance of Wm. Jay, Savannah Architect."[24] Jay had come to be known as a gifted architect of somewhat mysterious origins who had designed several extraordinary buildings in Savannah. Any picturesque structure in the city was a candidate for attribution to Jay, and, in the early years of the twentieth century, there was no more captivating site in the city than the Reid servants's quarters and carriage house. As a consequence, legend, which is often a very reliable source in Savannah, has maintained that this was a building by Jay, if not by his hand then certainly made in the spirit of his work.

---

[22] Ibid.

[23] Georgia Writers' Project of the W.P.A., 255; "Colonial Quarters of Old Reid Mansion, State St. Built 1775, Savannah Ga," postcard, c. 1905, VJD.

[24] Gamble, "Romance of Wm. Jay, Savannah Architect," May 8, 1932.

CHAPTER 17

SAVANNAH THEATER

Savannah had been hungry for a theater for decades before Jay arrived in late 1817. The town had relished performances from its early days and never gave way to puritanical impulses to ban them. The first record of this activity has been dated to September 1781, but this was certainly not the first event. By 1774 the Filature, a building constructed for the ultimately unsuccessful enterprise of manufacturing silk, was designated as a place for public performances of all sorts. By 1781 a small theater had been constructed on Broughton Street, then as now the central commercial district.[1]

An affection for the stage flourished in spite of a devastating fire in 1796 that slowed plans to build a new theater. And there were remonstrations by the usual foes of the dramatic arts, those evangelical preachers who believed that theatricals were the work of the devil. Prominent among the avenging clergy was Henry Holcombe, a Baptist minister who arrived in the city in 1797 and led campaigns against "his Satanic majesty's forces, called 'Stage-players.'"[2] However, the Reverend Holcombe did not prevail. In Savannah performances continued through lean economic times and perilous times of war.

Jay arrived in December 1817, and in less than one year he designed and saw to the construction of a very grand theater. How this could happen in such a short period of time has always been something of a mystery. It now seems likely that Jay came to Georgia with plans for such a building in his portfolio having entered but not won a competition for a London theater. And, what is now quite clear is that the groundwork for the Savannah project—the acquisition of a site and a plan for funding—had already been accomplished before Jay came on the scene.

In 1918, Thomas Gamble told the story of the planning for the theater:

---

[1] Patrick, 1–2.

[2] Ibid., 23, 51.

> In 1810 there was an abortive effort to provide the city with a new theater. "Friends of the Drama" [a group of seven citizens]...sought to secure subscriptions to stock at $100 a share. A few thousand dollars was raised and then the project was abandoned.... The close of the war of 1815 [the War of 1812] and the resumption of commerce with profitable customers abroad lifted Savannah speedily to an exceptional level of prosperity.... So it was that when the movement for a theater in keeping with the new dignity of Savannah was broached in 1816 it met with a more ready response than some years prior.

In 1816 shares to support the project were quickly subscribed by government officials and prominent citizens, and trust lots facing Bull Street on Chippewa Square were granted by the city.[3]

While there is no good evidence of when and how the project was awarded to Jay, there is ample evidence that it was. Work began on April 23, 1818, and opening night occurred on December 4. Soon after the opening, Jay was announced in the press as "the architect, Mr. JAY, who has displayed great taste in the out-fit [of the new theater]," an immodest proclamation since Jay was likely the author of this article.[4]

PEREGRINUS

It appears that most of what we know about the original design of Jay's Savannah Theater was first reported by Jay. A description of this building survives in great detail in a long newspaper article of December 9, 1818. The author is named "Peregrinus," Latin for "foreigner."[5] There are quarrels about whether or not this piece was written by Jay, but the case for Jay as its author is strong. This is a long account, replete with details that would have been best understood by the architect. Further, there are certain comments about contemporary architecture that reveal Jay's experiences and convictions. Finally, the name "Peregrinus" described Jay's status in Savannah. Here he was a foreigner, an outsider.

This article appeared five days after the opening of the new theater on

---

[3] Gamble, "Savannah Theater, One of the First in America," Nov. 17, 1918.

[4] "Dismantling the Theater," *SMN*, June 3, 1895; W. Jay, arch., attrib., Peregrinus, Dec. 9, 1818.

[5] The Latin term *peregrinus*, literally "from abroad," designated a subject of Rome from any of the provinces of the empire who was not a Roman citizen.

December 4. Peregrinus prefaced his review with these words: "The Savannah Theatre belongs to the Grecian order of architecture, and though not so capacious [spacious] as some houses of the same description in the northern cities—yet it may vie with and even excel most of them in taste and elegance."[6] Here was Jay's announcement that this was a building in the modern Grecian style, reflecting Savannah's growing prominence in national affairs.

How did Jay come to design a theater? From the evidence of this project, it is clear that he was familiar with the art of performance on a stage, and he may have known it from his childhood. Cyrus Jay recalled that his father "had never, during the whole course of a long life, been in a theatre"—evangelicals regarded such places as unsavory. But Cyrus remembered that his father's library contained "the works of several of the great dramatists, with which he was well acquainted" and that among his friends and admirers was a very large number of celebrated actors.[7]

In London, Jay must have experienced theaters, because the architectural form came to interest him. Good evidence of that survives in his plan for the Albion Chapel, which would come to be cited by a well-known critic for its theatrical aspect. Later in America he allowed to be published the claim that he had "built" the New English Opera House in London in 1815–1816.[8] A likely truth is that Jay, just beginning his professional life, submitted a design for this theater in 1815 in collaboration with two very close friends. His friends prevailed in this competition, but he did not. It is probable that Jay knew before he left for Savannah that plans to build a theater in that city were well advanced. When he arrived in December 1817, he carried with him a portfolio, the usual baggage of artists whose most valuable possessions are drawings of proposed or accomplished work. Jay's portfolio might well have contained an unrealized plan for a London theater.

Jay could have known from his brother-in-law Robert Bolton, then residing in Liverpool, or from Bolton's partner Richard Richardson, for whom Jay had designed a residence, that support for a theater in Savannah was well advanced. All he had to do was to appear on the scene, unfurl his London design, which represented the most modern stylistic and structural solutions

[6] W. Jay, arch., attrib., Peregrinus, Dec. 9, 1818 (hereafter cited in text).

[7] C. Jay, *Recollections*, 175–76.

[8] Elmes, *Metropolitan Improvements*, 170; "Mr. Jay, the celebrated Architect…," Apr. 22, 1822.

for a theater, and make the appropriate changes for a building that would be somewhat smaller in scale. This scenario would explain why this complicated and elegant building was raised in Savannah in the astonishing time of just seven months.

THE EXTERIOR OF THE SAVANNAH THEATER

Peregrinus offered no description of the exterior of the theater. Late-nineteenth-century photographs of the building show that it was a large rather plain block form, with windows at three levels and a pitched roof. In Augusta, Georgia, just a few years later, Jay proposed the following design for a theater facade, offering a hint of what may have existed in Savannah: "It is of the Grecian order—the front will exhibit four Antae pilasters [attached piers], supporting an entablature of the Corinthian order—in the centre will be three doors, leading to the vestibule."[9]

THE ARRANGEMENT OF THE INTERIOR

A guide to the city printed in 1823 offered this concise report: "*The Theatre* is a handsome building...one hundred and eighty feet long, and sixty feet wide. It has a pit, two tiers of boxes and a gallery, and will contain about eight or nine hundred persons."[10] Peregrinus said, "The plan of the interior of the building is semi-circular, following the choice of the ancient Grecian and Roman Theatres in this particular, being not only better adapted to the climate, but also better calculated for seeing and hearing, than the eliptical [*sic*] form used in modern Theatres." In this matter, Jay was somewhat defensive—the winning design for the New English Opera House in London was elliptical.

The seating was arranged in three regions, as revealed by the admission fees: the pit, the boxes, and a gallery. Admission to the pit (the ground level in front of the stage) and to the boxes cost one dollar, and gallery seats were fifty cents.[11] These prices defined two classes of accommodations. Separate entrances were provided to each of these regions, calculated in part as a safety measure to provide a quick exit in the event of fire. But this plan also allowed

[9] "Mr. Jay, the celebrated Architect...," Apr. 22, 1822.
[10] Kayser, 37.
[11] [Theater opening], *Columbian Museum and Savannah Daily Gazette*, Dec. 4, 1818.

for entry without long, quarrelsome lines, and it avoided the mixing of different groups of patrons. One of the unique features of the New English Opera House in London was the separation of the classes of theater-goers in an extreme fashion, both in access and in the regions of seating.

The boxes were arranged in two "tiers" or ranks at the second level. A "dress circle" of nine boxes at the center was flanked on both sides by boxes that stepped down in a lower tier to the sides of the stage. At the third level was the gallery, the top floor at the back of the house, the usual location of the "cheap seats." Peregrinus observed that the boxes and the gallery were supported by cast iron columns, which were "fluted, with gilt capitals and bases, uniting an air of great lightness, with strength." Likely these columns and other elements of construction and decoration were imported. An actor visiting in 1834 was told that the design and materials for the theater had come from England.[12]

The building was fitted with a place for libations in the lobby. According to Peregrinus, "[T]here are a large lobby and rooms for refreshment in the front of the building." When Jay submitted his proposal for a new theater in Augusta in 1822, he predicted that the revenue of the saloon would be as large as the receipts of the theater. Conventionally, theaters were leased to managers for a set amount, usually for a term of several years, and profits for the managers were derived from successful programs and full houses. Owners of the theaters gained additional revenue from the attached saloons.

THE ORNAMENT OF THE INTERIOR

The interior decoration of the Savannah Theater was brilliant in colors, sumptuous in textures, and elaborate in iconography, all of it described with enthusiasm by Peregrinus. The colors reflected the Regency's affection for the play of brilliant contrasts: "The stage doors and boxes [are] panelled [*sic*], and with golden mouldings—the arch is decorated with green and gold, on a white ground—the seats in the boxes are covered with crimson cloth—those in the pit are green—and an orange velvet cushion is carried round the circles." The whole effect must have been spectacular. The pit was a field of green. The iron columns, painted white, had gold capitals and bases. The boxes,

---

[12] Power, 2:118.

rimmed in orange, had crimson seats and white ceilings. Crimson, green, orange, and gold—powerful colors.

Ornaments "generally symbolical of the amusements of the place" included, at the lower boxes, "Golden Eagles [emblems of Jupiter], with wreaths of green foliage, relieved on a white ground." At the dress circle, the boxes were separated by panels bearing the motifs of lyres and wreaths, both attributes of Apollo as the patron of the arts. But surely the most remarkable decorations were paintings of classical subjects by William Etty for the nine boxes of the dress circle.

Etty was Jay's dear friend, and the story of their relationship has been told. It is tempting to conclude that the paintings Etty sent to Savannah for the dress circle of Jay's theater were simply copies of the compositions he had prepared for the London project in 1815, but clearly they were not. The New English Opera House had been established to promote native talent in music. That theater, in its plan (the outline of a lyre) and in its cycle of decoration, was dedicated to music. Etty's paintings for that venue were described as "classical subjects, illustrating the history of music."[13] Those images must have featured Apollo, among whose several responsibilities were music and song. He would carry the lyre as his symbol and be attended by the Muses, the very origin of the word "music."

Peregrinus described in some detail the nine paintings by Etty in Savannah. They were "basso relievos," paintings in imitation of low relief sculpture rendered in monochrome gray or brown, by "Mr. Etty of London." In subject matter, these works did not represent any particular narrative. A few alluded to the origin of the theater in ancient Greece, but most were simply popular classical and literary subjects that would have been familiar to many members of the audience, such as the adventures of Bacchus (Dionysus) and the misadventures of Venus and Cupid.

Only one of the Savannah compositions relates specifically to an early painting by Etty shown at the Royal Academy. Exhibited in 1821, *Cleopatra's Arrival in Cilcia* made a great sensation, gaining for the artist the attention that had eluded him.[14] Based on descriptions of Cleopatra's voyage to meet Marc Antony as told in Plutarch's *Lives* and later by Shakespeare in *Anthony*

[13] "New English Opera-House," *New Monthly Magazine and Universal Register*, July 1, 1816, 542.

[14] Graves, 3:65.

and Cleopatra, this work displayed Etty's mastery of the nude form with a great profusion of writhing, fleshy figures.

Etty's paintings for Jay's theater remained in place for many years. In 1918 Gamble wrote that they were removed from the building just before the Civil War.[15] These panels have disappeared, although it is sometimes whispered that they must be tucked away in some Savannah attic.

THE STAGE

As most theaters of the time, the Savannah Theater had a proscenium stage framed by an arch. Here the arch was elliptical rather than half round, to reduce the height of the opening. And, as in ancient examples, the stage was flanked by a door at each side, giving additional access to the front of the stage. This configuration is confirmed in a letter written by an actor visiting Savannah in 1878: "The theater is the oddest old building you ever saw.... The proscenium is very old & odd too and has an opening each side for the stars to answer calls without disturbing the curtain."[16]

Originally the stage was raked, or sloped upwards.[17] This arrangement had been conventional for the English stage since the Middle Ages; the purpose was to tilt the stage to afford the audience a better view. But, actors had to walk on a slope, which caused unnatural postures and gaits; and interactions between actors who were "upstage" or "downstage" could become contentious. By the late nineteenth century, it was usual to build a flat stage and rake or terrace the auditorium seating.

Special care had been taken in the matter of acoustics. Peregrinus said, "[F]or the sake of sound, the partitions and ceiling are all hollow." Some of the very large houses in London were criticized because the acoustics were so poor that actors had to strain their voices to be heard. The New English Opera House had as a particular innovation a "light" ceiling, conceived to give vibrancy to sound.[18] Clearly, this was a refinement of the modern theater with which Jay was familiar.

---

[15] Gamble, "Savannah Theater, One of the First in America," Nov. 17, 1918.

[16] Overstreet, 10.

[17] "Dismantling the Theater," *SMN*, June 3, 1895.

[18] "New English Opera-House," *New Monthly Magazine and Universal Register*, July 1, 1816, 542.

Above, portrait painted by William Etty in 1817;
below, signature from Savannah shipping records in 1818.

"Stewing Alive" in the heated bath,
drawn and engraved by Robert Cruikshank, 1825.

"A Regency Affair,"
drawn and engraved by Robert Cruikshank, 1825.

Facade.

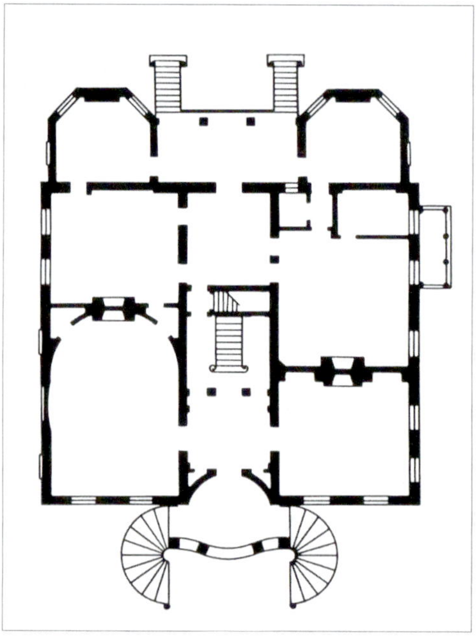

Plan of the main floor.

Entry hall.

Dining room.

The "Lafayette Balcony" on the south flank of the house.

Facade.

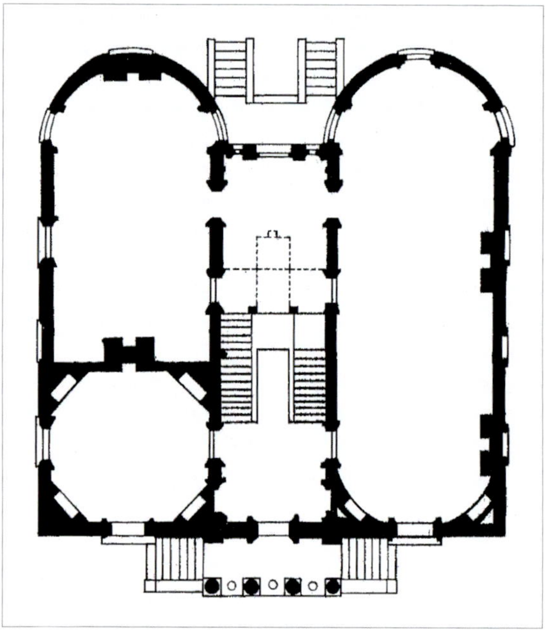

Plan of the main floor.

The "Oak Room."

Facade.

Facade.

Full view of the painting, from Bay Street (foreground) at the river looking down Bull Street (center).

Detail showing the ruins of Jay's custom house, east of Bull Street on the street just south of Bay Street.

City Hotel on Bay Street, west of Bull Street.

Detail of Bay Street showing City Hotel.

Above, street facade with entry at left;
below, view of the side piazzas behind the screen wall.

Facade of McBee House at Ashley Hall School.

Detail of Jay's structure, sepia-toned photograph
by W. Dennis Moss of Cirencester, ca. 1915.

THE AUDIENCE

At the close of his long description of the theater, Peregrinus appended this report:

> The audience have generally behaved with great decorum, and the few exceptions have been instantly marked by the strongest reprobation of the well disposed...[W]hen public etiquette, is better understood...then there will be no struggle for seats and no contest, but each one will feel himself called on, by the best disposition of the heart; a desire to respect the rights of his fellow citizens. Without this a visit to the theatre would terminate in a feud for places; instead of that harmonized feeling; that unity of soul, which constitute the highest pleasure of the Drama.

In this era, audiences for theatrical performance were increasing in size and expanding to groups in society for whom the experience was novel. Members of these audiences were often more animated than what was happening on the stage, given to moving about, shouting, and throwing fruits and vegetables. The role of the drama critic was evolving to take on not only the merits of the play and the accomplishments of the actors, but also the proper deportment of those in attendance. The theater was seen as a great opportunity to develop a shared sense of culture, "that unity of soul" in the words of Peregrinus.

And finally, for Peregrinus there was the important matter of dress: "It is rather to be regretted that a little more attention to *full dress*, was not bestowed by the ladies and particularly in the first or *dress circle* as it is emphatically called. A well dressed audience, adds to the lustre and charm of the whole entertainment, and gives that tone of fashion and ease, which every society in its infancy must want."

THE AFTERMATH OF THE SAVANNAH THEATER

Savannah had gained a theater of which the city could be proud. A corporation known as "Stockholders of the Savannah Theater" was granted by the state legislature in December 1818. This action provided for the election of five trustees to manage the affairs of the theater, among whom was Alexander Telfair. By early 1819, a flood of documents began to appear. First there were reports that funds had been transferred to Jay, though in insufficient amounts. Then by 1821 came the regrettable news that the project was mired in debt. However, there was work yet to be done. Some elements of the building were incomplete.

There had been one civic snafu. Three days after the opening on December 4, 1818, city council passed the following resolution, albeit by only the vote cast by the mayor to break a tie:

> Whereas it is the duty of this Council to preserve, as far as possible the public morals of this community and to keep the Sabbath holy and free from the general business and engagements of life; And whereas theatrical exhibitions on Saturday evenings lend to the injury of the public morals and frequently intrude upon the duties of the Sabbath; Be it resolved that Council cannot suffer the Manager of the theatre in this City to open the same on Saturday evenings for representation.

At the following meeting just one week later, the ban was rescinded without further comment.[19]

In March 1822, before Jay departed for England, Telfair issued a report to the stockholders of the Savannah Theater that summarized the vicissitudes of the project from the time of its opening in late 1818. The cost of the building, according the accounts of the builder, was "$16,047.69 ½." But the theater was still unfinished, and a large debt remained. In fast summary, Jay assumed the mortgage of the theater but signed it over to Richard Richardson in July 1821. At the time, Richardson was better able to bear the debt than Jay, but soon Richardson would collapse into bankruptcy. A sheriff's sale of foreclosure took place in May 1823, and the property was sold to an investor from New York for the bargain price of $5,100.[20]

RENOVATIONS, FIRES, AND SARAH BERNHARDT

Jay left the country in 1822, abandoning the Savannah Theater to its fate. As for most theaters of the era, it was a bumpy ride. Financially, these were very fragile institutions. Use took its toll, and costs of maintaining or revital-

---

[19] Savannah City Council Minutes, Dec. 7, 14, 1818, SMA.

[20] "Dismantling the Theater," *SMN*, June 3, 1895; A. Telfair, "Report to the Stockholders," Mar. 29, 1822, Savannah Theatre Collection, GHS; W. Jay, "Assignment of Mortgage of the Savannah Theatre to R. Richardson," July 1821, and "Record of Sheriff's Sale of the Savannah Theatre to F. Dupau," May 1823, CCRO.

izing these buildings were substantial. In Savannah, renovations were accomplished in 1854, 1867, 1870, 1881, 1888, 1894, and 1895.[21] And, through the nineteenth century, as the appetite grew for ever more spectacular events, costs of sets and costumes soared. Further, a "star system" emerged that obliged theater owners to book well-known actors and actresses who commanded large fees.

Then there was the nemesis of all theaters, fire. The Savannah Theater suffered devastating fires in 1906, 1944, and 1948. This was the condition of the theater in 1913: "The theatre is externally very little altered, since it was first erected, the walls being almost as they were originally built. The building has several times been renovated, and, after the fire of September 21, 1906, when it was, with the exception of the outer walls, almost totally destroyed, it was completely remodeled."[22] Two fires in 1948 finally brought down most of the walls of Jay's theater, leaving only a remnant of the wall on Drayton Street. A new building was raised on the site in the style of Art Deco in 1950.

Perhaps the last account of the building that Jay designed is this report from Tyrone Power, an Irish actor who performed in the theater in 1834: "Here [in Savannah] is a very well designed and well-built theatre, but...a good deal the worse in consequence of neglect: the materials and design were, I understood, all imported from England, at a prodigious cost when the smallness of the population is considered; but it is now, I fancy, rarely occupied."[23]

Nonetheless, the building had an auspicious beginning and a remarkably long life. Luminous stars came to perform in Savannah. One of these was the great French actress Sarah Bernhardt, who came in 1892 with her usual entourage and offered a great truth about Savannah, according to this news report: "[Bernhardt] has with her her Tasmanian 'possum, the mother of which Sarah killed herself in Australia, and her big St. Bernard dog. Her parrot is dead. As she is not playing 'Cleopatra' in the south she left her snake north.... [According to her] 'I haf never been south before...I like ze country, all I haf

[21] In 1854 the depth of the stage was reduced, a second gallery for whites and a gallery and boxes for blacks were added, and a heating system was installed. In 1870 a saloon was built near the entrance; in 1881 the seating circles were enlarged, and in 1894 electric lights were provided. In 1895 the building was extended to increase capacity by 400 persons (Lerski, 147).

[22] Harden, *A History of Savannah and South Georgia*, 1:390.

[23] Power, 2:118. William Grattan Tyrone Power was the great grandfather of another Tyrone Power, the American film star of the 1930s–1950s.

seen [of] it. I like Savannah…it ees so deeferent from ze rest.'"[24]

CONTEMPLATING "A SHRINE"

One person who knew well the story of the Savannah Theater believed that the building deserved to be designated "a shrine of the American theater." Charles Coburn was born in Macon, Georgia, in 1877. By his account, he grew up in the Savannah Theater, attending performances as a very young boy, then hired to hand out programs when he was thirteen, and appointed manager at eighteen. By the age of twenty, he was committed to the life of the theater and left for New York City to realize that goal. He had a long career, first on the stage and later in films, becoming well known as a character actor. By 1931 the theater that had made his life possible had been reduced to service as a movie house. When the structure was being rebuilt after the fires of 1948, Coburn argued for a restoration of a stage for live performance, to nourish a new generation of actors and patrons.[25]

Gamble had asserted the theater's claim to historic status when he wrote in 1918, on the occasion of the building's centennial,

> [The Savannah Theater] enjoys today the unique distinction of being the oldest building erected as a theater and continually used [as] such in the United States…[T]here should be some suitable recognition of the centennial of its opening, and a bronze tablet should tell the passerby, native or visitor, that before him stands the oldest theater in the United States, perhaps in the western hemisphere, for I have found no record of any other that has been in unbroken use for theatrical purposes for one hundred years.[26]

After the fires of 1948, Jay's walls no longer stood. Only the footprint and some remnants of the foundation were left. The Art Deco structure built in 1950 continued life as a movie theater until 1981 when new management reclaimed the theater for live performance. In recent years, this building has been the site of popular musical reviews, and the notices proudly declare that this is the nation's oldest continually operating theater.

---

[24] [Sarah Bernhardt at the theater], *SMN*, Jan. 23, 1892.

[25] M. Armistead, "Savannah Theater," *Georgia Review*, Spring 1953, 54.

[26] Gamble, "Savannah Theater, One of the First in America," Nov. 17, 1918.

CHAPTER 18

SAVANNAH FREE SCHOOL

In 1819 Jay was commissioned by the board of directresses of the Savannah Free School Society to construct a building in which indigent white boys and girls would be educated. This project is revealed in records of the organization, minutes of the city council, and several newspaper accounts. There are few hints of the appearance of this building that was lost to fire in 1852. Still, it is possible to make some very good guesses about the ground plan and the interior arrangement of this structure because the society subscribed to a well-known educational initiative of the day.

The Savannah Free School Society was founded in late 1816. In December 1818, the organization was incorporated by an act of the General Assembly of Georgia "for the purpose of affording education to the children of indigent persons…to dispense the benefits of education, religion and morality to a number of children of both sexes, in the city of Savannah, and to train them to habits of industry and usefulness." Among the 223 men and women listed as members of the society were some familiar names, including Jay's noisiest cheerleader, William Scarbrough.[1]

The "Rules of the Society" declared that membership was by subscription or payment of an annual fee. The business of the group was conducted by thirteen directresses who were chosen annually. A review of applicants to the school was performed by the directresses to certify that these children were truly needy. And the rules specified that the mode of instruction at the school was founded on "Lancastrian" principles.[2]

A LANCASTRIAN SCHOOL

Joseph Lancaster was an English Quaker. His mission was to educate the growing numbers of destitute children who were being cast aside in the tumult of the Industrial Revolution. But, there were these challenges: The number

---

[1] Lamar, 844–48.

[2] "Rules of the Society," Dec. 9, 1816, Savannah Free School Society Collection, GHS.

of students in need was daunting, the method of instruction had to be offered at very low cost, and the curriculum had to be engaging and rigorous to capture and keep the attention of these children who were often poorly disciplined.

Lancaster devised a method based on peer tutoring. A large open classroom, sometimes populated by several hundred students, was overseen by one teacher or master. This teacher trained a number of clever students to serve as monitors or tutors. Each tutor was assigned to a small group of classmates, usually ten, to teach units of reading, writing, or arithmetic. The method featured rote learning of content printed on cards with copy work done on slates. The economies were evident. One teacher could oversee the education of hundreds of students in one room by a method that required few textbooks.

From 1803 Lancaster wrote a number of books and pamphlets to describe his method and its efficiency. These materials provided detailed information about the manner of instruction, the elements of the curriculum, and the physical plan for the school room, including the size and shape of the room, the location of the desks, and the regions of the room designated for the gathering of the small groups led by monitors.

The content of the instruction was understood to be Christian and Bible-based, although Lancaster was careful not to identify the scheme with Quaker doctrine. Strong support came from evangelicals, both Anglicans and dissenters, for whom the education of poor children was an important goal in the reform of society. And, while the program was directed to children mired in poverty, the method was seen to have such merit that some youths from families of means gained admission by paying tuition. Likely one of those students was Cyrus Jay, the middle son of the Reverend Jay, who was sent to a Quaker school for his early education to gain habits of "order, and self-control."[3]

A LANCASTRIAN SCHOOL IN SAVANNAH

The directresses of the Savannah Free School Society were well familiar with the work of Lancaster. Their rules defined the mode of instruction for their school as "Lancastrian." Efforts were made to secure a teacher from the

---

[3] Rev. Jay, *Autobiography*, 96.

North who had been trained in this method, and students who were distinguished in deportment and in their studies were chosen as monitors.[4]

Classes commenced in February 1817 in a room at the Chatham Academy. This school for the children of good families was located in a new building completed in 1813 not far from the site later awarded by city council to the Free School. By April 1818, over ninety pupils had been admitted, and in March 1819 there were almost 200 pupils.[5] A visitor to the school in early 1819 wrote a long report for a local newspaper, observing,

> This school is conducted upon the Lancastrian system—and was first founded, and is still supported by an association of ladies, who visit it by turns, to ascertain the improvement of each scholar.... It was pleasing beyond any thing I had seen before: to see a child, as soon as it acquired a grain of knowledge, in turn communicate it, to a destitute fellow child.... Although these ladies do not pretend to have invented this mode of instruction, yet the merit of applying it to the poor children of Savannah is wholly their own.... The future good effects it will have upon society are incalculably great.[6]

"A BUILDING...SUFFICIENTLY SPACIOUS"

In June 1817, city council granted land to the Savannah Free School Society for the construction of a dedicated building. The city surveyor was directed to lay out a lot for this use in April 1818, and in June title for Lot 39 in Brown Ward was issued to the society. These actions were acknowledged in a local newspaper by the directresses who offered "warmest thanks to the Mayor and Aldermen of the city of Savannah" for their patronage of the "feeble exertions" of the society "for the benefit of the indigent," a project which all hoped would be "ultimately crowned with success."[7]

---

[4] "Rules of the Society," Dec. 9, 1816, Savannah Free School Society Collection, GHS.

[5] "Minutes of the Society," Feb. 10, Apr. 17, 1817; Apr. 16, 1818; Mar. 1, 1819, Savannah Free School Society Collection, GHS.

[6] "A Stranger in Savannah," *Columbian Museum and Savannah Daily Gazette*, May 1, 1819.

[7] Savannah City Council Minutes, June 1817 and Apr.–June 1818, SMA; [Grant of land to the Free School Society], *Columbian Museum and Savannah Daily Gazette*, June 8, 1818.

Jay was retained to design and build this school. The "Third Annual Report of the Savannah Free School Society," published in a local newspaper in January 1820, included these comments:

> The board have contracted with Mr. Jay for the erection of a building, on the lot granted them by the corporation, sufficiently spacious for the accommodation of an increasing number of pupils. It is in a state of considerable forwardness, and it is believed will be ready for the reception of the school at the commencement of the next quarter. The cost of the building will be twenty-two hundred dollars.

Then, on February 15, 1820, came this notice, "The dedication of the new building appropriated for the Savannah Free School, will take place on Wednesday next at 1 o'clock."[8]

The only certain representation of Jay's building is its footprint on a map prepared by Edward A. Vincent for city council and delivered in March 1853. This map showed the "Free School" on Lot 39 in Brown Ward (at the center of which is Chippewa Square), at Whitaker Street (a major north-south artery) and West Perry Street, in a region which had been designated for development only a few years before. Vincent portrayed the structure as a long, narrow rectangle filling the western third of the lot. With the device of close cross-hatching, this was identified as a brick building.[9] Affirmation of this material came in a note from the directresses of the Free School published in a local newspaper to thank "Mr. McAlpine" (Henry McAlpin) for his donation of "five thousand bricks, to aid in building a school house for the institution."[10]

A large, long, narrow classroom suited perfectly the requirements of a Lancastrian school. Lancaster had written, "The best form for a school-room is a long square, or parallelogram. All the desks should front the head of the school, that the master may have a good view of each boy at once.... At the

---

[8] "Third Annual Report of the Savannah Free School Society," *Savannah Daily Republican*, Jan. 7, 1820; "Notice [Dedication of the Free School building]," *Columbian Museum and Savannah Daily Gazette*, Feb. 15, 1820.

[9] E. A. Vincent, Map of the City of Savannah, 1853, VJD. This map must have been drawn before Jay's building for the Free School Society burned in 1852.

[10] E. Roberts, [Donation of bricks], *Savannah Republican*, May 18, 1819. By 1818 Henry McAlpin had established brick kilns at the Hermitage, his plantation located three miles west of the city on the Savannah River.

head of the school there should be an elevated platform for the master's desk."[11] Images of Lancastrian schoolrooms survive in early books by and about Lancaster and his methods. Typically they reveal a long rectangular hall, two stories in height, with ample windows set high on side walls to fill the room with light but without the distraction of views of the street. Several long rows of desks are fixed in the center of this room, each row having places for fifteen to twenty students, with all students facing forward in the room. In the wide side aisles, the floors are marked by semicircles to designate the "stations" where the small groups of students, usually ten, retired with their tutors for lessons and drills.[12] Surely these were features of Jay's building.

THE LIFE AND DEMISE OF THE SAVANNAH FREE SCHOOL

By July 1820, the Savannah Free School occupied its new building with an enrollment of nearly 300 students. The coming years would bring fluctuating enrollments, declining subscriptions, and the departure of several teachers (two by death). At least one goal was met in November 1827 when a teacher from New York trained in the Lancastrian mode was hired, but by the following July that fellow had fallen ill and was obliged to resign. In November 1841, the twenty-fifth annual report of the society declared that, since 1817, 1,210 pupils had been taught at the school. Even in the face of declining enrollments and revenues, the school continued in a relatively prosperous condition thanks to the diligence of the directresses, the long tenure of one particularly devoted teacher, and the proceeds of smart investments in banks and railroads, which largely replaced the dwindling subscriptions.[13]

Jay's building burned on June 6, 1852, swept up in a neighborhood fire. In November of that year, the school opened at a new location at Drayton and Charlton Streets.[14] Most of the functions of this institution ended in 1856 with the opening of the Massie School, a facility directed by city government and designated as a free school for poor children.

In a history of educational institutions in Georgia, the Savannah Free School is remembered for "its long life, excellent management, and general

[11] Lancaster, 1–3.

[12] Cubberley, 91, fig. 19.

[13] "Minutes of the Society," July 3, 1820; Nov. 5, 1827; July 7, Dec. 1, 1828; Nov. 1841, Savannah Free School Society Collection, GHS.

[14] Ibid., Nov. 29, 1852.

success." It succeeded where other "free schools" failed in realizing the commitment to needy children, in sustaining responsible oversight for the school, and in keeping the public well informed about programs and finances.[15] In the record of Jay's work, this project is a reminder of his versatility and his commitment to the important work of raising public buildings.

[15] Orr, 72.

CHAPTER 19

UNITED STATES CUSTOM HOUSE

The announcement that new research had revealed Jay to be the builder of a custom house in Savannah came in April 1987 on the 150th anniversary of his death.[1] The attribution of a project to Jay is always a cause for celebration in this city, and this event further illuminated why the young English architect had made his way to Savannah. He would be remembered for a number of private residences, but his goal had been to design important public buildings.

The source of this discovery was a great heap of documents from the archives of the federal government. In the early years of the nineteenth century, the U.S. government had just begun to multiply the number of its departments and to grow the stacks of paperwork required to get the business of the nation done. The archives of these early years were found to contain a number of reports of the first custom house in Savannah. This building had been commissioned in May 1819 and was ready for occupancy eight months later when it was destroyed in the calamitous fire of 1820. Too few of Jay's Savannah projects have survived these nearly two centuries. This one was ruined before his very eyes.

THE U.S. CUSTOMS SERVICE: THE FIRST FEDERAL AGENCY

Jay was selected for this work by one of his most obliging patrons. For Archibald Stobo Bulloch, the architect had designed and built what some believe to be his most original private residence in Savannah (later known as the Bulloch-Habersham House). In 1810–1822 Bulloch was the collector of customs for the port of Savannah. In this era, this was a presidential appointment, and Bulloch served two presidents, James Madison (in office 1809–1817) and James Monroe (in office 1817–1825).

---

[1] This announcement was made by John Duncan, professor of history, Armstrong State College (later Armstrong State University), and Elisabeth Evans, a graduate student in the program of historic preservation (D. Anderson, "Jay Building Discovered by Professor, Custom House Burned in Savannah's 1820 Fire," *SMN*, Apr. 27, 1987).

Among the first acts of the first Congress was the creation in July 1789 of the first agency of the federal government. This was the U.S. Customs Service, a field organization of collectors at fifty-nine designated ports of entry in eleven states. The responsibilities of these collectors included the assessment and gathering of duties (taxes) on the tonnage (cargo capacity) of ships coming into American ports and on imported goods carried by these ships. In September 1789, with the establishment of the Department of Treasury, the collectors reported to the secretary of the treasury.

For many years, this was the largest federal agency, and it was known to operate with exemplary efficiency. The costs of the Revolutionary War had left the new country bankrupt, but the work of the collectors begun in 1789 eliminated the enormous national debt. By the mid-1830s, port duties funded most governmental operations, and they continued to be the primary source of federal funding until the establishment of personal income tax in 1913.

In the early nineteenth century, a collector of customs had broad authority to survey incoming and outgoing traffic at a port, to assess and collect duties, and to report matters of concern to the federal government. In most locations, the collector was the only agent of the federal government in the area. Each collector was paid based on the amount of duties gathered. In 1821 Bulloch was paid $2,458.59, a substantial sum compared to most, though less than collectors at the more trafficked ports of New York (where the collector earned $4,234.83) and Charleston ($3,002.74).[2]

A CUSTOM HOUSE FOR THE PORT OF SAVANNAH

As collector, Bulloch was responsible for securing and maintaining facilities to house the operations of the port of Savannah. Earlier arrangements had been unpretentious. The first "House of Customs," built in 1763, was "a wooden hut," the location of which is unknown. In 1789, at the beginning of the Federal era, this office was moved to "Commercial row," a mixed-use building constructed by the merchant Robert Bolton, near the center of the business district.[3]

Now in the boom years following the War of 1812, the port of Savannah was thriving, and it was clear that new facilities were needed. Bulloch was on

[2] Force, 3:42, 52, 53.
[3] A. Wilson, 181.

his own to manage all aspects of this project, including site selection, appointment of an architect/builder, approval of the design, and supervision of the construction. In the early nineteenth century, there was no central agency to direct the design and construction of federal buildings, although finances were managed by the Treasury Department. Bulloch may have begun his campaign to build a proper custom house for Savannah as early as 1816. Existing facilities were inadequate, and it seems clear that Bulloch realized that the construction of a federal building in Savannah was an opportunity to declare the new prominence of the city of in the affairs of the nation.

In April 1817, Bulloch made application to the city council "to obtain a cite [*sic*] for a Custom house," but two weeks later the application was withdrawn.[4] The explanation came in May in a letter from Bulloch to William Harris Crawford, then secretary of the treasury to whom Bulloch reported. Crawford was a fellow Georgian who had served first in the Georgia House of Representatives, then in the U.S. Senate where he was quickly elected president pro tempore. He had been called by President Madison to serve as ambassador to France in the last two years of the Napoleonic Empire, then as secretary of the War Department in the aftermath of the War of 1812, and finally as secretary of the treasury in 1816, a post Crawford would occupy until 1825.

Bulloch's letter to Crawford in May 1817 detailed the current state of planning for a new custom house. The delay, he wrote, was "owing to my having met with some difficulty in procuring a suitable site for the Custom House." He explained that some lots were overpriced and others did not have clear titles. However, he had identified two possibilities. He wrote, "One is composed of an original City Lot Sixty by Ninety feet and has some old wooden buildings on it which the proprietor stipulates to remove and will take Ten Thousand Dollars for the same." The second prospect consisted of two lots, costing $20,000, with "a comfortable wooden house upon it." Bulloch estimated that, for $3,000 in renovations, this structure might serve as a custom house, but it would be necessary to build a fireproof warehouse for an additional $10,000 for a total cost of $33,000.[5]

---

[4] Savannah City Council Minutes, Apr. 21 and May 4, 1817, SMA.

[5] A. S. Bulloch to W. H. Crawford, May 20, 1817, U.S. Treasury Department Archives, Custom House at Savannah, GA, Records (1817–1822, 1836), National Archives, Washington, D.C. (hereafter cited as USTA/CH).

Bulloch offered his opinion that the smaller site was "sufficiently roomy & I will add that the popular opinion is with me in giving the preference to the erecting a beautiful convenient and durable edifice." He added that he had sent to Crawford "a plan of a custom House to contain Ware Houses underneath which will be sufficiently Roomy to answer the convenience of this District for a number of years." He named as the "architect" for this plan a Mr. Robbins, and he urged that Robbins be dispatched "Northward" to purchase materials so that work might begin in October 1817.[6]

This letter revealed Bulloch's interest in raising a building both "beautiful" and "durable," declaring that "popular opinion" was with him in meeting these goals. It is a hint to us of the environment into which Jay came in December 1817. He longed to do important work, to make public buildings which would, in his words, replace Savannah's "tawdry profusion" of structures.[7] It would seem that, in this matter, Jay's ambition to promote the "art" of architecture was shared by Bulloch and "public opinion."

"THE ARTIST WHO PLANNED THE CUSTOM HOUSE"

Reports of what happened next in the planning for this building are missing, but this much can be surmised: "Mr. Robbins," probably a carpenter/builder in the city,[8] was replaced by Jay, and a new plan designed by an "Artist" was sent to Crawford. In December 1818, Bulloch wrote to Crawford, "Accompanying this you will receive a plan and enclosed an estimate of a suitable edifice for a Custom House for the port of Savannah.... [Further] I have contracted with the Artist who planned the Custom House for the erection of suitable Warehouses." Ominously, Bulloch observed that the cellars must be built "of the best materials to be fire proof."[9]

A contract between Bulloch and Jay was recorded on May 27, 1819, promising the following features of the building: exterior dimensions of forty-eight feet by forty-two feet six inches, two stories in elevation, with substantial brick walls (eighteen inches thick in the basement and fourteen inches in the second story), finished with the "best Roman Cement" (stucco) at the exterior and with "Laths & plaster" at the interior, roofed with "the best slate," fitted

[6] Ibid.

[7] W. Jay, arch., attrib., A Friend to the Fine Arts, Feb. 10, 1818.

[8] "Mr. Robbins" was likely Daniel Robbins, a carpenter/builder in Savannah.

[9] A. S. Bulloch to W. H. Crawford, Dec. 31, 1818, USTA/CH.

with stone sills for the doors and windows, and having floors of "the best pitch pine." Accompanying the building would be a brick wall to enclose the entire lot, also finished with "Roman cement," with gates at each side of the building.[10]

There are no surviving views of the completed building—it was gutted in the great fire of early 1820. However, the ruined shell of the structure is portrayed in a painting of 1837, and its footprint is shown on a map of 1853. The map by Edward A. Vincent, documenting later construction raised on the foundation of the 1819 custom house, reveals that Jay's structure was centered and forward on the lot, fronting on Bryan Street at the northeast corner of Johnson Square. The plan was a T shape, having a more narrow center section with a wider extension at the rear to accommodate the warehouses. Half to one-third of the lot behind the building was free of construction allowing for expansion as needed.[11]

Work proceeded at a good pace to fulfill the contract, which called for the project to be "commenced and prosecuted and finished with all convenient speed and dispatch." Receipts signed by Jay show that he was paid in four increments in 1819: $5,050 on January 26, half of the amount due for the construction of the warehouses; $5,050 on May 27, payment in full for the warehouses; $4,500 on May 27, the first payment for the custom house; and $4,500 on August 30, the second payment for the custom house.[12] Jay was busy at least through the end of October 1819, as recorded in the minutes of the city council for November 1, 1819: "William Jay [reported for] obstructing Bryan Street & not having light fined [$] 30 & Costs."[13]

A FEARSOME FIRE AND FEDERAL HARASSMENT

The Savannah Custom House and warehouses were completed in late 1819 or early 1820, and a transfer of records to the new facilities had begun

---

[10] "Articles of agreement…between A. S. Bulloch…and W. Jay," May 27, 1819, USTA/CH.

[11] J. L. F. Cerveau, *View of Savannah*, 1837, watercolor, GHS; E. A. Vincent, Map of Savannah, 1853. VJD.

[12] "Articles of agreement…between A. S. Bulloch…and W. Jay," May 27, 1819; "Received from A. S. Bulloch…for Erecting a Custom House and Warehouses at Savannah…[signed] William Jay," four receipts (Jan. 26, May 27, May 27, and Aug. 30, 1819), USTA/CH.

[13] Savannah City Council Minutes, Nov. 1, 1819, SMA.

before the great fire of January 11, 1820, consumed much of the city. The building stood in the path of the fire, and when the flames had done their work, what was left was a rather remarkable ruin. The masonry walls stood to the roof line, and they continued to stand until 1837 when they were portrayed by Joseph Louis Firmin Cerveau in his topographic view of the city painted from the vantage point of the clock tower of the Exchange on Bay Street. The brick shell of Jay's custom house remained standing until 1847 when the property was sold.

The fire of 1820 in Savannah was such a catastrophe that it was broadcast far and wide in the national press, eliciting sympathetic responses from individuals and municipalities. Generosity was forthcoming from many quarters, but apparently not from the federal government. Among those reduced to pleading for special consideration in managing obligations to federal accounts was Isaac Minis, a wealthy merchant. On January 15, 1820, just four days after the fire, Minis wrote to Crawford,

> The late destructive Fire has...embraced in its destruction, my dwelling, [and] much merchandize [*sic*].... My object in now addressing [you] is to receive the most extended term of time, and to place me on the most liberal view that can be taken of the destressed [*sic*].... [T]he amount of loss is so very great, as to render poor those whom a few hours previous to the fatal Morning of the 11 Jan[uar]y were wealthy.[14]

It seems that, at the time of this fire, the accounts for the new custom house in Savannah were in something of a muddle, for which Bulloch and Jay would pay a terrible price. There is evidence that the project was being held to a high standard of scrutiny by federal officers, and Bulloch and Jay, both eager and ambitious men, were insufficiently responsive. In early January 1819, Crawford wrote to Bulloch acknowledging a request for $5,050 for work on the warehouses. Crawford approved the request but admonished Bulloch, saying, "As it is not usual to make advances in such cases, until some progress has been made in the work, it is hoped that you have taken a Bond with approved security for the faithful performance of the contract."[15] The first payment was made to Jay on January 26, 1819, but the "Articles of Agree-

[14] I. Minis to W. H. Crawford, Jan. 15, 1820, USTA/CH.

[15] W. H. Crawford to A. S. Bullock [*sic*], Jan. 8, 1819, USTA/CH.

ment" were not drawn until May 27, 1819. Jay continued to receive incremental payments for work on the warehouses and the custom house through August of that year. In the aftermath of the fire, federal officials ascertained that records of costs and payments for goods and services were incomplete.

In September 1820, some months after the fire, Savannah was seized by an epidemic of yellow fever. In the throes of this new catastrophe, Bulloch wrote to Joseph Inslee Anderson, the first comptroller of the treasury,

> Sir, I have received your letter covering a bond to be executed by me for the faithful discharge of the duties of Collector of the Customs for the port of Savannah. The bond would have been executed and forwarded before this period had not the City of Savannah been visited by a calamity as distressing as unexpected. A fever which continues to baffle all medical skill prevails among the inhabitants, carrying off as many as seventeen on some days of a population of perhaps one thousand. The people continue [to evacuate] in search of country quarters hoping to escape the calamity.[16]

So, the bond earlier requested by Crawford had not been obtained. Fifteen months later, in December 1821, Anderson wrote a terse note to Bulloch, summarizing the advances from the Treasury Department of $29,100 ($10,000 for the lot and the remainder for the construction of the custom house and the warehouses), concluding, "As there has been no settlement on that Account, you are requested to transmit without delay a Statement of it accompanied by the requisite vouchers."[17] Bulloch might have claimed that the vouchers were lost in the fire, but there is no record of his reply.

Anderson commissioned an audit of the project. The report, dated August 15, 1822, detailed the advances of funds to Bulloch and charged both Bulloch and Jay with the obligation to cover all costs of the lost buildings. Bulloch was forgiven the $10,000 for the lot, since that purchase of land had been properly recorded. A receipt dated January 29, 1821, survives to testify that Bulloch had received those funds, made the purchase of the lot, and forwarded the titles to the land to Crawford.[18] By August 1822, Jay was gone

---

[16] A. S. Bulloch to J. Anderson, Sept. 21, 1820, USTA/CH.

[17] J. Anderson to A. S. Bulloch, Dec. 20, 1821, USTA/CH.

[18] R. Harrison, Report to the Comptroller of the Treasury, Aug. 15, 1822, USTA/CH; "Received of A. S. Bullock [*sic*]...for erecting a Custom House and Warehouses in Savannah," Jan. 29, 1821, USTA/CH.

from America and back in England, and by the end of that year he had resolved not to return to Savannah.

Bulloch was held to account for the losses and suffered a brief term of imprisonment in early 1824.[19] Ultimately he was credited with the amount he had paid to Jay and cleared of the charges against him. In 1842 Secretary of the Treasury Walter Forward reported to the U.S. House Committee on Commerce, then considering the construction of a new custom house in Savannah. Of Bulloch's debt, he said, "On the settlement of Mr. Bullock's [*sic*] account, he has received credit in the sum of ten thousand dollars, (the amount paid for the lot,) and also for nineteen thousand one hundred dollars paid by him to William Jay, contractor for the erection of the building. With the latter sum said Jay now stands debited on the books of the Treasury."[20] Of course, Jay, having died on the island of Mauritius in 1837, was well beyond the reach of the U.S. government.

OLD RUINS AND NEW BUILDINGS

Newspaper reports in 1822 and 1824 reveal that, after the fire, the custom house was situated in "Bolton's centre building" on Commercial Row, suggesting that the transfer from that location had never been completed. In 1825 city council received a proposal to fit a portion of the Exchange to receive the offices of the custom house, with rent to be paid by the federal government; and in early 1826, that move was made.[21]

While the ravaged shell of Jay's custom house lingered in Savannah, with the passage of some years, the federal government seems to have forgotten about that adventure altogether. In March 1834, members of Congress appealed to the federal government for funds to build a new facility in Savannah. It took a couple of years for the Secretary of the Treasury Levi Woodbury to unearth the records of the structure of 1819–1820. He reported that, while the costs of construction had been advanced by Bulloch to Jay, the building

---

[19] President Monroe proposed to William H. Crawford in Feb. 1824 that Bulloch be released from confinement and his case submitted to the attorney general; a declaration by Monroe in Mar. 1824 ordered the discharge of Bulloch from confinement on the condition that he settle his debts to the U.S. (Preston, 2:920).

[20] "Custom-House—Savannah, Georgia," Mar. 19, 1842, *U.S. Congressional Serial Set*, vol. 403, n.p.

[21] E. Evans, "Lot 9, Jekyl Tithing, Derby Ward," 1987, 11–12, VJD.

was consumed by fire before ownership was transferred to the federal government. He concluded that it was indeed appropriate to raise a new custom house at Savannah, although he could not recommend the project because the Treasury Department was at that time very short of funds for new buildings. Undeterred by the matter of insufficient funds, Congress recommended in May 1836 that the old lot be sold and a new site purchased.[22] But, in the ordinary ways of government, the sale of the old lot, the purchase of a new one, and the allocation of funds for a new building took decades.

In June 1847, the lot on Bryan Street "with the ruins of the custom house heaped upon it" was sold by the government of the United States to the Georgia Historical Society. This organization, founded in 1839, set about to build a library to contain a growing collection of books and documents.[23] In 1848 a structure in the Gothic Revival style was built on the site. The architect was John Norris, a New Yorker who trained as a mason but became a skillful architect. He had come to Savannah having won the commission for a new custom house at Bay and Bull Streets, which would be constructed in 1848–1851.

The Gothic confection made for the Georgia Historical Society was raised on the foundation of Jay's building, taking the distinctive T shape. No doubt this was a measure of economy. But, nostalgia and not economy was on the mind of Henry Rootes Jackson when, in July 1848, he remembered the old custom house at the laying of the cornerstone for the new one. Jackson gave what was to be the last tribute to Jay's building, saying, "His [Norris's] genius seems to possess the power to *renovate* as well as to *originate*, and while he is about to erect the most beautiful and substantial building between Washington and New-Orleans for our new Custom House, he has embraced the skeleton of the old, burned to death this generation past, and it is growing into life and youth and beauty beneath his magical touch."[24] Jackson's comment about Norris's embrace of "the skeleton of the old" for the construction of the library may have been simply poetry, one of Jackson's many gifts. But

---

[22] L. Woodbury to G. W. Owens, Apr. 18, 20, 1836, USTA/CH; "Custom-House – Savannah," May 17, 1836, *U.S. Congressional Serial Set*, vol. 295, n.p.

[23] Harden, *A History of Savannah and South Georgia*, 1:409; E. Evans, "Lot 9, Jekyl Tithing, Derby Ward," 1987, 13, VJD.

[24] H. Jackson, [Laying cornerstone of new custom house], *Georgian*, July 19, 1848.

this comment suggests that at least some of those old walls, still standing in 1837 when Cerveau painted them, might have lingered in the structure commissioned by the Georgia Historical Society.[25]

The society moved into the Gothic Revival building in 1849, occupying the upper floors with commercial enterprises below. By 1870 the organization once again found that its collections required more space, and in the following year the library was moved to temporary quarters. A permanent home was found in 1875 in Hodgson Hall, at the northeast corner of Forsyth Park, a building prompted by Margaret Telfair Hodgson to honor her husband, William Brown Hodgson. The old Gothic Revival building, which may have contained remnants of Jay's 1819–1820 custom house, continued to be occupied by various commercial establishments, first banks and later a bar.[26] Sometime in the early twentieth century, this building was lost, run over or swallowed up by new development.

[25] The mortar in Jay's standing brick walls may have been weakened in the fire, but it is likely that the foundation below grade had survived in good condition. Norris's building for the Georgia Historical Society was brick, stuccoed, and scored to resemble stone masonry construction.

[26] Harden, "Georgia Historical Society," 7–11; A. Wilson, 159.

CHAPTER 20

"A NIOBE OF CITIES": THE FIRE OF 1820

In the early morning of January 11, 1820, a small fire began in a livery stable near Market or Ellis Square, at the northwest corner of Savannah's historic district. The flames were whipped by winds across a city built largely of wood and just then parched by drought. By midday, much of Savannah lay in ruins. Nearly 400 structures had burned to the ground, and losses were estimated as high as five million dollars. Widely reported in the national press, the conflagration was said to have been the most awful fire to strike an American city up to that time.[1]

A week later, a local newspaper gave the details of this terrible event. The path of the fire had been across the business district turning "the center of wealth and industry" into "a heap of worthless ruins." The fire began in the early hours of a Tuesday morning. The alarm was sounded, citizen groups and fire companies fought the flames valiantly, but their efforts were thwarted by strong winds that carried burning cinders across the town. The news report observed, "When we consider the mass of wooden buildings which had been exposed for years to the influence of the sun, and the almost total absence of rain for several months past, it is surprising that the progress of the devouring element should have been arrested at all before it had swept every house in the direction of the wind."[2]

The fire consumed the commercial district, destroying the properties and holdings of the market and retail stores along with the imported goods waiting to be processed at the custom house. Among the residences lost to the fire were a very large number of double tenements, displacing scores of families. Ninety-four lots were leveled, taking 321 structures of wood and thirty-five of brick. The newspaper article concluded, "Alas! never did the sun set on a gloomier day for Savannah, or on so many aching hearts."[3]

From its settlement in 1733, the city had been alert to the threat of fire.

---

[1] Coulter, "Great Savannah Fire of 1820," 2, 7.

[2] Harden, *A History of Savannah and South Georgia*, 1:288.

[3] Ibid., 289.

In early planning, wooden chimneys had been banned, and all homeowners were required to keep buckets equal to the number of fireplaces and ladders for access to roofs. This vigilance did not deter a fire in 1796 that destroyed two-thirds of the city, including most of the original structures. Over the next two decades, the city formed bucket brigades and acquired at least six fire engines propelled by hand power. In early 1819, city council put in place an ordinance to prohibit the storage of gunpowder in buildings in populated districts, and a bill was introduced to encourage new building in brick or stone.[4]

None of these measures suppressed what E. Merton Coulter called the "uncontrolled and devouring conflagration" of early 1820, a catastrophe compounded by "two explosions of gunpowder illegally stored [in Market Square]...which demoralized fire-fighters and scattered the flames in all directions." Two days after the fire, Mayor Thomas U. P. Charlton said,

> A moiety [half] of this once beautiful city, is LITERALLY IN RUINS...The plan of our city has been universally admired for its symetry [*sic*]—its beauty—its fitness for all the purposes of health, cleanliness and circulation of air. Years of prosperity had given a splendor to the appearance of this now devoted [destroyed] city...[where] affluent merchants and citizens [had built]...expensive warehouses, and elegant mansions.[5]

JAY'S LAMENT

No one could speak with more professional knowledge and personal conviction about the ruin of city buildings than the architect of Savannah's most "elegant mansions." Ten days after the fire, Jay gave his estimate of the tragedy in a local newspaper. His opening words painted a poignant image of ruined Savannah with lines of poetry borrowed from Lord Byron:

> She was happy—and the language of many was
> I lov'd her from my boyhood—she to me
> was as a fairy city of the heart,
> Rising like water columns from the sea;
> Of joy the sojourn—and of wealth the mart.
> She has become a Niobe of cities,

---

[4] Coulter, "Great Savannah Fire of 1820," 5; Savannah City Council Minutes, Mar. 18 and May 17, 1819, SMA.

[5] Coulter, "Great Savannah Fire of 1820," 1, 9.

a chaos of ruins; who can trace the void,
or who can bend him over the fallen pile,
without remembering her former greatness;
she was rising a model, she has fallen a monument.[6]

The first and last lines of Jay's poetic tribute were his invention. The intervening six lines came from *Childe Harold's Pilgrimage*, Canto IV, by George Gordon, Lord Byron, published in 1818. The image of "a fairy city of the heart" referred to contemporary Venice where Byron had lived in winter 1816 and embraced as a delight. The motif of Niobe referred to contemporary Rome, which Byron toured in 1817 and recalled as a once great city laid in ruin by "[t]he Goth, the Christian, Time, War, Flood, and Fire."[7]

A distraught Jay declared,

> In a calamity so dreadful as the late fire, which laid prostrate much of our city, it behooves every one to offer his assistance: the benevolent man his charity, and the scientific his genius.... The object of this address, is a subject which has met my most serious consideration, and it is offered to the public, founded on experience and sanctioned by practice, it is a plan to erect fire-proof stores.

What ensued was Jay's account of recent advances in the fireproof construction of commercial buildings in England, methods that "not only prevent fires from without, but defy fires from within." These were discoveries made in the cotton mills of the late eighteenth century, when friction from the spinning machines ignited the cotton dust, which smoldered causing brick walls to heat and the timber frame to burn. Jay concluded, "[I]t is a fact worthy of remark, and one long attested, that a building in which wood is admitted is not fire-proof."

According to Jay, this was the solution:

> To remedy the evil complained of, and to offer security to the public, the present mode of building is proposed to use Iron instead of timber, to make the floor joists of cast-iron, cast in two lengths, united in the middle, and supported by areas, iron columns of the same material...the cellars would

[6] W. Jay, arch., "Savannah, January 21st, 1820," Jan. 22, 1820 (hereafter cited in text).

[7] Byron, 12, 42–43.

> be turned in groined arches [crossed barrel arches] in brick work...the roof to have iron rafters, crossed by small iron rods, on which the the tiles would rest, for I prefer tiles to slates, thinking them less liable to burn.... The shutters and sash frames to be of iron, and the latter, in retail stores or fancy shops, would be a security against burglary...to avoid so many openings, they are neither useful nor ornamental, in buildings devoted to commerce they are unnecessary.

Jay offered a rebuttal to the cost of his proposal, saying,

> I am aware, that many will object to this method, on the supposed difference of expense, and which I contend is not much more, if calculated, and much less than is supposed, if the difference of the durability be considered, the one is perishable, and the other unperishable, the appearance is much improved by the neatness of the materials, while considerable room is gained.

He announced his plan of action as,

> The subscriber respectfully informs the public, that in a few days he will exhibit plans and models illustrative of the present designs, and he further begs leave to observe, that he has made arrangements with Mr. M'Alpin [Henry McAlpin], who lately has erected a foundery [*sic*] for casting, so that the subscriber is willing to undertake any building on the principle stated, or in his way offers his professional services.

Jay expressed himself in the two imperatives of his own profession: art and science. Here the art was poetry, and Jay borrowed familiar lines by the most popular poet of the age to describe the anguish of the event. He offered as a remedy for the catastrophe in Savannah his own knowledge of recent developments in the science of construction, the new materials and methods of structural engineering which were believed at the time to prevent or at least diminish the ravages of fire.

JAY'S EMBRACE OF POETRY

Jay chose to reveal his grief in the company of Lord Byron, using lines from *Childe Harold's Pilgrimage*, Canto IV (1818), words familiar to many of Jay's readers. The first two cantos of *Childe Harold* had been published together in 1812 and resulted in Byron's immediate fame. This work was the first of Byron's long narrative poems, and it was the first to feature a Byronic hero, a charismatic and conflicted adventurer. Eagerly anticipated, Canto III appeared in 1816 and Canto IV in 1818.

Jay turned to two passages in Canto IV, a description of contemporary Venice to evoke the former beauty of Savannah and an account of the ruins of ancient Rome to measure the ravages of the fire. Like Venice, Savannah had been "a fairy city of the heart." Now charred rubble, the place had become like Rome a "Niobe of cities." Byron had selected Niobe, Queen of Thebes, to symbolize unbearable loss. In ancient Greek legend, Niobe had mocked Latona, the mother of Apollo and Diana, boasting that she had seven sons and seven daughters. To preserve their mother's honor, Apollo and Diana drew their arrows and slew the fourteen children of Niobe. Now childless, Niobe fled into the mountains where she changed to stone and her tears became an unending stream. For Jay, this image conveyed Savannah's losses.

JAY'S CLAIMS FOR SCIENCE

In this article, Jay offered his "science" to help in the rebuilding of the city, a reminder of his announcement in early 1818 that architects were both artists and scientists.[8] In particular, he offered "a plan to erect fire-proof stores" in the devastated commercial district using cast iron structural components. He cited methods developed in England in the early 1790s to control fires in the textile mills. The conventional wisdom of the time was that cast iron was fireproof, but it is not because the material degrades and collapses when subjected to very high heat.

As a student in London, Jay became aware of the history of addressing the threat of fire in English towns and cities. The matter had been studied with particular care in the wake of the great fire of London in 1666. The usual precautions were discussed, such as reducing the crowding of structures and replacing timber construction with brick and stone. And, as one means to cope with the inevitable ravages of fire, the industry of fire insurance was established in the late seventeenth century. David Riddall Roper, Jay's first teacher in London, was an architect and surveyor who, in 1805, was appointed surveyor to the Albion Fire and Life Insurance Company. Founded in that year, Albion was prominent in the growing industry of insurance.[9]

In Jay's own work, there is early evidence of the use of structural cast

[8] W. Jay, arch., attrib., A Friend to the Fine Arts, Feb. 10, 1818.

[9] Elmes, *Topographical Dictionary of London*, 7.

iron. His 1815 proposal for the New English Opera House in London likely incorporated cast-iron columns to support the galleries—those elements were present in his 1818 design of the Savannah Theater. Given what can be known of the plan and elevation of the Albion Chapel, it is reasonable to assume that in 1815 Jay used cast-iron columns in that structure. And, there is ample evidence of the use of cast iron for structural details, such as stairways and balconies, in Jay's Savannah houses in 1816–1819.

In addition to these conventional uses of cast iron, Jay had surely seen some of the most ingenious explorations of the material in construction and ornament in 1814 during his time in Liverpool pursuing the commission for the Wellington Rooms. By the early nineteenth century, most of the iron foundries in England made products for industrial and military uses. But John Cragg, proprietor of the Mersey Iron Foundry in Liverpool, had a great interest in extending the possibilities for cast iron. In 1813 Cragg engaged the services of the architect Thomas Rickman to design three churches in the Gothic style using cast iron for both structural components and ornamental elements. These were the "iron churches" of Liverpool built in 1813–1816 by Cragg near the location of his foundry on the River Mersey. Likely Jay was alert to this and other work by Cragg, including a patent granted in 1810 for a method of producing cast-iron rafters for "houses, warehouses, and other buildings."[10]

"ARRANGEMENTS WITH MR. M'ALPIN"

As evidence of his readiness to design and construct fireproof buildings in the commercial district, Jay declared that he would soon present to the public "plans and models" of his proposals. And he announced arrangements with a local foundry where iron for these projects could be cast. He identified the owner of this shop as Henry McAlpin. A native of Scotland, McAlpin arrived in Savannah in 1812 with the plan to pursue the occupation of architect/builder for which he had been trained. In 1815 he acquired an estate on the Savannah River just west of the city, a property then known as Hermitage Plantation. The site was near timberlands (a sawmill had been located here since 1776), and it had significant deposits of clay (brick-making had been undertaken here as early as 1798). McAlpin took possession of the property

[10] Picton, 2:82–83; J. Cragg, "Patent…Improvements in the casting of Iron Roofs," *Repertory of Arts, Manufactures, and Agriculture*, 132-35.

in 1819 and soon established a steam-driven sawmill, a brick manufacturing plant, and a foundry.[11]

In 1819 McAlpin was described in the press as "a brickmaker."[12] The products were the now much-prized Savannah gray bricks. Made of a regional clay said to be gray (but actually grayish red-brown in color), these bricks were large, 1.5 times the conventional size. They would come to play an important role in the rebuilding of Savannah after the fire of 1820. Notice of the opening of McAlpin's "Cast Iron Foundery [*sic*]" came in a local newspaper in January 1821: "WHERE Castings of all descriptions is done in the neatest manner & at as short a notice as the nature of the work wanted will allow, and of the very best materials."[13] The reference to McAlpin by Jay has been taken by some to suggest a collaboration between these two men, but Jay routinely turned to English suppliers for materials that came quickly and efficiently on the ships of his Savannah patrons.

THE AFTERMATH OF JAY'S ENTREATIES

Nothing came of Jay's proposal to rebuild the commercial district of Savannah. He gained no contracts for work, nor did he establish a relationship with McAlpin. Savannah merchants did not rush to Jay to commission fireproof buildings perhaps because they could not justify the increased costs of construction. There were deep fissures in the local economy even before the fire came to deal a crushing blow. And, to heap sorrow on sorrow, in 1820 between May and November came a fierce outbreak of yellow fever. As the disease took its toll, hundreds died, and thousands fled the city.

There were daunting obstacles to recovery, yet newspaper articles appeared just one year after the fire to affirm that Savannah had rallied. This was a report of January 11, 1821: "A stranger would hardly believe on viewing this city, that so many superb edifices could have been erected in the time [since the fire]…. Hardly a vestige of that terrible conflagration now remains by which it can be traced."[14] Three months later, an article appeared having a ring of Jay's voice, echoing themes of the announcement he made soon after

---

[11] Savannah Unit, Georgia Writers' Project of the W.P.A., "Hermitage Plantation," *Georgia Historical Quarterly,* Mar. 1943:64–71.

[12] Ibid., 71.

[13] H. McAlpin, "Cast Iron Foundery [*sic*]," *Georgian,* Jan. 30, 1821.

[14] "11 January, 1821," *Georgian,* Jan. 11, 1821.

his arrival in late 1817:

> Upon the buildings nearly finished, both public and private, the proverbial spirit of emulative taste is conferring a degree of external elegance that will compete with many of greater magnitude.... There is something peculiarly pleasurable in witnessing a revolution so remarkable...[in] the growing prosperity of commercial enterprise, and the beauty of architectural refinement.... It is the triumph of public spirit, when wealth is joined to liberality, and unite to encourage architectural excellence, where classic simplicity is blended with modern taste, to embellish our buildings.[15]

The flames had touched none of Jay's houses, and the Savannah Theater was unsinged. The U.S. Custom House, which he had just completed, was gutted—only the brick walls stood. That structure might have been rebuilt in the aftermath of the fire, but quarrels about liability caused the building to languish in its ruined state until it was forgotten altogether. The Savannah Branch of the Bank of the United States, which Jay had designed for Richard Richardson, was insufficiently advanced to be affected by the fire. Construction of the bank began in 1820 and was completed in the following year. And, work on the City Hotel, the design of which may be attributed to Jay, did not begin until after the fire. Soon Jay turned his attention to Charleston, South Carolina, but with only moderate success; and to Augusta, Georgia, with no result at all. By mid-1822, he had returned to England.

---

[15] "Improvement of Savannah," *Georgian*, Apr. 18, 1821.

CHAPTER 21

SAVANNAH BRANCH OF THE BANK OF THE UNITED STATES

The report of Jay's Savannah Branch of the Bank of the United States mirrors the peaks and valleys of his professional career.[1] Here was an elegant design of a public building that gained wide attention, predicting for Jay a future of new clients and more commissions, yet none of this promise was realized. In the wake of this project came a national financial crisis, in which a central player was this very bank, the Bank of the United States, bringing calamity to some of Jay's most important Savannah clients and prompting the decline of his own fortunes. At least this structure might have survived to be a reminder of the exquisite character of Jay's art in the arena of public architecture, but it did not. In 1892, Jay's bank acquired an unhappy second story, and in 1924 it was demolished to make way for an unremarkable office building.

According to a notice published in a London art journal in 1819, Jay had traveled to Savannah to accomplish work of a particular sort, "public buildings of his own designs."[2] In his short stay in the city, he did design a theater, a school for indigent children, a custom house, perhaps a hotel, and a bank. Of all of these, the structure most likely to achieve notice in the history of American architecture was this bank. It is now occasionally remembered as an early example of the Greek Revival in this country although Jay's style was certainly Grecian by way of the Regency. It was a beautiful building, and we are left to wonder why Jay did not receive the recognition he deserved.

JAY'S BANK: AN "ELEGANT STRUCTURE"

Contemporary testimony affirms that this was a handsome building. It was raised in those fretful months following the great fire of January 1820

---

[1] There were two charters of this bank, the first in 1791–1811 and the second in 1816–1836, sometimes misidentified as "First Bank of the U.S." and "Second Bank of the U.S."

[2] Elmes, "Notice of Works in Hand…Foreign and Domestic," *Annals,* Oct. 1819:487.

when evidence of recovery was welcomed. A news report in late March 1821 declared, "The neatness and uniformity of the new buildings...astonish every one who knew the place before the late memorable fire.... The United States Bank, claims to be noticed.... [It is] being executed, in a style of architecture and workmanship, surpassing any public building before seen in Savannah."[3]

By mid-April, Jay's bank was being readied for service. According to a newspaper account, this was the exterior of the building: "The principal front of this elegant structure is viewed from the south, and finished with a symmetrical portico, sustained by 6 massive columns, in the Grecian Dorick [*sic*] order; a double range of stone steps lead up to the grand entrance, at the extremity of which, are placed broad pedistals [*sic*] for statuary. The rear of the building is ornamented by a collanade [*sic*] of similar extent with the front projection, but less magnificent in the decoration."[4]

This same report described the interior as "spacious and commodious." The central banking hall was surmounted by an oval dome "supported by a handsome cornice, bordered by a species of Etruscan ornament," surely the anthemia (lotus or honeysuckle blossoms) which had become Jay's signature decorative detail. Among the furnishings of the room were mantelpieces of "dark, and highly polished Kilkenny [black] marble," a popular export quarried in southeast Ireland.[5]

Members of the public were invited to tour the premises: "The interior is completed, and *will be opened for the transaction of business, on Monday next, 23d inst.* [April 23, 1821]. In the interim those who wish to gratify their taste for architectural science, will have an opportunity, as the banking house is now open for the inspection of the public." A copper plaque affixed to the cornerstone carried this inscription: "Corner Stone of the Branch Bank of the United States laid May 8, 1820/ Rich[ar]d Richardson, President/ James Hunter, Cashier/ Will[ia]m Jay, Architect/ John Retan [and] Rob[er]t Wright, Builders."[6]

No doubt Jay's capture of this commission was the consequence of his close association with Richardson, for whom he had designed a splendid

[3] "Amidst all the shipwrecked hopes...," *Georgian*, 30 Mar. 1821.

[4] Ibid.

[5] Ibid.

[6] "New U. States Bank," *Georgian*, Apr. 19, 1821; "Historical Society Given Jay Tablet," *SMN*, Apr. 20, 1932.

home as his first Savannah project. Richardson, a principal in the Bolton cotton house, had been appointed to the board of directors of the Savannah branch of the Bank of the United States in 1817 and elected president in the same year. That this bank would occupy an elegant structure could surprise no one. The Bank of the U.S. would prove to be a formidable patron of architecture, because its directors understood with unusual clarity the symbolic significance of important public buildings.

THE BUMPY HISTORY OF THE BANK OF THE UNITED STATES

Banking in the United States developed first as private or state enterprises with no broad code of regulation, issuing a variety of banknotes sometimes insufficiently supported by reserves of specie (gold or silver). In 1791 Congress chartered a national bank for a term of twenty years. This enterprise had been promoted by Alexander Hamilton, the first secretary of the treasury. Hamilton believed in the need for the federal government to regulate the industry of banking by controlling the issue of banknotes, guaranteeing the reserves of specie to assure the value of the notes, and directing lending policies that would sustain growth in the economy. This plan was supported by President George Washington against the objections of Thomas Jefferson, then secretary of state, who thought that the federal government had no constitutional authority to establish a central bank.

Jefferson's position was embraced by the directors of the growing number of private and state banks, who opposed federal tampering with their practices. So, when the national bank's first charter expired in 1811, President James Madison, who supported Jefferson, did not renew it. But the crush of debt incurred during the War of 1812 obliged Madison to prompt a second charter of the bank in 1816, again for a term of twenty years. Opposition forces again prevailed in 1832, and an early bid to extend the second charter was vetoed by President Andrew Jackson. Jackson's dislike of the Bank of the U.S. was visceral, opposed as he was to any concentration of power over the important affair of the management of money. Operations of the bank ceased in 1836.

From its origin, the Bank of the United States was headquartered in Philadelphia. It had as one of its responsibilities the important function of receiving and managing monies paid to the federal government from customs duties in the lucrative shipping trade. For that reason, branch offices of "discount and deposit" were opened in seaport cities: Boston, New York, Baltimore, and Charleston in 1792; Norfolk in 1800; Washington City (District of Columbia) and Savannah in 1802; and New Orleans in 1805. There was strong opposition to this enterprise from the beginning, but these quarrels were muted in Georgia. In fact, the establishment of a branch in Savannah in 1802 was welcomed. Banking and credit were essential to the conduct of trade, particularly to sustain the production and sale of the large money crops of rice and cotton. But Georgia came late to the enterprise of banking—the first bank charter issued by the state was in 1807 to the Planter's Bank. Before the arrival in 1802 of a branch of the Bank of the U.S., Georgia was dependent on the banks of Charleston, South Carolina, an unwelcome state of affairs.

By the time of the second charter of the Bank of the United States in 1816 and the opening of a Savannah branch in the following year, the banking environment in Georgia had become more complex. Additional bank charters had been issued by the state to the Bank of Augusta in 1810 and the Bank of the State of Georgia in 1815. However, regulation of these state banks was problematic, and currency was often unsettled. During the War of 1812, Georgia banks had difficulty gaining deposits from the Northern banks and the federal government. These circumstances forced Georgians once again to rely on Charleston institutions. So, when Congress authorized the second charter in 1816 for another term of twenty years, the establishment of a branch in Savannah was welcomed by state authorities and by the state banks. And, for a short time, a general atmosphere of congeniality and cooperation prevailed.[7]

A BRANCH OF THE BANK OF THE U.S. IN SAVANNAH

The Savannah branch of the Bank of the United States first opened in 1802 as an office of "discounts and deposits," with Joseph Habersham as president and a board of directors composed of men prominent in the community. That office was closed in 1811, but it reopened in January 1817. Richardson was named as one of the thirteen directors. In February he was elected president, and in early 1820 he was "unanimously re-elected President."[8]

---

[7] Govan, 2–5, 46–49.

[8] W. Murphey, "Banks and Money in Savannah, Georgia, 1733 to 1865," Mar. 1943, 20, in Thomas Gamble Collection, Live Oak Public Library, Thomas Gamble

This second Office of Discount and Deposit began operations in May 1817 at a location on Bay Street, just west of Bull Street. It is likely that plans were underway for a fine new building when the great fire of January 1820 swept through this district. By April 1820, property at the corner of East St. Julian and Drayton Streets had been purchased, and construction was ready to proceed. The following advertisement was posted in a local newspaper: "TO MASONS AND CARPENTERS: Proposals will be received by the undersigned until Monday, the 24th inst. [April 24] for the workmanship of a BANKING HOUSE, intended to be erected in this city. The building to be got under cover by the lst of July, and to be completed by the 1st Dec., next....Plans and drawings may be seen anytime during the hours of business by applying to James Hunter, Cashier."[9]

DESIGNING A BANK

In the early nineteenth century, a bank was a building type relatively new in the history of world architecture. While the practice of banking (receiving, securing, and lending money) has ancient roots, the construction of buildings specifically dedicated to the commerce of managing money dates to the late seventeenth and early eighteenth centuries. In 1694 the British Parliament established the Bank of England with the aim to manage the national debt in times of war. By 1732 buildings were being raised in London for the functioning of this bank, with broader responsibilities for national economic security and development. In 1788 this complex of structures came under the supervision of John Soane, who became professor of architecture at the Royal Academy in 1806.

While the Bank of the United States was attended by controversy from its establishment in 1791 to its close in 1836, this institution left in its wake a powerful expression of a specific architectural style as an emblem for the enterprise of banking. The first building for the Bank of the U.S. was constructed in 1795–1797 in Philadelphia, designed by a gentleman architect in the Georgian style then fashionable. When the second charter was issued in 1816, a new home for the bank was needed. By this time, the architectural

---

Collection, Savannah, GA; Anderson, "Second Bank of the United States, Savannah Branch," *Georgia Numismatic Association Journal*, Autumn 2006:*3*, 6.

[9] "[U.S. Bank] To Masons and Carpenters," *Savannah Republican*, Apr. 13, 1820.

identity of the country had grown, first led by Jefferson whose admiration for the classical architecture of Rome shaped many early federal structures. In the early years of the nineteenth century, the Greek style was preferred, and the most admired of the ancient building types was the Greek temple form. This was a simple rectangular structure with a pitched roof and a porch at one or both of the gable ends. The porch (portico) was surmounted by a triangular pediment and supported by a row (or two) of monumental columns. This model became ubiquitous for both public and private buildings, and for banks this design was iconic.

For many architectural historians, the signal building of the Greek Revival in this country is the Bank of the U.S. constructed in Philadelphia in 1819–1824. In 1818 the directors of this bank issued these guidelines for the design competition: "The building will be faced with marble, and have a portico on each front, resting upon a basement or platform of such altitude as will combine convenience of ascent with due proportion and effect. In this edifice, the Directors are desirous of exhibiting a chaste imitation of Grecian Architecture, in its simplest and least expensive form."[10] By this time, there was consensus that the most perfect ancient Greek structure was the Parthenon on the Acropolis in Athens built in the fifth century B.C. For his winning entry to the competition, William Strickland provided a respectful but spare version of this model by eliminating the lateral colonnades and all of the sculptural decoration.

There is no report of a competition for the design of the Savannah branch of the Bank of United States. Richardson may have known of the potential for this project as early as 1817—he had been elected president of this branch bank in February of that year. In fact, this may have been one of a number of planned public buildings suggested to Jay to entice him to make the journey to Savannah.

JAY'S DESIGN FOR THE SAVANNAH BRANCH OF THE BANK OF THE UNITED STATES

What Jay provided for the branch bank in Savannah was a Grecian design in the manner of Soane, who had announced to his students two governing principles: the superiority of Greek architecture and the requirement never

---

[10] Whiffen and Koeper, 1:153.

to imitate the ancients, only learn from them and make something new. Soane held that Greek buildings exemplified perfection, leaving to later generations "only the humble task of imitating" these works. But he declared that imitation was "the road to mediocrity," concluding, "He that only copies or imitates will always be left behind."[11] So, quite unlike Strickland's composition that paid homage to the Parthenon, Jay's design for Savannah did not quote any specific ancient temple. The elements of Jay's building, such as the proportions of the structure and the size and character of the colonnaded portico, were derived from measures and ornament of ancient Greek examples; but this composition was new, ingenious, and "modern."

Two early views of Jay's bank survive. A drawing by Joshua Shaw was made in 1820 before the building was raised, so this image is certainly Jay's plan for the structure. The second view, made in 1825 by William Goodacre, documents the completed project. Unsurprisingly, Jay's conception for the building was more elegant, lighter in form and more refined in detail than the finished structure, which had heavier elements and little applied ornament.

In Shaw's sketch, Jay's design is a one-story, flat-roofed structure, with a substantial center hexastyle portico featuring six grand Doric columns. But, the frieze does not contain the conventional Doric elements of trigylphs (three grooves, reminders of the crossbeams of early wood construction) and metopes (the intervening spaces, sometimes filled with figural sculptures). Instead there are six laurel wreaths, each one positioned above a column. The laurel wreath was a popular motif in the Regency. Formed of branches of the bay laurel, it is an emblem of Apollo, who had among his several attributes "truth" and "light" (i.e., enlightenment), promising advertisements for a bank.

A bank strives to convey both accessibility and security, and Jay's design manages to achieve both of these aspects. A welcome to the building is expressed by the colonnade of the portico, but the structure is rendered secure by the lack of apparent openings. The entry is held in the shadow of the colonnaded porch, and the two flanking wings contain lovely round-headed wall niches but no windows. Jay had a particular notion about the use of windows in business establishments. In his proposal to rebuild Savannah's commercial district following the great fire of 1820, he said this about windows, "[A] circumstance of considerable importance is, to avoid so many openings [win-

[11] Soane, Lecture I:37; Lecture XI:249.

dows], they are neither useful nor ornamental, in buildings devoted to commerce they are unnecessary, and in buildings for civil purposes they had better be avoided. In the finest specimen of architecture you cannot find them, they distract the eye, and destroy that repose which is so essential in architecture."[12]

There are a number of refinements in this original design. The cornice is formed of two end blocks, each one relieved in real and perceived weight by an incised rectangle. The profiles of the cornice moldings are complex and sculptural. The columns appear lithe and elastic, more narrow at the top than at the bottom and swelling slightly just below the midsection, evoking the ancient method of entasis. But these and other elements of Jay's proposal did not survive in the completed building, likely victims of cost that great enemy of elegance.

Goodacre's view of the building drawn in 1825 represents the finished structure. The general configuration of the original design was sustained. The roof appears to be fashionably flat. The central portico with six Doric columns is flanked by broad bays, each one having a central round-headed motif. However, in the completed building, certain refined elements of design and ornament are stripped away. The cornice of the portico is greater in size and appears heavier—the incised rectangle is now in the center element, rather than at the ends, making the end blocks appear to be larger and weightier. The frieze is empty—the delicate wreaths are nowhere to be seen. The columns now appear heavy and rigid. Openings (windows and doors) are readily apparent inside the colonnade, and those lovely niches of the end wings have been pierced by windows. It is still a fine composition, but perhaps not quite what Jay had hoped for.

Jay's bank did not survive, but the design endures in the drawings by Shaw and Goodacre, English artists who took up the task of documenting examples of the early progress of American architecture. Both images were engraved and used as illustrations in popular publications. Shaw's depiction of this bank appeared in two travel guides to commercial districts in the United States, and Goodacre's view was included in a popular survey of American cultural, political, and natural histories.[13] By these means, this structure was signaled as an emblem of the city of Savannah, the state of Georgia, and the American South.

---

[12] W. Jay, arch., "Savannah, January 21st, 1820," Jan. 22, 1820.

[13] Shaw, 115; Kayser, fig. facing 34; Hinton, fig. facing 2:554.

REGRETTABLE CONCLUSIONS

Jay's building for the Savannah Branch of the Bank of the United States was open for business in late April 1821. In little more than a year, the architect was headed back to England where he would weigh the decision to return to Savannah. By late 1822, he had determined to remain in England to seek his fortune in the newly fashionable spa town of Cheltenham not far from the family home in Bath. As Jay contemplated his prospects for continuing work in this country, he surely took into account the depressed economy in the U.S., which in an awful irony was caused in some measure by the Bank of the United States.

By 1819 a crisis arose that is now remembered as the Panic of 1819, often signaled as the first grave economic collapse in this country. There have been many explanations for this calamity. Some propose that it was simply the first event in what would come to be understood as the "boom and bust" cycle of modern market economies. But an accusing finger is often pointed at the policies of the Bank of the U.S. This federal institution attempted to quell speculation then occurring in land, commodities, and industries by establishing greater control over loads of debt and by regulating the issue of banknotes which too often were not supported by specie. As the Bank of the U.S. called in loans and required state banks to act accordingly, the banks and their borrowers crumbled in heaps. In Georgia in 1817, the operations of the Savannah branch had begun in some spirit of cordiality, but as the Panic ensued sentiment in Georgia turned against the federal bank.

In these fretful circumstances, there is some wonder that this bank designed by Jay got built at all. The project may have been in progress from as early as 1817, but the Panic of 1819 and the awful event of the great fire in 1820 interrupted the work. Another blow came when Richardson, concerned about the posture of the Bank of the U.S. in relation to local industry, resigned his position in early April 1821 to become president of the Planter's Bank just two months later.[14] Richardson was gone from the Savannah branch before the fine new building that he and Jay had envisioned was opened in late April.

By 1822 the Savannah Branch of the Bank of the United States was almost bereft of business, having quarreled with the state banks about how banknotes were to be received and valued. The unsettled banking climate and

---

[14] [R. Richardson at Planter's Bank], *Georgian*, July 27, 1822.

the specific turmoil in Savannah did not recover until 1824–1825.[15] Among those ruined in this economic tsunami were Richardson, William Scarbrough, and Archibald Stobo Bulloch. The wrecked economy and the loss of these three extraordinary patrons must have weighed heavily in Jay's decision not to return to Savannah.

In the early decades of the nineteenth century, portraits of Jay's bank were distributed in the images drawn by Shaw and Goodacre, yet this design did not come to play an important role in the history of American architecture. Architects in this country came to embrace a more austere Greek Revival style, particularly for bank buildings. Jay's Grecian design by way of the Regency, an ingenious and elegant composition, stood quite apart from the ubiquitous classical pedimented temples that would come to crowd the American landscape by the middle of the century.

Sadly, Jay's lovely Savannah bank went the way of most commercial buildings. First, his initial design was altered, perhaps to constrain costs. When the second charter for the Bank of the United States was terminated in 1836, the Savannah building was occupied by a parade of banking institutions. With each new tenant, there were changes to the structure, the most grievous of which was the addition of a second story in 1892. In the early twentieth century, what remained of Jay's bank was acquired by a real estate company, then destroyed in 1924 to be replaced by an entirely ordinary office building.

---

[15] C. Anderson, "Second Bank of the United States, Savannah Branch," *Georgia Numismatic Association Journal,* Autumn 2006:6.

CHAPTER 22

CITY HOTEL: THE CASE FOR JAY

One of the most remarkable building projects in Savannah during Jay's brief time in the city occurred in 1821–1822. This was the construction of the City Hotel, built on speculation prompted by a local entrepreneur, raised on Bay Street in the first block west of Bull Street, nearly in the shadow of the Exchange and within view of Savannah's very busy waterfront. It was a noisy statement of the prosperity and ambition of the city, a building designed primarily for business travelers who came to this place to arrange for the purchase, transport, and sale of goods. Now, instead of the unpredictable accommodations at taverns, inns, and boarding houses, here was a proper establishment with private rooms and first-class amenities.

This was one of the earliest purpose-built hotels to be constructed in the country, probably the first in the South. At its opening, the City Hotel was declared to have the most elegant rooms, the best bar, and the finest table in town. The place became legendary. In the forty-four years of its operation, this was the site of important meetings, magnificent banquets, and some infamous confrontations, prompting one historian to title his review of the hotel "Ease and Elegance, Madeira and Murder."[1]

The client for this project was Eleazer Early, an associate of Richard Richardson in the enterprise of the Savannah branch of the Bank of the United States. The builder was Amos Scudder, a busy local contractor who has been linked with at least two Jay projects, the Savannah Theater and the Bulloch House. The designer of this building is unknown, although it has long been speculated that Jay was the architect of the City Hotel.

The arguments against Jay are easy to make. No written records or persistent oral traditions have linked him to this structure, and an attribution based on stylistic analysis is difficult to make. The building was refurbished and renovated several times in its long life as a hotel. By 1865 hotel operations had ceased, and the two lower floors were converted to stores and the upper floors to offices. In 1907 the building came to be occupied by a moving and

---

[1] Bell, "Ease and Elegance," 551–76.

warehouse company, which filled the place with stacks of furniture and mounds of debris. By the mid-twentieth century, just as Savannah was learning to care for its remarkable architectural inheritance, the former City Hotel was largely a shell, stripped of the ornament of its early days and bereft of many of the features that might signal the work of Jay.

However, there are good reasons to name Jay as the architect of this building. The date is right. Likely the planning began early in 1820, in the months following the fire, at least two years before Jay left the country. The work was prompted by Early, cashier of the Savannah branch of the Bank of the U.S., just as Jay was designing that building. Then, as the last good bit of evidence, there is the building itself. Though largely deprived of its original ornament, the bones of the structure survive, and certain elements of the plan are so unique that they may well be credited to Jay.

THE CLIENT

Eleazer Early was the second son (one of eight children) of Joel Early, who settled in northern Georgia in 1791 on lands still claimed by the Creek Indians. Here he prospered at farming, gained influence in politics, and saw to the classical education of his three sons.[2] His eldest son Peter practiced law, served in the U.S. House of Representatives in 1803–1807 and was elected governor of Georgia in 1813–15. Equally ambitious, Eleazer made himself busy about the business of making his fortune, often relying on the political connections of members of his family and those of his wife Jane Meriwether Patterson, whom he married in 1803.

In March 1817, he was named cashier of the Savannah branch of the Bank of the U.S. By 1820 he had been appointed postmaster for Savannah. And, in 1821 he gained from the state of South Carolina "the exclusive right and privilege of running a line of stages [coaches] for the conveyance of travellers, from Hamburgh [a new market town] directly down the north side of [the] Savannah river, to some point adjacent to the town of Savannah, in the State of Georgia…for the term of fourteen years."[3]

---

[2] Early, 293–95.

[3] McCord, 8:321–22.

THE BUILDING

Why might Early have conceived of a hotel for Savannah? Hotels were then rare in this country and always expensive undertakings. They were linked to the commerce of a region, because these establishments provided for the meeting of planters and manufacturers with merchants who arranged for the transport and distribution of products. Early was eager for success, and in this building he planned to accommodate his own professional commitments: the Savannah post office; a terminus for the coach route to Hamburgh, South Carolina; and temporary quarters for the Savannah branch of the Bank of the U.S.

Early chose a site on Bay Street not far from the Exchange, where much of the business of the city was conducted, and close to the busy waterfront. A building may have existed at this location, which Early might have planned to convert to a hotel—in mid-1819 some sort of construction was underway here.[4] Then, in January 1820 this region was swept by the great fire. That catastrophe may have been the occasion for clearing the site and securing a plan for a new structure. The project would have been a challenge for any designer, including someone as well trained as Jay. In this era, the purpose-built hotel was still a novelty in this country and abroad.

The building was open for some operations in January 1821. For the evidence of what it looked like, we have only the much-altered surviving structure and an image seen in the topographic view of the city painted in 1837 by Cerveau.[5] Cerveau portrayed the hotel as a block shape, four-stories in elevation at the front and seven bays across (marked by the openings of windows and doors). The building was surmounted by an attic under a well-pitched roof, and the gable ends (at the sides of the structure) each carried two end chimneys.

It was a simple white facade, known to be brick painted with stucco, symmetrically composed. At the center of the ground level was an entrance, perhaps double doors, flanked by windows and smaller doors (probably leading to the ground floor offices of the post office and the temporary quarters for the Bank of the United States). The three first floor entries were posed under a colonnaded piazza (a covered gallery), likely of cast iron, with classical

[4] Lerski, 159.

[5] J. L. F.Cerveau, *View of Savannah*, det. City Hotel, 1837, watercolor, GHS.

columns. The piazza extended over all seven bays and was surmounted by a balcony. Resting on the tops of the three center windows of the third level was a rectangular sign bearing the name "City Hotel."

In Cerveau's view, the building was quite simple, but it was handsome in its proportions. Taller by one story than the adjacent buildings, the City Hotel appeared large and important by the regularity of its features, by its white coat of stucco, and by the number of openings (windows and doors) and their massing. The windows at the fourth level were diminished in height as compared to those below, making the building appear to be more compact. The south elevation fronting the lane (the service road at the rear of the building) was not pictured by Cerveau, but its appearance can be deduced from what remains. Here the building was two and a half stories, also symmetrically composed. There were fanlights above the single central entry and above a central second-story window.

Because so many changes were made to the building in later years, it is difficult to reconstruct its interior plan and its ornament. But enough survives to tell us that the building was based on a central hall plan. Near the entry, a large stairway, contained within a circular masonry cell, led to the upper stories. Since it is likely that ground floor offices housed the post office and the temporary quarters for the bank, this great stairway probably gave access to hotel operations on the upper floors, with the reception area at the first landing. In this scheme, the dining hall, bar, and other common areas would have been arranged at the second level, with guest quarters above. The attic may have contained rooms for servants, and the basement was probably the location of the kitchen, the larder, and the laundry.[6]

THE PROPRIETORS

At the beginning of 1821, Early contracted a five-year lease with Orran Oates Byrd of Charleston to operate a hotel at these premises. Byrd was an experienced innkeeper who had directed the Planter's Hotel on Meeting Street in Charleston. A large and popular establishment, this was an "inn" made from a preexisting structure, resulting in a jumble of public and private rooms to accommodate travelers. Byrd was also the proprietor of the Planter's

[6] In 1985 Herbert Brito made a series of drawings for a reconstruction of the old City Hotel (Bell, 575).

Hotel on Sullivan's Island near Charleston.[7]

On January 30, 1821, Byrd announced the opening of Savannah's City Hotel in a local newspaper. He proclaimed that the establishment offered guests "every requisite for their comfort and convenience," including a post office on the premises, only a quick walk from the Exchange, with the provision of liquors "of the finest quality, with RELISHES, CIGARS *etc.*" By mid-May 1822, the hotel was in full operation, according to this notice: "Travellers and constant boarders will be well-attended to...and the eating establishment will at all times be furnished with the very best viands [foods] the market can afford. The bedding is of the first order and attentive servants are provided to procure every comfort that can be had for those who may call for them."[8]

For residents of Savannah, the hotel was, along with Jay's bank, welcome evidence of recovery from the fire of January 1820. A newspaper review in March 1821 called the City Hotel "magnificent and spacious." Promised were excellent accommodations and fine food and drink.[9] This soon became the preferred residence for men and women of means who came to Savannah for business or pleasure, and it was the meeting place of choice for the local "swells" or members of the fashionable set. Success for this enterprise must have seemed assured.

Regrettably, Early and Byrd were soon disappointed by their investments. The construction and fitting up had taken place in a treacherous financial environment. Both men suffered rounds of legal action against their debts. By 1824 Byrd was gone, forced to give up his shares in the hotel; by 1831 Early had abandoned Georgia. For the next several years, the enterprise endured several rounds of new management and refurbishment, including very substantial exterior and interior restorations in 1830–1835.[10] Finally, in 1865, hotel operations ceased, and the building was let for other purposes.

THE SEARCH FOR JAY IN THE SHADOWS OF THE OLD CITY HOTEL

A problem in attributing this building to Jay is that it survives in such a poor state. After it closed in 1865, the space was chopped into shops and

[7] Lerski, 159; Miles, 92.

[8] [City Hotel], *Georgian,* Jan. 30, 1821; "City Hotel," *Georgian*, May 13, 1822.

[9] "Amidst all the shipwrecked hopes...," *Georgian*, Mar. 30, 1821.

[10] Lerski, 165–67.

offices, leaving little evidence of the original plan and ornament. By 1907 the building housed a storage and transfer company. In 1948 a newspaper reporter, curious about the history of this building, visited this establishment. He found the structure to be in a miserable condition and filled with debris. However, there were the remains of a handsome central stairway leading to a second floor landing. At the second and third floors were large rooms furnished with fine marble fireplace mantels, "silent evidence of the luxury the planters and merchants of a century ago could afford." Some elements recalled the work of Jay. A "great arch" in the main hall opened to other arches along a central passage, doors were curved and framed by "fluted wood," and the construction was sound, having brick walls "eighteen or more inches thick, with strong mortar."[11]

When James V. McDonough made his survey of this property in the late 1940s, he offered a tentative attribution of the design to Jay "because of the free use of curved walls…and the heavy arched door frame and unique stairway from the second to the third floor [a configuration requiring a "bridge" similar to that used at the Richardson House]." When Hanna H. Lerski saw the building in the late 1970s, the new occupant was an office supply store. She found a staircase with "the delicate wavelike motif [the Vitruvian scroll] on the outer side of the steps," very like the ornament at the Richardson House; "woodwork of very high quality," including sliding doors and curved doors, all having panels in the pattern favored by Jay; and "the ingenious capture of the staircase within curved walls." Still, she concluded, "The evidence for attributing the City Hotel to Jay is convincing but not quite decisive."[12]

Perhaps the most compelling case for Jay as the designer of this building was made by J. Everette Fauber Jr. In 1965, Fauber was commissioned by the Telfair Academy to make a study of the Richardson-Owens-Thomas House. He looked at the sorry remains of the City Hotel with the eye of an architect and a preservationist. He said,

> [T]he old City Hotel has certain earmarks of William Jay. The stair from the second to third floor…is, in a way, reminiscent of Jay's bridge in the Owens-Thomas House.… The doors from the hall into the rooms around the stairhall, set in concave and convex walls at the corners of the stairhall and the entire symmetrical treatment of the building in plan around the

---

[11] A. Gerecht, "City Hotel Dim Reminder of Old Days," *SMN*, Jan. 18, 1948.
[12] McDonough, 69; Lerski, 158, 165.

> rather large center hall, the fenestration and division of the outside walls, and the relation of solids to voids, etc. certainly reflect the hand of a sensitive designer such as Jay.

He concluded, "I think it is highly likely that William Jay had something to do with the design of the old City Hotel."[13]

A "GEM...CAST ASIDE"

The building still stands on Bay Street, a less proud occupant of the block than it once was. Worn down by the years, the structure has been humiliated by the loss of its gracious piazza and by the large display windows that have pierced the facade at street level. The building houses a popular eatery on the ground floor where they serve burgers and brew. Occasionally detectives of paranormal activity are admitted to the upper stories where members of the very large community of Savannah ghosts are said to appear now and again.

The City Hotel deserves to be remembered as, in Fauber's words, "highly likely" a design by Jay, offering more evidence of his virtuosity and of the role he played in shaping Savannah. But perhaps no one has recalled the significance of this structure with more sensitivity than did Judge Richard H. Clark, a native of Savannah. Clark was a respected jurist, a great student of local histories, and an inveterate teller of stories about his beloved state. His memory of the City Hotel reached back to the early 1830s. It was, he said, "a small brick structure...most patronized by the wealthy and refined," known for "hospitality, good cheer and conviviality." But he ended on this sad note: "This little gem of a hotel, like some conspicuous military officer, has been reduced to the ranks [demoted]...and cast aside for a more pretentious rival. Its epaulets and sword and sash have been removed.... It has been put to common uses, sadly in contrast with the high life which once made it the abode of the grand and lovely of the land."[14]

---

[13] K. Haeberle, "Detective Probes Museum," *Savannah Evening Press*, July 18, 1965; J. Fauber to Walter Hartrich [*sic*], Sept. 18, 1965, Walter C. Hartridge Collection, GHS.

[14] Clark, 79.

CHAPTER 23

JAY ELSEWHERE IN GEORGIA

Outside of Savannah in Georgia, there are records of only one house credited to Jay and only one public project proposed but not built. Given Jay's prominence in Savannah, his standing with certain important and influential patrons, and his desire for work, it seems likely that he sought commissions elsewhere in the state. But, Georgia was young, the last of the English colonies in what had become the United States. Founded in 1733, Georgia had not yet reached the century mark when Jay arrived. Fine architecture of the sort Jay proffered was possible only in the environment of abundant wealth and social ambition. When he arrived in late 1817, these conditions had been met in only three locations, all of them settlements prompted by Oglethorpe in the early years of the colony: Savannah, Darien, and Augusta.

A HOUSE BY JAY IN DARIEN, GEORGIA

Sixty miles south of Savannah, Darien had been settled in the mid-1730s by the brave and industrious Highland Scots from Inverness, who were recruited by Oglethorpe to defend the new colony from incursions by the Spaniards. By 1742 these soldiers had removed this threat and set about to realize the natural riches and strategic location of the region. The town was blessed at the beginning by the location at the mouth of the Altamaha River, just ten miles from the Atlantic Ocean. Nearby dense forests of yellow pine and cypress would make it a center of the timber trades (lumber and naval stores, the by-products of the pines such as turpentine, pitch, and rosin). Rice flourished in the river marshes, and in the uplands rich soil and ingenuity produced a variety of crops, including sea island cotton and sugar cane. A busy ocean port conveyed these products to markets in this country and abroad.

The founders of Darien were abolitionists, and they would be brought only reluctantly into the plantation age. But, after the ban on slavery was repealed in 1751, plantation culture took hold, and fortunes were made in this region by the labor-intensive cultivation of rice and later cotton. Then in 1863 the undefended town was burned to the ground by federal troops in an act of vengeance which satisfied some but left others haunted by remorse. Much was lost here, including a house said on very good authority to have been designed by Jay.

THE HOME OF DR. JAMES MCGILLIVRAY TROUP

According to Spencer Bidwell King Jr., in 1801 the town of Darien was composed of three stores and eight houses. But just as Jay was beginning work in Savannah, Darien was set for a boom. In 1818 this place was designated as the seat of McIntosh County and awarded a bank charter. As evidence of the recent prosperity of this place, King noted that the home of James McGillivray Troup "was built by the leading architect of the period, William Jay, who also did some of Savannah's finest homes."[1]

The claim for Jay's hand in this project appears in a family history. In the "Memoirs of Ophelia Troup Dent," written in 1902 by Mrs. George Dent for the benefit of her grandchildren, she reported, "In 1824 my father began building his beautiful tabby house, with the same architect, Jay, who had put up the old Habersham [Bulloch-Habersham] and Owens [Richardson-Owens-Thomas] houses in Savannah. I was the first child born in this house."[2] The date given is troublesome, because Jay left this country in 1822 and did not return. But the account is credible given the circumstances of this place and this patron.

At the time of Jay's arrival in Georgia in late 1817, Darien's port rivaled those of Savannah and Charleston, and a bank was being established that was for a time one of the most influential financial institutions in the state. The gentleman who was reported to have built a home designed by Jay was Dr. James McGillivray Troup. A respected physician and a founder of the new bank, he later served terms as mayor and state senator. Further, from the time of his marriage around 1813 to Camilla Brailsford, a woman of fine South Carolina stock and substantial means, he came into possession of vast lands. At the time of his death, his holdings were counted as over 7,000 acres, which he managed for the cultivation of rice in the tidal low lands and cotton in the high lands.[3]

How might Troup have come to know the work of Jay? James Troup was

---

[1] King, 7, 9.

[2] Dent, "Memoirs of Ophelia Troup Dent," app. 82.

[3] B. Sullivan, *Early Days*, 150–51; Vanstory, 81.

born in Savannah. His daughter reported that he studied medicine with Dr. Benjamin Rush in Philadelphia, the best known physician in the country. To begin his professional life, Troup returned to Savannah, probably in 1811 or 1812, where his elder brother George Michael Troup was settled as a lawyer and a man of considerable influence. George served as a member of the U.S. House of Representatives (1807–1815), a U.S. senator (1816–1818 and 1829–1833), and governor of Georgia (1823–1827). A pugnacious fellow, Governor Troup saw to the removal of the Creek Indians from state lands without tribal or federal authority. He is said to have responded to his brother's desire to take a position in Savannah's hospital that "he [George] did not hold office to enrich his family." James was advised to go to Darien, "then a promising town."[4]

As Darien and the good doctor prospered, James Troup, who surely knew the fine houses designed by Jay in Savannah, sought to have one for himself. The date when this house was built can be fixed between late 1824 and early 1827.[5] A likely prospect is that he secured a design from Jay before the architect left this country in mid-1822. Then, some few years later, Troup had this house constructed in Darien by a local builder using the familiar regional material of tabby (a concrete of sand, oyster shells, lime from burned shells, and water).

No certain trace of Troup's house in Darien remains—it was a casualty of the raid on the town by federal troops in 1863. Of the appearance of the structure, we have only the persistent legend that it was remarkable. In an account of old Darien published in 1956, Burnette Vanstory reported that two of Darien's houses "were considered showplaces…[one of which was] the beautiful Troup house upon the promontory known as Cathead, a serene tree-shaded point overlooking the river and marshes on the west side of Darien." The precise location of this house has been a matter of some dispute. Buddy Sullivan believes that the house sat "overlooking Cathead Creek on the first bend, north of its merger with the Darien River."[6]

Of the appearance of the house, we have only hints offered by Troup's

[4] Dent, app. 81.

[5] Ibid., app. 82. Dent said that she was the first child to be born in this house, in Jan. 1827. Her brother Daniel Heyward Brailsford Troup was born elsewhere in Oct. 1824.

[6] Vanstory, 80; B. Sullivan, email to SLU, July 5, 2012.

daughter Ophelia. Writing in 1902, she reported that her father's house was designed by the architect of the Bulloch-Habersham and Richardson-Owens-Thomas Houses, then both still standing in Savannah and admired as examples of tasteful design. Both of these houses took the form of a block of three stories, the first below grade to accommodate kitchen and service areas, with reception and dining rooms at the main level and bedrooms above. Both featured a portico of classical design, a central hall plan with a prominent stairway near the entry, and two rear curved bays. Likely Troup's house included those elements.

"A TABBY HOUSE"

Tabby construction would have posed challenges for a Jay design, and this was, as Troup's daughter said, "a tabby house." Tabby was a ready product in this area, made of materials at hand. It was durable in this setting where wood was likely to rot and where structures could be buffeted by high winds and sometimes assailed by hurricanes. And it was a tested product with a vigorous supporter in the person of a fellow of enormous influence in the region.

Thomas Spalding was a direct descendant of the Scottish founder of Darien. He would come to be recognized as "the leading citizen of McIntosh County," a founder of the bank, committed to development in the region. Troup's daughter reported that Spalding and her father were cousins and that "friendship quite eclipsed the cousinship." One of Spalding's passions was tabby, and he was the first to make a careful study of the material and the means by which it was employed.[7]

Spalding's procedure of "tabby casting" is described by Sullivan:

> [O]ne-foot boards [were] spread apart and fastened with wooden pins at the top and bottom, the lower pins resting upon the previously cast portion of tabby wall. The mixture of sand, water, lime and oyster shell was mixed in equal proportions [forming a loose compound] and poured between the wood mold boards, which extended around the entire outline of the walls of the structure. Upon the pouring of a layer of tabby the level of the wall rose about a foot higher.

Walls were two to three feet thick, and the building was finished with stucco to hide the marks of the wooden pins that appeared at each level of the

---

[7] Dent, app. 81; B. Sullivan, *"Old Tabby,"* 7.

casting. Counting the process of forming the molds, pouring the mixture, and allowing it to set before proceeding to the next level, Sullivan estimates that the construction of a large house took two to three years.[8]

The block form of Jay's Savannah houses would seem to adapt readily to Spalding's method. But the elegance of Jay's work is in the details, in animating the block with string courses, moldings, setback corners, and window reveals. Those sculptural elements would have been difficult, perhaps impossible, to render in the process defined by Spalding. A good guess is that the exterior of the Troup House was formed of plain surfaces with some applied ornament.

Troup's daughter reported that one aspect of the design was troublesome. The Darien house had "a flat roof." By the mid-1820s, a flat roof was still fashionable, but this form is problematic in terms of wear. In any climate where rain is expected, a flat roof does not drain, and tabby (particularly Spalding's very loose mixture) was likely to absorb moisture. Jay's houses had roofs of shallow pitch hidden behind parapets to appear flat. The roof of the Troup house was likely a flat surface, a form Spalding recommended to give less resistance in the high winds of this coastal region. But, as Sullivan observes, the flaw was that "without an application of tar each year the roof was subject to leaks." And apparently it was this defect, among other circumstances, that drove the Troup family from this home in the 1840s. Troup died in 1849, but the family left the home in Darien before that year, moving to a country home to better manage the plantation crops.[9]

THE LOSS OF THE HOUSE: "A WHOLE TOWN ON FIRE"

The house of Dr. Troup said to have been designed by Jay was lost in June 1863 when the town of Darien was burned to the ground by two regiments of federal troops formed of black soldiers and led by white officers. The 54th Massachusetts, commanded by Robert Gould Shaw, the son of prominent Boston abolitionists, was a well-trained and storied force later commemorated in sculpture, poetry, music, and film.[10] The regiment's first foray was

[8] B. Sullivan, *"Old Tabby,"* 16.

[9] Dent, app. 83–84; B. Sullivan, *"Old Tabby,"* 15.

[10] Sculptures include the Robert Gould Shaw Memorial (1897) on Boston Common designed by Augustus Saint-Gaudens and a bust of Shaw (1864) by Edmonia Lewis. Shaw and his regiment were commemorated in verse by Robert Lowell, Paul

the raid on Darien. But, in this affair Shaw was subordinate to Colonel James Montgomery, who commanded the 2nd South Carolina, formed just a few months earlier than Shaw's force. Montgomery's battle style had been forged in the 1850s in "Bleeding Kansas." His plan, which Shaw opposed, was to loot thc town and leave nothing but ashes.[11] According to an eyewitness, one of Shaw's officers, "[W]hen we reached Darien...[n]ot a soul was to be seen.... It was a beautiful town, and never did it look so both grand and beautiful as in its destruction. As soon as a house was ransacked, the match was applied...[and] the whole town was in one sheet of flame. It was a magnificent spectacle, but still very few were found to gloat over it."[12]

A PROPOSAL FOR A THEATER IN AUGUSTA, GEORGIA

In April 1822, Jay visited Augusta, Georgia, to present a proposal for a theater in that town. Most of his Savannah clients had been brought down by a weak economy and the city's devastating fire in early 1820. Some of his Charleston clients seem to have bristled at the costs of employing the young English architect. Augusta was a promising location for Jay to make a new stand. It was an enterprising place with a history and reputation almost as long and large as Savannah. Jay had started with a theater in Savannah, and he must have calculated that such a project might work for him in Augusta.

The town was founded by Oglethorpe in 1736, only three years after the settlement of Savannah. Located at the navigable head of the Savannah River, 130 miles northwest of Savannah, it was adjacent to territories held by Indian tribes with whom Oglethorpe formed alliances and promoted trade. In the years after the Revolutionary War, Augusta vied with Savannah for political and economic importance. Both were, now and again, capitals of the state. Augusta served as the seat of government for Georgia in 1779–1781 and again in 1785–1795. In the 1790s, the town prospered, first as a tobacco market and later as a center for the trade of cotton. As sure signs of its importance, Augusta was visited, as Savannah was, by presidents Washington and Monroe in 1791 and 1819, and by the Marquis de Lafayette in 1824.

Laurence Dunbar, and Benjamin Griffith Brawley; in music by Charles Ives; in the motion picture *Glory* (1989), filmed in Savannah.

[11] Moore, "The Invasion of Georgia...A Rebel Account," 7:297.

[12] Moore, "The Invasion of Georgia...A National Account," 7:295.

Jay may have made his way to Augusta through contact with Joseph Vallence Bevan, the son of an Irishman who had settled in Savannah by 1804 and gained success as a planter and merchant. This father, also a Joseph, had close personal and business ties to Robert Bolton, the head of the Bolton cotton house, and Richard Richardson. At the death of the senior Bevan, Richardson administered the estate while the younger Bevan returned from studies abroad. The matters of settlement were contentious, and Joseph was obliged to remain in Savannah in 1819–1821.[13] In this period, he surely met Jay.

In 1821 Bevan purchased the *Augusta Chronicle and Georgia Gazette* and established himself as the editor. In late April and early May of the following year, three articles appeared in the newspaper describing Jay's proposal to build a theater in Augusta.[14] Bevan may have written these pieces, but more likely these are Jay's own reports of his plans. These published accounts are valuable in that their clarity and completeness give us further insight into a proposal he may have submitted for the New English Opera House in London and a better understanding of the elements of his design for the theater in Savannah.

On April 22, 1822, a long article began on a laudatory note:

> Mr. JAY, the celebrated Architect, is now in our town, on his way to Washington City [D.C.]; and we fondly hope that the inhabitants of this place will give him an opportunity of erecting in it, some monument of taste worthy of himself, and corresponding with the rising importance of Augusta. He built the Church in Moorsfield [Moorfields], the New English Opera, in the Strand, London, and the Wellington Rooms, Pleasant Square, Liverpool; but is better known to most of us, on account of those elegant structures he has reared in Savannah.[15]

For Augusta, Jay proposed a complex of a theater and two shops as rental properties. Drawings were available for viewing, and the building was described as follows:

> It [the theater] is of the Grecian order—the front will exhibit four Antae pilasters [appearing as side posts or pillars], supporting an entablature of the Corinthian order—in the centre will be three doors, leading to the vestibule, in which is the Box office…[Y]ou ascend a small flight of steps

---

[13] Coulter, *Joseph Vallence Bevan,* 30–33.

[14] Ibid., 49.

[15] "Mr. Jay, the celebrated architect…," Apr. 22, 1822 (hereafter cited in text).

> to the lobby landing, in front of the dress circle, and on the right to the staircase to the second tier—at the back of [the] second tier is a large and spacious saloon for refreshments, so far removed from the audience, that they will experience no inconvenience.

The plan for seating and access included these features:

> The first or dress circle, will be divided into nine boxes, the backs of which will be enclosed and made perfectly warm in the winter.—The pit will have no entrance through the boxes, but kept entirely distinct, preventing the confusion which frequently takes place in the lower tier.—One advantage will be derived from this design—the staircases and lobbies are distinct from the Theatre—the ingress and egress is easy, the vestibule having five entrances.

For the stage: "The plan of the Theatre is of the most approved and modern shape—the Proscenium of the stage is formed by four Corinthian columns, supporting an arch from which springs the dome of the Theatre—between the columns are the stage doors." And in the matter of ornament:

> The lower tier of boxes will be decorated with a series of designs, illustrative of Painting and Music, from the earliest ages of barbarism, to their present union on the stage. The boxes will be supported with small cast iron columns, gilded, and which will support arches in the upper tier—the other boxes will have characteristic ornaments. The decorations in the Theatre will be gold on white ground, contrasted with a rich crimson, which will be the color of the back of the boxes.

And, in closing: "[T]he ceiling will have a panelled [*sic*] dome, from which will be suspended a large chandilier [*sic*], to light the theatre, the plan now universally adopted in Europe. It has been the peculiar care of the artist to afford to each person a view of the stage, and a hearing of the actor—to combine utility with elegance: it is calculated to hold eight hundred dollars." The final note may have been in error, giving "eight hundred dollars" for "eight hundred persons"—the Savannah Theater accommodated an audience of one thousand. Or, this comment may have referred to estimated revenues for a full house.

Three days later, on April 25, Jay presented a report of costs for this project, careful to note that these "estimates" were "not the objects of speculation, but predicated on facts." He offered two options: one for a site on Broad Street to include "fire proof" stores and a theater, for a total of $37,300, and one for a site on Greene Street with two small wooden houses (properties for rent) and a theater, for a total of $30,200. For each of these proposals, he estimated the annual income to be $4,000 for the project on Broad and $3,000 for the project on Greene. He made no secret of his preference for the Broad Street lot because the site there would have "a more imposing effect on the view." A meeting was called for "citizens" on Saturday, April 27, "for the purpose of deciding upon the proper site, and making all other necessary arrangements."[16] There is no evidence that such a meeting took place.

On Monday, May 6, the following notice appeared:

> We understand, that Mr. Jay, the architect, from the nature of his engagements, will be obliged to leave this place for the north in a day or two. In the mean time [*sic*] the Drawings and Prospectus of the proposed New Theatre will be left at the Bookstore of Messrs. J. & H. Ely, for inspection; where persons who feel a disposition can have an opportunity of subscribing for the stock. Further—we are authorized to state, that Mr. Jay will return in the fall to carry the design if possible into effect; that any deficiency in the amount he will make up, and that bonds will be entered into, not only for the amount of expenditures, but the actual receipts of the income.[17]

Jay did not return to Augusta, and there is no further report of his proposal for this theater.

[16] [Public meeting to review plans for a theater], *Augusta Chronicle*, Apr. 25, 1822.

[17] "Mr. Jay…to leave this place for the north," *Augusta Chronicle*, May 6, 1822.

Telfair House porch.

Alexander Telfair.

Mary Telfair.

"And a Little Child Shall Lead Them,"
Parlor mantelpiece by John Frazee, ca. 1818.

Telfair Academy of Arts and Sciences,
View of the new museum in 1888.

Rendering for the stairway in the entry hall.

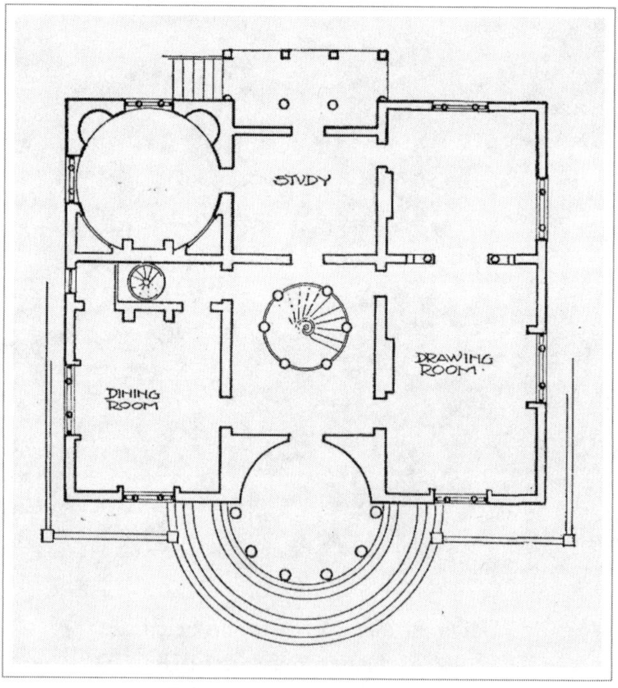

Plan of the main floor.

Facade.

Side view of the porch.

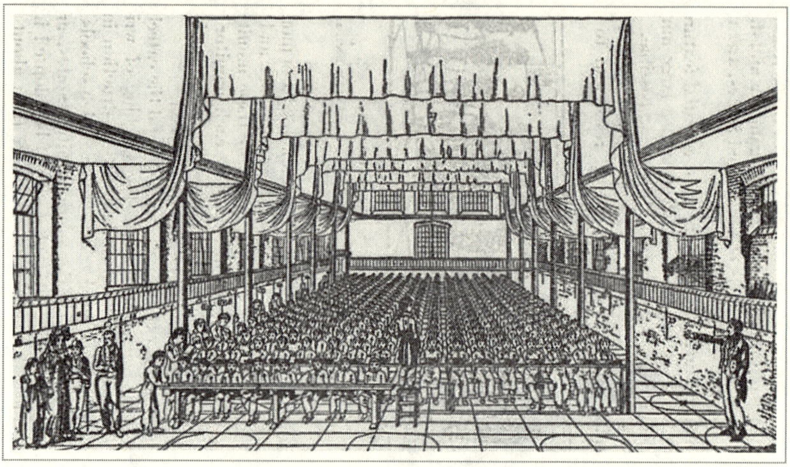

Plan for a Lancastrian School.

Facade.

Interior, ca. 1880.

Jay's design for the facade.

The design as constructed.

Jay's Sumterville courthouse, altered by Robert Mills.

Jay's stock designs for a courthouse (left) and a jail (right).

Colombia (later Columbia) Place.

Paragon Parade.

Facade of Duffield and Weller's Public Library.

A dodo.

Paul and Virginia by Saint-Pierre.

Entry to Central Market.

Independent Chapel.

Little Willy teaching another child to read.

Mrs. Harriet Newell.

"Owens-Thomas House Portico,"
Christopher A. D. Murphy Jr., etching.

Staffordshire gravy tureen,
J. & W. Ridgway, Hanley, England, ca. 1830.

PART FOUR

JAY IN CHARLESTON, SOUTH CAROLINA

CHAPTER 24

CHARLESTON

Jay began the year 1820 with this announcement in a Charleston, South Carolina, newspaper: "WILLIAM JAY, offers his services to the inhabitants of Charleston, and the State generally, in his profession as an ARCHITECT. Any commands left at his Office in Jones' Building, St. Michael's Alley, will meet with immediate attention. January 1."[1] Why did he establish this office, and why at this time?

Jay had accomplished two very full years of work in Savannah. He had received commissions for several elegant homes and at least four important public buildings, but he must have concluded that there were few remaining opportunities for him in Georgia. Perhaps he had worn out his welcome in that place. The evidence suggests that his Savannah projects were ambitious, exacting, and frequently costly. There was a limited audience for Jay's renderings of distinctive private residences. And, in the uncertain economic climate emerging by 1819, the city had initiated very few public projects.

On January 11, 1820, ten days after the opening of his Charleston office, a great fire swept through Savannah. That catastrophe should have assured work for Jay in the rebuilding of the ruined commercial district. Shortly after the fire, he had declared in a Savannah newspaper his eagerness to participate in the recovery of the city by raising new fireproof buildings, but there is no evidence that he gained any new commissions for public or private projects in Savannah. Of two later projects, a bank building had been planned before the fire, and the genesis of a hotel is unknown.

Given these Savannah circumstances and Jay's ambition, there is little wonder that he set up shop in a new location. The wonder is that he had not done so earlier. He surely knew that there were few trained architects in this country. But he may not have known how these professionals, usually from London or Paris, had struggled to find work. In the U.S., local jurisdictions

[1] W. Jay, arch., "Notice [Office opening]," *Charleston Courier*, Jan, 1, 1820. The Jones's Boarding House, managed by Jehu Jones as rooms for travelers and long-term residents, began life as a home built for William Burrows in 1772–1774.

seldom had revenues to support public buildings, and private clients were often reluctant to hire trained architects whose fees were greater than those of ordinary builders.

Jay did made a mark on Charleston. He is credited with at least three private residences, an art academy, a proposal for a group of public buildings in the city, and designs for a number of district courthouses and jails throughout South Carolina. But the circumstances of his service in Charleston were in stark contrast to what he had experienced in Savannah, and these matters help to explain why his time in South Carolina was so brief and why knowledge of his work there soon slipped from memory.

FINDING JAY IN THE HISTORY OF ARCHITECTURE IN CHARLESTON

Jay's term in Charleston was probably less than two years, and his labor there was quickly forgotten. For decades most architectural historians recorded only a vague recollection of the tenure of "an English architect" in South Carolina at the beginning of the nineteenth century.

An early hint of Jay in Charleston came in 1902 in the pages of *"The Georgian Period," Being Measured Drawings of Colonial Work,* a survey of the beginning of American architecture. For accounts of Charleston and Savannah, the author was Corinne Ruth Stocker Horton (Mrs. Thaddeus Horton). She had no background in architecture or architectural history, but she was a Southerner, a journalist, and an amateur photographer. And she had a discerning eye and an affinity for the formative style of the Greek Revival. In her report of Charleston houses, Horton did not name Jay (as she would do in a subsequent review of Savannah), but she credited the design of one grand residence, the Witte House (later McBee House at Ashley Hall School), to "an English architect, in 1810." In articles for popular magazines in 1903 and 1904, Horton drew attention in text and photographs to this building and the Weyman House (later the Ancrum House), two Charleston mansions now attributed to Jay.[2]

Just a few years later, *Architectural Record* profiled early American buildings in the South, featuring Charleston in 1906 and Savannah in 1907. Both articles were written by J. Robie Kennedy Jr., a native of Alabama and an

[2] Horton, "Charleston, Between Ashley and Cooper," 10:41; Horton, "Classic Houses of the South," 389, 392; Horton, "Georgian Houses of the Far South," 264–65.

architect working in Washington, D.C. In his report of Charleston, Kennedy did not mention Jay. But, like Horton, he admired the Greek Revival style, and he focused on the Witte House, which he described as "[p]erhaps the best of the Greek Revival houses in Charleston." In his later survey of Savannah, he named Jay, identifying the four signal houses as "forerunners of the classic revival which only a few years later was to deluge the South." And he made the observation that Jay had prompted in Savannah a "taste and refinement" in architecture which had prevailed for almost a century.[3]

In these early commentaries, both Horton and Kennedy placed Jay in Savannah. But, they did not locate him in Charleston, perhaps because there was no local lore remembering Jay in South Carolina.

In 1917 the first book on Charleston's domestic architecture appeared. The authors of *Dwelling Houses of Charleston, South Carolina* were Daniel Elliott Huger Smith and Alice Ravenel Huger Smith, father and daughter, descendants of a venerable Charleston family. There was no mention of Jay; in fact, there were few references to named architects. However, this book included a discussion of the one house now assigned with certainty to Jay, the William Mason Smith House.[4]

In 1927 Albert Simons and Samuel Lapham Jr., architects and natives of the city, published a survey of the early architecture of Charleston, a volume intended to be the first in a series documenting historic structures in the eastern United States. Charleston had been chosen for this project of the American Institute of Architects because of the city's large and remarkable inventory of surviving old buildings. The text included the names of architects and builders known to have worked in Charleston, but there was no reference to Jay, nor was he cited in a list of "Signatures and Identified Works" of early architects and builders. However, two of the houses now attributed to him were represented in photographs.[5]

It was not until 1945, with the publication of *Architects of Charleston* by Beatrice St. Julien Ravenel, that Jay got his due, a full chapter recording what was then known of his life and work. Of her book, Ravenel said, "Much has been written about the architecture of Charleston, South Carolina, but the

[3] J. R. Kennedy Jr., "Georgian Work in Charleston, South Carolina," 292–94, J. R. Kennedy Jr., "Georgian and Greek Revival Work in the Far South," 215, 218.

[4] A. R. Smith and D. E. Smith, 3.

[5] Simons and Lapham, 199, 208, 215–16.

architects who brought it about have remained largely neglected." By "architects," she meant the very wide range of individuals who had designed and raised buildings in the city: carpenters and masons, builders or contractors, gentlemen architects, and professional architects. She found that the greatest number of these "architects" were native Charlestonians, who were influenced by prevailing English styles: Georgian in the eighteenth century, the Adam style by 1800, followed by the Classic Revival and the Greek Revival.[6]

The two heroes of Ravenel's account were natives of the city. The first was Gabriel Manigault, "Charleston's best-known amateur architect." The second was Robert Mills, who had claimed for himself the title of "the first American architect," being by his account the first to be native-born and professionally trained. According to Ravenel, Mills had accomplished important projects in Charleston, but he was acclaimed for his work in the District of Columbia, which included the Old Post Office, the Patent Office, the Treasury Building, and the Washington Monument. She concluded, "His work in Washington won him a national reputation, and he is thought of, not as South Carolinian, or even as Southern, but as American."[7]

Ravenel confirmed Jay's presence in Charleston by citing the newspaper notice of the opening of his office here in January 1820. For her account of the young English architect, it appears that she relied on the discoveries of Savannah historian Thomas Gamble, published a dozen years before.[8] She perpetuated the myth that Jay was a rebellious son of a Bible-thumping preacher, saying, "Lively and witty in the midst of a strictly brought-up household, the child was doubtless happier away from home than in it (after childhood, he was there very little)." And she recited what was then known of Jay's experiences: the significance of Bath in the development of his style, his apprenticeship to an unnamed architect and surveyor in London, and his voyage to America prompted by the marriage of his elder sister to a member of a prominent Savannah family.[9]

Ravenel affirmed the "[v]ague but persistent" rumor that Jay had been active in Charleston, particularly in relation to the design of a small number of residences. She did this based on her own study of Jay's surviving work in

[6] Ravenel, 3, 8, 107–15.
[7] Ibid., 55, 135.
[8] Gamble, "Romance of Wm. Jay, Savannah Architect," May 8, 1932.
[9] Ravenel, 107–108.

Savannah, from which she formed her own impression of his style. She said, "Jay handled decoration fearlessly, and these houses, in Regency style, own a wealth of detail, striking staircases, curved rooms, porticoes, and balconies." As one example of her assessment of Jay's ingenuity, of the entry hall of the Richardson-Owens-Thomas House, she described as "superb" the use of "deliberately restrained pilasters...to set off the gilded Corinthian capitals of the columns."[10]

Later research added bits and pieces to the story of Jay in Charleston, but most of this record is still based on Ravenel's observations. Only one surviving Charleston residence, the William Mason Smith House, can be attributed to Jay with certainty given the evidence of a signed receipt for construction material. A summer house on Sullivan's Island (now lost), advertised for sale by Jay, may or may not have been his design. One public building, an art academy known to be by Jay, did not survive. The Joseph Turpin Weyman House (the Ancrum House) has been attributed to the young English architect based on its resemblance to the William Mason Smith House, but it no longer exists. Claims are made for Jay as the designer of McBee House at Ashley Hall School (variously known as the Patrick Duncan, James Nicholson, James Pringle, George Trenholm, or Charles Witte House), and the Aiken-Rhett House. These are based on dating, stylistic analysis, and the very good authority of Ravenel, who knew the history and character of Charleston residences as no one else did.

CHARLESTON AS A PLACE OF OPPORTUNITY FOR JAY

During his time in Savannah, Jay had surely gained an impression of Charleston. Founded in 1670, the colony of Carolina was sixty-three years older than Georgia. It had been established as a proprietary settlement to realize profits for friends of Charles II. By 1680 Charles Towne (later Charleston) had been moved to its present peninsular location where the Ashley and Cooper Rivers join, overlooking a bay opening to the Atlantic Ocean, a location chosen for defense and to prompt the development of a port. The city flourished, sustaining strong ties to England and fostering rich traditions of culture and the arts, circumstances that must have pleased Jay.

In 1820 Charleston counted nearly 25,000 souls, more than half of

---

[10] Ibid., 108, 115.

whom were black. It was the largest and most prosperous city in the South, and the fourth-largest city in the nation (after Philadelphia, New York, and Boston). By contrast, the population of Savannah in 1820 was approximately 7,500, more than half of whom were black. It was counted as the eighteenth-largest urban area in the U.S. At the time of Jay's arrival, both cities had experienced a rush of success and gained an appetite for building.

Charleston's industry was well known. In 1826 Robert Mills reviewed the condition of the city in his *Statistics of South Carolina*. He observed,

> The growth of this city was very tardy in the beginning, and previous to the revolution. Since that eventful period its progress has been proportionably rapid, especially between the years 1800 and 1820. The commercial prosperity which it then experienced produced a spirit of enterprise among the citizens that resulted in favor of public and private improvements; hence the erection of a number of large private houses, stores, &c.[11]

Given these circumstances, there was much in Charleston to attract an ambitious young English architect not long removed from his experiences in London.

In some ways, Charleston and Savannah were alike. Both cities had active ports trading in the products of plantation agriculture, both with close ties to England. In both locations, men and women of means enjoyed the benefits of frequent travel abroad, making them aware of the latest in European fashion and eager to acquire goods of English manufacture. However, there were some rather serious differences between Charleston and Savannah for which Jay may not have been prepared.

THE CHALLENGES FOR JAY IN CHARLESTON

Had Jay analyzed the situation with care, he might have realized that Charleston would not be easy for him to conquer. In its longer history, the temperament of its people, and the lay of the land, it was very different from what he had found in Savannah. In Charleston, Jay would never have the success that he had achieved in Savannah.

In 1786 the capital of South Carolina was moved from Charleston to Columbia, 115 miles northwest and well inland. But Charleston retained its

---

[11] Mills, 391.

position as the most populous and prosperous city in the state. It was the center of political influence, and it had fostered a culture that embraced the arts. And, while Charleston may have seemed to occupy a similar position to that of Savannah in Georgia—also a founding city, also deprived of governmental functions when the capital of the state moved to Milledgeville in 1804—the character of Charleston was quite different from that of Savannah.

According to Maurie D. McInnis, "Both in spirit and reality, Charleston's society was rigidly hierarchical." An aristocracy grew from the "landed wealth" of the planters, who enjoyed high social status. Further, "Membership in the aristocracy was available only through birth or family association; members of the aristocracy were not self-made."[12] By contrast, Savannah's beginning had been non-aristocratic by design. The Georgia colony had been established to give opportunities to able and ambitious members of the working class, and that unique "spirit and reality" prevailed. Counted among Jay's most important patrons in Savannah were successful self-made men who became his fierce supporters.

From the record of his several activities in South Carolina, Jay came prepared to make a success in this new place. He worked hard to gain work here. By mid-December 1820, he had closed his office in the Jones's Building, moved to a new location on Tradd Street, and was occupied with projects through 1821.[13] But, by April 1822 he was in Augusta, Georgia, seeking a commission for a theater. Some weeks later, he was gone, back to England, where he soon resolved not to return to any part of the United States of America.

A hint survives of the tone and temper of Jay's tenure in Charleston. One of his colleagues here was John S. Cogdell, a prominent lawyer in the city and a gifted amateur painter and sculptor. He served with Jay on the board of directors of the South Carolina Academy of Fine Arts, for which Jay had designed a building. It was a fine structure by all accounts, but the cost was wildly over budget. In September 1821, Cogdell wrote to another member of this board, proclaiming his unhappiness with the architect "Mr. J.," saying, "I begin to think we sh[oul]d have done better with an architect less *brilliant*."[14]

---

[12] McInnis, 24.

[13] "Mr. Morse [Location of his painting studio]," *Charleston Courier,* Dec. 19, 1820, W. Jay, arch., attrib., "A Marine Villa," *Charleston Courier,* Jan. 3–5, 1821.

[14] McInnis, 137.

There were several buildings in Savannah that provided ample evidence of Jay's skills and his taste, and his clients there might readily have used the word "brilliant" to describe his work. But, Charleston, in its longer history and established conventions, posed challenges for Jay for which his eagerness and ingenuity provided no remedy. He was, it seems, quite at odds with this place and unable to gain the success he had hoped for.

CHAPTER 25

JAY'S CHARLESTON HOUSES

In Savannah, Jay had come upon a uniquely lovely and functional town plan. A series of wards composed of regular lots fronting a central square resulted in well-defined neighborhoods, each one having a congenial scale and a pleasant open space at the center. Three of Jay's great houses occupied prominent places on these squares, sites that allowed for the full expression of his elegant style. But Charleston was different. Both the town plan and tradition imposed certain constraints on house types and styles.

CHARLESTON'S TOWN PLAN

In 1680 Charles Towne (later Charleston) was moved to its present location on a peninsula between two rivers and near the ocean. Here the land was limited in mass, but the terrain was conveniently flat although much of it was low and subject to frequent flooding. Settlement of this area was directed by a plan, the Grand Modell, prompted by Anthony Ashley Cooper, 1st Earl of Shaftesbury, one of the eight lords proprietors." While it was not as remarkable as the plan that would shape Savannah fifty-three years later, the scheme for Charleston had advantages. It was a plan, a clear alternative to random occupation. An irregular grid of eight blocks fronted the Cooper River at the east, providing public use of the waterfront and determining the shape, size, and arrangement of lots. There were two prominent avenues running north-south, King and Meeting Streets, and these were crossed by Broad Street running east-west. A central square at the crossing of Broad and Meeting Streets was designated for important civic and religious buildings.

The grand residences of Charleston were the town homes of plantation owners, and early development here resembled that of Georgian towns in England. Houses were joined structures, often with relatively little street frontage on deep lots. By the time Jay arrived in 1820, few attached townhouses remained. Some lots had increased in size, but generally they were narrow and deep with side and rear yards. Most houses, with their gardens and outbuildings, were concealed behind high walls for privacy and security.

This was the Charleston seen by William Dean Howells when he visited in 1915. Howells was quick to declare that this was "not quite like any other city." He observed that the very great number of graceful homes and gardens were private places, evidence of "a compact history" in which members of the city's fine old families, constituting a "vast cousinship," "meet one another in constant ease and intimacy."[1]

CHARLESTON'S HOUSE TYPES

As the early joined houses were lost to the treacheries of fires, storms, redevelopment, or neglect, these buildings were replaced by two types of structures. Now associated uniquely with Charleston, the "single house" and the "double house" differed in their orientation to a site and in the configuration of the ground plan, but they were similar in the adaptations to the terrain and to the semi-tropical weather. These two plans shared several elements:

A raised basement protected the quarters above (two or more stories) from flooding and from the grime and noise of the city streets. This first or ground level was sometimes posed as a cellar, accommodating storage or service areas. In some structures, the first level contained living quarters, such as a sitting room and a breakfast room, and the first springing of a central staircase. At the second or main level ("first floor") were an entry with a reception hall and public rooms, including a parlor, where formal dining could be accommodated, and drawing or "withdrawing" rooms. At the third level ("second floor") were private rooms and bed chambers. Though sited differently on their lots, the single house and the double house were both accompanied by outbuildings, such as a detached kitchen with slave quarters above and a carriage house with stables. The properties included ornamental and kitchen gardens and a work yard.

Both plans incorporated long porches (verandas), often at multiple levels. In Charleston, these were and still are called "piazzas," from the British use of the term for covered arcades at the sides of public squares. A single house carried these porches on a side of the building. At a double house, the porches generally graced the front of the structure. In both plans, the piazzas faced ornamental gardens and were located at the south or west to shade adjacent living quarters and to catch prevailing winds, remedies for the hot and sultry

[1] W. D. Howells, "In Charleston," 747, 756.

climate. In some seasons of the year, these porches were quite literally outside rooms, extensions of the space of the residence.[2]

The single house took its name from the width of a single room. From the street, it suggested the form of a row house, but it was actually a conventional central-hall plan turned at ninety degrees on the lot. It appeared as a free-standing rectangular structure with an end fronting the street. The facade sat at the side, adorned with piazzas, overlooking a side garden. The upper floors were composed of galleries of single rooms, with windows at both sides allowing for cross ventilation. The piazzas or long porches were positioned to shade the rooms from a hard sun and to catch prevailing breezes.

In this configuration, the element of the house facing the street was not a conventional facade. The formal entry, piazzas, and side garden were screened by a high wall where a gate (often of wrought or cast iron) offered only a glimpse into the property. To enter the house, one passed through this gate then proceeded to a front door, usually in the center of the piazza of the first floor (the level above the raised basement). On the interior, there was a central stair hall with a room at each side of this hall. Public rooms, such as the drawing and dining rooms, were on the first floor, and private rooms or bed chambers were on the second floor.

The double house was a more traditional form, a plan that would have been familiar to Jay. Taking its name from a structure two rooms deep, this was a detached house with a facade, usually incorporating piazzas, fronting the street. Also a central-hall plan, the public rooms were on the second level, with private chambers above. By the time Jay arrived in 1820, the city was expanding into the northern part of the peninsula, a region known as Charleston Neck. Here there were large lots, allowing houses to be set well back from the streets, gaining privacy from distance and plantings rather than high walls. These properties suggested plantation estates, and here versions of the double house occasionally evoked the suburban villas of Regency London.

---

[2] Horton credited the "enormous two and three story covered verandas" to wealthy immigrants from the West Indies, calling these "San Domingo houses." But both Ravenel and Nichols concluded that the development of these piazzas was unique to Charleston (Horton, "Charleston, Between Ashley and Cooper," 10:29–30; Ravenel, 4; Nichols, 48).

CHARLESTON HOUSES ATTRIBUTED TO JAY

The two house types, the single house and the double house, were well established by the time Jay appeared on the scene. As a consequence, he confronted in Charleston certain fixed notions about the forms and functions of residences. Obviously, these established models imposed constraints on architects working in this city, and further there was a Charleston habit of not engaging architects for the design of homes. According to Gene Waddell, "About 99 percent of Charleston's houses do not have known architects. Charlestonians seem to have been quite content to use plans that had been adopted for local conditions by trial and error and that had proven their worth."[3] In Savannah, by contrast, Jay had the benefits of the regular geometry of the ward plan, the ample size of the joined trustee lots, the prominence of a site facing a small city park, and patrons not bound by local conventions.

Then, there was the serious matter of style. Though its origins reach into the seventeenth century, Charleston is often called a Georgian town because of the very large inventory of eighteenth-century residences. These old houses survived due to pride of place and pride of family. Rather than building new residences, there was a convention of adapting family homes for each new generation by constructing additions to the structures and changing patterns of exterior and interior ornament. In these circumstances, Jay faced two challenges: First, old families rarely commissioned new houses; and second, an affection for the Georgian style (and its successor, the Adam style) offered limited opportunities to an English architect working in the very modern manner of the Regency. Against these odds, five houses in Charleston, three of which survive, have been attributed to Jay.

William Mason Smith House, 26 Meeting Street, 1820–1821. According to Beatrice St. Julien Ravenel writing in 1945, "Vague but persistent tradition says that the dwelling, now 26 Meeting Street, was built by 'an English architect,' perhaps Jay."[4] Now there is certain evidence of Jay's work at this house. In the early 1990s at Middleton Place, a plantation about fifteen miles northwest of Charleston, a remarkable document was found. In the papers of Wil-

[3] G. Waddell, intro. to A. R. Smith and D. E. Smith, xxxiii.
[4] Ravenel, 115.

liam Mason Smith was a receipt for the cost of "14 thousand best slates selected and delivered in good order on the premises in Meeting Street," dated December 2, 1820, signed by Jay.[5]

Even without this evidence, several structural and stylistic features argue for attribution to a trained and clever architect familiar with modern methods and materials, and to an artist thoroughly conversant with the Grecian style of Regency London. This was a Charleston single house with several unique features. The three-story brick building was stuccoed in the modern fashion, with the modern profile of a flat roof with a low parapet. At the street, the center two bays of the four-bay front pressed forward and included a front door. Windows, resembling those at the Scarbrough House in Savannah, were round-headed, set in reveals, each with a panel carved in the Greek key pattern below the sill.[6] The interior featured high ceilings, arched windows and doors, and ornament of the sort familiar in Jay's Savannah houses. And, the masonry construction was of such high quality that the core of the house survived the disastrous earthquake of 1886, an event that destroyed many of the buildings in town.[7]

Jay's patron here was William Mason Smith, a fellow of considerable status and means in the community. He was the son of the Reverend Robert Smith, the first Protestant Episcopal bishop of South Carolina and the first principal (president) of Charleston College (later the College of Charleston). William was a wealthy planter, owner of a large plantation called Smithfield some fifty miles west of Charleston. Both that residence and this one on Meeting Street were remembered as centers of culture.[8]

Smith's Charleston home was to be built at a prominent location in the old town, on a site suited for a single house, a design much admired for its comfort and privacy. No doubt this was the plan Smith requested for his residence. But, as Ravenel observed, an architect might find the imposition of this plan to be unwelcome:

> As a practical solution of the problem of keeping cool, before the invention

[5] "The Premises in Meeting Street," *Middleton Place Foundation Notebook*, Winter 1993–1994:3.

[6] These panels were destroyed in one of Charleston's hurricanes.

[7] Stockton, 42, 49.

[8] D. E. Smith, A. R. Smith, and Childs, 279–81.

> of artificial ice, electric fans, and air conditioning, it [the single house] offered little room for improvement, and therefore, little scope for the imagination. The nineteenth century enlarged the scale and played tricks with the piazzas, but the plan, being complete, remained unchanged. Few architects are content with repetition.[9]

For Jay there were several problems with the composition of a single house. The plan resulted in an asymmetric positioning of the house on the lot, quite at odds with good classical practice. The front of the house at the street stood for little, since the entry to the residence was located in the middle of a long piazza set on the side of the building. The view of the house from the street was distressing to the eyes of a classicist, since it lacked focus (there was no doorway) and balance (the piazza stretched along one flank made the building appear to be lopsided).

These elements could not have pleased Jay, but fundamentally architecture is an art shaped by the needs and desires of a patron. Jay's response was to take this apparently intractable plan and change it to meet his standards of form and function. He solved the problem of an insignificant street front by extending this portion of the structure to four bays, with a center block of two bays flanked by wings of one bay each. At the north bay of the center block, he provided a proper entry door, giving street access to the home rather than deflecting visitors to a door at the side of the house. The south wing of this street front was a sham, a fake masonry wall matching the wing at the north and sharing identical openings. The purpose of this screen wall was to mask the view of the piazzas from the street.

Jay's design was pleasing when one stood directly in front of the building. Now there was at least the appearance of a classically symmetrical composition. Only as one came upon the house obliquely was it apparent that the front wing at the south was pure trickery. Some later observers asserted that this screen wall was beneficial in adding privacy to the piazzas. However, there were critics. Persuaded of the rightness of the original conception of a Charleston single house, some called Jay's screen wall a theatrical exercise and an abomination of a beloved architectural form that needed no improvement.[10]

There were innovations for the interior of this house as well. To provide

---

[9] Ravenel, 7.

[10] Simons and Lapham, 104.

access to the house directly from the street, the stair hall was moved to the front and side at the north, freeing the interior space and allowing for the development of large double drawing rooms at the second level. This variant on the single house plan gained some popularity in the early nineteenth century, sometimes identified as the "side-hall single house." Still, Jay's plan respected the old form, providing rooms that enjoyed cross ventilation and piazzas that, weather permitting, could extend the living space of the home.

In 1917 Daniel Elliott Huger Smith and Alice Ravenel Huger Smith observed that the William Mason Smith House "had certain architectural features not previously seen here [in Charleston]." They named, among these innovations, the door at the street giving access to an entry hall; the circular stairway at the side of the entry hall; and folding doors in rooms on the two lower floors, making these spaces more versatile. It was, the Smiths said, "very well built," having survived natural disasters and the conflagration of the Civil War.[11]

This project appears to have been something of a trial for Jay's client. Concerning another matter, John S. Cogdell wrote to a friend that he wished "Mr. J.... had remained in Savannah.... I know Mr. W. M. Smith is quite out of humour about his house."[12] The reason for Smith's displeasure is unknown. Perhaps it was because Jay insisted on more costly materials than Smith had anticipated, or perhaps it was because Jay fiddled with this time-honored house plan.

Joseph Turpin Weyman House (Ancrum House), Meeting and Charlotte Streets, 1820–1822. According to Ravenel, "Tradition holds also that the dwelling at the southeast corner of Meeting and Charlotte Streets, no longer standing, was built by the 'the same architect' who designed 26 Meeting Street."[13] She observed only that a number of elements of this building resembled features of the William Mason Smith House. In 1904, for *House and Garden* magazine, Corinne Horton surveyed this structure then owned by the Ancrum family. In her view, this was one of the most elegant residences in the city, combining Charleston's affection for the Georgian style with the later style of the Greek Revival. Citing the southern porch "upheld by four Doric

---

[11] A. R. Smith and D. E. Smith, 204.
[12] McInnis, 350, n. 36.
[13] Ravenel, 115

columns," she said, "Viewed from the immediate front, Ancrum house is formal Georgian, nothing more. Viewed from another position, it takes on all the dignity and charm peculiar to any façade beset with white columns."[14]

The house was commissioned by Joseph Turpin Weyman, a merchant who was to suffer financial reversals. He held this property for only a few years, after which it changed hands many times. Acquired by the federal government in 1938, it was demolished ten years later to make way for a post office. Now much lamented as one of those great houses lost to "progress," the Weyman House is generally acknowledged to be the work of Jay.

McBee House, Ashley Hall School (Duncan, Nicholson, Pringle, Trenholm, Witte House), 172 Rutledge Avenue, c. 1820–1822. According to Ravenel, this remarkable structure deserved to be credited to Jay. She said, "The building in Charleston which most resembles Jay's work is No. 172 Rutledge Avenue, now Ashley Hall School for Girls. A Regency villa, it was built when the area was still suburban. It has a riot of curved lines, the curved rooms and curved doors characteristic of his [Jay's] houses, an oval staircase and an apse under the portico." A grand estate, this house was, in the best sense of the Regency word, "showy"; by tradition the building had been credited to "an English architect."[15] Conventional wisdom has held that "Ashley Hall is probably Charleston's outstanding example of a suburban Regency Villa."[16] The patron here was Patrick Duncan, a Scot. He was not a member of the old society of Charleston, nor was he a planter. He gained a very substantial fortune through banking and real estate, and it seems that he had an appetite for the Regency style.

If Jay were the designer of this splendid residence, he was working within the idiom of the Charleston double house. This plan addressed the issues of topography (the prospect of flooding) and the weather (most of it hot and sultry) and provided for two rooms at each side of a central stair hall at each level. As Ravenel observed, the double house was a more traditional form, typical of eighteenth-century houses in England and throughout the American colonies. And this more conventional plan offered "more opportunity for

---

[14] Horton, "Georgian Houses of the Far South," 264–65.
[15] Ravenel, 115.
[16] E. M. Burton, "Ashley Hall," 1, 1946, VJD.

variation."[17]

Part of the grand effect of this residence was its presentation in the landscape. Duncan's mansion was built in Cannonsborough, a suburban area just north of the city, a region of creeks and marshes which in the late eighteenth century had been filled to promote development. Here a structure of the double house plan was set on a lot of nearly three acres. The facade at the south fronted the roadway, but privacy was achieved by a screen of trees and shrubs.

There were two stories and an attic over a high basement, with a roof of relatively low pitch. The building was constructed of brick, finished with white stucco scored to resemble limestone blocks. As a testament to the prospect that the design and construction had been guided by a trained architect, the house suffered only minor damage in the earthquake of 1886, the foundation having been prepared with a mass of unfired clay brick.[18]

If this is a design by Jay, as many are willing to concede, this facade is as grand and as fanciful as any he made. Here a monumental portico was raised over an arcade, now closed but originally open. A grand piazza with four colossal Ionic columns, rising from a balustrade, defined a veranda at the second level. At the center of this space, and extending through two stories, was a great exedra (niche) that contained an entry to the main floor and an ironwork balcony opening to the center hall of the second floor (at the third level). This exedra was an enlarged version of the entry apse that Jay had used in Savannah at the Richardson House and again at the Bulloch House. At each side of the upper balcony were smaller semi-circular cast iron balconies, originally extensions of two bedroom suites, each one anchored at the base by a conical pendant. Surmounting this portico was a pediment carrying three lancet windows, a Gothic motif echoing the mullions of the round-headed window in the pediment of the Bulloch House.

On the interior, the four levels (ground to attic) were accessed by a great oval, cantilevered stairway in the form of a rising elliptical curve, reaching to an oval skylight. Entry to the house was gained through the arches at the ground level, where the first springing of the stairs was located in the center hall. Although later changes obscured the original design of this ground floor, likely the chambers at the sides of the center hall were a sitting room and a breakfast room.

---

17 Ravenel, 7.

18 MacDonald, 5.

At the second level (main floor) were the public rooms. The stair hall was flanked by a parlor, which might function as a formal dining room, and a double drawing room. Particularly in these spaces, echoes of Jay's style could be seen in curved walls and doors and the application of elegant ornament. The double drawing room was judged to be so fine that, in the mid-1950s, agents of the Metropolitan Museum of Art in New York City sought to purchase the room to represent the Regency style in this country.[19] At the third level, the stair hall was flanked by two bedroom suites, accommodating Duncan and his friend James Nicholson, an attorney who shared occupancy of this house. Each suite was composed of a front private parlor and a rear bedchamber.

The case for Jay as the designer of this structure was prompted early in the twentieth century by the visits to Charleston of Corinne Horton and J. Robie Kennedy Jr. Both writers named this building as a remarkable monument of the Greek style, more modern than the Georgian and Adam styles. And, perhaps sensing the inadequacy of the label "Greek Revival" for what they found here, both compared some elements of ornament to the splendors of Byzantium. Here they cited features that would come to be associated with Jay: an ambitious plan, raised at great cost with the goal of extravagant display; and on the interior, a profusion of arches and curved walls, and a remarkable central stairway, oval in form and self-supporting at each stage.[20]

The attribution to Jay seems strong. Elements of the plan and ornament are, as Ravenel observed, characteristic of Jay's work, and he was the only architect in the region with good Regency credentials. Still, no documents have been found to attach him to this project, and debate about who designed this building persists.

One point of contention has concerned records indicating that this building was completed around 1816, a date too early for Jay. However, there is some evidence that this structure was not built until after April 1820. The source is the report of William Faux, a British traveler. Faux often observed the character of public and private architecture as evidence of how well people lived in America. In April 1819 in Charleston, he met Duncan, whom he

[19] The offer of $100,000 was declined by Caroline Pardue, then headmistress of Ashley Hall (ibid., 11).

[20] Horton, "Charleston, Between Ashley and Cooper," 10:41; J. R. Kennedy Jr., "Georgian Work in Charleston, South Carolina," 293–94.

described as "a rich, knowing old gentleman, living in a garden of the choicest flowers and fruits," but there was no mention of a remarkable residence. A year later, in April 1820, Faux again visited Duncan "and took a final leave of him and his beautiful gardens"; still there was no report of an extraordinary building.[21] These entries suggest that Duncan's fine home was built after April 1820, allowing for the prospect that Jay was the architect.

How might Jay have come to Duncan's attention? His Savannah patrons may have recommended him. Or, after his arrival in South Carolina, Jay became quickly involved with Joel R. Poinsett, one of Duncan's neighbors in the district of Cannonsborough. Poinsett was a prominent citizen of Charleston, and he directed two enterprises with which Jay became involved. In January 1820, Poinsett was named president of the South Carolina Board of Public Works, a program for which Jay served as architect. In 1821 Poinsett was elected president of the board of the South Carolina Academy of Fine Arts, a board on which Jay was a member and for which he designed a building.

In 1984 Mills B. Lane IV, a Savannah scholar of Southern architecture, cited the unique character of this house and concluded, "This extraordinary design may have been the work of William Jay."[22] In that same year, an article in a Charleston newspaper declared the building to be an example of the Regency style and according to "authorities" the work of Jay.[23] In 2004, Ian MacDonald, writing a history of the house, argued for Jay on the basis that the Regency style portrayed in this structure was not in evidence in this country until it came with Jay in late 1817. MacDonald determined that this building was considered to be the finest example of the Regency style in Charleston and "perhaps, in the United States,"[24] a claim with which custodians of Jay's surviving Savannah houses might take issue.

When Duncan left in 1829 to take up residence in Liverpool, England, the house was conveyed to his friend Nicholson, who continued to live here until his death in 1836. In 1838 the building was purchased by James Reid Pringle, customs collector for the port of Charleston. In 1845 the new owner was George Alfred Trenholm, head of the city's leading cotton house whose

21 Faux, 43–44, 405.

22 Lane, *Architecture of the Old South: South Carolina*, 129.

23 E. McDowell, "Ashley Hall's McBee House Displays Regency-Style Detail," *News and Courrier*, Sept. 17, 1984.

24 MacDonald, 3–4.

very substantial wealth extended to holdings in banks, real estate, and railroads. From 1879 to 1907, this was the home of Charles Otto Witte, who had emigrated to the U.S. from North Rhine-Westphalia and gained a fortune in trade, banking, and real estate.[25] In flourishes worthy of the Regency, Witte made a number of changes to the grounds, including extensive gardens and, perhaps for the amusement of his six daughters, a "zoo" populated by "a tame bear named Frederick" and "an alligator named Wishy-Washy."[26]

In 1909 the house was purchased from the Witte estate by Mary Vardrine McBee, a native of North Carolina and a graduate of Smith College and Columbia University. Prompted by the work of her parents in educational reform, she conceived of a plan to establish a school for Southern girls to prepare them for entry into the prestigious colleges and universities of the Northeast. The mission appealed to the Witte daughters, and the property was sold to McBee for considerably less than the asking price. The school was named Ashley Hall, and initially the old mansion accommodated most of the functions of the institution. Later this building was named McBee House to honor the school's founder.[27]

Aiken-Rhett House (Robinson, Aiken, Rhett House), 48 Elizabeth Street, after 1817. Ravenel included in her list of houses that might be attributed to Jay "the Robinson-Rhett house, built sometime between 1817 and 1825 and therefore in Jay's American period." Comparing it to the Patrick Duncan House, she called this structure also "a striking one," and she fixed on the double staircase with iron balusters just inside the entry as the element "strongly reminiscent of his [Jay's] work."[28]

Of the houses attributed to Jay, this is the least compelling case, in part because there is little remaining evidence of the original design. The house was built sometime after 1817 for John Robinson, a merchant and real estate

---

[25] Hemphill, 1:436–40.

[26] MacDonald, 17–18

[27] Strauch, 11–12; B. Hicks, "Ashley Hall: 100 Years Strong," *Post and Courier*, Oct. 8, 2009. At its beginning in 1909, the school enrolled forty-six boarding students in grades 10–12. Former First Lady Barbara Pierce Bush was a member of the class of 1943. By 2010, it was no longer a boarding school, and the programs had been extended to include a coeducational preschool and a kindergarten-through-senior-year curriculum for girls, enrolling over 600 students.

[28] Ravenel, 115.

investor who raised several houses on Judith Street. If Jay designed this building, this was his composition: Built as a double house of twelve rooms, there were three stories and an attic above a high basement, topped by a hipped roof of low pitch. The interior was a conventional central hall plan with two rooms on either side of a stair hall on each of the three floors of living quarters, and the basement contained a cellar and storerooms. The construction was brick covered with stucco, with the basement or ground level incised to resemble masonry blocks. Quoins appeared at the corners of the upper stories. The facade at the south had piazzas with Doric colonnades at the second and third levels. The central three bays of this five-bay front were crowned by a pediment (at the attic level) pierced by a semi-circular window.

In 1825 Robinson suffered financial reversals, and this property came into the possession of William Aiken Sr. Aiken was a native of Ireland who prospered in Charleston as a wealthy merchant and president of the South Carolina Canal and Railroad Company. At his death in 1831, the house passed to his widow and his son William Aiken Jr. Over the next twenty-five years, Aiken Jr. enlarged the house several times, moved the facade from the south (on Judith Street) to the west (on Elizabeth Street), and remodeled the interior in Victorian modes, leaving little trace of the original plan and ornament.[29] It is this much-changed structure that survives as a house museum, property of Historic Charleston Foundation, to commemorate William Aiken Jr., who was governor of the state in 1844–1846.

Marine Villa, Sullivan's Island, c. 1821. In January 1821, this notice appeared in the *Charleston Courier*:

> To be Sold by Private Contract, A MARINE VILLA, pleasantly situated on Sullivan's Island, on the east side of the Fort, from which it is well protected on one side, and has a commanding view of the ocean. Great care has been taken in selecting the materials, and it is framed expressly to withstand a gale. It is erected in the Gothic order, and consists of a Saloon [drawing room] 30 by 20 feet, two Chambers 16 by 14 feet, and two Verandas 14 by 13 feet; the principal story is 13 feet, and stands 8 feet out of ground. Further particulars may be known, and the drawings seen at the

29 "Aiken House given to Museum," *Charleston Museum Members' Newsletter*, Dec. 1975; "Robinson-Aiken House, Charleston, South Carolina," 1958, 1962, HABS.

office of Mr. WM. JAY, Architect, Tradd-street. Jan. 3.[30]

Sullivan's Island, located at the entrance to Charleston harbor, was rich in history by the time Jay arrived in 1820. It was the site of events both terrible and proud. In 1707–1796, Africans brought to North America to be sold as slaves were quarantined here. And, in June 1776 the Battle of Fort Sullivan (later Fort Moultrie) was fought here, defeating British forces attempting to lay siege to Charleston. By 1809 a brick fort had been raised for coastal defenses, and Jay described this "marine villa" as "on the east side of the Fort."[31] In June 1819, Faux described the summer residences on Sullivan's Island as constructed of wood and "built on wooden posts or pillars, so that the sea may flow (at high-tide in winter) underneath."[32]

A question has persisted about whether Jay was the architect of this "marine villa" or was simply representing the house for sale on speculation. Ravenel offered this opinion: "Since Jay's known work in Savannah shows no Gothic influence, it seems likely that he found this order already well established in Charleston (where it had long been popular for coach houses and similar buildings) and adapted himself to the fashion."[33] In truth, Gothic forms and sensibilities were often embraced by Regency designers. In Savannah there are hints of Jay's affection for the Gothic in the passages of colored glass at the Richardson House and the lancet mullions of the attic window of the facade of the Bulloch House. And, there is certain evidence that Jay knew the Gothic well from his childhood adventures in Tisbury, Wiltshire, in the neighborhood of Fonthill Abbey.

THE CONSEQUENCES FOR JAY IN CHARLESTON

Ravenel closed her report of Jay with the lament that "Jay's influence in Charleston was small." However, she claimed that his brief stay had not been forgotten. She quoted a review published in 1847 in a Charleston newspaper of a popular book on the history of architecture. The reviewer had complained that "'an allusion at least' should have been made to 'the private edifices

---

[30] W. Jay, arch., attrib., "A Marine Villa," Jan. 3–5, 1821.

[31] Fort Moultrie was decommissioned in 1947. The site is now managed by the National Park Service.

[32] Faux, 82–83.

[33] Ravenel, 109.

erected by the late Mr. Jay in Savannah.'"[34] For Ravenel, here was evidence that Jay was remembered in the region although it is odd that the Charleston reporter had called for the recognition of Jay's work in Savannah and not for his efforts in South Carolina.

For *House Beautiful* in 1903, Horton began her article titled "Classic Houses of the South" by naming the Bulloch-Habersham House in Savannah as "[p]erhaps the most refined, elaborate, and carefully planned specimen of the Greek Revival in connection with domestic architecture of America." She concluded her survey with a house now attributed to Jay, known to her as the Witte House (later McBee House at Ashley Hall School), of which she said, "On the whole, it is perhaps the most ambitious private house of that period in the South or in America."[35]

To this day, Savannah evokes the Regency, because subsequent architects gained from the examples of Jay's work important lessons of scale, massing, and ornament. But in Georgian Charleston, the Regency played a smaller role. Its presence was so unremarkable as to be unreported in some early histories. In 1927 Albert Simons and Samuel Lapham Jr. identified certain "ante-bellum dwelling houses" in Charleston, which they dated to after 1825. They found that these structures had been "dismissed" as "early Victorian." These houses shared

> a tendency toward the grandiose and magnificent, tempered by an almost academic classicism...the use of porticos of the colossal order...[ceilings of] an unprecedented loftiness, with tall, narrow windows extending to the floor, giving access to balconies, or protected by cast-iron grilles of anthemion patterns...[stairs rising] in a great hemi-cycle...[built in] an age of dominant and forceful individuals, who, in the character of their homes, expressed their personalities without reserve.[36]

This list of characteristics now seems familiar to us as evidence of the Regency style and the hand of a young English architect named Jay.

---

[34] Ibid., 114.

[35] Horton, "Classic Houses of the South," 389, 392.

[36] Simons and Lapham, 176.

CHAPTER 26

SOUTH CAROLINA ACADEMY OF FINE ARTS: AN "AGREEABLE" BUILDING

In an uncharacteristic display of approval for the work of someone other than himself, Robert Mills, native son of Charleston and self-proclaimed "first American architect," wrote this about Jay's only public project in the city:

> The next specimen of the Greek style, is the facade of the academy of fine arts. The appearance of this edifice is upon the whole agreeable, and exhibits the hand of the artist: passing through the portico you enter a vestibule, on each side of which are two rooms for statues, &c. In front a large opening leads you into the exhibition room, where a rich feast in the painting department of the fine arts meets the eye. The room, in its plan, is a perfect square, lighted from the top.[1]

The "artist" whose "hand" Mills detected in this building is not named, yet it is improbable that he did not have knowledge of this London-trained architect, a skillful interpreter of the modern Grecian style of Regency England. Jay was younger than Mills by a decade, but in a very short time he had accomplished an enviable body of work in Savannah. In Charleston, Jay confronted a number of obstacles, one of which may have been Mills. But, in the somewhat remorseful tale of the South Carolina Academy of Fine Arts, Jay met a number of challenges, and Mills was not among them.

THE FOUNDING OF THE SOUTH CAROLINA ACADEMY OF FINE ARTS

Anna Wells Rutledge traced the beginnings of this academy to the period just following the American Revolution, citing a plea published in 1784 in a Charleston paper for "an establishment for THE ARTS…those Arts which will afford entertainment, recreation, liberality of sentiment, and a refinement of knowledge." By 1816 a large community of professional and amateur artists (painters, engravers, and sculptors) had grown in Charleston, but there was no academy for properly training artists and no gallery to display

---

[1] Mills, 411–12.

their works. In that year, an exhibition at the South Carolina Society Hall was noticed as a "*small* beginning to *progress* the Fine Arts in our State" with the hope that "in time, Charleston may also boast of its *Academy of Fine Arts*."[2]

An account of the founding of the South Carolina Academy of Fine Arts was given by William Dunlap in *History of the Rise and Progress of the Arts of Design in the United States* (1834), the first history of the arts in this country. For the report of this organization, Dunlap quoted John S. Cogdell, a Charleston lawyer and gifted amateur artist who had participated in this venture: "In January 1821, my friend [Samuel F. B.] Morse had several conversations with me about the practicability of establishing an academy. We agreed to have a meeting...Mr. Morse moved that the honourable Joel R. Poinsett take the chair; Mr. Jay, that Mr. Cogdell act as secretary. Mr. Morse then submitted a resolution asking of the council a site in the public square for the building, and we adjourned."[3]

According to Cogdell, he and Morse were the principal organizers, but Poinsett was immediately named as chair and then president of the enterprise. Jay was cited as a participant in the first public meeting—he nominated Cogdell for the post of secretary. Members of the community of artists in Charleston were "invited" to serve as "directors" of the organization. Jay was listed among this number as "Wm. Jay, architect."[4] This report suggests that Jay was right at the center of this affair. And it seems that, by the time of the first public meeting, he had secured the commission for the design of the structure. But Jay was surely drawn to this enterprise by more than the opportunity to raise a building.

A COMMUNITY OF ARTISTS

By his own report, Jay was "an artist," probably by inclination as well as by training. He had an affection for the visual arts evidenced by his friendship with William Etty, the English painter who in 1821 was just beginning to realize success in London. As a student, Jay heard John Soane make it quite clear that architecture was an "art" connected intimately to painting and sculpture.[5] To affirm his status as an artist, Jay participated in exhibitions at the

[2] Rutledge, 137–38.

[3] Dunlap, 2:284–85.

[4] Ibid.

[5] Soane, Lecture VII:174.

Royal Academy displaying drawings of proposed projects. The large community of artists in Charleston must have pleased him, as nothing of the sort had yet emerged in Savannah.

And who were his colleagues in this venture? Among the eleven original officers of the South Carolina Academy of Fine Arts, three were Europeans (Jay, Joshua Canter, and William Shiels); two had just come to Charleston from Savannah (Jay and Charles C. Wright); four had trained or participated in the programs of the Royal Academy in London (Jay, Morse, John B. White, and Shiels), which provided the model for the Charleston institution.

In these years of the late eighteenth and early nineteenth centuries, the Royal Academy had a very particular relationship to the growth of the fine arts in the United States. During all of the years when Jay was a student and a young professional in London (1807–1817), the president of the Royal Academy was an American. Benjamin West, born to a Quaker family in Pennsylvania, had trained as a history painter in Italy. In London by 1763, his work caught the attention of George III. In 1768 West was among a group of artists who gained the support of the king for the establishment of the Royal Academy of Arts, and he became the second president of the institution, serving from 1792 for most of the years to his death in 1820. For American students, who had no native schools of art, West's attention prompted what came to be known as "the American school" in London. Prominent among this group were several painters associated with Charleston, including Samuel F. B. Morse.

Samuel Finley Breese Morse. Jay may have known Morse before they both arrived in the American South to seek greater opportunities for work, Jay in late December 1817 and Morse in late January 1818. They certainly shared many experiences of life and art. Morse, born in Massachusetts, was the son of Jedidiah Morse, a well-known Congregational minister but now remembered as the author of the first survey of American geography.

In 1811 Samuel Morse made his way to London where he attended the Royal Academy.[6] Contacts provided by his father, who was well known to

---

[6] According to Paul Staiti, Morse was "the only academically trained artist on the Board," but there were four: Morse, Jay, White, and Shiels (Staiti, "Samuel F. B. Morse in Charleston 1818–1821," *South Carolina Historical Magazine,* Apr. 1978:109).

English evangelicals, included at least two important associates of the Reverend Jay. William Wilberforce and Henry Thornton were cousins, both men of considerable means, members of Parliament, Evangelical Anglicans committed to the cause of abolition, and frequent visitors to Bath where they were often in the company of the Reverend Jay.[7]

At the Royal Academy, Morse became fixed in his commitment to history painting, but he was obliged to earn his living in the more popular and more lucrative specialty of portraiture. In 1815 he was persuaded by his father to venture to Charleston, known to be a place of some affluence, where Jedidiah had taken an early turn in the ministry and where there were friends and family members.[8] But, Samuel's stay was not long. Caught in the same poor economy that sent Jay packing for England in 1822, Morse left Charleston in that year to rejoin his wife and children in New Haven, Connecticut. By 1824 he had moved to New York City where he would turn the lessons of the Charleston experiment to good effect as the founder and first president of the National Academy of Design. By the 1830s, his attention was increasingly drawn to science and technology, and his passion became the manufacture of a practical electromagnetic telegraph and signal code.

John Stevens (later Stephano) Cogdell. Cogdell played a central role in the organization and administration of the Charleston academy. Born near Charleston, he was a lawyer by profession, serving four terms in the state House of Representatives. However, he was by passion and conviction an artist, and he gained commendable skills as a painter and sculptor. He traveled often to Philadelphia, Boston, and New York to see art collections and visit with artists.[9] His political, business, and artistic abilities and connections equipped him to tend to the establishment and sustenance of the academy in Charleston.

Joel Roberts Poinsett. Poinsett was the only member of this group who was not an artist, neither a professional nor an amateur. He was a Charleston native although he had spent very little time in this place. He was widely educated in medicine, law, and military science; an amateur botanist; proficient in several languages; and one of the most widely traveled Americans of the day. He was, according to a late nineteenth-century account, one of a "small

---

[7] E. Morse, 1:90, 140.

[8] Prime, 106–22.

[9] Dunlap, 2:218.

but brilliant body of Americans who, with plenty of means…travelled with very observant eyes…in portions of Europe, then little visited by cultivated people of any country…[gaining] admission into the highest social circles in the countries in which they travelled and…[coming to know] everybody worth knowing."[10]

In 1809 Poinsett was appointed by President James Madison to go to Chile to assess the struggle for independence from Spain. By 1815 he returned to Charleston, resolved to serve his home district: in the state House of Representatives (1816–1819), as president of the South Carolina Board of Public Works (1818–1820), and in the U.S. House of Representatives (1821–1825). And, during this period he was selected to be the president of the South Carolina Academy of Fine Arts.

Charles Fraser. Fraser was a native of Charleston, obliged by his guardians (his father had died when Charles was quite young) to become a lawyer. In 1818 he gave up the law to pursue his passion for painting. He became a master of the technique of painting "in little" with watercolor on ivory. One of these miniatures was a portrait of Jay (now lost).[11]

In Dunlap's early history of American art, Fraser was described as "a gentleman of polished manners and fine feelings," known for his own remarkable work and for his support of other artists. Oddly, Fraser appears to have been little involved with the South Carolina Academy. A letter from Cogdell to Morse in 1821 observed that Fraser seemed to resent that Poinsett and not he had been named president.[12] The comment survives as not altogether surprising evidence that there were, from the beginning, disagreements about the mission and the methods of the academy.

Joshua Canter. Canter was a Danish Jew who had trained as an artist in Copenhagen. He immigrated to Charleston in 1792 and established himself as a painter and as a teacher of drawing. He was, as reported in Dunlap's history, "devotedly attached to the art," but his talent had languished for want of "professional competition" then lacking in South Carolina.[13]

John Blake White. White gained only brief mention by Dunlap as "a native of Charleston, South Carolina" who had studied under West in London

---

[10] Stillé, 4.

[11] Severens and Wyrick, 124.

[12] Dunlap, 2:150–51; Severens, "Charles Fraser" in Severens and Wyrick, 14.

[13] Dunlap, 1:426–27.

but took up the law and practiced his art only "as an amateur."[14] He was born in South Carolina to a distinguished family. In 1800, after studying law, he sailed for England to enter the Royal Academy, returning to Charleston in 1803. As were other artists who had been inspired by West, White longed for a career painting historical subjects, but he was obliged to begin as a portraitist. When painting earned him a poor living, he took up the law to support his family.

Charles Cushing Wright. Likely Jay had met Wright in Savannah. Born in Maine to poverty resulting from the early death of his father, Wright lived by his wits and various trades until he apprenticed himself to a watch and jewelry maker and learned the craft of engraving on metal. In 1818 while attempting to settle in New York City, he met a gentleman from Savannah and was persuaded to set up his shop in that place. When his studio was destroyed in the fire of January 1820, he moved to Charleston and purchased a die-sinking shop where dies (stamps for pressing images into metal) were fabricated. In 1824 he moved back to New York where he earned a reputation as the premier maker of commemorative medals.[15]

William Shiels. Like Jay and Morse, Shiels was a trained artist with recent experience at the Royal Academy in London. A Scot, he traveled to London in 1808 to pursue history painting, but he was often reduced to the business of making portraits. In June 1817, Shiels departed for New York and then moved south to Charleston by 1820, enjoying success primarily as a portrait painter in both locations. He moved to Savannah in 1823, but like Jay he soon abandoned America.[16] By 1826 he was back in Edinburgh, a founding member of the Scottish Academy modeled on the programs of the Royal Academy in London.

James Wood and Charles Simons. In his effort to name all of the artists, native and foreign, who had contributed to the rise of the arts in this country, Dunlap resorted to "lists" of architects (curiously, Jay did not make this list), sculptors, engravers, and painters in an appendix to the second volume of his history. In "Engravers, Of Whom My Limits Will Not Permit a More Detailed Notice," Dunlap included "James Wood, of Charleston, S.C." and "Charles Simons, of Charleston, S.C.," noting only that both were directors

[14] Ibid., 2:471.
[15] Ibid., 2:440–42.
[16] Rutledge, 131.

of the South Carolina Academy of Fine Arts. Newspaper notices confirm that both artists were active in Charleston: Wood in 1825, Simons in 1820–1835.[17]

"A FRIEND TO THE ARTS"

A charter for the South Carolina Academy of Fine Arts was granted in 1821. The group received no public funds, so private support was solicited. It is likely that, as at the Royal Academy in London, receipts of annual exhibitions were expected to cover most of the costs of operations. Members were charged a subscription fee. Each artist member was expected to present a painting, sculpture, or engraving to the academy, a conventional way of gathering a teaching collection of art works for the use of students. And there were rules, very like those adopted by the Royal Academy, to govern the election of officers and to provide for the management of the institution.

In February 1821, just a few days after the declaration of the charter, a report of the new academy appeared in a local newspaper contributed by "A Friend to the Arts." Three years earlier, in February 1818, "A Friend to the Fine Arts" had written to a Savannah newspaper concerning the regrettable state of architecture in that city and the prospects for improvement. That writer was certainly Jay, who had arrived in Savannah only a few weeks before.[18] The "Friend" writing in Charleston in 1821 could well have been Jay. This "Friend" wrote,

> Under the guidance of its enlightened and highly respectable President [Poinsett], who is no less remarkable for his public spirit, than for his attainments in the Arts and Sciences, and with its valuable code of Rules, it must soar to perfection.—The attainments likewise of its Secretary and board of Directors, are well known and duly appreciated in this community.... This infant institution, it is hoped, will receive at its commencement, the support of many of our wealthy inhabitants; as on that, and the acquirements of others in the Fine Arts, its future success and glory must depend.[19]

Jay would be anxious to heap praise on the "enlightened and highly respectable" Poinsett to whom he had been obliged in another South Carolina

---

[17] Dunlap, 2:469; Rutledge, 191, 218, 227.

[18] W. Jay, arch., attrib., A Friend to the Fine Arts, Feb. 10, 1818.

[19] Rutledge, 138.

enterprise, the Board of Public Works. His projects in Savannah had been tied to the fortunes (and misfortunes) of the city's "wealthy inhabitants." And he could claim particular knowledge of the "valuable code of Rules" for the academy in Charleston, surely modeled on the "Instrument of Institution and Laws of the Royal Academy of Arts in London" set forth in December 1768.[20]

As yet another proof of Jay's commitment to the Charleston academy, there is this: He was certainly responsible for the nomination of his friend William Etty as an honorary academician. Etty's first biographer, Alexander Gilchrist, declared that this designation greatly pleased Etty, who always included it in the list of his awards. The date at which this occurred is not clear, but Etty wrote to his brother from Venice in early 1823 that the Imperial Academy of Fine Arts in Venice had made him an "Honorary Academician," noting that "Charleston, America, gave me the first Diploma; Venice the second."[21] This comment suggests that the Charleston award to Etty came in 1821 or early 1822, when Jay was still active in this project and before he left the country in mid-1822.

A FINE BUILDING, A DISAGREEABLE PROJECT

The optimism of "A Friend to the Arts" was not shared by Morse, who wrote to his wife in January 1821 that his prospects in Charleston had declined. He had reduced his prices, but he received no new commissions. Discouraged, he said, "[T]here has been formed here an Academy of Arts to be erected immediately.... What this is going to lead to I don't know.... I feel not very sanguine as to its success, still I shall do all in my power to help it on as long as I am here."[22]

By early April, Morse had returned to his family in New Haven, Connecticut. In mid-April, Cogdell sent him this report: "I promised to apprise you of all going on: the Society of which you are a Director—has re[ceive]d a savage *shock*: the Citizens began to Clamour—a Protest was presented to the City Council last Monday from Mr. H[enr]y Ravenel ag[ains]t the building going up so near his residence on the Square...and the Council then Resolved to direct us to suspend our operations on the Square." First awarded a site on the civic square (later Washington Square), a prime location near City Hall,

[20] Royal Academy of Arts, *Abstract of the Instrument of Institution,* 3-32.

[21] Gilchrist, 1:163, 253.

[22] E. Morse, 1:235–36.

the organization was obliged to move. With funds short, the decision was made to rent a site just a few blocks away, near the Charleston Theater.[23] Here Jay again took up the labor of directing the construction.

According to the grudging praise of Mills, the building was a fine structure in "the Greek style." It may have been the first public building in Charleston to be raised in that style. And it was remarkable in that there were at that date virtually no models in this country (or elsewhere) for a purpose-built art academy.[24] Jay's solution, if Mills's description is to be trusted, was to provide big rooms with good light, just what was needed for exhibitions and lectures or classes. A further description survives in a letter written by Cogdell to Thomas Jefferson in July 1821: "Our building after the Grecian temple is nearly finished, a portico—12 feet wide by 30: and columns—a front room for statuary 30 by 20: and the main room lighted by a dome 45 by 35." A local news report of 1823 noted the presence of "four handsome fluted Doric columns."[25]

That this building significantly exceeded the anticipated costs of construction was a matter of considerable consternation. By September 1821, Cogdell's reports to Morse were grim. The directors had budgeted about $1,500, but the expenses were three times that amount. To Morse, Cogdell moaned, "[A]las! I wish I had never seen that Gentleman."[26] In the very near future, his wish would be granted. By mid-1822, Jay was gone, headed back to England.

THE DEMISE OF THE ACADEMY

The South Carolina Academy of Fine Arts had some successes, but ultimately it failed. Cogdell described these travails to Dunlap:

> The legislature granted a charter, but my good sir, as they possessed no

---

[23] Rutledge, 139; McInnis, 136–37.

[24] The first design of a purpose-built art gallery is credited to John Soane. His Dulwich Picture Gallery in Dulwich, South London, was accessible to students of the Royal Academy in 1815 and open to the public in 1817. Jay would have known of this remarkable building, and he may have seen it. Soane's design featured natural light from overhead skylights. At the Charleston academy, Jay's "main room" was "lighted by a dome."

[25] K. Severens, 37; McInnis, 137.

[26] McInnis, 137.

> powers under the constitution to confer taste or talent, and possessed none of those feeling[s] which prompt to patronage—they gave none to the infant academy. We have had as splendid exhibitions as I have seen in any other city....The institution was allowed, from apathy and opposition, to die, and the property has been sold recently to pay its debts; but Mr. Poinsett and myself, with a few others, have purchased [it] with a hope of reviving the establishment.[27]

There were certainly many miscalculations in the conception of this academy. There were no public funds to support the activity, so it was dependent on gifts, subscriptions, and entry fees to lectures and exhibitions. The timing was poor, coming in the midst of an economic setback from which the region did not recover for many years. And, although there was an artistic community of substantial size, it was probably too small and too diverse in its commitments to support such an organization. Of the original group of eleven officers, six were gone by 1826. Still, the institution persevered for nine years. Rutledge gave this report of its demise: "Despite discouragement...the Academy continued, and the advertisements and open letters in regard to its *modus operandi* were almost daily appearing in all the papers. There were amusing letters, dull letters, encouraging letters, indignant letters, and even verse in regard to its purpose and its management; at times there were letters even accusing it of failure and then letters denying its insolvency."[28]

One of the local newspapers offered this vivid obituary when the academy closed its doors:

> Departed this life on the 30 of June last [1830], the ACADEMY OF FINE ARTS, of this city, where it was resolved to sell out its fixtures, interests, chattels, and possessions in order to satisfy the debts incurred by the inadequate and useless endeavors to tame, civilize and restore [this city] to something like the features and conditions of humanity.... It was born on the 21st of January, 1821, and died, as we have before stated, on the 30th of June of the present year, living, as will be seen, nine years, the term commonly allot[t]ed to an oyster (if not eaten.) before decay.[29]

Subsequently, Jay's building was put to other uses, and it survived until it was consumed by fire in 1861.

---

[27] Dunlap, 2:285.
[28] Rutledge, 139.
[29] Ibid., 140.

CHAPTER 27

JAY'S PURSUIT OF PUBLIC COMMISSIONS IN SOUTH CAROLINA AND HIS NEMESIS, ROBERT MILLS

In December1819, Jay was appointed to the South Carolina Board of Public Works,[1] a curious assignment for a young English architect with ties to Savannah. This board was instructed to address matters of concern that had gained prominence with the election of President James Monroe in 1816. Having trounced England not once but twice, in the Revolutionary War and the War of 1812, the United States was now poised to undertake some determined nation-building. In the states, efficient transportation systems (roadways, riverways, and canals) were required to move people and products, and administrative and judicial buildings were either missing, inadequate, or derelict.

The time was ripe for "internal improvements," but a federal scheme to accomplish this work was fraught with difficulties. Projects funded by the federal government were supported by unpopular taxes and tariffs. Southerners opposed tariffs as punishing to Southern markets. And an unhappy truth was that grants of federal monies more often drifted to the North than to the South.

In 1817 South Carolina began a program to advance projects funded by state resources. The legislature established the office of Civil and Military Engineer and appointed John L. Wilson, an accomplished engineer and surveyor. A state grant of $1,000,000 over four years was designated for the development of transportation systems and the construction or refurbishment of courthouses and jails for judicial districts. Wilson worked to advance this ambitious program, but after only two years his position was abolished.[2]

---

[1] [Board of Public Works meeting], *Charleston Courier*, Feb. 5, 1820.
[2] Waddell and Liscombe, 19 n. 7; Kohn and Glenn, xi-xiii.

JAY'S ROLE ON THE BOARD OF PUBLIC WORKS

The South Carolina Board of Public Works, formed in December 1819, was led by three distinguished citizens of the state, one named as president and two as commissioners. These officers served in the public interest without salaries, and they supervised the work of two departments: Roads, Rivers, and Canals; and Public Buildings. These units were led by "acting commissioners," salaried agents who reported to the officers of the board. Jay was named "Architect." He served without salary and worked at the direction of the officers, but he had no relationship with either of the two departments.[3]

Officers of the board included Joel R. Poinsett as president, a South Carolina native who was nationally known for his service in international affairs; and as commissioners, William R. Davie, a former governor of North Carolina who had retired to a plantation in northern South Carolina, and Abraham Blanding, a lawyer who had moved to South Carolina in the late 1790s. As salaried "acting commissioners," Wilson, who had first led the office of Civil and Military Engineer, now took charge of the Department of Roads, Rivers, and Canals; and the Department of Public Buildings was led by Thomas Baker, a building contractor.

What was Jay's role in this group? The three officers of the board were focused to the development of transportation systems, and neither of the acting commissioners had experience as an architect. Jay was the only member of this group with the knowledge and skill to prepare proposals for buildings; but he was not salaried, nor did he have any responsibility for project development.

Why would Jay have been drawn to this assignment? He accepted an unsalaried position, but he must have thought that important commissions for public buildings throughout the state would be forthcoming, with the prospect of an appointment as supervising architect for the state, a district, or a municipality. He knew from his training in London that such assignments could guarantee a living wage for an architect and relieve him of the onerous labor of casting about for commissions. And Jay knew, as a truth of his profession, that important statements of the art of architecture were public buildings.

---

[3] [Board of Public Works meeting], *Charleston Courier*, Feb. 5, 1820

It is unknown how Jay came to be appointed to this board. In early January 1820, he opened an office in Charleston and advertised his desire to accomplish work for the state and the city. A few weeks later this notice appeared in a Charleston newspaper: "A beautiful *Model* of a series of Buildings, designed by Mr. Jay, the Architect, for the East and North sides of the Public Square on Broad and Meeting-streets, and submitted to Council for their approbation, may now be seen at the City Hall."[4] No evidence survives to tell us what Jay proposed or if his plans were given any consideration.

At a meeting of the South Carolina Board of Public Works in late January 1820, several building projects were identified for construction in that year, including four new district courthouses and four new district jails.[5] Ten days after this meeting, Jay was asked to draw plans for these structures. William H. Gibbes Jr., secretary and treasurer to the board, wrote to Baker: "Immediately upon the receipt of your Letter of the 3d inst [February 3, 1820] I wrote to Major [John] Wilson requesting him to get Mr. Jay to make out a Plan for a Court House and Gaol [*sic*] and forward it as soon as Possible. The Board are of opinion it will be best to construct all the Buildings upon the same Plan. As soon therefore as Major Wilson can get the Plans finished, they shall be sent you."[6]

For this work, Jay was paid $300 for two sets of plans, each one comprised of eight drawings.[7] These renderings survive along with written specifications for construction. Jay had no responsibility for the implementation of these projects. All matters of construction—site selection, the award of contracts, and the procurement of supplies and labor—were advanced by appointed district commissioners who reported to Baker.

---

[4] W. Jay, arch., attrib., "Notice [Services offered]," *Charleston Courier,* Jan. 1, 1820, W. Jay, arch., attrib., "A beautiful *Model* of a series of Buildings," *Charleston Courier,* Feb. 11, 1820.

[5] "Public Works," *Southern Patriot and Commercial Advertiser*, Feb. 4, 1820.

[6] W. Gibbes to T. Baker, Feb. 9, 1820, South Carolina Department of Archives and History, Superintendent of Public Works and Internal Improvements Papers (1820–1821), Columbia, SC (hereafter cited as SCDAH/SPW).

[7] "Bill of Wm. Jay Archit. for Plans of Court Houses, Goals [*sic*] furnished the Board" and "Board of Public Works [Payment] To William Jay," May 17, 1820, South Carolina Department of Archives and History, Legislative Papers and Petitions Collection (1817–1827 and 1837–1941), Columbia, SC. (hereafter cited as SCDAH/L).

Then, just one year after the commission of the Board of Public Works, the group was reorganized. On January 6, 1821, a new board was constituted as follows: Poinsett continued as president, and Blanding took the salaried position of acting commissioner for Roads, Rivers, and Canals (or superintendent of Public Works) replacing Wilson.[8] The second salaried position of acting commissioner (or superintendent) for Public Buildings, which might have been taken by Jay, was awarded to Robert Mills. Jay was gone from this group.

ENTER "THE FIRST AMERICAN ARCHITECT"

Surely one of the reasons why Jay and the record of his work for the South Carolina Board of Public Works got lost in accounts of the early history of American architecture can be summed up in two words: Robert Mills. Mills, a native of Charleston, declared himself to be "the first American architect." By way of clarification, Beatrice St. Julien Ravenel observed that Mills claimed to be "the only native-born American who had studied to be an architect, the others having entered the profession from various trades."[9]

By making this announcement, Mills was taking full advantage of a theme of early nineteenth-century American politics. The United States had detached itself from England by the extreme discomfort of two bruising wars. The country was now eager to reject and expunge British influences and to promote native accomplishments. An obvious impediment for the training of architects was the lack of an American academy. But Mills forged his own course of study and laid claim to the designation as the first native-born and native-trained professional in the practice of architecture.

In William Dunlap's *History of the Rise and Progress of the Arts of Design in the United States* (1834), the profile of Mills is very long. His prominence in this publication was likely a fine example of self-promotion, because it was Dunlap's practice to send questionnaires to the artists soliciting information. As reported by Dunlap, these were Mills' credentials:

Mills was a native artist, born in Charleston and educated at the College of Charleston. He was first tutored in architecture by James Hoban, designer

---

[8] [Board of Public Works meeting], *City Gazette and Commercial Daily Advertiser*, Jan. 6, 1821

[9] Ravenel, 117.

of the executive mansion (later the White House) in Washington City. Subsequently he conducted his own grand tour of "all the principal cities and towns in the United States" to learn from examples of the practice of building in this country. Upon his return, he studied in the library of President Thomas Jefferson, who was "highly pleased to find an American directing his attention to the acquisition of this useful branch of science." Soon Mills was introduced by the president to Benjamin Latrobe, "then recently appointed architect of the capital," to whom he was apprenticed and in whose office he focused on the discipline of engineering. By 1821 he was "invited to his native state to enter into her service, in prosecuting a system of internal improvement there," receiving the appointment as "one of the acting commissioners of the board of public works, and engineer and architect of the state."[10]

Why was Jay now gone from this enterprise? He may have hoped to gain a salaried position but was unsuccessful. Or, he may have learned, as Mills soon would, that the prospects for success in this endeavor were not good. As it happened, these public building projects were something of an awful muddle given the vicissitudes of state supervision, local building committees, inadequate funding, and uncertain sources of quality supplies and competent labor. As various reports would testify, this was difficult and frustrating work, requiring almost constant travel into far-flung parts of the state over very poor roads. Negotiations with local officials were troublesome and time-consuming, and financial support from the state was not abundant. Further, the board had come to focus on transportation systems, depriving the program for public buildings of attention and funding. It is possible that, in these circumstances, Jay willingly and gladly fled from the board.

JAY VERSUS MILLS: THE SOUTH CAROLINA COURTHOUSES AND JAILS

No report survives of a meeting between Jay and Mills; although, it seems improbable that they did not, at the very least, pass in the street. Jay had arrived in Charleston in January 1820, opened his office and taken his post on the Board of Public Works. Accounts of his work in the city place him here at least into 1821. By early 1821, Mills had taken up his assignment as superintendent of Public Buildings, which included advancing some projects using

[10] Dunlap, 2:221–22, 224.

Jay's stock designs for district courthouses and jails.

In the matter of the South Carolina courthouses and jails, what can be credited to Jay and what to Mills? In the usual reports of these structures, Mills receives all of the accolades. In 1935 Mills's biographer Helen Mar Piercc Gallagher wrote that Mills was appointed "State Architect" in December 1819 and that he prepared the stock plans.[11] The story persisted for decades that Mills drew the standard plans for courthouses and jails and wrote the specifications or standards for construction.[12] In truth, Jay's plans and specifications preceded Mills's arrival, and they addressed many of the significant issues concerning these projects, including innovations for fireproof construction and jail reform.

THE CHARACTERISTICS OF JAY'S DESIGNS

With the formation of the Board of Public Works in late 1819, Baker, as acting commissioner for public buildings, assessed the condition of existing courthouses and jails. He observed that most of the existing structures had been raised in recent years but were so poorly constructed that they required repair or replacement. Most were wood and vulnerable to fire, and rooms were too small and too few in number to suit their functions.[13]

Jay's stock plans were available by May 1820, and they addressed Baker's concerns. These buildings were two stories in height with chambers that satisfied designated functions. The courthouse plan located the courtroom at the first level, which was entered from the street through a lobby, with offices raised above. This was an efficient plan for public access to the courtroom and for economy in construction, having the larger and taller chamber at the first level and the smaller and less trafficked offices above.[14] The construction was brick with stone trim, materials more durable than wood and resistant to fire. The designs were simple but handsome. At each three-bay facade, the central

---

[11] Gallagher, 51.

[12] R. Toth, "Architect Robert Mills and His Influence on Criminal Justice Structural Design," *Judicature*, Jan.-Feb. 2007:177–80.

[13] T. Baker, "Report…for 1820," in Kohn and Glenn, 35–36.

[14] Jay's specifications for the courthouses of Colleton and Sumter called for a first story of eighteen feet in height and a second story of twelve feet (Waddell and Liscombe, 21, n. 17).

bay contained the main entry to the building. The courthouse design incorporated classical elements, such as pilasters and round-headed windows; and the scheme for a jail was appropriately unembellished.

MILLS' REFORMS OF JAY'S DESIGNS

In January 1821, Mills became superintendent of public buildings, inheriting a number of projects guided by Jay's stock plans. The records of the Board of Public Works suggest that Jay's plans were carried out in a few cases. In some instances, construction was so far advanced that Mills was deprived of the opportunity to alter Jay's proposals. Sometimes Mills halted work to respond to local concerns or to impose his own ideas.

In one particular aspect, Mills changed Jay's plans for a courthouse if construction had not begun or was not too far advanced. To address the complaint that courtrooms were "exposed to the noise and confusion of the streets, into which they immediately open," Mills moved the courtroom to the second level.[15] To accomplish this, he lowered the height of the first level and located the offices there, employing a system of brick vaulting to support the floor above and to enhance the fireproofing of the structure. For the courtroom at the second level, the height of the ceiling was raised.

Access to the raised courtroom might have been accomplished by way of an interior staircase, but that would draw crowds into the building, a distraction for residents of the offices on the first level. Mills's solution was functional, aesthetic, and symbolic. He added a monumental classical colonnaded porch at the second level. An open arcade below provided entry to the offices of the lower level. An exterior grand stairway, usually divided, led to the elevated porch above the arcade. At the center of the porch was the entry to the courtroom. This design became Mills's hallmark. The new plan was responsive to the complaint of the intrusion of street noise into the courtroom, and the facade was an imposing statement of classical elements. Still, these changes—vaulting at the first level, greater height at the second level, and the addition of a raised monumental porch—were more complex and certainly more costly than the simpler plan proposed by Jay.

[15] T. Baker, "Report...for 1820," in Kohn and Glenn, 36.

ON FIREPROOFING

Jay's designs were to be constructed of brick with stone trim. Mills carried the matter of fireproofing further by insisting on a scheme of vaulting the first level of the structure in brick.[16] Jay's plan may have been constrained by guidelines given to him. Certainly, he was concerned about the issue of fireproofing, particularly for public and commercial structures, and he was well informed about the methods of deflecting or retarding fire.

On January 11, 1820, a devastating fire leveled a swath of Savannah, including the business district. Ten days later, Jay wrote to a local newspaper broadcasting his offer "founded on experience and sanctioned by practice" to erect fireproof buildings. Citing English technology developed in the 1790s to protect the fire-prone textile mills, he named various methods, such as brick construction with all timber elements replaced by cast-iron and cellars of groined arches fabricated in brick.[17] Why did Jay not include all of these features in the South Carolina stock plans? Probably for the same reasons that his offer to contribute to the rebuilding of the commercial district of Savannah was unsuccessful: The direct cost was too great, and corporate will was weak. It seems that, in South Carolina, Mills prevailed in this matter as Jay did not.

ON JAIL REFORM

Another element of innovation credited to Mills was in the design of the jails. However, Jay was well aware of the principles of prison reform initiated in England in the late 1770s by John Howard. Howard was a well-known dissident who conducted a lifelong campaign for the reform of prison practices and architecture. He spoke for more humane treatment of prisoners in larger cells having good sources of light and ventilation, and he called for cells in sufficient numbers to provide for the separation of debtors from felons.[18] In 1817 James Elmes, the architect and architectural critic, published *Hints for the Improvement of Prisons.* This work probably informed both Jay's stock plans for the South Carolina jails drawn in 1820 and his design of a large

---

[16] Mills's method at the Fireproof Building in Charleston was "masonry vaults made of brick shells solidified with concrete and reinforced with iron bars" (Waddell, 1:165).

[17] W. Jay, arch., "Savannah, January 21st, 1820," Jan. 22, 1820.

[18] J. Howard, 40–48.

prison on Mauritius Island in 1836, recognized by British officials for its "accordance with the [standards] of prison discipline which are recommended for adoption in this Country."[19]

ON PROFESSIONAL STANDARDS

In his report for1820, Baker announced to the Board of Public Works that he had secured stock plans for courthouses and jails and "specifications" to define "[t]he style and finish, and the degree of strength and neatness" for each project.[20] These instructions survive and may be credited to Jay. They reveal an important contribution to this public building program as the first professional statement of standards for materials and methods of construction.

The declaration of "Specifications and Workmanship" adapted for each project offered directions for an array of workers, including bricklayers, plasterers, stonemasons, carpenters, blacksmiths, painters, and glaziers. In each section, there were detailed measurements and materials specified for construction to satisfy concerns for strength, durability, and appearance. For example, the bricklayers at the Colleton Courthouse were addressed as follows:

> The building is to be of Brick, Fifty by forty feet from out to out. The Foundation to be sunk a proper depth but not less than 2½ feet and laid on piling if necessary, and to be raised 2½ ft. above the surface of the ground. The wall to be of the thickness of 3 bricks or 29 In. The first story to be 18 feet in the clear.... All of which brick work to be done with bricks of the best kind, & laid in good strong mortar having at least 1½ barrel of unslacked stone lime or 25 bushels of shell lime to the thousand bricks.[21]

Careful detail was given of the measurements and means of fastening all aspects of the timber frame. Base moldings and door and window jambs were specified for all areas. The floors were "to be laid with narrow boards free from sap, planed, tongued, grooved, and nailed from the top." The plasterers were instructed to cover ceilings and some interior walls with "3 Coats of Mortar."

---

[19] "Report from the Inspectors of Prisons," London, June 16, 1837, National Archives of Mauritius, Public Record Office and Colonial Office Correspondence Collections (1835-45), Coromandel, Mauritius (hereafter cited as NAM/PRO-CO).

[20] T. Baker, "Report...for 1820," in Kohn and Glenn, 25.

[21] W. Jay, arch., attrib., "Specifications for the Colleton Courthouse and Jail," May 18, 1820, in Waddell and Liscombe, 42.

The exterior steps at the entry and all of the sills of doors and windows were stone. For the courthouse, the entry door was "a double door 4½ [feet] wide," the entry to the courtroom "a double door 6 ft. wide & double wrought to have an el[l]iptical fan light above, sashed & glazed." Paint colors for the courthouse included "Mahogany colour" for the doors of the first story and the desks of the judges and clerks, and "chocolate colour" for the doors and details of woodwork at the second level. And always there was the final admonition "that in finishing the work whether of Bricklayers, Carpenters, Blacksmiths or Painters & Glaziers it must be done in the best possible manner…[with materials] of the best quality."[22]

JAY'S DESIGNS IN THE DISTRICTS

Among the courthouses and jails to have adopted Jay's stock designs were those in seven districts (later identified as counties): Beaufort, Chester, Colleton, Fairfield, Marlborough (later Marlboro), Pendleton (relocated to Anderson), and Sumter. A few of these projects were completed in the form proposed by Jay; some were altered by Mills. Records of these survive both in the archives of the Board of Public Works and in a rather extraordinary book by Mills.

In 1826 Mills published *Statistics of South Carolina*, written as a companion to the *Atlas of the State of South Carolina* presented in the previous year. The *Atlas* was the first state atlas to be published in the U.S. It included a state map and twenty-eight district maps taken from surveys done by Wilson as civil and military engineer in 1817–1819. In the *Statistics of South Carolina*, Mills assessed the prosperity of each district and commented on the condition of regional courthouses and jails.

Coosawhatchie Courthouse and Jail, Beaufort District, 1819–1820. Mills hailed Beaufort as the founding precinct of the state, Port Royal being the site of the first settlement in 1670.[23] Beaufort District was established in 1768, but the seat of the district was moved in 1791 to a more central location at Coosawhatchie. By the late eighteenth century, this coastal region was a major supplier of sea island cotton, a superior long-fiber variety often grown in recovered salt-water marshes.

[22] Ibid., 42–44.
[23] Mills, 365.

Jay's stock designs for a courthouse and jail were adopted in early 1820. In early February 1821, a local commissioner reported to Poinsett that the work was nearly completed and done to the satisfaction of the local commissioners. Mills described the buildings at Coosawhatchie as "a neat substantial brick court-house and jail." In December 1836, the court moved from Coosawhatchie to Gillisonville, and Jay's structures were sold.[24] Neither building survives. Jay's courthouse was burned in 1865 as General William T. Sherman torched his way from Savannah through South Carolina.

Chesterville (later Chester) Courthouse and Jail, Chester District, 1820–1821. Located near the North Carolina border in the foothills of the Appalachian Mountains, Chester was designated a judicial district in 1785. In 1820–1821 a courthouse and jail were built according to Jay's stock plans. Mills described these as "a handsome court-house and jail."[25] Neither building survives.

Walterborough (later Walterboro) Courthouse and Jail, Colleton District, 1819–1822. Colleton is located between the coastal districts of Charleston and Beaufort. The town of Walterborough was settled in 1784 by owners of nearby rice plantations. The town was designated the judicial seat of the district in 1817. In 1820 a courthouse and jail were begun with Jay's plans, but both were redesigned by Mills.[26]

In May 1820, a contract for construction of the courthouse was drawn locating the courtroom at the street level with offices above. By June 1821, Mills had moved the courtroom to the second story, increasing the height of that level, with offices below, and a grand colonnaded portico with stairs was added for exterior access to the courtroom.[27] This building survives. Although it was reconstructed in the mid-nineteenth century and again in the early twentieth century, it has been preserved as an example of Mills's courthouse design. The jail was replaced in the mid-nineteenth century and destroyed by fire in 1884.

---

[24] W. Martin to J. Poinsett, Feb. 3, 1821, SCDAH/SPW; Mills, 368; Beaufort District, SC, Public Buildings, Petition, Nov. 1841, SCDAH/L.

[25] Mills, 491–92.

[26] Ibid., 506.

[27] Hampton, 7–8.

Winnsborough (later Winnsboro) Courthouse, Fairfield District, 1821–1822. Fairfield District is located in the Upper Piedmont region of South Carolina, just south of Chester District. The town of Winnsborough was settled in the mid-eighteenth century, and it was designated the judicial seat of this district in 1785. In the 1790s the area became a center for the production of upland cotton, a heavily-seeded short fiber cotton that flourished after the invention of the cotton gin in 1793.

A courthouse was begun in 1821–1822 with a plan by Jay, but it was redesigned by Mills.[28] If there are remnants of Jay's conception here, they are to be found in the core two-story structure, stucco on brick, with a three-bay front. Characteristic of Mills is the colossal colonnaded portico in the Doric style, with prominent curving stairs of cast iron leading to the second-story entrance. The building survives, although it was altered and enlarged in 1843.

Bennettsville Courthouse and Jail, Marlborough (later Marlboro) District, 1822–1824. Marlboro is located at the northeast boundary of the state, created as a judicial district in 1795. The court was moved in 1819 to a more central location at Bennettsville, and in 1820 Jay's designs for a courthouse and jail were adopted. However, bids for the work were too high, so the process was delayed. Ultimately both buildings were redesigned by Mills.[29]

Mills's description of this courthouse provides a useful summary of the components of his design. He wrote,

> [A] handsome court-house and jail were erected here of brick, rough-cast, to imitate stone-work. The offices under the court room are all vaulted, and made fireproof; all the rooms in the jail are also made indestructible by fire. The court-house presents, in front, a portico of Doric columns, surmounted by a pediment, raised on an arcade one story high. To the platform of the portico you ascend by a double flight of circular steps, from which you pass through a vestibule previous to entering the court room. On each side of the vestibule are two jury rooms, which open into the court room only, over which are the galleries.[30]

---

28 Mills, 539.

29 Waddell and Liscombe, 22, n. 22.

30 Mills, 631–32.

What Mills did not report was that serious construction problems vexed these two projects. The jail did not survive, and the courthouse was judged to be unsound and was taken down in 1851.[31]

Pendleton Jail, Pendleton District (relocated to Anderson District), 1820–1821. At the northwest boundary of the state, in the most mountainous region of South Carolina, Pendleton became an independent judicial district in 1798. Mills offered no comment about the jail built to Jay's plan, however he did observe that a new courthouse of his design was in progress.[32] However, in 1826, Pendleton District was divided into two districts, Anderson and Pickens.

Jay's jail would have a storied history. Land was secured for the project in December 1819, and the structure was completed in mid-1821 and declared to be "a good, strong jail." When the district was divided, Jay's jail was purchased at auction for use as the Female Academy, believed to be the first formal school for girls in the state. According to an early history of the academy, "This was a brick building, strong and sturdy—walls twelve inches thick."[33] In 1904 public schools were established, and the Female Academy was closed.

By 1919 the building had come into private hands and was renovated as a residence. As a nod to the origin of the place, it was named "Marshalsea" after an infamous London prison described by Charles Dickens in *Little Dorrit* (1855–1857). This structure survives. Traces of the original design can be seen in the well-constructed block of two-stories and a three-bay front with a central entry, now behind a long front porch added in the mid-nineteenth century.[34]

Sumterville (later Sumter) Courthouse and Jail, Sumter District, 1820–1821 and 1820–1830. This region near the center of the state was first settled in the 1740s. Designation as a judicial district in 1800 impelled the building

[31] "Report of the Committee on Public Buildings, Marlboro," Nov. 26, 1827, SCDAH/L.

[32] Mills, 674.

[33] Pendleton District Historical and Recreational Commission, 31–32; Klosky, 93; R. Boggs, 3.

[34] Pendleton District, Historical and Recreational Commission, 32.

of a courthouse and a jail in Sumterville, 100 miles north of Charleston. Jay's stock designs were adopted in 1820, and these buildings were noticed by Mills as "a handsome court-house and jail" although the jail was not completed until 1828–1830.[35]

Anne King Gregorie credited this courthouse to Mills, "who loved the classics and designed his courthouses as 'temples of justice.'" In 1989 John Poindexter corrected the record with this explanation: "Robert Mills did not design the [courthouse] building. That honor goes to English architect William Jay." Poindexter had discovered that Jay's plan was adopted in 1820 and Mills made no changes to the design. In August 1821, Mills was obliged to certify the completion of the building although he probably never visited the site. The "classic portico" in the manner of Mills cited by Gregorie was added at a later date.[36]

In December 1837, an assessment was made of the condition of this courthouse. The description of the existing plan corresponds to Jay's design, verifying that this was not a building changed by Mills: "The Court room is inconveniently fixed on the first floor...[with access] directly on the street...[subjecting] the court much more to interruptions, from noises without and from the intrusion of idle and disorderly persons."[37] In response to this complaint, the building was renovated in 1839–1840 in the mode characteristic of Mills's designs, moving the courtroom to the second floor and adding the classical colonnaded porch and grand entry stairs. Abandoned by 1906 and sold to house a bank, this building was demolished in the 1960s.

CONSEQUENCES FOR JAY AND MILLS

Of these six courthouses and six jails, all began guided by Jay's stock plans and specifications. But only three courthouses and four jails were completed with his designs, and only one jail survives—though turned to other uses and much altered. Still, these projects reveal the contributions that Jay made to this early initiative of internal improvements. In the matter of design, he brought classical clarity and simplicity, and in the drafting of specifications, he prompted professional standards for construction.

---

[35] Mills, 742

[36] Gregorie, 91, 96; J. Poindexter, "The Myth of the 2nd Courthouse," *The Item* [Sumter, SC], Jan. 22, 1989.

[37] Sumter District, "Alteration of the Court House," Dec. 1837, SCDAH/L.

Jay's tenure in this enterprise was brief, no more than one year. Mills fared very little better. He took the salaried position as superintendent of public buildings in 1821. By December 1822, the legislature had abolished the Board of Public Works, providing only for the completion of existing projects. By December 1823, Mills had been replaced by a fellow who was a clerk of court and a part-time contractor. In December 1824, the position was eliminated.

Jay left this work without a whimper. Mills's abbreviated term of service was chronicled with considerable indignation in a local newspaper in 1824:

> Architecture...can accurately be known by those only, who have studied it professionally.... We have such a man, a native of South-Carolina. We invited him from Baltimore, where he was profitably employed and remunerated, into the service of this State. As superintendent of public buildings, Mr. Mills...saved the State upwards of $30,000, and yet erected very superior edifices. Upwards of a year since, the Legislature thought proper to substitute another gentleman in his place...and at the last Session, they abolished the office altogether—leaving the design and superintendence of the public buildings to gentlemen not professional men, but chosen because they enjoy the good opinion of the Legislature.[38]

[38] Ravenel, 123.

CHAPTER 28

AN ACCOUNTING OF JAY VERSUS MILLS

In Charleston, both Jay and Mills struggled in a climate not yet ready to embrace the profession of architecture with its unique assertion of mechanical skills and conceptual knowledge. But a competition between these two artists would occur in another arena, and that was in the matter of style.

In 1944 Talbot Hamlin defined this contest between Jay and Mills as he drew this portrait of Mills:

> So far as I know, Robert Mills was the first American designer who realized that the new country demanded a new, an American, architecture. The country's needs were her own, her materials were peculiarly hers.... No mere borrowed or derivative architecture could ever fill these needs or use these materials in the best and most appropriate way.... The young country was full of pride—pride in her birth, pride in her rapid development economically—and full of confidence in her future. Her separateness from Europe had never been more deeply felt...Mills was merely true to his time in feeling that his architecture must be, above all, American.[1]

Mills's commitment to a native style was so central to his work that he did not shy from using the issue as a bid for attention. In 1814 he promoted his design for a monument to George Washington in Baltimore, Maryland, saying, "Being an American by Birth and having also the honor of being the first American who has passed through a regular course of Study of Architecture in his own Country, it is natural for me to feel much Solicitude to aspire to the honor of raising a Monument to the memory of *our illustrious Countryman*."[2] Mills won this competition. History, politics, and public relations were on his side.

Mills had revealed his agenda in a letter to President Thomas Jefferson in 1808, saying, "My wish is to endeavor to show to the European who visits us from the metropolis of his country, that the *American* talent for *architecture*

---

[1] Hamlin, *Greek Revival Architecture*, 55.

[2] Bryan, 68.

is not a whit inferior to the Europeans, under the same advantages."[3] To accomplish this goal, Mills crafted for himself a curriculum of sorts comprising apprenticeships, field studies, and surveys of literary sources. By these means, he claimed to be a professional architect and the first American to achieve that status.

A CASE IN POINT: THE FIREPROOF BUILDING

Charleston's Fireproof Building is a well-known monument in American architecture. It is a signal work by Mills, often declared to be "the first Greek Revival building constructed in Charleston." And this structure is recognized as a pioneering example of fireproof construction in this country.[4] A part of the history of this important building is a drawing of it rendered by Mills around 1828. Curiously, this drawing is different in character than the completed structure, having notes of elegance and grace not ordinarily found in the work of this architect whose usual compositions were more muscular. As a further complicating matter, the drawing was made at least six years after the beginning of construction in 1822.

So, what is the relationship of this late drawing to the conception of the building? And given the more refined character of this sketch, might Mills have been influenced, even in some small measure, by the presence in Charleston of a young English architect working in the Regency style?

Planning for the Fireproof Building began soon after Mills returned to South Carolina to take up his appointment as superintendent of public buildings for the Board of Public Works. This structure was a state project to be constructed in Charleston (the capital had been moved to Columbia in 1786) to house designated state offices and records.[5] In October 1821, Mills began corresponding with the city council about a proposal for a fireproof repository of records, and by the close of that year the state legislature had authorized the construction of this building. The plan for this project was completed in

---

[3] Liscombe, 9.

[4] Waddell, 1:165. Mills employed these methods of fireproofing in this building: "The rooms for offices are vaulted with brick, and the roof covered with copper,...[and] the sashes and frames are all of iron with the shutters" (Mills, 410).

[5] Mills named as these residents of this building "the secretary of state, treasurer, comptroller general, ordinary, tax collector, register of mesne conveyance, master in equity, commissioner in equity, attorney general, surveyor general, etc." (Mills, 411).

spring 1822.[6]

For much of the time of construction, Mills was not at this site in Charleston. He was living in Columbia, attending to the design and building of the South Carolina Asylum (1822–1828), a facility for the care of the mentally ill. He also was overseeing work on district courthouses and jails. For the Fireproof Building in Charleston, a carpenter-builder was hired to direct the labor, and the building was ready for occupancy in December 1826.[7] Mills, who had provided the design, was neither in charge of this project nor a regular presence at the site.

Motifs of the Regency style are evident in the drawing, but for the most part these features are suppressed or missing in the building. In 1944 Hamlin observed the differences between Mills's drawing and the existing building. He believed that construction had advanced in the ordinary way from this sketch to the finished product. He concluded that, in raising this building, Mills had abandoned his original vision and opted for a more austere or "cruder" but more powerful expression than that represented in the drawing. Some decades later, Gene Waddell came to a different conclusion. He documented a number of changes ordered during the construction when Mills played no role in the oversight of the project, and he traced the effects of a number of subsequent restorations and renovations. Further, Waddell learned that the drawing was made on paper watermarked 1828, offering the possibility that this was either a copy of an earlier design or a rendering of the structure as Mills wished it had been built.[8]

In recent years, architectural historians have associated some aspects of the Fireproof Building with the Regency style, but the sources of these elements are in dispute. Waddell has determined that the stylistic influences on this building were Andrea Palladio by way of Thomas Jefferson's library and "the tradition of simplified, but carefully proportioned Regency exteriors" gained from Benjamin Latrobe.[9] Maurie D. McInnis observes, "The stuccoed exterior and the exterior form of the building alluded to the city's cultural links

---

[6] Waddell, 1:165–66, 168–69.

[7] Ibid., 169.

[8] Hamlin, *Greek Revival Architecture*, 49; Waddell, 1:169–73, 181 n. 31.

[9] Waddell, 1:167–68. Waddell and Liscombe observed that Jay's use of windows "within reveals" (the distance between the outer wall to the window jamb) was distinctive and that Mills seemed to have emulated this motif in the Fireproof Building (Waddell and Liscombe, 20, n. 13).

with Regency England. In the use of Greek Doric details, Mills revealed the interest in the new archaeological styles emanating from Europe."[10] Of course, what is missing in these comments is any reference to the fact that a Regency architect of considerable accomplishment was on the scene in Charleston just as Mills was preparing his design for the Fireproof Building.

COLLIDING ARCHITECTS

Jay and Mills made architecture out of very different experiences. Mills did not study or travel abroad, so the buildings he saw were often provincial or eccentric. Jay grew up in Bath, the most elegantly planned town of the eighteenth century, and he trained in London, the site of a long history of architectural achievement just then being made new by a frenzy of building. He pursued a path of study that included an articled pupilage with an industrious London architect/surveyor, and he had access to a course of instruction in architectural history and theory by way of the lectures of John Soane at the Royal Academy. Further, Jay learned his art in the rarefied atmosphere of Regency England, a time of refined taste and yearning for elegance.

Hamlin noted the contrast between these two architects. He praised Jay as having "almost perfect taste." He said of Mills, "His taste was far from impeccable; his forms are frequently over-heavy, blocky, even stodgy." But, Hamlin concluded that Mills made "American architecture," buildings born of the unique spirit and character of the American people.[11] There is no mistaking the truth that Jay was an English Regency architect, but he believed that his art transcended geographic boundaries. He came to America eager to raise beautiful buildings in this new and promising place. By contrast, Mills was a prideful American, determined to fill this landscape with architecture that declared American values.

As notice of Jay's work in Charleston grew in the mid-twentieth century, some expressed regret that he had not stayed there longer and done more to ornament that city. In 1945 Beatrice St. Julien Ravenel observed, "Though Jay's plan [for a series of buildings at the public square in Charleston] would have prevented Mills' beautiful Fireproof Building from being erected…this refusal to follow Jay's design would seem to have been Charleston's loss."[12]

---

[10] McInnis, 100.

[11] Hamlin, *Greek Revival Architecture*, 54, 201.

[12] Ravenel, 110.

Charleston's loss—and Savannah's gain—was duly noted in 1959 at a celebration of the gift of the Owens-Thomas House to the Telfair Academy. Organizers of the event offered this commentary:

> It is to the everlasting credit of the Savannahians of that day [the early nineteenth century] that they recognized the genius of Jay, for he was to set the style for the city's finest period of architectural achievement. He left us after a residence here of about three years to go to Charleston.... Proud as they are of Robert Mills, South Carolinians have been known to suggest, even in print, that the political preference for the designs of their native son over those of the young Englishman may have been, architecturally speaking, Charleston and South Carolina's loss.[13]

We are left with only a theoretical collision of Jay and Mills in the American South in the early years of the nineteenth century—they may never have met. But this aura of competition suggests why Jay's success on these shores was limited. He had the professional misfortune to have arrived ready for service just at the moment when Americans were eager to reveal their native mettle. At this time and in this place, he had a liability he could not shake: He was English. And worse, he was young and "modern," pledged to the Grecian style of the Regency. In Charleston, he crossed paths—figuratively, if not literally—with "the first American architect."

After Charleston, Jay gave up on America, probably for many reasons: In Savannah he ran out of wealthy clients. In Charleston he ran headlong into the wall of the politics of art. Clever as he was, this was a rampart he could not breach. After Charleston, Mills, who was both talented and dogged, would realize his unique opportunities as "the first American architect." As early as 1822, Mills was actively seeking employment elsewhere—in Virginia, Maryland, and Washington, D.C.[14] By 1829 he had left Charleston, going first to Baltimore. In 1836 he gained the appointment in the nation's capital as architect of public buildings, a position he held until 1851. There he would accomplish his goal to achieve "the first American style" of architecture.

---

[13] Godley, Hawes, and Gignilliat, 11.

[14] Bryan, 84

PART FIVE

JAY'S DEPARTURE FROM AMERICA AND HIS RETURN TO ENGLAND

CHAPTER 29

"WOULD THAT HE HAD STAYED"

In 1981 George Everard Kidder Smith lamented, "William Jay…in Georgia and South Carolina left a definite imprint on United States architecture. Would that he had stayed."[1] What Jay left behind was so extraordinary that one wonders what might have been built had he settled in this country. So, why did he leave America?

Having arrived at the end of 1817, Jay began work in Savannah in early 1818. He achieved quick success with the fawning admiration and financial backing of a few ardent patrons. By the end of 1819, some of his supporters were already sliding into debt, and his opportunities in Savannah were declining. In early 1820 came the disastrous fire, but Jay's bid to help rebuild the business district failed. Further, court records suggest that by early 1820 he was mired in debts he could not cover.[2]

By early 1820, Jay had opened an office in Charleston, South Carolina, and begun what he must have thought would be a profitable practice in a place with a longer history and older fortunes. But, for several reasons Charleston was difficult for him, and here again he incurred debts that he could not honor.[3] By the beginning of 1822, Jay was hungry for work, and new projects eluded him in Savannah and Charleston. In April he traveled to Augusta, Georgia, where he proposed to build a theater. A local newspaper of April 22 announced, "Mr. Jay, the celebrated Architect, is now in our town, on his way to Washington City." On May 6 the paper reported that Jay had "engagements" in "the north" but would "return in the fall" to advance the theater project. According to a later account, "The newspaper never mentioned the

---

[1] Kidder Smith, 161.

[2] "Simon Sainsimon vs. William Jay," Nov. 20, 1818; Apr. 29, 1820; Jan. 3, 26, 1821; "Daniel Sutherland vs. William Jay and Richard Richardson," Jan. 4, 1820, and Dec. 27, 1821, Chatham County Superior Court, Court Records (1818–1823), Savannah, GA (hereafter cited as CCSC).

[3] "John Horlbeck vs. William Jay," Feb. 10, Apr. 28, and Oct. 29, 1821; Feb. 2, 16, 1822, SCDAH/L.

theatre or William Jay again."[4]

WASHINGTON CITY

A visit to Washington City (later Washington, D.C.) in 1822 by an architect seeking work might have seemed to be a promising venture. After all, this was the capital of a nation just then taking its place on the world stage. Very little of this important city had been built, and two central structures, the Capitol and the president's house (later the White House), had been burned by the British in 1814. Now eight years later, the Capitol was still incomplete, and other facilities were needed to accommodate the blossoming agencies of government. Jay could presume that the skills of a trained architect would be in demand.

Likely he did not know that building in the federal city had developed only by fits and starts since the work began in 1792. There were the usual governmental quarrels about who was in charge and about the costs of materials and labor. By 1822 there had been at least six architects—some trained and some not—in charge of the work on the Capitol.

By 1803 the project had come into the hands of Benjamin Henry Latrobe, an Englishman who had been trained in London as an architect and engineer. Latrobe, who emigrated to this country in 1796, is generally considered to be the first professional architect to work in America. He was named by President Thomas Jefferson as the first surveyor of the public buildings, and he presumed that he would be allowed to direct projects in a professional manner. But, buffeted by politicians and bureaucrats, he resigned in 1809, returned in 1815, and resigned again in 1817. Subsequently, Charles Bulfinch of Boston was appointed by President James Monroe as architect of the U.S. Capitol. Self-trained but diligent and graced with an accommodating manner, Bulfinch brought the project to completion in 1829.

In Savannah, Jay had the luxury of working for clients who had full confidence in his skills and whose resources were large, at least temporarily. In Charleston, he had not been so fortunate, and his relationships with clients were sometimes strained. Given what we know of his work habits and standards, it seems very unlikely that he would have found success directing a fed-

[4] "Mr. Jay, the celebrated Architect…," Apr. 22, 1822; "Georgia Advertiser," *Augusta Chronicle*, Apr. 25, 1822; L E. Peters, 113.

eral project in Washington City where an architect might be told by a politician or a functionary how his design could be improved and how it should be built.

A DESIGN FOR A PRESIDENTIAL VILLA

There is no evidence that Jay applied for any government project. In fact, there is no certain report that he spent time in Washington City, although he may have intended to do so because he presumed that he would be received by the president. In early 1819, Jay had met James Monroe in Savannah. Following that meeting, at some time not certain, he supplied Monroe with a set of drawings for "a villa and outbuildings" for a country home that Monroe wished to build at Oak Hill in Loudoun County, Virginia, thirty miles northwest of the District of Columbia.

Soon after his inauguration in March 1817, Monroe set out on a tour of the northern states, and in March 1819 he began a tour of the southern states. He arrived in Savannah in May, and on this occasion he met Jay. This meeting and its consequences were reported by Monroe to a friend and associate in a letter of June 12, 1822.[5] This friend was Joseph Gardner Swift, the first graduate of the United States Military Academy at West Point in 1802, trained as an engineer-surveyor. For a time, Swift had directed programs to rebuild Washington City after the War of 1812. By 1822 he was surveyor of the port of New York.

Monroe needed someone to act on his behalf in a troubling matter, and he wrote to Swift,

> When in Savannah in 1819 I observed several buildings erected with great taste, with columns in the grecian stile [*sic*] of architecture. On enquiring by whom they had been erected, the credit was given to Mr Jay, an English gentleman then at that place. I expressed my approbation of his taste & talent, & observed that I should be glad to have a sketch of one of the buildings, that I might show it here, as a specimen of his work. I thought also, as I intended to erect something for myself, that I might get a hint that might be useful to me. Mr. Jay called on me & I spoke to him.[6]

---

[5] J. Monroe to J. G. Swift, June 12, 1822, Joseph G. Swift Papers, U.S. Military Library Archives, U.S. Military Academy, West Point, NY (hereafter cited as USML).

[6] Ibid.

Jay had designed a temporary pavilion in Savannah where Monroe was entertained at a grand celebration, and he was the architect of the very fine home of William Scarbrough where Monroe was received as a guest during his stay in the city. Likely Monroe saw the Richardson House, and he may have seen other Jay houses that were well enough advanced in construction to give an impression of the young English architect's work. Surely there was a conversation about architecture, a topic which interested Monroe just as it had fascinated his mentor Jefferson. And, at that time the president was contemplating the construction of a new country home on old family property at Oak Hill.

This is how Monroe remembered his meeting with Jay:

> Mr. Jay called on me & I spoke to him…though I have no very distinct recollection of what passed, being in a crowd, & little able to attend minutely to a circumstance of this kind.… This occur[r]ed in June [May, not June], & in Nov[embe]r, or the last of Oct[ober] following [in 1819], I received a very handsome sketch containing the ground floor, second story, front, & back elevation, of a house, & a plan also for a stable. On the last month [May 1822] I received a note from him, containing an amount, for this sketch, amounting to $150, which I now transmit to you.[7]

Jay's bill, which Monroe sent to Swift, read as follows: "For a design of a Villa in the grecian [sic] order/ making a complete set of drawings of the same/ a set of drawings for out buildings—furnishing the same—$150 [.] New York [,] May 19th, 1822 [signed] William Jay."[8] Now Monroe was in a stew, and he pleaded his case to Swift: "The truth is the drawing has been of no use to me. The improvements which I am making in Loudoun, Virg[ini]a, was sketched partly by Col [George] Bomford, & partly by Captain [James] Hoban, & partly by ourselves, or rather on suggestions from us all. This drawing was always out of our view. My improvements will cost $5[000] or [$]6000 at most, & for this plan, I have paid not one cent."[9]

---

[7] Ibid.

[8] W. Jay to J. Monroe, May 19, 1822, Joseph G. Swift Papers, USML.

[9] "Col. Bomford" was George Bomford, a graduate of West Point in 1805. In 1817 President Monroe engaged Swift and Bomford as consultants to review Latrobe's plans for the rebuilding of the Capitol burned by the British in 1814. "Captain Hoban" was James Hoban, an Irish architect who had immigrated to the U.S. in

We have no record of Jay's account of this exchange. It seems evident that Monroe had spoken of the project at Oak Hill, which Jay either took as an invitation to supply plans or caused him to act presumptuously hoping for a good outcome. Monroe claimed that he was a victim of a social event. Now quite defensively, Monroe declared that the plans had been of no use at all in the design of his country home.

These were Monroe's instructions to Swift:

> I wish you to see Mr. Jay, & to confer with him on the subject. I am not in circumstances to make sacrifices, of any kind; what is just & fair I am willing to do. I take it for granted that the drawings can be of no use to him, or I would willingly return it to him, that he might profit of it, & I have too much respect for his feelings to wound them in this mode. As a specimen of taste, I will deposit it in [the] Capitol, or have it placed in a frame, in some part of this house [the president's house] as he may prefer. And whatever you think I ought to pay for it, after conferring with him, I will pay. But weigh with all the circumstances of the case, & decide accordingly to the principles of strict justice. Let me hear from you soon.[10]

There is no account of how this matter was resolved, and these drawings are now lost.

Jay's presentation of this bill to the president is curious. Two and a half years had passed. Certainly Jay's resources were stretched at this time, and he may have considered this action to be simply the calling in of a debt. Or, he may have used this as a method to catch Monroe's attention, to prompt a memory of their meeting in Savannah as a means to solicit work in Washington City. If what he wanted was Monroe's sponsorship, his method was impolitic. As a tactic, the posting of this bill failed spectacularly and invited only Monroe's ire.

Jay probably did not know that Monroe was, and had been for some years, rather desperately low of funds and certainly in no position to build a residence of such fine appointments as the houses Jay had designed in Savannah. Monroe had spent most of his life in service to his country, and that labor was not very remunerative in those days. He had been appointed to two diplomatic missions abroad, first to France and later to England, during which

---

1785. In 1792 he won the design contest for the president's house and remained in Washington City to take on a number of federal projects.

[10] J. Monroe to J. G. Swift, June 12, 1822, Joseph G. Swift Papers, USML.

he had incurred large personal debts. Debt plagued him to the end of his life.[11]

Susan Holway Hellman suggests that Monroe, who loved all things European, likely admired Jay's modern Regency villas in Savannah but was probably deterred by the cost. And Oak Hill was a home in the Virginia countryside. A more conservative style suited that place, as a Regency villa would not. The final design was an amalgam of many proposals from friends, architects, and engineers upon which Monroe ultimately set his own imprint.[12] The result was a fine Federal-style structure in brick with a very grand Greek Doric pedimented two-story portico, occupied by Monroe when his second term as president ended in 1825.

FAMILY MATTERS

Jay's note to Monroe was dated May 19, 1822, and sent from New York City. Likely he was in residence in that city with his sister Anne and her husband Robert Bolton at the home of Robert's younger brother James McClean Bolton. Robert had come to New York to settle the affairs of the family business, a complicated matter under the terms of his father's will.

In 1820–1821 the cotton shipping business suffered considerable losses as a result of fractures in the economies of England and the United States. Further, these were tumultuous times for textile manufacturing in Manchester, the destination for the loads of cotton that moved from Savannah to Liverpool. Workers protesting the loss of jobs to mechanization often brought the mills of Manchester to a halt, leaving Liverpool cotton merchants with inventories they could not sell. Caught in these events, the stock of Bolton's firm depreciated greatly in value. Ultimately he was obliged to remit his stock to his creditors.[13]

Later in 1822, Robert and Anne returned to England, and Jay may have joined them on that voyage. The Boltons settled near Weymouth in Dorset, on the southwest coast of England, where Robert once again pursued his goal to take up an evangelical ministry. This change in the affairs of his brother-in-law may have influenced Jay's decision not to return to the U.S. Bolton had been the essential contact for Jay's work in Savannah—Jay's first patron was

---

[11] Ammon, 408, 553.

[12] S. H. Hellman, email to SLU, Jan. 29, 2009.

[13] R. Bolton, *Genealogical...Account of the Family of Bolton,* 155–57.

Richard Richardson, Bolton's brother-in-law and business partner. Now Bolton was relinquishing all of his business interests in Savannah and committing to life as a preacher of the gospel in England.

In the coming years, Jay maintained close contact with his eldest sister and her husband. In 1827 he took a wife from Henley-on-Thames, forty miles west of London, where Bolton had been appointed minister of the Independent Chapel in 1824. In 1829 Jay was commissioned by Bolton to renovate this chapel. And, in 1836 both Bolton and Jay determined to leave England to seek more remunerative opportunities abroad, Bolton in the northeastern U.S. (he did not return to Savannah) and Jay in Mauritius.

There were other circumstances to influence Jay's decision to abandon America. When he arrived in Bath in late 1822, he may have been met by pleas that he remain close at hand. According to the report of the Reverend Jay, some thirty years after the date of his marriage, his beloved wife, Anne, began to suffer ill health in the form of "oppression in breathing" that resulted in "sudden, painful seizure." Anne's declining health can be dated to 1821–1822. This had been and would remain a very close and loving family. Through the years, the Reverend Jay's adult children and his grandchildren were often at the family home in Bath, and he described as "trials" the times when his two oldest children (Anne and William) were in America and out of his reach.[14]

In the recollections of the Reverend Jay by his middle son, Cyrus, there is a notice of the gift Jay brought to his father on his return to England. This gift conveys something of the devotion of this eldest son, and it is a reminder of what America meant to this family. Describing his father's library—the hundreds of volumes it contained and the pleasure his father took in being there—Cyrus observed that a much loved and familiar feature of the room was this particular object: "Over the door of the library was suspended a painting by an American artist, representing the seat and grounds of General Washington at Mount Vernon. It was presented to Mr. Jay by his eldest son."[15]

---

[14] Rev. Jay, *Autobiography*, 99, 93.

[15] C. Jay, *Recollections*, 139. By 1822 landscape painting was emerging as a specialty in American art, and there was a brisk market in souvenirs of the nearly sainted George Washington who had died in 1799.

Below the painting was posted a poem written by the Reverend Jay, revealing his affection for the place that for a time had captured his son. These are the opening lines: "There dwelt the *Man*, the flower of human kind,/ Whose visage mild bespoke the noble mind;/ There dwelt the *Soldier*, who his sword ne'er drew/ But in a righteous cause, to freedom true."[16]

The admiration for Washington and the adventure of America was a view commonly held by nonconformists who relished the promise of freedom of religion and who had opposed what they took to be George III's heavy-handed dealings with the colonists that led to the Revolutionary War.

THE "DEAR NATIVE LAND"

Beyond family, there was the issue of country. In these years following the War of 1812, there was renewed interest in the matter of what it meant for English men and women to emigrate to this place. One example of this concern was Howard Hinton's *History and Topography of the United States of North America...Including All the Information Necessary for Emigrants of Every Class* (1830–1832). Hinton's goal was to inform prospective settlers about what they might expect to find on the other side of the Atlantic Ocean, in all matters of human history, natural history, economic development, and peculiar manners of speech and behavior.

Hinton took care to analyze the history of immigration to the U.S. He found a record of substantial and steady population increase that, in his view, could be well supported by the availability of land, resources, and opportunity. The vast majority of these immigrants had come from the British Isles, particularly in the "extraordinary years" of 1817 and 1818 when the numbers were two or three times what they were in the years before or after. In 1817, the year in which Jay traveled to the U.S., 18,000 came from Britain, a much greater number than the previous annual average of 7,000. However, Hinton warned prospective emigrants that there were significant cultural differences. For example, in the matter of deportment, there was a "friendly and social intercourse...in a far higher degree than the present state of Great Britain will now permit to its inhabitants."[17]

A number of published travel narratives in this era raised the serious question of whether or not an Englishman should leave England and take up

[16] Ibid., 139.

[17] Hinton, 2:305, 415.

residence in America. William Faux, who traveled here in 1819–1820, offered a conventional view: "Very few emigrants, whatsoever may have been their disgusts and evils in the old country, or their successes in the new, can forget their 'dear native land.' ...This seems an indestructible feeling; the incurable mania of the British exile." He concluded, "Are those English people who are now in America happier than they were in England? I will take upon me to pronounce, that in the aggregate, they are not."[18]

Jay had met resistance from some in Savannah and many in Charleston. Now back with his family in Bath, he may have realized that in some measure he had fallen victim to a clash of cultures. He might have determined, as others had done, that he simply would not find his way as an Englishman in these lost colonies.

THE PERPLEXING PROBLEM OF "AMERICAN" ARCHITECTURE

Finally, Jay may have recognized the forces just then mustering in the U.S. to devise an architectural style that was thoroughly "American" and the growing hostility to English influences—and perhaps to English architects. In his 1834 account of the early history of American art, William Dunlap offered the opinion that English models had been of very little use in the development of architecture in the United States, that contemporary English architects were lacking in "invention and taste, and even common sense." According to Dunlap, American architecture was making its own way quite successfully in the capable hands of native artists such as Robert Mills, who boasted that his training had been undertaken wholly in his own country.[19]

Unsurprisingly, English observers had a different view. In 1832 Hinton offered this opinion of American architecture: "[I]n the mechanical arts they [Americans] are inferior to no nation of the globe, as their ships, steam-boats, and engines of all kinds, bridges, canals, and rail-roads, abundantly testify." In the matter of architecture, Hinton determined that some progress was being made by those who made "the tour of Europe, to inform their minds and cultivate their taste." There was, he thought, some hope for the future.[20]

---

[18] Faux, 330–31, 424.
[19] Dunlap, 1:335.
[20] Hinton, 2:406.

"HE TRUSTS *NOT* TO RETURN"

Evidence of Jay's journey back to England in late 1822 survives in letters from the painter William Etty to his brother. In sum, this correspondence reveals that Jay arrived in England while Etty was in Venice and that he planned to return to America before Etty would make his way back to England. But, by mid-1823 Etty reported this news: "A letter from Jay tells me he trusts *not* to return (to America): a very amusing letter. He seems the very man he used to be. I long to see him."[21]

Apparently Jay's decision to stay in England did not come quickly or perhaps easily. No doubt he weighed many factors. In the end, he may have been persuaded by this: As luck would have it—or so it may have seemed to be luck—a new spa town not far from Bath was just beginning a building boom. Jay made his way to Cheltenham, and by the end of 1822 he had found work in great abundance.

[21] Gilchrist, 1:172.

CHAPTER 30

CHELTENHAM

By late 1822, Jay had found work in Cheltenham not far from Bath. Some have wondered why he settled in this place, but the choice was perfectly in keeping with his credentials and with his character. As his experiences in the American South had shown, Jay was a master of the Grecian style of the Regency era, and he was ambitious. Those qualities, along with family connections, had taken him to Savannah, Georgia, at the very moment when that place was experiencing a rush of prosperity.

Jay arrived in Cheltenham at the time of a building frenzy. This was a spa town in Gloucestershire, fifty-five miles north of Bath, and it was just then gaining prominence as the fashionable resort in England. Likely Jay was drawn to this place through family connections, as he had been in Savannah—the Reverend Jay was a frequent visitor to Cheltenham with influential friends in the community. What Jay could not have predicted was that his experience here would be very like what had happened to him in America. He would enjoy some quick success only to be buffeted by a tumultuous national economy. But failure here would bring him to his knees.

CHELTENHAM WATERS

Cheltenham was primarily a drinking spa. A natural spring containing salts of iron had been discovered in this region in 1716, and by 1740 the waters at Cheltenham were cited as perhaps the best in the country.[1] The mineral elements, which had the properties of an emetic (inducing vomiting) or a purgative (promoting evacuation of the bowels), existed in a dilute state. According to a medical reference of 1835, the "exceedingly mild" Cheltenham waters could be taken for a long period of time and were recommended for persons who had lived for some years in hot climates and suffered "diseased liver."[2] This analysis would result in the settlement here of scores of British merchants and military officers who had served in India, but the most significant

---

[1] T. Short, 79.

[2] Forbes, et al., 4:465.

impetus for development of this spa was the visit in 1788 of George III. At the onset of an affliction now believed to be porphyria, an inherited condition involving a low production of hemoglobin, the king suffered from skin irritations, cramps, shortness of breath, and a general anxiety about his health. His physician recommended taking the waters at Cheltenham, bringing considerable attention to this spa.

A PLACE OF "HIGH CELEBRITY" AND GREAT BEAUTY

In 1800 Cheltenham had around 3,000 residents and 2,000 visitors. By 1826 the population of the town had grown to 20,000 with 15,000 visitors.[3] As the popularity of the place grew, the number of wells (spas) increased. The most prominent were the Old Well (the Royal Well) opened by 1720 and the Montpelier Spa opened in 1808. A "New Spa" at Pittville, just north of the city, was in planning by 1824 and opened in 1830.

In 1826 Samuel Young Griffith, author of a guide to the city, announced grandly, "Cheltenham has for some years past been progressing towards a station of high celebrity. The rank it now holds amongst its rivals is such as the most enthusiastic could not have dared to predict." Here were to be found the usual amenities of a spa: facilities for "taking the waters," theater productions and other programs of entertainment (concerts, dances, and spectacles), shops, and libraries. But what set Cheltenham apart from other spa destinations was the remarkable character of the architecture. According to Griffith, "[M]any of its mansions may almost be termed palaces; and its elegant villas are innumerable." From a distance, one saw a "galaxy of white buildings." So quickly had this "new town" been built that it was "almost miraculous…like the instantaneous production of the magic lamp, or the fairy's wand!"[4]

JAY'S CONNECTIONS AT CHELTENHAM

This altogether agreeable place had been known to the Reverend Jay at least since 1809 when he preached at the opening of Cheltenham Chapel. The Reverend Rowland Hill had prompted the construction of this large chapel because Cheltenham was becoming crowded with men and women of

[3] Hembry, L. Cowie, and E. Cowie, 33.

[4] Griffith, 1:v–viii.

substantial wealth but feeble faith. Modeled on Hill's Surrey Chapel in London, it welcomed both members of the Church of England and dissenters.[5] That the Reverend Jay was the featured speaker at the dedication of this building is a reminder of his long association with Hill.

Cheltenham became a place of retreat for the Reverend Jay. According to a history of the town published in 1863, he was "some time a resident, besides being an occasional visitor." In 1820 he came here to recover a sense of well-being after the death of his youngest child, his daughter Statira.[6]

JAY'S WORK IN CHELTENHAM

No doubt Cheltenham was well known to the eldest son of the Reverend Jay. It was a spa town very like the place in which he had been born. It was a frequent resort for family and friends and a refuge for his father. Here Jay might have expected to settle into the long career that had eluded him in the American South. And, in the very short span of five or six years, Jay did accomplish a significant amount of work in Cheltenham, in the new suburb of Pittville, and in nearby Cirencester, just as he had done in Savannah and Charleston.

But aside from his ambition and industry, there were important differences in these experiences. In the American South, Jay enjoyed, both to his benefit and his peril, the unique position of being the only trained architect in the region. In 1825 a city guide listed Jay as one of five architects in Cheltenham, casting him in a competitive environment.[7] Further, in Cheltenham he was primarily involved with speculative schemes in the design and construction of residential terraces or parades (joined residences), a very different enterprise than the commissioned public buildings and private residences he had built in Savannah and Charleston.

For a time, the record of Jay's work in Cheltenham was lost. Now several projects are attributed to him, and these tell us much about his successes and his tribulations during this chapter of his life.

---

[5] "Religious Intelligence," *Evangelical Magazine*, Sept. 1809:394; Sidney, 81.

[6] Goding, 325; C. Jay, *Recollections*, 128.

[7] Architects named were Jay, Forbes, Hayward, Jenkins, and Edwards (Williams, 195).

DUFFIELD AND WELLER'S PUBLIC LIBRARY AND LITERARY SALON, FACADE, 1822

Jay's first assignment in Cheltenham bears the marks of a Bath connection. Charles Duffield was a bookseller in Bath, the proprietor of the Royal Union Library. With Thomas Edmund Weller, he came to own a public library at Cheltenham, Duffield and Weller's Literary Saloon, located in an old abandoned assembly hall (ballroom), which they renovated in 1822. Likely Duffield was an acquaintance of the Reverend Jay, who busied himself at writing books and collecting them for his own very large library.

By late 1822, it would have been known that the eldest son of the Reverend Jay was at home in Bath, just when Duffield was seeking a design for the facade of his building in Cheltenham. Perhaps as a coincidence, in 1809 Jay had exhibited at the Royal Academy in London a drawing titled "Design for a public library," a composition that may well have survived in the architect's portfolio.[8]

Libraries were prominent attractions in spa towns. Griffith described these establishments in Cheltenham in his guidebook of 1826:

> There can be no more rational or agreeable recreation—no more pleasurable means of diversifying the amusements of the day, than reading-rooms afford: the tables piled with the London and provincial newspapers, periodical publications, reviews, &c. and surrounded by shelves, loaded with all the literature of every age, and of almost every country...[an] accommodation thus afforded to visitors...for a trifling subscription.[9]

Duffield and Weller's was only one of several commercial circulating libraries in Cheltenham. But according to Griffith this one was the most grand by virtue of its programs (including band concerts), collections (all of the most current newspapers, journals, books, maps, and prints), and accommodations. He said, "[Here is] a scale of splendour and liberality seldom equalled, and the arrangements are all marked by taste and judgment.... [This library] is not surpassed by any literary establishment in the kingdom. The long neglected premises...have become one of the principal ornaments of the town."[10]

---

[8] Graves, 4:238.
[9] Griffith, 1:69–70.
[10] Ibid., 71–72.

The interior was composed of a grand salon, a circulating library, and a reading room. The presentation of the reading room was credited to John Henderson Grieve, the leading scenic designer for Covent Garden, the most popular London theater of the day. According to Griffith, "This room has a peculiar and very elegant effect…[in] the semblance of an Ionic temple." Griffith described the facade as "a handsome portico of the same order [Ionic], extending along the entire front; and surmounted in the centre by a fine colossal figure of Minerva." The record of this composition survives in an engraving published in Griffith's guidebook citing Jay as the designer and dated by an inscription of "A.D. 1822." The facade bears the marks of Jay's style in its ingenious but tasteful array of classical motifs.[11]

PARAGON BUILDINGS, 114–124 BATH ROAD, 1823–1826

According to Oliver Bradbury, this was probably the first large-scale project by Jay in Cheltenham.[12] Here were six three-story houses built on the east side of Bath Road as linked semidetached pairs. The very name Paragon Buildings suggested dwellings of the finest quality. The accommodations were described in a notice for the sale of one of these units in 1826: "TO BE SOLD (And immediate possession given), A WELL-FINISHED HOUSE, No. 6, PARAGON BUILDINGS, Bath Road. It consists of a large Dining Room, with Drawing Room, seven Chambers, and suitable Culinary Apartments, and possesses the advantage of a large Garden, and a suitable situation for Coach House and Stables. For Particulars, apply at the Office of Mr. WM. JAY, Architect."[13]

A feature of this design is Jay's interpretation of the composition of a row of linked houses. Here, to break the otherwise monotonous reach of a parade of six houses, three buildings (each containing two residences) are joined by low and recessed entries. At each of these double entries are flanking pilasters and a center post with capitals carved with anthemia (the stylized blossoms of lotus or honeysuckle). The post supports a lintel ornamented by a course of dentil molding, and it is crowned by a large classical urn. It is an artful design and a model of the Grecian style of the Regency in which ancient Greek elements were used in new and often surprising combinations.

---

[11] Ibid., 72; illus. between 72, 73.

[12] Bradbury, "Paragon Buildings, Cheltenham, Gloucestershire," 141–49.

[13] "To Be Sold," *Gloucester and Cheltenham Herald*, Jan. 21–Aug. 12, 1826.

Also at the Paragon Buildings are remarkable elements of cast and wrought iron. Amina Chatwin drew attention to the "wrought balconies of Anthemion design...lacelike and beautiful." Jay is now understood to have played an important role in the presentation of ornamental ironwork in Cheltenham. Chatwin observed that the use of ironwork flourished here in the 1820s and 1830s. It was, according to her, a time of "the full flowering of wrought iron balconies and verandas of a most varied and complex nature, alongside the introduction of cast panels from distant foundries."[14] It is a reminder that in 1818–1822 Jay had introduced ornamental ironwork to Savannah.

CAMBRAY PARADE, A CONTESTED SPECULATIVE DEVELOPMENT NEAR BATH ROAD, 1825

Most of Jay's work in Cheltenham took place in a fast-moving world of speculative development. Some schemes were realized, others were not, and competition for these projects was fierce. One such adventure involving Jay concerned the development of a tract of land on speculation to supply housing for permanent residents as well as visitors to the spas. Cambray Parade was to be located on a street formed as a crescent springing from Bath Road.[15] A quarrel about who was in charge of this project was documented in a series of reports in the *Cheltenham Journal* in early 1825. First came this notice of January 31: "We are informed, by a correspondent, that a 'new Street,' upon a magnificent scale, comprising upwards of two hundred houses of the first magnitude, is about to be commenced in the Bath Road...built upon a plan under the superintendence of Mr. Edwards, architect."[16]

In the next edition of the newspaper came this "correction": "We are requested...to state that 'part of the improvement...may receive Mr. Edward's attention, but that [another section]...has been placed under the professional care of Mr. William Jay, of Bath-street.'" That announcement fired the pen of Mr. Edwards, who hurled this reply to the editor of the paper: "I cannot conceal my astonishment, that any person having the slightest regard to truth, should put forth such an incorrect and garbled statement. The idea of the intended 'New Street' originated with me...I designed it, drew the plans,

[14] Chatwin, 6, 28, 32.

[15] Bradbury, "William Jay's English Works After 1822," 189.

[16] "A 'New Street,'" *Cheltenham Journal*, Jan. 31, 1825.

traced it on the land, and am now preparing elevations.... The plans are in my office."[17]

Some retort must have been issued from Jay in the following week, because Edwards replied with a full load of invective:

> Having just seen another garbled and scurrilous epistle of Mr. Wm. Jay's...the remarks used by him (as well as the man) are too contemptible to notice, and reminds me of a bird of the same name, which, however noisy and gaudy in its plumage, is disregarded by the sportsmen...I agree with Mr. Jay, that architecture is a science, and if we are to form our judgment on the specimens given by him in Priory-street, Bath-road, &c., we may fairly say...that he was never intended by nature for science...[I]f he ever possessed any science, he must have left it in Yankee Country, or that the motion of the ship on his return upset his brain.[18]

In the end, this venture was not realized, not by Edwards or by Jay.

The method of speculative development was fraught with peril for architects. It was a practice that had been roundly condemned by John Soane, who declared that the system had become "abominable and fatal to the advancement of architectural taste, and, what is more important to sound construction, whereby not a year passes without lives being lost from this wretched practice."[19] Lives or livelihoods and reputations were lost when speculative ventures collapsed. Soane detested this practice, particularly as it had the potential to ruin the careers of young architects. There is no evidence that any of Jay's projects in America compelled him to carry all of the debts incurred, but this method was common in the rapid development of new suburbs and resort communities in England. When a speculative project was successful, substantial financial gain could be achieved. When such a plan faltered or failed, the results were disastrous, as Jay would learn.

A TERRACE OF THREE HOUSES, 13–17 PRIORY STREET, 1825

This short terrace has been identified as "probably by *William Jay*."[20] There are marks of Jay here and there. At the center house and the one at the

---

[17] "To Correspondents," *Cheltenham Journal,* Feb. 7, 1825, H. Edwards, "To the Editor," *Cheltenham Journal,* Feb. 14, 1825.

[18] H. Edwards, "To the Editor," *Cheltenham Journal,* Feb. 28, 1825.

[19] Soane, Lecture X:226.

[20] Verey, *Buildings of England, Gloucestershire 2*, 262.

right, the windows of the first floor rest on rectangular panels of a fluting pattern Jay would use at Watermoor House in Cirencester, but this ornament is missing for the house at the left. Distinctive ironwork survives only at the house on the right. Other elements are inconsistent, suggesting that over time individual owners modified or changed the once coherent design. What exists now is an awful muddle.

Most disconcerting is the fact that this terrace of three houses sports a lopsided crown of only two triangular shapes clearly meant to echo the pediments of ancient Greek temples. It is what remains of a solution to this very interesting problem: How can a short terrace of only three houses be made to appear important? A satisfying answer would have been a composition of three pedimental shapes at the roofline, each one separated by an anthemion antefix (an upright ornament on the eaves of the roof) of the sort surviving here between the center dwelling and the one at the left. Such a design of pediments and antefixes might well have been posed by someone as clever as Jay.

COLOMBIA (LATER COLUMBIA) PLACE, 1–6 (LATER 112–222) WINCHCOMBE STREET, 1825–1826

A modern guide to English architecture in this region refers to this structure as "the excellent Columbia Place."[21] It may be the most complete surviving example of Jay's work in Cheltenham, and it is a superb example of his capacity for invention. This parade of six houses was built near the entry to the "New Spa" of Pittville just then in development. This project was commissioned by one Thomas Thompson. Little is known about Thompson other than that he became wealthy by supplying cavalry equipment to revolutionaries in South America. In the years 1817–1825, many British merchants and veterans of the Napoleonic Wars sought to make fortunes by providing aid to rebel forces in South America seeking freedom from Spain and Portugal. As another benefit of his commerce with Simón Bolivar, the liberator of Colombia, Thompson was granted the lucrative rights to operate the salt mines at Zipaquirá.[22]

In 1829 Edward Billings, an associate of Thompson, wrote, "Mr. Thompson on his return [to England] happening to visit Cheltenham for the

---

[21] Ibid., 279.

[22] Parks, 113.

benefit of his health, proceeded to employ some of his surplus gains in the erection of five [six] capital houses near the entrance gates to Pittville, which he designated Columbia [Colombia] Place."[23] There is a reference to this project given by Jay's brother Cyrus in his book on the adventures and misadventures of London lawyers. Cyrus said,

> I was concerned for a gentleman of the name of Thompson, who, after making a small fortune in South America, returned to England...for the restoration of his health. He remained for a short time in London; but [he was advised]...to take the waters at Cheltenham.... One morning, on his way to the wells, he saw a piece of ground which was to be sold for building on. He consulted me about the purchase...[and] sold some portion of the ground to a builder.[24]

In the report of this affair, Cyrus did not name his brother as a participant in this affair, but the "builder" was surely William.

In 1976 plans for a terrace of houses signed by Jay were discovered and determined to be early drawings for Columbia Place.[25] The similarities between the existing building and these sketches are significant. Both are terraces of six residences with the two end structures turned at an angle to flank a long porch. In the drawings, the windows and doors at the ground level are all formed of tall arches set in reveals. At Columbia Place, all of the arches are gone, likely to reduce the costs of construction. Perhaps as a way to make up for the loss of those elegant arches, Jay produced a design that is part Gothic, part Baroque, and a measure of whimsy—"showy" in the best sense of that Regency word.

Across the midsection of this building is an open colonnaded porch or veranda at the ground level, at the perimeter of which are all of the front entries to the residences. The uprights here are square piers pretending to be proper columns. Each one stands on a base, wears a sort of capital, and is dressed on its four sides with inset panes to capture light and shadow. Across the front of the building, there are twenty-one of these piers arranged not in

---

[23] E. Billings, "A Journal of Mr. Edward Billings, 1829," in A. Miles, *History of Cheltenham*, c. 1920, 4:211, Cheltenham Public Library, Reference Department, Cheltenham, England.

[24] C. Jay, *The Law*, 4–5.

[25] Verey, "The Architect and Architecture of Watermoor House," 168–69.

the even and equal measure of ancient classical columns but rather in the Baroque rhythm of doubled uprights. At the balcony above is a march of small arches rather like diminutive Roman arcades with details evoking triumphal arches and medieval castle crenellations at the roofline. The effect of these ornaments is that of pierced stonework, a Gothic confection.

To this structure, Jay added the embellishments of wrought and cast iron, most of which exploit the patterns of anthemia—in grilles at the basement windows, as free-standing shapes at the front of the veranda, and as dividers along the shared balcony. Chatwin said of these elements at Columbia Place that they were "daring and unusual…[including] the first panels in the town to make cast iron successful in its own right." She observed, "This is like nothing that has gone before…. It is strong, sure, and inventive, using the new method in its own way; here cast iron has found its own nobility."[26]

In the twentieth century, Columbia Place came to be appreciated as a unique design for a terrace, both in the composition of the whole and in the ingenious details. In 1979 Christopher Bishop observed, "Columbia Place is the most unusual of all the Cheltenham terraces." Chatwin said of the ironwork on this building, "It must have been very 'modern' and was not always appreciated."[27] In fact, so remarkable was this building in the landscape of Regency Cheltenham that it drew the attention and the ridicule of an infamous journalist of the day.

Of all of Jay's work in Cheltenham, Columbia Place was the structure most often noticed by contemporaries. Occasionally it earned praise, as here in a guidebook of 1834: "On the north side of the town…is a handsome row of buildings called Columbia Place…. The appearance of the houses is showy and architectural, and contrasts advantageously with the humbler dwellings by which it is surrounded."[28] But Columbia Place was also the target of the acid pen of William Cobbett, one of the most colorful journalists of the day. In 1802–1835 Cobbett published the *Weekly Political Register* in which he dispensed his views about the degradation of English country life brought about by the Industrial Revolution. For a regular column titled "Rural Rides," Cobbett made a visit to Cheltenham on September 30, 1826, in which he took particular notice of Jay's "Colombia Place."

---

[26] Chatwin, 38–39.

[27] Bishop, 3; Chatwin, 39.

[28] Davies, 159.

Cobbett declared, "Cheltenham…is what they call a 'watering place'…. To places like this, come all that is knavish, and all that is foolish, and all that is base; gamesters, pickpockets, and harlots; young wife-hunters, in search of rich and ugly old women, and young husband-hunters in search of rich and wrinkled or half-rotten men." Persuaded to survey the architecture, he said, "I learned from a coal-carter [a coal merchant], which way we had to go, in order to see '*The New Buildings*'…. There is a new row of most gaudy and fantastical dwelling places, called 'Colombia Place.'" The residents of the town remembered Cobbett's abuse of Cheltenham. On a tour of the area in 1830, he planned to give a lecture here, but he was denied a venue, and his effigy was paraded through the streets and burned not far from Columbia Place.[29]

In a curious turn of events, some years later Jay's brother Cyrus reported, "I was acquainted for many years with the late celebrated political writer, William Cobbett, who frequently was a guest at my house in Sergeant's Inn [London]." Cyrus observed that Cobbett was an admirer of the Reverend Jay, and that his father was an avid reader of Cobbett's newspaper.[30] However, Cyrus made no mention of the invective that Cobbett had once heaped upon his brother William's work in Cheltenham.

PROPOSALS FOR CHURCHES AND CHAPELS

Given Jay's obvious connections to religious interests of the time, it is no surprise that he was linked to at least two plans to develop church and chapel projects in Cheltenham.

Proposal for "A New Church or Chapel," 1825. In 1825 the Reverend Charles Jervis, curate of the parish of Cheltenham, advanced a plan to add "a new Church or Chapel."[31] The time was right. The population of Cheltenham was expanding quickly with the popularity of the spa. In the town, there were only two properties of the Church of England: the medieval parish

[29] Cobbett, 460–61; [Announcement of Cobbett's lecture], *Cheltenham Journal*, June 7, 1830, [Cobbett's arrival], *Cheltenham Journal*, June 14, 1830.

[30] C. Jay, *Recollections*, 50–53.

[31] Rev. C. Jervis to Cheltenham Church Commissioners, May 30, 1825, Gloucestershire Archives, Records of the Cheltenham Church Commissioners/Church Building Commission, Gloucester, England (hereafter cited as GAG).

church of St. Mary, and Holy Trinity, a "chapel of ease" completed in 1823 to accommodate members who lived at a distance from the parish church. Further, there was an increasing presence of nonconformity in Cheltenham. In 1818 Parliament had established the Church Building Commission to provide government funds to aid in the growth of the Established Church.

On May 30, 1825, Jay wrote to the Reverend Jervis,

> I am willing to dispose of the ground required for the new Church—for which I ask £600. [T]his situation possesses many advantages. [I]t will require little enclosure which is very expensive, and the Building will have only two sides decorated. I give up the best part of the Ground and it will be my wish to make the whole correspond so as to be ornamental as well as useful. I shall be happy to present a Design suited to the situation of the Ground, and also to show the other improvements intended, and am ready at any time to attend the Board.[32]

On the same date, the Reverend Jervis directed this query to the Cheltenham Church Commissioners, "I have the offer of two Sites, one from the Reverend the Rector of Lincoln College, Oxford at £500—the other from a Mr. Jay an Architect at £600—I prefer the latter." On December 8, Jervis wrote again to the commissioners, this time with considerable enthusiasm,

> I am happy to be enabled to inform you that my scheme for the erection of a Free Church in this town is, with the promised aid of the Royal Commissioners, likely, speedily to be carried into effect.... Finding it expedient to have some sketch of the proposed church for public inspection, I have been offered several *gratuitously* by a very able architect of this town, who is very ambitious of being employed in the work, and who has even offered to raise me a thousand pounds among the tradespeople in furtherance of my object. May I be allowed to accept his services?[33]

There are no further records of this project. Perhaps Jay's proposal was not met with enthusiasm by others. Or, he may have fallen victim to a bruising prejudice. His father, whose name he bore, was well known to leaders of the Established Church and reviled by many of them. The Reverend Jay repre-

---

[32] W. Jay, to Rev. Jervis, May 30, 1825, GAG.

[33] Rev. C. Jervis to Cheltenham Church Commissioners, May 30, Dec. 8, 1825, GAG.

sented the kind of threat to the Church of England that was not easily managed because among his many admirers were some very prominent Anglicans. In any case, Jay's petition to develop this project stalled, and the final blow came in late September 1826 with the death of the Reverend Jervis at the age of forty-four.[34]

Plan for the Renovation of Highbury Chapel, c. 1826. Jay is linked to this chapel by the testimony of a letter written by his father in August 1826 to "Thomas Wilson, Esq., Office, City Road, London." The aim of the letter was to recommend the services of his son for the renovation of a chapel in Cheltenham recently purchased by Wilson.[35] Although there is no evidence that Jay came to be involved in this project, the letter reveals much about his relationship with his father, his appetite for this work, and aspects of the enterprise of chapel building in the 1820s.

Thomas Wilson was well known to the Reverend Jay. Wilson had inherited and increased a family fortune built on the manufacture of silk ribbons. At the age of thirty-three, he retired to give his attention and much of his money to evangelical causes. Among his several obligations, he served as treasurer of the London Missionary Society, an organization in which the Reverend Jay played a prominent role. Formed in 1795, membership included Independents/Congregationalists, Baptists, Presbyterians, and Evangelical Anglicans, with the aim "to spread the knowledge of Christ among heathen and other unenlightened nations." Early missions included South and Central Africa and the islands of Madagascar and Mauritius.[36]

Wilson was also treasurer of Hoxton College (later Highbury College), one of the first of the nonconformist academies dedicated to training preachers for the growing numbers of evangelicals. He took a strong interest in the fortunes of the young men training for these ministries. Often a beginning pastor took up his service in a region where there was no proper meeting place. Wilson helped finance a number of these projects to restore or rebuild existing structures or build new ones.

---

[34] "Rev. C. Jervis, A. M., expired on Thursday last," *Cheltenham Journal*, Oct. 2, 1826.

[35] Rev. Jay to T. Wilson, Aug. 9, 1826, Hull Museums Collections, Social History Archives, Hull, England (hereafter cited as HMC).

[36] Ellis, 26.

In August 1826, the Reverend Jay wrote to Wilson,

> My Dear Sir, I have just received a line from my son who resides at Cheltenham, as an architect, to say, that you have just purchased Mr. Snow's chapel; and requesting me to ask of you the favor of employing him in any alterations you may wish; especially as he had been engaged by Mr. Simeon and Mr. Murtlock before, when they designed it for a church or chapel of ease. He thinks that while it would benefit him, it w[oul]d be also a saving to you. I am sure you may depend upon his *cleverness* and *integrity*. I should be much obliged myself, if you are not already engaged; and at the opening, or at any future period I will give you a sermon there when it is in my power.[37]

The building to which the Reverend Jay referred had been built in 1817–1818 for the Reverend Thomas Snow, an Anglican of a somewhat alarming evangelical disposition. By 1826 he had repented of his wayward ways and taken up a more conventional ministry elsewhere. At Snow's departure, this chapel was first purchased by the Reverend Charles Simeon of Cambridge, a leader of the evangelical movement in the Established Church, who sought to open it as a chapel of ease. In his letter to Wilson, the Reverend Jay noted that his son had been engaged by Simeon to prepare a new design for the building. But, Simeon's plan failed, and the building was put up for auction.

In 1827 Wilson provided the funds necessary to purchase and refurbish this building for service as an Independent chapel.[38] There is no evidence that Wilson directed the renovation of this chapel although he often did. Nor is there evidence of the participation of Jay in this project or any other managed by Wilson, a somewhat surprising observation given Wilson's connections with the Reverend Jay. However, there are some clues to suggest that Jay was not a good candidate for this labor. Wilson was known to be a man of simple tastes. In his memoir of his father, Joshua Wilson observed that it was his father's plan in chapel projects "to provide sittings for as many hearers as the space would allow," with comfort a secondary consideration and appearance of little or no concern at all. These buildings were generally "extremely plain, though substantial" and of "no architectural pretensions."[39] To a certainty, Jay

[37] Rev. Jay to T. Wilson, Aug. 9, 1826, HMC.
[38] J. Wilson, 392–93.
[39] Ibid., 322.

would not have been successful executing projects characterized by "no architectural pretensions."

CHAPTER 31

THE PROMISE OF PITTVILLE AND A CASCADE OF TROUBLES

Soon after 1820, a new development began to emerge just north of Cheltenham. Pittville Estate was a grand speculative adventure, and Jay was quick to participate in this extraordinary project. The plan was devised by Joseph Pitt, who had been born into inauspicious circumstances in Little Witcombe, a village near Cheltenham. As a boy, he caught the eye of an attorney who took him on as an apprentice. In 1780 he began his own legal practice in Cirencester, just fifteen miles southeast of Cheltenham, and accumulated considerable wealth, land, and a seat in Parliament. According to a friend, "[Pitt was] one of those fortunate members of the legal profession, whom great sagacity, lucky opportunity and the skill of seizing on favourable circumstances have elevated from a very humble to a very prosperous situation in life."[1]

In 1789 Pitt began buying land around Cheltenham, perhaps as he realized the prospect for growth in the wake of the visit of George III in the preceding year. By 1820 he had amassed nearly 100 acres on the north side of Cheltenham, and he began to plan for a "New Town," the center of which would be a "New Spa." The development was named "Pittville," and from the beginning Pitt was at the center of all aspects of planning and construction on the estate, incurring debts that he carried to his grave.[2]

The proposal for the new town called for 600 houses, a mix of parades or terraces (unified compositions of row houses) and villas (free-standing, individual residences). The goal was to accommodate people of means, some full-time residents and some seasonal visitors. Designed as a garden suburb of Cheltenham, Pittville had a central "Long Garden" flanked by roads, long blocks of housing, a crescent, and two squares. Just beyond this residential district was an artificial lake and an impressive promenade leading to the Pump Room, the center of spa activity at the northern reach of the estate.

According to an early twentieth-century account of this development,

---

[1] Witts, 42.

[2] Blake, n.p.

Pitt was "a great amateur of art," a collector of "beautiful pictures." His vision for Pittville was very grand, a blend of nature and art shaped by his own "eye for effect."[3] To lay out this new town, he commissioned local architect John B. Forbes, an able fellow who had trained at the Royal Academy in London. Forbes drew the general plan for the estate, including roads, walks, gardens, and lots for terraces and villas. And he designed the Pump Room (1825–1830), an imposing classical building with a great dome and majestic colonnades.

Pitt developed the common roads, walks, and gardens; he provided water, sewers, and gas lighting. Building lots were sold to individuals for the construction of private houses or to architects or builders who raised structures on speculation. Attached to the purchase of these lots were annual fees for the maintenance of the estate and restrictive covenants regarding the placement and exterior appearance of the houses, including the types of material (brick, usually faced with stucco scored to resemble limestone blocks, and slate roofs) and the placement of front gardens and iron railings. Interiors were configured and finished as the owners desired.[4]

JAY'S CONTRIBUTIONS TO PITTVILLE

For Jay, Pittville offered the opportunity to participate in the building of an entire community, a new and modern resort guided by the vision of a very wealthy man who was "full of culture and devoted to art."[5] And Jay, who understood his own métier to be an art, made at least two worthy contributions to Pittville in the design of a terrace and the construction of a villa.

Pittville Parade, Design for a Complex of Seventeen Units, Completion of Numbers 2 and 4, Evesham Road, 1825–1826. Pittville Parade is believed to be the earliest residential construction in the new town. This is a block of seventeen houses on the west side of Evesham Road, a prominent site very near the entry to Pittville. The design of this terrace is attributed to Jay based on a

[3] Humphris and Willoughby, 156–57.

[4] Blake, n.p.

[5] Humphris and Willoughby, 159.

drawing prepared by R. Mackay in 1826.[6] The first offering for sale of building lots in the town occurred in September 1824. In October, Nathanial Colt, a draper (a dealer in cloth goods), made an agreement with Pitt to purchase the entire block at this site. Subsequently, the two southernmost plots were resold to Jay and the remaining fifteen plots to James Watts, a painter.[7]

It was Pitt's usual method to have plans drawn by an architect, then building lots were sold to builders who were obliged to follow the proposed design.[8] For Pittville Parade, Jay may have drawn a plan as early as October 1824 when the block was first sold. Certainly the proposal was in place in 1825 because construction began at the site in that year. Jay acquired the plots for and completed two of these houses (Numbers 2 and 4) in 1825–1826.

Mackay's drawing of Jay's design was a fair depiction of what the parade was intended to be. The view took a raking perspective from the vantage point of the southernmost units, offering good detail of the two houses known to have been completed by Jay. For the entire structure, the architect had as his challenge to break the monotony of a very long row of seventeen joined houses. All of the units were three-bays wide (two windows and a front door at the ground floor) and three stories in elevation over a basement.

Jay's solution was to create a symmetrical design, with five units crowned by an elaborate cornice at the center. At each end were three houses composed as an entity, with four monumental pilasters (Doric at the left and right and Ionic at the center) serving as anchors for the long parade. Between these end groups and the prominent central group were three quite plain houses with facades articulated only by a unifying string course.

Echoes of Jay's design for Pittville Parade survive only in the two southernmost houses known to have been completed by him. The work at this complex proceeded in fits and starts. By the end of 1825, Watts had finished two houses and partly built five more. However, he was caught in the banking crisis of 1825 and was declared bankrupt by January 1826. His holdings were taken by one of his creditors and resold to a builder who completed the terrace

[6] R. Mackay, "Pittville Parade," design by William Jay, drawing, 1826, formerly Cheltenham Art Gallery and Museum Collection, Cheltenham, England, now presumed lost.

[7] Cheltenham Art Gallery and Museum, entry #5.

[8] Howes, 58–59.

in 1831–1835.[9]

Glenmore Lodge, Wellington Square, 1826–1827. At the western edge of Pittville, two large garden squares were developed, and lots overlooking these were prime locations for private villas. These squares were named for two important figures of the day, the dukes of Clarence and Wellington. The Duke of Clarence was William Henry, the third son of George III, who became William IV in 1830 upon the death of his eldest brother George IV. The Duke of Wellington was Field Marshal Arthur Wellesley, a distinguished military officer who was revered for his role in the final defeat of Napoleon at the Battle of Waterloo in 1815.

Glenmore Lodge is presumed to be the earliest building on Wellington Square and one of the first free-standing residences in the new town. It was built for Alexander Limond, one of a number of military officers who retired to Cheltenham; he had served in India as a Lieutenant Colonel of the Madras Army. Limond married in 1823, and perhaps to honor his Scottish wife, he gave his fine home on Wellington Square the good Gaelic name of Glenmore (the Great Glen).[10]

Attributed to Jay based on elements of the style, this structure is a familiar Regency block comprising two floors over a basement, stucco on brick with a flat roof. Like Jay's Savannah houses, this building has relatively plain surfaces with expressive contours and volumes. On the first floor is a reception room terminating in a bow at the east end with large windows overlooking the square. "Gothik" windows at the second level of the east elevation have tracery patterns of overlapping pointed arches.[11] A unique element is the sweeping flourish of a false gable at the north facade, structurally meaningless because this roof is flat but clever because it hides a prominent chimney for an interior fireplace.

THE PACE OF THE WORK AND THE WEIGHT OF THE WORRIES

Once again Jay had come to a place that seemed to be brimming with opportunity. He arrived in late 1822 to participate in a great rush of building.

---

[9] Cheltenham Art Gallery and Museum, entry #5.
[10] Ibid., entry #11.
[11] Verey, *Buildings of England, Gloucestershire 2*, 284.

Census figures for 1801 gave the number of houses standing at 710, with fifteen in construction; by 1826 the count of houses was 4,027, with 774 in construction. Notice of projects attributed to Jay in Cheltenham and Pittville survives in a variety of public documents. For example, a report of improvements in Cheltenham in 1825–1827 cited Jay as the builder of "two houses in Priory Street," "1 house in Mr. Godsals field, Bath road," "5 Houses in Columbia place," and "a building on the South side of the colonnade."[12]

Further evidence of Jay's work comes in advertisements posted in local newspapers. However, notices appearing in 1826 hint at the trouble to come. In December 1825, the country was hit by a tremendous financial crisis. In just a few weeks, the halcyon days of speculation came to a fast end with the failure of credit lines and the collapse of many banks. By early 1826, it was clear that the building boom in Cheltenham and Pittville was caught in a worrisome stall.

Jay often met adversity with a determined optimism, no doubt inherited from his famous father. On Saturday, January 14, 1826, came this entry in the *Gloucester and Cheltenham Herald*, an advertisement masquerading as a news report:

> The works at Pittville are in progress, though necessarily suspended by the rigour of the season, & checked perhaps, in a temporary degree, by those commercial embarrassments which Cheltenham has not had the good fortune to escape. This quarter of the town must add much to its beauty & convenience, and cannot fail, we think of sharing largely in those general advantages to which it will contribute.—Some very elegant houses are completing on various spots, under the superintendence of Mr. William Jay, a gentleman whose architectural merits are most admirably displayed in every task he has hitherto undertaken.[13]

The regrettable truth was that, in the company of many other builders, Jay had overextended his resources. To recover, he needed to sell or rent all of his holdings. Newspaper notices of available properties appeared weekly in 1826 from late January through mid-August, sounding as drumbeats through this difficult time. Dozens of anxious posts included the instruction to "enquire [*sic*] at the office of Mr. WM. JAY. Architect" for sales or rentals at the Paragon Buildings, Columbia Place, a dwelling "with a good Shop" in the

[12] Griffith, 1:17; *An Act for Better Paving... Cheltenham*, n.p.
[13] "Works at Pittville," *Gloucester and Cheltenham Herald*, Jan. 14, 1826.

High Street, "A Most desirable Piece of GROUND...in the Bath Road," "Lots, for Building" in the High Street, and Oakland House "an excellent detached residence, with...twenty acres of meadow land" near the High Street.[14]

JAY'S ACCOMPLISHMENTS IN CHELTENHAM AND PITTVILLE

Cheltenham flourished as a Regency city gaining prominence in the early years of the nineteenth century. Remarkably, over two centuries very few Regency buildings have been lost, and among the surviving structures are a handsome handful credited to Jay. Henry Davies, writing in 1843, cited among the fine residences of the region these now attributed to Jay:

> Descending the Bath road...we pass in succession two or three rows of excellent private dwelling houses, among which are...[the Paragon] Buildings.... [Proceeding up Winchcomb Street] we pass...at the very top of the street, on the left, *Columbia Place*, a row of private houses much superior in external appearance to those already passed.... The grand drive to the Pittville Spa...forms the principal northern outlet of the town, and, for a considerable distance, is flanked on either hand by buildings of the best description...*Pittville Parade* stands out most prominently, forming as it does a peculiarly neat and uniform range on the left.[15]

Five years after the national financial collapse in 1825, building resumed in Cheltenham and continued apace into mid-century. But by 1841, the report was that "the reputation of Cheltenham as a Spa is on the wane." With the decline of Cheltenham, Pittville was doomed. According to an early twentieth-century report, "Pittville appears to have been never really well patronised. Its distance—three quarters of a mile from the High Street and further still from the other spas—was against it. Cheltenham's days as a fashionable spa were coming to a close. Mr. Joseph Pitt therefore found the Fates against him."[16]

By these accounts, the lasting success Jay might have had in Cheltenham and Pittville was thwarted by more than failing banks in 1825. The spas here had fallen victim to capricious fashion. By 1830 the popular resort for the

---

[14] [Sale of Jay properties], *Gloucester and Cheltenham Herald,* Jan. 21–Aug. 12, 1826.

[15] Davies, 196–97.

[16] Granville, 2:284; Humphris and Willoughby, 158.

fancy crowds was Leamington Spa in Warwickshire, forty-five miles northeast of Cheltenham, visited twice by Victoria (in 1830 as princess and in 1858 as queen). Cheltenham and Pittville had been congenial settings for Jay's skills and sensibilities, and here he had found an abundance of work. He had arrived in late 1822, and very soon the wind was at his back. But, events and circumstances would crush him, and he would be gone from this place by 1830.

CHAPTER 32

WATERMOOR HOUSE

Watermoor House in Gloucestershire, designed and built by Jay in 1825–1827, is just fifteen miles south of Cheltenham. The location is now a district of Cirencester, but when this residence was constructed, it was fashioned as a country house in a region more rural than suburban. For a century, this structure accommodated families of means and standing who settled here in the southern Cotswold Hills.

In the early nineteenth century, this area was crowded with fine country homes, but now many are gone. Victims of the changing circumstances of their owners, some of these houses have been demolished, and some have been reduced to the rank of vacation rentals. Of the few estates remaining in the region of Watermoor House, a near neighbor is Cirencester House claimed by the Bathurst family since 1695 and the site of the finest forest landscape in England. Just down the road a dozen miles to the southwest is Highgrove House, the country estate of Charles, Prince of Wales; and nearby is Gatcombe Park, the country home of Anne, Princess Royal.

Watermoor House has been called "perhaps his [Jay's] most important surviving work in Europe."[1] The claim is easily made because so little by Jay is known outside of the American South. But, this house is an unsatisfying treasure. Some plans for this project survived, and they reveal that what was built was much changed from Jay's original design. Later a jumble of additions began to swallow up the original structure. Finally, after little more than a century of existence as a fine country house, the building was given over to institutional use, first as an Anglican school for young women and later as a residence for seniors.

Still, among a profusion of sundry attachments and renovations, hints of the original structure remain—it was a close cousin of Jay's Savannah houses. This was a Regency villa, a compact block of two-stories over a basement, with an apparently flat roof. A three-bay facade featured a Greek unpedimented porch, and corners were emphasized by setbacks. On the interior were

[1] Bishop, 3.

good quality finishes and a grand stairway illuminated by a skylight.

OFFERING JAY A PLACE IN THE HISTORY OF ENGLISH ARCHITECTURE

Notice came slowly to this house by Jay. The first careful studies of Watermoor House date to the 1970s when the history of this building and an account of its architect were recovered by David Verey and Christopher Bishop, both important figures in the historic preservation movement in this region of England.

Verey was the first to draw attention to Watermoor House. Trained in architecture at Cambridge, Verey was a native of Gloucestershire, and he wrote the two surveys of this area for *Buildings of England*, the series directed by Nikolaus Pevsner.[2] In 1970, for the first edition of *Gloucestershire 1: The Cotswolds*, Verey observed, "Watermoor House by *William Jay*, c. 1840, two-storeyed and ashlar-faced, has a large porch with fluted Doric columns in antis and a wreath-embellished frieze."[3] The architect was identified, although the date was mistaken—Jay, who worked here in the 1820s, died in 1837.

In 1976 Verey presented a paper on Watermoor House at the gathering of a regional archaeological society, in which he conveyed the regret that so little was known about Jay and his work in England. He offered his assessment that Jay's "Soanian [referring to John Soane] tastes and natural talents" had fostered a creative approach to design. And he cited an observation by a colleague, saying, "According to John Cornforth, Jay's houses are certainly the most interesting in Savannah, and if that town were as well-known as Charleston to English visitors Jay might not seem so detached from English architectural history."[4] By the early 1970s, John Lewley Cornforth was gaining recognition as the expert on the architecture and interior decoration of English country houses. His comment on Jay's undeserved obscurity underscored the worth of recovering the history of Watermoor House.

In 1979 Christopher Bishop was engaged to study this building, which

---

[2] This series of forty-six volumes first appeared in 1951–1974. Verey was given responsibility for *Gloucestershire 1: The Cotswolds* and *Gloucestershire 2: The Vale and Forest of Dean,* both first published in 1970.

[3] Verey, *Gloucestershire 1: The Cotswolds*, 182.

[4] Verey, "The Architect and Architecture of Watermoor House," 168.

was by then a home for seniors. He was asked to assess its condition and propose a course for its restoration. Trained as an architect, he spent much of his career involved with historic preservation. Like Verey, Bishop was a native of this region, and like Verey he was surprised by what he found at Watermoor House. It was, he said, "a good quality Regency Villa," displaying taste and ingenuity and accomplished by an architect virtually unknown in England. He concluded, "William Jay was one of the more unusual architects of his generation, both in his designs and in his life history."[5]

THE PATRON

This house was commissioned by Joseph Randolph Mullings. Mullings had been born in Devizes in the county of Wiltshire, educated in Devizes, and admitted to practice as a solicitor there in 1820. Soon thereafter he settled in Cirencester, thirty miles north of Devizes. There he had the good fortune to become the protégé and later the associate of Joseph Pitt, the developer of Pittville Estate. In 1823 Mullings married and acquired the three-acre plot that would be the site of Watermoor House.[6]

It is assumed that Jay came to the attention of Mullings by way of Pitt, but there may have been familial connections. Devizes was a market town in the center of the Reverend Jay's ancestral lands in Wiltshire. Throughout his life, he was a frequent visitor to towns and villages in Wiltshire, and Devizes was the home of the Reverend Richard Elliott, a lifelong friend who was also a seasonal supply to Surrey Chapel in London.[7]

However the connection was made, it is likely that the relationship between this patron and this architect was congenial. Mullings and Jay were the same age, and both were ambitious and industrious. Mullings was just beginning a practice of law, and in the coming years he would assume positions of responsibility in this district. First elected to Parliament in 1848, he served there for most of the remaining years of his life. Ultimately he was a magistrate (judge), first in Gloucestershire and later in Wiltshire. Mullings was remembered in an account written in 1882 as having "no adventitious claims of birth, or rank, or fortune…[but rather] native talent, nursed and rendered productive by great industry and indomitable perseverance, which in this free

[5] Bishop, 3–4.
[6] Ibid., 1.
[7] Wallace, 118–19.

country is open to the humblest born pursuing the same course."[8] Here at the beginning of his career, his prospects for success were reflected in the construction of a fine house on a very remarkable site.

THE PLACE

At Watermoor, Jay was commissioned to design a country house on a plot of land within the precincts of a Roman town dating to 43 A.D. By the early fourth century, Corinium Dobunnorum had a population of around 15,000, the second-largest town of Roman Britain, the largest being Londinium (later London). Public buildings here had included a central forum (marketplace), a basilica (law court), temples, and baths; south of the town center was an amphitheater, oval in form and fitted with seating to accommodate as many as 8,000 spectators. The residence for Mullings was built in the district of the basilica and not far from the amphitheater.

Watermoor House took its name from the land. This had been a river floodplain of marshland or moors. In the first and second centuries, Roman engineers constructed drainage ditches to control flooding and built up the ground level to support the development of the town. According to legend, these circumstances prompted the name "Watermoor," a watery moor.

From the time of Roman settlement, this district grew wealthy from the wool of the sheep of the Cotswolds. When the Romans left in 408 A.D., the medieval village of Cirencester emerged, and by the mid-fourteenth century this town was the principal market for Cotswold wool from which was woven the best cloth produced in Europe. By the early sixteenth century, Cirencester had come to look like a prosperous place. Its public buildings and fine private homes were constructed of Cotswold stone, an oolitic (formed of spherical grains) limestone dating from the Jurassic period. In this region, the stone, which has been quarried since ancient times, is yellow and weathers to a golden color, and it is abundant. This is the stone that would be used to face Watermoor House.

But, fortunes turned. By the late eighteenth century, textile mills powered by the rivers of Stroud a dozen miles away replaced the looms of Cirencester, and soon cotton took the place of wool in the manufacture of cloth.

---

[8] Stratford, 128–29.

Desperate to attract new industries, in the early years of the nineteenth century the civic leaders of Cirencester raised funds for infrastructure projects by selling parcels of undeveloped land in what had once been the Roman town. One of these plots came to Mullings and his new bride as a gift from her grandfather.[9]

THE PLANS

Drawings signed by Jay survive for "Mr. Mullings House." They include a depiction of the facade behind a gated front wall and a plan for the first floor of the house. The design for the facade shows three stories on a raised basement, a symmetrical three-bay front with tall windows at the first two levels and short windows at the third. At each side of the entry is a tall, round-headed window set in an arched reveal. There are notations for ironwork, including shallow balconies at the two windows of the first level and a central veranda flanked by two small balconies at the second level.[10] Most of this design was not realized. Of the proposed three upper stories, only two were built. The windows of the ground level were not rendered as arches, and the elements of ironwork were eliminated.

For the interior, only a plan for the first floor survives. In this scheme, the front door opened into a broad hall that continued to the center or core of the building. Just inside the door at the left was a "private room" and at the right a dining room. Behind the dining room was a drawing room linked by double doors to a library at the back of the house. The staircase was located at the center of the structure behind the "private room" and not visible from the front door.[11]

THE CONSTRUCTION

When Bishop studied the house in 1979, he discerned "a small, four square Grecian Villa…with some unusual detailing."[12] Essentially this was the

---

[9] Bishop, 1.

[10] W. Jay, arch., "Plans for Mr. Mullings House," Architect William Jay Papers (1825-1830), Gloucestershire Record Office, Gloucester, England (hereafter cited as GRO)..

[11] Ibid.

[12] Bishop, 1–5 (hereafter cited in text).

familiar Regency design of two stories over a basement with the kitchen located below, reception and dining rooms on the main floor, and the bedrooms above. Joining the house to this landscape, it was faced in ashlar (squared and coursed stone) of the locally quarried golden limestone.

Among the "unusual detailing" included a handsome unpedimented porch, conceived as an unexpectedly deep passage, and two fluted Doric columns supporting a full entablature with a frieze showing a laurel wreath posed above each column, a pattern Jay proposed for the bank in Savannah. At each side of this porch are one-story bays, each one pierced by two long widows with apron panels of a ribbon of flat fluting, an element Jay used in Cheltenham. At the southwest corner of the building is a familiar setback, and it is likely that the other three corners were treated in a similar fashion. The south flank of the building is composed of four bays articulated by three giant order pilasters, recalling the design of the sides of the Savannah bank.

Bishop observed that the interior had "the usual fittings of a good quality Regency Villa," such as carved marble fireplaces and fine woodworking details. In particular, he admired the top-lighted stairs: "The staircase is the most memorable feature, as the soffits [the underside] of the steps form a continuously carved band of stone rising round an open well. The handrail is mahogany supported by an unusually masculine wrought iron balustrade—quite unlike the normal Regency style. Above the staircase is a domelight."

It is unknown why some of Jay's recorded design for this property was abandoned, but cost is always a good guess. Further expense would have been incurred by the addition of a third story, the construction of great arched windows at the first level of the facade, and the components of ornamental ironwork. Likely money was in short supply for this project. Here Jay's client was not yet a man of substantial wealth, and in 1825–1827 the national economy was in distress, making it difficult to secure loans to cover the costs of materials and labor. Nonetheless, Mullings took possession of a fine house in 1827.

WATERMOOR HOUSE AFTER JAY

Jay's original structure was much changed over the years. When Bishop surveyed the house in 1979, he offered some proposals concerning the nature of the alterations as they may have been prompted by various residents:

Joseph Randolph Mullings, in residence 1827–1842. Mullings commissioned this work from Jay in 1825 and took up residence here in 1827. As he prospered and his family grew, the house was enlarged. According to Bishop, a large north wing, containing kitchen quarters on the ground floor and additional bedrooms above, was added by Mullings as early as 1835. In 1842 he abandoned Watermoor House and moved to Eastcourt House, an old estate seven miles south of Cirencester which had come to him at the death of his mentor Joseph Pitt. Watermoor House remained in Mullings's hands for twelve more years.

Captain (later Vice Admiral) Charles Talbot, in residence c. 1842–1866. In the early 1840s, the house was leased to Talbot, a colorful character who had a long and distinguished military career, including his rout in 1845 of the Sharif Osman, perhaps the greatest Malay pirate of the day. In 1854 Mullings sold Watermoor House to Talbot, who increased the holding from three acres to twelve and greatly expanded the gardens.

The family of Charles Richard Pole, in residence 1866–1897. In 1866 the house was sold to "C. R. Pole," a descendant of the Poles of Wyck Hill House in Gloucestershire. Bishop proposed that Pole was responsible for a number of additions, including a large ballroom with a saucer dome, a chapel, a colonnaded loggia at the southeast corner, and two one-story bays flanking the portico of the west facade. However, the bays of the facade have apron panels of the sort Jay used in Cheltenham, so these features are surely original to the house. And, the chapel has been dated to 1908 and credited to an architect active in Cirencester after 1900.[13]

Members of the Cripps family, owners of the house 1897–1908. Members of the Pole family lived here until 1897 when the property was sold. Ownership passed to the Cripps family, a numerous clan with roots in Cirencester reaching back into the sixteenth century. Various Cripps became prominent in business and civic affairs, and their holdings included cloth mills, a brewery, land investments, and banking services.

The member of this family with the most certain interest in Watermoor House was Wilfred (or Wilfrid) Joseph Cripps. He was a barrister, an owner

[13] Verey, *Gloucestershire 1: The Cotswolds*, 246, 277.

of the brewery, and a landowner; but his consuming passion was archaeology. He was a member of the Society of Antiquaries of London, established by royal charter in 1751, and he was well known for his research and writing about finds in Cirencester. In 1897–1898 Cripps financed and directed excavations near Watermoor House that would prove his calculation of the site of the long-lost Roman basilica.[14]

The family of Thomas Arthur Fitzhardinge Kingscote, in residence 1908–c. 1939. By 1908 Watermoor House came into the hands of Thomas Kingscote. The Kingscotes were an old family, holders since the eleventh century of an estate known as Kingscote Park ten miles southwest of Cirencester. Thomas was the fourth son of the lord of the manor and the son of a second wife, so he had little prospect of inheriting the family estate. Still, he was successful as a courtier in the royal household. His second son became a legendary polo player, and the family may have been drawn to this place because of its prominence in that sport.[15] The Cirencester Park Polo Club had been founded in 1896 on the grounds of the Bathurst estate.

The Kingscotes were the last family to live in Watermoor House. Thomas died in 1935, and his wife was gone from this place by 1939. By the late 1930s, the suburb of Watermoor was becoming crowded with commercial establishments, and the onset of World War II would take a toll on the life of the landed gentry in the Cotswold Hills. Watermoor House might have suffered the indignities of abandonment or demolition, the fates of many of the old country houses in this era, but the structure was saved by the occupation of two particular enterprises.

St. Michael's Convent School, c. 1939–1949. Around 1939 Watermoor House was acquired by the Sisters of the Society of the Holy and Undivided Trinity as a new home for an established "upper school" (offering secondary education) for young women of privilege. First located in Oxford, St. Michael's was so successful that the sisters were compelled to move it to a larger

---

[14] "Recent Discoveries," *Reliquary and Illustrated Archaeologist,* 1898, 212–16.

[15] This second son was Maurice John Kingscote, a star polo player who won the Roehampton Trophy (the oldest cup in the sport in Great Britain) in 1922, 1923, and 1929.

facility. They chose Watermoor House, and the structure was adapted to accommodate all of the programs of the school and to house the sisters and their students.

Watermoor House, a residential and respite care house, 1952–present. By 1950 Watermoor House had been abandoned, and some community leaders expressed concern about the future of the property. A rescue of sorts came in 1952 when the building was acquired to become a residential care home for the elderly. To fit this new use, the interior was carved into several "flatlets" or suites, but funds were not available for needed repairs. By the time Bishop studied the property in 1979, he observed considerable deterioration of the structure. Subsequently the property was recognized as having historic significance, protecting it for the future and prompting a number of restoration projects. The building survives in good condition, and the grounds are now a community park, recognized as one of the largest undisturbed areas of Roman settlement remaining in Great Britain.

THE SIGNIFICANCE OF WATERMOOR HOUSE FOR THE STORY OF JAY

Enough of Jay's Watermoor House has survived to reveal his unique accomplishments. Bishop said, "His [Jay's] proportions and detailing are so idiosyncratic—almost perverse on occasion—that his mixture of tradition and innovation can only be compared to Soane among his contemporaries." He pointed to the unusual composition of the entry to the house: "While the design is essentially a simple distyle in antis [two columns at the front of a recessed porch adjacent to square piers], the whole character has been changed by making the anta [the piers] only half as wide as they are deep. This has the effect of giving them a narrow face to the visitor, but a broad depth flanking the columns."[16] Verey perceived essential elements of Jay's style as he praised the design of this facade, calling it "severely simple" in the use of "proportion, scale and subtle detail" to achieve the aspect of "dignity."[17]

In the known body of Jay's work, this is the only house planned for the English countryside. Over nearly two centuries, the original design was much compromised. First it was built at the time of a national economic crisis when

[16] Bishop, 4.

[17] Verey, "The Architect and Architecture of Watermoor House," 169.

money was short, then it was subjected to an array of changes and additions by a succession of demanding residents. The wonder is that enough of Jay's hand survived here to have delighted the likes of Verey and Bishop and to have prompted community leaders to preserve this structure as a fine country home in the Cotswold Hills.

CHAPTER 33

"WILLIAM JAY, A BANKRUPT"

On August 19, 1828, the name of "William Jay, of Cheltenham...Architect and Builder" was published as "a Bankrupt." In the parlance of the day, he had been "gazetted." The notice of his financial embarrassment was posted in the *London Gazette*, which since 1665 had been the journal of record for statutory notices. Bankruptcy was a serious matter; indeed, it was a crime because it undermined the good conduct of commerce essential to a prosperous society. So grave was this offense that, over long centuries, English law did little to address the plight of debtors whose condition often seemed more hopeless than that of all other perpetrators of crime.

Debtors' prisons were still being built in England in the first decades of the nineteenth century. Until 1820 the death penalty was held as the ultimate punishment for fraudulent bankrupts although few had paid that price in long memory. But certain views of the problem were changing. Debt was still a most serious matter, but the law now considered the amount of loss. Small debtors (those who owed less than £100) might gain release from prison by declaring a condition of insolvency and allowing all of their present and future assets to be assigned to their creditors. Those whose debt amounted to more than £100 gained the legal status of "a bankrupt," and a proceeding of bankruptcy was conducted. That was Jay's fate.

Increasingly it was seen that larger sums of indebtedness were not only a hazard but a necessity in an era of rapid development. In a booming economy, progress in many sectors was made through speculation. Worthy projects and their financial rewards were often achieved only at the exercise of great risk carried aloft by credit, which in turn increased the earnings of banks and investors. Bankruptcy might be the outcome of a failed business plan, or it could be the result as in Jay's case of a collapse of the banking system. In the latter case, many argued that the responsibility for failure should be shared by the individual and the society which allowed and even encouraged speculative ventures.

THE PANIC OF 1825

In Cheltenham, Jay worked on speculation, and he was caught in a catastrophic failure of the banking system in late 1825. From the time of his arrival here, he made many efforts to be successful. He developed several properties, contributed to the development of others, and represented some for sale. Had the boom of the early 1820s lasted for just a few more years, Jay could have realized considerable financial gain. But, as they had in Savannah, forces quite beyond his control crossed his path and brought him down.

Jay was a victim of the Panic of 1825, one of the unhappiest events in English economic history. According to one report, it was "a classic example of a speculation-fueled crisis."[1] After 1821 opportunities for speculative investment with the promise of quick fortunes were abundant. In England the inventions and industries of the Industrial Revolution unleashed a flood of new products and revolutionized transportation systems (roads, canals, and railroads). Land acquisition and development boomed as new wealth brought demand for places of residence and retreat. Investors grew besotted with projects that were either unrealistic, in which case the prices of stocks became wildly inflated, or fraudulent, with the result that the stocks had no value at all. A consequence was that in December 1825, the Bank of England found itself long on loans and short on specie (gold) and so ceased payment on notes. This action caused the Panic of 1825, resulting in the collapse of several large London banks and dozens upon dozens of small banks across the country.

THE CONSEQUENCES FOR AN "ARCHITECT AND BUILDER"

As a victim of this catastrophe, Jay was not alone. The bank failures that emanated from the Panic of 1825 led to the bankruptcy of hundreds of companies and thousands of individual investors. Architects and builders who worked on speculation had borrowed money and mortgaged assets to pay suppliers and workers, all on the promise of sales, which would cover debts and realize substantial profits. When the economy collapsed, the housing market crumbled as prices fell and buyers disappeared.

In this era, many architects succumbed to bankruptcy. Some recovered and built their practices anew, but others failed and were not heard from

[1] Haupert, 511.

again. John Nash, who became the favorite architect of the prince regent, began in 1775 as a builder working on speculation. He was driven into bankruptcy by 1783. Robert Mills, who stole Jay's thunder in South Carolina, succumbed to bankruptcy in 1821, a consequence of his involvement in an unsuccessful development of row houses in Baltimore, Maryland. Ultimately, both Nash and Mills were rescued by gaining civil service appointments.

The published record gives some clues about how Jay managed the awful event of his bankruptcy. In a series of ten notices posted from August 19, 1828, through August 28, 1832, the *London Gazette* carried the full report of his indictment and the ensuring transactions. In the usual process, commissioners interviewed the debtor, kept the accounts of assets and debts, rendered decisions about the claims of creditors, and determined the penalty. This routine had the goals of satisfying creditors and punishing the debtor. But often the disposition of properties was negotiated, and a prison term might be brief or made more comfortable or avoided altogether. The facts seem to be that Jay complied with the order to make a full disclosure of his circumstances. Both his assets and his debts were substantial. So, as certain properties held by Jay were sold, profits were realized, and the claims against him were mitigated. The resolution of this matter took four years.[2]

Surely Jay received treatment as fair as might be procured in those days. He had two lawyers, one from Cheltenham and one from London. Likely these were men of good standing, probably recommended by his own two brothers who were solicitors, Cyrus in London and Ernest in Bath. Further guidance could be offered by his younger sister Arabella's husband, Garfit Ashton, a solicitor and clerk of the peace in Cambridge. There is no evidence that Jay was imprisoned during or after these proceedings.

THE CONSEQUENCES FOR JAY'S FAMILY

What this episode meant for Jay's personal life can only be surmised. Just at this time, there was very much at stake. In March 1827, he married Louisa Coulson of Henley-on-Thames.[3] She may have been a member of the Inde-

---

[2] "William Jay, of Cheltenham, in the County of Gloucester, Architect and Builder," *London Gazette*, Aug. 19, Oct. 3 (two declarations), and Dec. 2, 1828; Mar. 13 and Apr. 14, 1829; Jan. 26 and Feb. 5, 1830; Aug. 18, 28, 1832.

[3] "Married...Mr. William Jay," *London Times*, Mar. 21, 1827.

pendent Chapel in Henley where Jay's brother-in-law Robert Bolton ministered in 1824–1836. At the time of his marriage, Jay must have thought that his prospects were good and that he would have the means to support a wife and children to come. During the adjudication of his bankruptcy, two children were born, a son in 1830 and a daughter in 1832.

There is no report of how this family was sustained through these years. It seems that for at least some of this time Jay prevailed on his sister Anne and her husband, Robert, in Henley. In 1833 Anne wrote in her diary, "December 31st—Never was affliction sent to one of thy children but for the good. This night I am closing the year 1833 in the most entire dependence upon thy Providence, pressed down with family cares, my 13 children all at home, my dear nephew and niece with us—now orphans—myself confined to my room…our remittances from abroad…smaller than usual."[4]

Soon some of Anne's children, having come of age, would leave her home. In 1833 her last child, a daughter (the thirteenth child living; an infant born in 1828 did not survive to baptism), was two years old, and her eldest born in 1814 was nineteen.[5] In three more years, her husband would resign his ministry in Henley and take most of this family to the United States, where he hoped to secure an appointment with a larger salary to provide for the professional training of his sons. The "dear nephew and niece" of her diary entry were certainly Jay's children, William (known as "Willy") at age three and Louisa at age one. None of Anne's other siblings had children, and members of her husband's family lived in the United States and Canada. The account of her distress, including the observation that Jay and his wife had "orphaned" their son and daughter by leaving them in Anne's care in a house full to the rafters with children, suggests that these were difficult times for both families.

And what support could Jay have drawn from his father, the Reverend Jay? For a man of faith, and in particular for an evangelical, debt was a serious moral failing and a grievous sin. At least one report survives of the Reverend Jay's judgment of the condition of bankruptcy. In 1939 A. W. Wills wrote a history of the Argyle Chapel in Bath. His own life in this chapel began in 1875, long after the death of the Reverend Jay in 1853, but he knew the legend

---

[4] W. J. Bolton, 151. Anne's diary, begun in 1815 and comprising more than nine volumes, is now lost.

[5] R. Bolton, *Genealogical…Account of the Family of Bolton*, 184–94.

of the famous preacher. He recalled that "every year scores of visitors came to 'Jay's Chapel'" from places as far away as Canada, the United States, South Africa, Australia, and New Zealand because they had been nurtured by the Reverend Jay's popular books. Wills conveyed the complaints of chapel members that the preacher was "in great demand—all over the country...and in consequence, was away from Bath more often than he was in it." A view prevailed that the Reverend Jay's "preaching fees" and the royalties on his very numerous books allowed him to live "in a princely fashion." In the words of Wills, "He [the Reverend Jay] was the uncrowned king of the Free Church world; and ruled and acted as such."[6]

Wills offered these words to describe the Reverend Jay's view of bankruptcy: "'Woe betide the unfortunate person who could not pay his creditors in full! There were absolutely no extenuating circumstances which would be considered. He had disgraced the whole community, and out he had to go!" Wills recorded an episode in which a father and son, both members of the Argyle Chapel, were declared bankrupt. They offered to resign their memberships, but the Reverend Jay refused their proposals and forthwith expelled them from the congregation. The action was, Wills concluded, "terribly hard."[7]

However, there is no evidence that the Reverend Jay abandoned his son through his time of trouble. In August 1826, as Jay was busy searching for revenue-producing projects, his father wrote to Thomas Wilson, an evangelical philanthropist who was directing a campaign to build Independent/Congregational chapels, to recommend his son for this work.[8] And, during the proceedings of bankruptcy, the Reverend Jay granted his son a loan. Among the bundles of documents that survive to chronicle this affair is an indenture (a formal contract) dated January 11, 1830. This is a notice of agreement granting to the Reverend Jay a sum of £650, identified as interest earned on stocks brought to the marriage by Louisa Coulson and now given by Jay to his father to repay a loan.[9]

---

[6] Wills, v–vi, 11, 13.

[7] Ibid., 51.

[8] Rev. Jay to T. Wilson, Aug. 9, 1826, HMC.

[9] W. Jay, "Indenture," bankruptcy papers of William Jay, Jan. 11, 1830, GRO.

THE CONSEQUENCES FOR JAY'S PROFESSIONAL LIFE

What did the declaration of bankruptcy mean for Jay's professional life? There are very few reports of his activity during this period until his appointment to a civil service position in Mauritius. Given the legal status of "a bankrupt," it would have been difficult for him to find work. The publishing of the names of bankrupts was undertaken for the purpose of warning all who might enter into agreements with these persons. In addition to the statement of record in the *London Gazette*, announcements of Jay's bankruptcy appeared in a number of newspapers in late 1828, including the *Cheltenham Journal*, the *Gloucester Mercury*, the *Bath and Cheltenham Gazette*, the *Bath Chronicle*, *Keenes' Bath Journal*, and the *Times* of London.

Following are the reports of Jay during this time in Henley-on-Thames in Oxfordshire and Bromley in Kent:

Henley-on-Thames, Oxfordshire. The only work that can be assigned to Jay with certainty in these years is at the Independent Chapel in Henley. In July 1824, Jay's brother-in-law Robert Bolton took the position of minister at this chapel. Henley is located forty miles west of London on the Thames River, and in the early nineteenth century this was an enterprising place. There had long been a large population of dissenters here, including manufacturers, merchants, and laborers. In 1827 Bolton made the decision to enlarge the existing chapel (built in 1719) by adding side galleries. Then, in 1829 he commissioned a complete renovation and expansion of the building. All of this work is credited to Jay.

A description of Jay's 1829 refurbishment of this building survives in this report of the opening: "The present place will comfortably seat 700 persons.... The ceiling, which is arched, is supported, the columns running from the floor. The vestry is divided off by a large Gothic screen, which, when thrown back, lays it nearly entirely open to the Chapel, giving a light effect to the pulpit, and affording over it an open gallery for the instruction and sitting of part of the Sunday Scholars." Jay was praised for his design: "Its appearance struck us as being a considerable improvement on the style of Dissenting Chapels in general.... The whole is remarkably simple and elegant, and does great credit to the taste of the architect, Mr. William Jay, from whose designs, and under whose superintendence, the alterations have been made."[10]

Of no surprise at all was the participation in the opening ceremonies of the Reverend Jay and the Reverend Rowland Hill—for many years Hill had taken an interest in Bolton's preparations for the ministry. The event, reported in a local newspaper, was described as a great success:

> On Tuesday last [June 2, 1829], the opening of the Independent Chapel (upon the occasion of its enlargement) was most numerously and respectably attended. The Rev. Mr. Jay of Bath, preached in the morning...The Rev. Rowland Hill preached in the evening.... The collection at the doors, toward defraying the expenses of the enlargement, exceeded the expectations of its warmest friends, amounting to 92£ 18s.... Much praise is due to Mr. Jay (son of the rev. gentleman) the architect, whose taste in style and effect is admirably shown in the beauty of this building.[11]

In 1836, just seven years after this celebration, the Boltons left for America; Jay, his wife, two very young children, and a baby departed for Mauritius. In 1867 the Henley Independent Chapel was renovated again, and in 1907–08 a new structure was raised on an adjacent site. Finally, in 1909 all trace of Jay's work here was lost when the old chapel was demolished.

Bromley, Kent (later London Borough of Bromley). By August 1828, Jay was mired in the resolution of his bankruptcy. When he left Cheltenham is unknown, but by 1830 he was in Bromley where his eldest child, William, was born. In 1832 the bankruptcy negotiations were resolved, and in that year Jay was listed in a Bromley directory as an architect at Mason's Hill.[12]

A borough of London since 1965, Bromley is just ten miles southeast of the city. When Jay arrived in the early 1830s, coaches to London ran several times a day, and Bromley was booming. A book published in 1832, titled *History, Antiquities, Improvements, &c. of the Parish of Bromley, Kent,* described "the general improvements of the town of Bromley, which have taken place

---

[10] "Old Independent Chapel at Henley Upon Thames," *Evangelical Magazine,* Sept. 1829:414.

[11] "Henley, June 5," *Berkshire Chronicle,* June 6, 1829. The cost of this renovation was £957, donated by "friends in Henley, Bath, Liverpool and London" (G. Peters, 84–85).

[12] Lerski, 250; "William Jay," *West Kent Poll Book* (1835), Bromley Central Library Archives, Bromley, England.

within the last 16 years," offering the quick conclusion that these "improvements" had been "very considerable." Among the subscribers to this book was one "Mr. Jay" of Bromley.[13] Perhaps this was the architect Jay who knew the value of advertising his presence in the community.

According to this report in 1832, development had occurred in the central district called Bromley Common where "there have been erected numerous houses of genteel structure and appearance." Mason's Hill, where Jay was located, "is also very much improved from the extremely neat erections that have taken place within the last few months."[14] Evidence that Jay had a hand in these projects is missing, but this was work at which he was very accomplished.

A REPRIEVE

It seems that Jay did not find steady employment with the prospect of providing for his young family until 1836. In that year, he followed a course of action taken by other architects who had found work on commission unreliable and work on speculation hazardous. He sought a position in the British civil service, and he was appointed civil architect and inspector of works in the department of the surveyor general on the island of Mauritius. For Jay, it was to be—just as Savannah and Cheltenham had been—both opportunity and risk. But, this time the consequences would be dire.

---

[13] C. Freeman, xii, 19.

[14] Ibid., 29–30.

PART SIX

JAY IN MAURITIUS

CHAPTER 34

ISLAND OF MAURITIUS

When prospects for work seemed bleak at the beginning of his career, Jay set off for Savannah, Georgia. It was a world away from his life in England. Nearly twenty years later, again with his career caught in a dreadful calm—and now with a wife, two very young children, and a baby—Jay made the decision to move to the island of Mauritius in the Indian Ocean. This place was two worlds away from life in England. What could he have been thinking?

Given inadequate opportunities for work to sustain his growing family, Jay must have concluded that a prudent course of action was to secure a government appointment. In 1836 he accepted a position in the British civil service in Mauritius. Much was known about this place. The English had taken this strategic holding from the French during the Napoleonic Wars, and the accounts of this island were beguiling in ways that must have suited Jay's spirit of adventure.

On a world map, Mauritius is a small dot. An island of volcanic origin in the southwest Indian Ocean, it is located 700 miles east of Madagascar (a large island, 250 miles east of Africa). It is much smaller in land mass (only about 700 square miles) than the role it would play in history. Still, human habitation came late to this place. Early sea-faring traders used the island only as a stop on the way to somewhere else, a place to provision with fresh water and whatever food could be found. When the Dutch arrived in 1598, they named the place Mauritius for Prince Maurice of Nassau, the head of state of Holland and Zeeland. Importing slaves from Madagascar for labor, the Dutch built a fort, appointed a governor, and set about to cultivate sugar, vegetables, and fruit. But the efforts at agriculture failed, and the Dutch finally abandoned the island in 1706.

The French came in 1715 and made a mark here that survives to this day. The place was named *Ile de France*, and the capital city of Port Louis was established on the northwest coast and soon became a busy seaport. The French constructed government buildings, hospitals, factories, and warehouses. Large plantations produced sugar, cotton, and indigo, crops harvested by slaves from Madagascar and Africa.

By the mid-eighteenth century, France and England were locked in conflict over control of the Indian Ocean and its access to the riches of India and Africa. The French often hired privateers or gave harbor to mercenaries who attacked English vessels returning with goods from India. Increasingly, the *Ile de France* played a conspicuous role in the skirmishes to claim this region. In December 1810, on one of the several fronts of the Napoleonic Wars, the British took Port Louis (by then named Port Napoleon). They claimed the island and renamed it Mauritius.

By the time Jay arrived in May 1836, Mauritius was known as one of the most important British colonies because of its strategic position on the sea route from England to India. The French threat to British domination of the Indian Ocean had been eliminated, and Mauritius could boast of the trappings of French culture and the efficiencies of English administration. Jay must have heard stories about this place. The French had left behind some handsome structures in Port Louis, including a college, a theater, and streets of charming houses. The countryside was dotted with pleasant villages and grand plantations. The natural landscape was beautiful, formed with mountain ranges, rivers, and streams. The lush vegetation included such exotic plants that French and English naturalists busied themselves supplying specimens of these to the great museums of Europe. It was, as described by Alexandre Dumas *père* in 1843, an Eden, a paradise, "the promised land, the land of our dreams, 'tis the pearl of the Indian Ocean! 'tis the Isle of France!"[1]

THE DODO AND PAUL AND VIRGINIA

In this idyllic setting, the fame of Mauritius grew in curious ways through the unrelated legends of a flightless bird and a pair of star-crossed lovers. This very small island in the Indian Ocean had once harbored the dodo, a bird so odd that it seemed improbable that it had ever existed. And this island had been home to Paul and Virginia, sweet children of nature made so real by an eighteenth-century French writer that these lovers were believed to have lived in this place.

The Dodo. At some time in a distant past, a type of primordial pigeon

[1] Dumas, 5–7.

landed on this island and settled in. Finding no predators, the bird feasted on fruit fallen to the ground and grew to a size estimated to be about three feet tall and weighing as much as fifty pounds. The Dutch were first to report sightings of this odd bird in 1598, describing its rump as *dodaersen* ("a fat bottom"). The creature was remarkably unlovely. A large head sported a hooded, bare face with an oversized hooked beak; puny wings showed no prospect of lifting this lump up into the air; and only a few curly plumes sprouted from that great round butt.

In 1688 came the last report of a living dodo. The early claim was that the dodo had disappeared because it was so poorly adapted to life as a bird. But scientists came to see that what had befallen the bird were humans—who were mean (they taunted and hunted the bird as sport), hungry (although the meat was reported to be disgusting), curious (several specimens were dragged away from Mauritius to be displayed at public and private menageries in places such as London, Prague, and Amsterdam), or careless (having imported cats, dogs, pigs, and rats, alien creatures that destroyed the ground nests of the dodo and consumed the chicks and eggs).

Paul and Virginia. By the time Jay arrived here in 1836, the dodo was gone and forgotten. What was then known about Mauritius was an account of young lovers written fifty years earlier, a fiction remembered as a true story. *Paul et Virginie* by Jacques-Henri Bernardin de Saint Pierre is not much read these days, but from the time it appeared in 1787 it was a wild success, quickly translated into many languages. It was the great love story of the age.

In fast summary of *Paul et Virginie*, in 1726 on this exotic island two French women settled, each one with the burden of a baby and no husband. Their children, Paul and Virginia, were inseparable. Knowing nothing of the treacheries of the larger world, they grew in a perfect state of nature. But, as a very young woman Virginia was sent to be educated in Paris. In the care of a wealthy aunt, she was abused and sent home by ship in the season of fierce hurricanes. When the vessel approached Mauritius, it was swamped by a storm, and Virginia's lifeless body washed ashore into the arms of Paul, who soon died of despair. The phenomenal success of the novel prompted a Paul-and-Virginia industry to take hold in Mauritius. A suitably lovely grave site for the fictional lovers was found, imposing tombstones were installed, and pilgrims came by the thousands to that place.

As testimony to the endurance of this tale, Commodore Matthew

Calbraith Perry, the American Navy officer sent by the government to open trade with Japan, stopped at Mauritius in 1856 and observed, "It is not to be supposed that, among those who read at all, there are many who are unacquainted with the beautiful story of Paul and Virginia by Bernardin St. Pierre." And, in 1899 Mark Twain declared, "Apparently, there has been only one prominent event in the history of Mauritius, and that one didn't happen. I refer to the romantic sojourn of Paul and Virginia here. It was the story that made Mauritius known to the world, made the name familiar to everybody, the geographical position of it to nobody.... It is the greatest story that was ever written about Mauritius, and the only one."[2]

THE ASSISTANT CIVIL ARCHITECT AND INSPECTOR OF WORKS

Jay was delighted to gain a civil service appointment to Mauritius. What he did not know was that he would come into a position made of a mountain of work. The French had left behind grand public buildings, but they were disheveled; the English were busy building roads and bridges to improve the general efficiency of communication and transport on the island. In May 1838, John Augustus Lloyd, the surveyor general and civil engineer who directed the department in which Jay served, reported that the volume of work he supervised was "perhaps unequalled in any other Colony."[3]

Had Jay been offered a glimpse of the correspondence preceding his appointment, he might have declined the offer to journey to Mauritius. The incumbent assistant civil architect and inspector of works had died in January 1835. Lloyd, eager to fill the position, wrote to his supervisor, the governor of Mauritius, requesting "that this appointment may be filled up as early as possible from England by some Engineer having a thorough knowledge of land & surveying & the manner of drawing up Estimates, specifications and reports and a good architectural draftsman, important branches in this Department at present resting on a single Individual." He added, "The yearly salary is £250."[4] The skills cited were numerous, but the compensation was paltry.

In April 1835, Charles Grant, a Scot born in India to the chairman of the British East India Company, was appointed secretary of state for war and

---

[2] Perry, 185; Twain, 2:292, 296.

[3] J. A. Lloyd to G. Dick, May 23, 1838, NAM/PRO-CO.

[4] J. A. Lloyd to W. Nicolay, Jan. 3, 1835, NAM/PRO-CO.

the colonies, and he was named 1st Baron Glenelg. When the matter of this position on Mauritius came to his attention, he directed an aide to appeal to the Treasury for an increase in this salary. The aide wrote, "It is indeed scarcely to be expected that any person who has attained such a degree of professional ability should be induced by so small a remuneration to accept a laborious office in a distant & expensive Colony." Rather quickly came the reply from Treasury that the request was denied based on "already large expenditures for this department."[5]

By January 1, 1836, Jay had been offered and had accepted this appointment in Mauritius.[6] It is not known how he came to secure this position. He was not credentialed as an engineer or surveyor, so he did not precisely fit the qualifications earlier articulated by Lloyd. However, Jay was an able draftsman, and in Savannah and Cheltenham he had accomplished the design of a number of public and private structures. One possibility is that Jay came to the attention of the Colonial Office through contacts in the London Missionary Society (LMS). Both his father and his brother-in-law the Reverend Robert Bolton were active in the work of the LMS. Since 1814 this organization had sponsored a mission on Mauritius.

Another prospect is that Jay made this connection through one of his Cheltenham patrons. Thomas Thompson was a British merchant for whom Jay designed and built Colombia (later Columbia) Place. Thompson had gained a fortune through his relationship with Simón Bolivar, the liberator of Colombia in 1819. No doubt Thompson had come to know a Brit, on the personal staff of Bolivar, who in 1827 had been directed to conduct the first survey of the Isthmus of Panama to chart a passage between the Pacific and the Atlantic. This fellow was John Augustus Lloyd, who in 1831 was appointed to the position of surveyor general and civil engineer on Mauritius, a position he held until 1851.

When Charles Darwin visited Mauritius in 1836, he was attended by Lloyd. Darwin reported, "May 3rd. In the evening Captain Lloyd, the Surveyor-general, so well known from his examination of the Isthmus of Panama, invited Mr. Stokes and myself to his country-house.... We staid [*sic*] at this delightful place two days.... [W]e were constantly tempted to exclaim, 'How

[5] J. Stephen to Treasury Chambers, London, Oct. 6, 1835; Treasury Chambers, London, to J. Stephen, Oct. 26, 1835, NAM/PRO-CO.

[6] Lord Glenelg to W. Nicolay, Jan. 1, 1836, NAM/PRO-CO.

pleasant it would be to pass one's life in such a quiet abode!'" Darwin had arrived at Mauritius on the *Beagle* on Friday, April 29, and he sailed from the island on Monday, May 9.[7] On the following day, Lloyd welcomed another voyager to the island, his new assistant civil architect and inspector of works.

THE ARRIVAL OF JAY

Jay, his wife, two small children, and an infant left from Liverpool on February 21, 1836, on the ship *St. George* set "direct" for Mauritius.[8] They arrived in Mauritius on May 10, after nearly three months at sea. Jay took up his work on May 16. By January of the following year, he was in distress and wrote this appeal to his supervisor Lloyd:

> When I accepted the appointment in England...I was not aware of the heavy expences I should have to meet, or that I should find every thing so much dearer than in England. A few Months of sad experience...proves that the Salary now allowed is not sufficient to meet my common expences.... You are fully aware of the difficult and many duties I have to fulfill...[T]he importance of many of the Buildings—and the inefficiency of the artisans require more than ordinary attention and inspection...I consider that all the Works should be constantly inspected and especially early in the morning so as to give directions for the day.... Since I have been appointed I have every morning visited the Public Works—I shrink from no duty and am always the cheerful complier of any wish you have or may require.[9]

Jay requested an increase in his salary, and Lloyd forwarded this matter to the governor with his own appeal for more support for the work of the department. Ten days later came the reply from the governor. He declared that his many efforts to increase salaries had been futile—there was no hope of securing a remedy for Jay. However, in an administrative sleight of hand, the governor announced that he was willing to receive from Lloyd a new plan for distribution of the funds allotted to the department.[10] That proposal came

---

[7] Darwin, 572–73.

[8] "Shipping Intelligence," *The Albion* [Liverpool], Feb. 23, 1836.

[9] W. Jay to J. A. Lloyd, Jan. 13, 1837, National Archives of Mauritius, Surveyor General's Department Collections (1836-1837), Coromandel, Mauritius (hereafter cited as NAM/SGD).

[10] G. Dick to J. A. Lloyd, Jan. 23, 1837, NAM/SGD.

to nothing. Just how poorly Jay was compensated for his work is clear from a report printed in 1836. Lloyd earned an annual salary of £800; Edmund O'Brien, the assistant surveyor general, earned £400; James White, clerk of works and draftsman, earned £397; and Jay, civil architect, earned £250. Below Jay were a master mason who earned £192; a storekeeper at £124; and two accountants at £144 and £120.[11]

"I SHRINK FROM NO DUTY"

As Jay had written in his appeal for an increase in his salary, he had accepted with some cheer the heap of work required of him. This load was tremendous, and it had been made more onerous by recent events. Jay had come to Mauritius at a very difficult time. Enslaved Africans had been on the island since the occupation of the Dutch and the beginning of a plantation economy in the early seventeenth century. Under the French, the number of slaves had grown as the sugar industry flourished on the island. When Parliament declared that the slave trade in all English colonies would cease by 1833, the plantation owners on Mauritius (most of whom were French) feared that the end of slavery would be an end to their enterprises. Ultimately, the British government agreed to pay the plantation owners a substantial sum of money in compensation. The deadline for abolition was extended to 1835, with the further provision in law that these newly freed persons were to remain in service to their former owners as "apprentices" for six years.

The results were an economic crisis (brought on by the tremendous outlay of funds to the plantation owners) and a severe labor shortage (most of the freed slaves fled the plantations rather than serve as apprentices). To solve the labor problem, the British devised an experimental program in 1835 to bring indentured workers from India, a system soon revealed to be little more than a new form of slavery. In this chaotic environment, much of the labor for projects of the department of the surveyor general was accomplished by indentured Indians, and Jay as inspector of works was obliged to supervise this new workforce.

By his own accounting, Jay had responsibility to plan for and oversee the construction of all government projects on the island. From June 1836 to June

[11] *Blue Book for Mauritius*, 1836, NAM/PRO-CO.

1837, this work included repairs and expansion for customs and port buildings, design and planning for new schools, an expansion of the supreme court house at Port Louis, new barracks for the police force of the colony, repairs and expansion of public offices at Port Louis, and construction of a civil hospital at Port Louis and dispensaries at Port Louis and Mahébourg.[12] But most of Jay's energy was directed to three major initiatives in Port Louis: a restoration of government house, a new prison, and a new central market.

Repairs to Government House, Port Louis. Completed during Jay's term, this work had been long in coming. The governor observed, "The substantial repair which Government House has undergone will prove, I have no doubt, an economy in the end, and I have only to regret that the work should have been so long deferred, as it has occasioned heavier expence...than had been calculated upon." In particular, Jay had restored the banqueting room.[13]

A New Prison, Port Louis. The design of this important project had been undertaken by June 1836. By January of the following year, the work was underway, and Jay submitted a progress report identifying himself as the "architect." In May the project came to the attention of Lord Glenelg, who observed that the plans "appear to have been drawn up with skill and attention," and the British inspectors of prisons reported that the project complied with "the general principles of prison construction...[and the standards] of prison discipline which are recommended for adoption in this Country."[14]

Jay had grown up in the era of prison reform, one of the several issues of social action promoted by evangelicals. He surely knew the work of John Howard, an eighteenth-century dissident whose recommendations for prison reform had influenced James Elmes's *Hints for the Improvement of Prisons* (1817). Likely Jay's stock plans for jails drawn in 1819–1820 for the South Carolina Board of Public Works and the design of this building in Port Louis

[12] W. Nicolay, "Minute [administrative report]," June 12, 1837, NAM/PRO-CO.

[13] Ibid.; "Return of all Public Works," 1837, NAM/PRO-CO.

[14] "The erection of the new Prisons," *Mauritius Government Gazette*, June 4, 1836, NAM/SGD; W. Jay, "Estimate of the value of the Work done at the Civil Prison," Jan. 18, 1837, NAM/SGD; Lord Glenelg to A. Y. Spearman, May 5, 1837, NAM/PRO-CO; "Report from the Inspectors of Prisons," June 16, 1836, NAM/PRO-CO.

looked to the work of both Howard and Elmes.

The completed structure in Port Louis contained ninety-two cells and was augmented by yards and outbuildings. Each cell was designed to be occupied by one prisoner, allowing for "the separation of felons from all other prisoners" and for assignments according to "the nature of the crime, the age, the conduct, the character &c. of each individual." Construction began in August 1836 and was completed by June 1837.[15]

Replacement of the Bazaar, or Central Market, Port Louis. The central market had been decimated in 1834 by a great hurricane, but its restoration had faltered for at least three reasons: the lack of someone in the office of the surveyor general with sufficient skill to formulate and draw appropriate plans, the existence of a committee of concerned and meddlesome citizens, and inadequate funding.

By October 1836, Lloyd had achieved two remedies for the languishing problem of the central market: He had the services of a skilled architect, and he had mustered the courage to set aside the several proposals submitted by the citizen committee. He wrote to the governor, "Thinking it more desirable to propose a new market place than to attempt any correctives to [the committee's] plan I have the honor to forward for His Excellency's inspection [new] plans and elevations.... These drawings being the entire performance of Mr. Jay, I beg leave to forward the description, in his own words of the new Bazaar."[16]

Jay's proposal included the following features:

> [T]he new Bazaar is divided into four compartments, two for vegetables and fruit, one for Fish and Poultry and one for Butcher's meat.... A neat Entrance and two lodges near the street are provided, one for the Clerk of the Market, the other for the use of the Police...[S]heds for the sale of vegetables should have a cast iron roof suspended on plain columns of the same material.... The roofs in three spans. The centre to form a covered way for foot passengers which will serve as a pleasant promenade being protected from the sun and rain.[17]

---

[15] "Return of the Gaols and Houses of Correction," 1837, NAM/PRO-CO; "Return of all Public Works," 1838, NAM/PRO-CO.

[16] J. A. Lloyd to G. Dick, Oct. 22, 1836, NAM/PRO-CO.

[17] W. Jay, "Description of a New Bazaar," [Oct. 1836], NAM/PRO-CO.

The citizen committee responded with grudging praise for "the elegant Plan designed by Mr. Jay and adopted by the Surveyor General." However, members of the committee raised the question of "whether an elegant Plan and durability of materials [particularly the components of iron and slate]...will counterbalance the great augmentation of expense and the consequent and unavoidable delay in rebuilding the Bazaar." Work began in January 1837. Apparently, Jay's plan was left intact, but the project was not completed until April 1845.[18] Remnants of Jay's design survive, including an entry to the market. Having endured the ravages of hurricanes and fires, this gateway has become a familiar landmark of Port Louis.

[18] E. Draper to G. Dick, Nov. 3, 1836, NAM/PRO-CO; "Return of all Public Works," 1837, NAM/PRO-CO'; "Financial Report," Apr. 1, 1845, NAM/PRO-CO.

CHAPTER 35

"LITTLE WILLY" AND THE LAST CHAPTER OF THE LIFE OF WILLIAM JAY

Because so little is known of the private moments of Jay's life, it comes as a surprise to find that much can be learned of his goings and comings in his final two years. This knowledge comes from two sources: *Little Willy*, a tract or pamphlet written by his wife about the death of their eldest child soon after they arrived in Mauritius, and the archives of the government of Mauritius where, in the usual manner of the British civil service, efficiencies and inefficiencies were recorded in lengthy reports in triplicate.

There may have been many reasons Jay brought his family to this place, including his spirit of adventure. But surely this move to Mauritius in 1836 was prompted in greatest measure by the need to provide for his family: Louisa, his wife of nine years; a son William, called "Little Willy," age six; a daughter Louisa, age four; and a baby son, Ernest, just six months old when this journey began. As an architect, Jay had been plagued by cost overruns, reluctant or insolvent patrons, and the failures of speculative schemes. Finally, in 1828, caught in a national economic collapse, he was declared "a bankrupt." In this dire circumstance, his prospects were poor. Work in the civil service must have seemed like a good option in a barren landscape of opportunities.

THE JOURNEY TO MAURITIUS

One can imagine Jay launching himself off to Mauritius with enthusiasm, even when there were early signs that this was not an entirely sound decision. The salary was meager, but Jay seemed to assume that the cost of living was low on this remote tropical island—and in this he was gravely mistaken. For his wife, there was only apprehension. The trip was arduous, and for Louisa it was compounded by the despair of leaving family and friends in England and by the stress of caring for a baby. This was her account of the journey to Mauritius:

> Just as my darling [Little Willy] had entered his sixth year, arrangements were made for our going abroad; and the anticipation of leaving England,

> and the prospect of the voyage itself, occasioned intense anxiety in my own mind and feelings.... During the long [eleven weeks], tedious, and, in some respects, dangerous voyage, the dear creature [Willy] was greatly affected by seeing the tears, which it was utterly impossible for me, despite my earnest efforts, to restrain.[1]

Settling into life on Mauritius would have been complicated in the highly stratified social, economic, and political environment of the mid-1830s. Most of the wealth and much of the political influence was held by the sugar plantation owners, many of them French and Catholic. In quite a separate circle moved officers and functionaries of the British government and military, most of them Anglican, who had been in place since the British took the island from the French in 1810. Here also were a few English dissenters, tradespeople or, like Jay, members of the civil service. In different districts altogether were large numbers of slaves brought from Africa by the French to work the plantations but nominally freed by the British in 1835. And, coming just as Jay arrived were Indians recruited by the British government as indentured laborers, a new form of slavery to replace the old one.

LOUISA

From the financial ruin that had come to Jay early in their marriage to this long voyage to a very foreign place, this was surely not the life that Louisa Coulson had hoped for when she married the eldest son and namesake of the Reverend William Jay of Bath. But, she revealed herself to be a very particular sort of early nineteenth-century wife. She was an educated, middle-class woman of an evangelical faith, deeply religious and committed to her work as a Christian mother. Such women were not uncommon in this age. Her mother-in-law, Anne Davies Jay, and her sister-in-law Anne Jay Bolton were very like her in character and spirit.

Evidence of who these women were and who they aspired to be survives in a great heap of books and articles. One category of this literature was the tract or "little book." These small volumes of moralistic tales had been prompted by the work of Hannah More, a friend of the Reverend Jay. In 1795–1797 More produced small books of Christian themes as guides to proper conduct, with the goals to spread the teachings of the gospels and to

[1] L. Jay, 28–31.

promote the agenda of social and political reform advanced by evangelicals.

The volume that Louisa wrote about the death of Little Willy in Mauritius was of this sort, a little book about an extraordinary child whose demise was counted as a Christian blessing. From a modest first appearance in 1837, this publication moved swiftly to a second edition with an introduction by the Reverend Jay, the child's grandfather. It remained in print through much of the nineteenth century, distributed by religious tract societies in England and America.

Louisa's account makes clear that she knew what her work on this earth was ordained to be. She wrote, "I received my little child as a precious gift from my heavenly Father; and knew that if I nursed him for God He would pay me my wages.... I felt so much the importance of maternal influence and watchfulness on the mind and character, that I considered that hour a lost one, in which he was not under my own notice." She knew precisely that her responsibilities were to care for her family and to direct the Christian education of her children. And she was pleased to report that her husband was her helpmate in achieving these goals. She declared, "However trifling, no request [to "dear Papa"] was ever granted without the previous inquiry, 'Have you asked Mamma?'"[2]

Little Willy is replete with examples of the extraordinary goodness of this eldest son. He learned Bible verses and hymns and recited and sang them when he thought they were needed to comfort his mother. In Mauritius, the family had three servants: an English woman, a black man, and a young black girl. Concerned that they should have "saved souls," Little Willy gathered them all for evening worship in the home, and he set about to teach the young black girl to read.

The remarkable character of this child was a matter of some amazement to his grandfather. In his introduction to the second edition of *Little Willy*, the Reverend Jay confessed that, because this boy was his own grandson, some might suspect him of a certain bias. But he had been persuaded by the observations of others who had known Little Willy that this was a true account of a rare child. So, he wrote confidently, "An infant more attractive, more engaging, more intelligent, and more pious, as far as piety could display itself in such early childhood, I have never seen."[3]

---

[2] Ibid., 14, 16–17, 20.

[3] Ibid., xi.

In mid-August 1836, just three months from the time of the arrival of this family in Mauritius, Little Willy fell ill. Louisa described the malady as first a slight headache. Then, as concern grew, "his devoted father walked the distance of four or five miles to procure medical advice." Over the coming week, more doctors were consulted, and the diagnosis came as "inflammation of the brain," perhaps typhus common in Mauritius during the nineteenth century. Louisa described the scene of her husband sitting at his son's side "every moment of the night, in the most intense, though silent anguish I ever witnessed." Then, "at the age of six years and eight months, he closed his eyes on earth and awoke in the realms of bliss."[4]

WILLIAM

In April 1837, just eight months after the death of Little Willy, Jay fell ill. His work had been hard and unrelenting, and there were grave personal matters in the death of his eldest child and the burden of a salary too small to meet the needs of his family. Further, it became clear that the department of the surveyor general was not a happy place. There were jealousies in the ranks, one of which involved a clerk of works who had begun his labor in 1824 and now reported to officers appointed a decade later. He was charged with poor performance of his duties, tardiness, occasional unauthorized absences, and "constant habits of intoxication." The clerk was suspended from service, but the unpleasant affair had involved Jay, who was obliged to describe and defend the conduct of his own labor. This sordid episode surely counted among the pressures that wore Jay down during this time.[5]

On April 14, Edmund O'Brien, the assistant surveyor general, reported to his superior John Augustus Lloyd that he had made a site inspection "in consequence of the illness of Mr. Jay." Three days later, Jay died in the late afternoon. The death certificate was signed by "Jean Lebrun, Missionary" and "Henry Austin Turner, Lieutenant in the Royal Artillery Corps."[6] The cause

---

[4] Ibid., 38, 43–44.

[5] E. O'Brien to J. A. Lloyd, Feb. 8, 1837, NAM/PRO-CO; G. Dick to J. A. Lloyd, Feb. 18, 1837, NAM/PRO-CO; W. Jay to J. A. Lloyd, Feb. 3, 1837, NAM/PRO-CO.

[6] E. O'Brien to J. A. Lloyd, Apr. 14, 1837, NAM/SGD; "William Jay," *Acte de Déces, Ile Maurice*, Apr. 18, 1837, in *Register of the Acts of the Civil Status of the District of Port Louis...Year 1837*, vol. 3, NAM/PRO-CO.

of death was not recorded. Years later Jay's old friend William Etty wrote in a letter, "William Jay, poor fellow, went out to the Mauritius, took a bilious fever, and died; leaving a wife and children."[7] Now obsolete in medical terminology, "bilious fever" was used in the nineteenth century to describe a condition characterized by raging fever and the excretion of bile by vomiting or diarrhea. Associated with any number of causes (including malaria, typhus, and yellow fever), "bilious fever" frequently resulted in death in temperate zones, particularly in certain seasons of the year. Europeans who lived in Mauritius called "the fine season" that time from May through mid-October when the heat was moderate and the winds were strong. "The bad season" came in late October and lasted through April, when heat, damp, and calm promoted the breeding and spread of disease.[8]

Eleven months later, Lloyd was the target of a serious challenge to his leadership by none other than O'Brien, his own assistant. In March 1838, O'Brien asserted that he had discovered irregularities in accounts, leading him to suspect that "this Department is conducted in a manner dangerous in its effects to public morality." He called for "a full and public inquiry" into the work of the department as guided by Lloyd. As a retort, Lloyd declared that O'Brien's malevolent character was revealed when he claimed shortly before Jay's death that Jay had stolen money from him by keeping a sum of £30 rather than posting it to England as he had been instructed to do.[9]

This accusation was the occasion for both men to speak of their recently deceased colleague. According to Lloyd, "Mr. Jay was a man of high talent, of upright and strongly religious principles which he appeared in every case to act up to. He possessed a most respectable family, was undividing in his attention and duties to his office. Such a man I respected and regarded. I regretted his loss both as a man and an Alt[ernate] Assistant in the Dept[ment]." Lloyd declared that O'Brien, in reporting the loss of his money, had fouled the memory of Jay. For his part, O'Brien was indignant that Lloyd had told this tale. He said, "It was enough to lose my friend and to find confidence misplaced without having had ashes disturbed to accuse me.... Mr. Jay died in my debt and I was offered payment but refused it and have received

[7] W. Etty to Mr. Bodley, Feb. 3, 1839, in Glchrist, 2:93.

[8] Lloyd, 367.

[9] E. O'Brien to W. Nicolay, Mar. 1838; J. A. Lloyd to G. Dick, May 23, 1838, NAM/PRO-CO.

the grateful thanks of his widow."[10]

"A LAST RESTING-PLACE"

Jay was buried beside his son in a place near Port Louis now known as the Western Cemetery. They were interred close to the grave of Mrs. Harriet Atwood Newell. This had become a hallowed spot, a destination for Christians coming to pay respect to the young woman who had been laid to rest here in 1812 and was venerated as a martyr in missionary service.

Harriet Atwood had been born into a family of good circumstances in Haverhill, Massachusetts. In 1812 she married Samuel Newell, a graduate of Andover Theological Seminary who had pledged his service to foreign missions. The young couple set out for India, as the first American missionaries. At Calcutta (later Kolkata) they were refused entry by officials of the British East India Company, who feared disruption of long-established trade agreements with native groups.

The Newells headed for Mauritius. Usually a six-week sail, the crossing took three months in a season of violent storms. During this journey, Harriet became ill and gave birth prematurely to a daughter who lived for only five days. Soon after landing at Mauritius, Harriet died. She was nineteen years old, taken from this earth before she could, as she declared in a letter to a friend, "lend my little aid in the promulgation of the Gospel."[11] She was buried in Mauritius and might have been mourned only by family and friends had it not been for a book compiled by her husband, which included a few of her letters and pages from her journal describing the last few months of her life. First published in 1814, this small volume moved quickly through a number of editions and was translated into several languages. It was read by thousands, and among this multitude was Anne Jay Bolton.

Anne must have been one of the first to read *A Sermon Preached at Haverhill, Mass. in Remembrance of Mrs. Harriet Newell, Wife of the Rev. Samuel Newell, Missionary to India...To Which Are Added Memoirs of Her Life*. To begin her diary in 1815, Anne wrote, "I have been reading a memoir of that devoted young Christian, Mrs. Newell, and trust it has been useful to me in leading me to examine myself." Early in 1815, Anne was twenty-four years

[10] J. A. Lloyd to G. Dick, May 23, 1838, NAM/PRO-CO; E. O'Brien to G. Dick, Sept. 28, 1838, NAM/PRO-CO.

[11] Woods, 98.

old, the young wife of an aspiring preacher with no permanent assignment, the mother of a young son, pregnant with her second child, and anxious about her future. Now, prompted by the sacrifice of Harriet Newell, Anne begged forgiveness for having been "wrapped up in the world and the things of the world."[12]

The grave of Harriet Newell soon became a place of pilgrimage. That Jay and his son should be buried in this place brought comfort to Louisa and the Reverend Jay. As Louisa said in *Little Willy*, "How singular that this little missionary [Willy] should have found a last resting-place so near that of the eminent servant of God (Mrs. Newell) who had consecrated all her powers to the work of spreading the tidings of salvation amongst the heathen."[13] And then, as fate would have it, her husband would rest at the side of his eldest son and namesake.

"MY LATE DEAR SON" AND THE DESIGN FOR AN INDEPENDENT CHAPEL IN PORT LOUIS

Jay's death was not reported in the newspapers of Bath until September 1837, and then the event was invariably noted as the passing of "the eldest son of the Rev. William Jay."[14] Jay's father received letters from two ministers, one from the London Missionary Society (LMS)—surely this was John Le Brun—and one from the Church of England Missionary Society.[15]

In March 1839, the Reverend Jay received another communication from Le Brun, to which he quickly penned a reply. Prepared in haste and with passion, it said,

> I have this moment received your application, & with immediateness & pleasure reply;—[that] you are welcome to make use of my Name in whatever way you deem most expressive of my earnest recommendation of this very important case—a case alas not less interesting to me [for] knowing that my late dear Son the civil architect to government in the Mauritius, had urged & promoted the design; & expressed a hope in his last letter that if the case should be introduced into England, I w[oul]d lend it my

12 R. Bolton, *Genealogical...Account of the Family of Bolton*, 175.

13 L. Jay, 45.

14 Notice of the death of William Jay: *Bath and Cheltenham Gazette*, Sept. 19, 1837; *Bath Chronicle*, Sept. 21, 1837.

15 Rev. Jay, *Autobiography*, 95.

Countenance.[16]

The matter concerned a project begun shortly after Jay arrived in Mauritius to take up his work as civil architect and inspector of works—he provided a design for a chapel for the nonconformist congregation of the Reverend John Le Brun.

Le Brun was born on Jersey in the Channel Islands, a Crown dependency since the early thirteenth century. Its location in the English Channel at 100 miles south of England and only fourteen miles north of France accounted for Le Brun's familiarity with French culture and language. That knowledge would serve him well in Mauritius, which was then French at its core. As a young man, Le Brun studied for the Independent/Congregational ministry and made a commitment to missionary service. In 1814 he was sent by the LMS to Madagascar, a large island nation in the Indian Ocean just off the southeastern coast of Africa. He arrived first in Mauritius, 700 miles east of Madagascar. There Le Brun sensed, as others had not, the needs of a particular community of slaves.[17]

The London Missionary Society was focused on Madagascar because that island was populated by a number of tribal groups whose members were "unbelievers," ripe for conversion. By contrast, Mauritius had no native population of any sort. Slaves had been brought from Africa to work on plantations, first by the Dutch in the seventeenth century and later by the French. When Le Brun arrived in 1814, he saw a population of slaves descended from slaves, who lived in unique circumstances of despair.

In his first year on the island, Le Brun established several schools for black children. By 1824 his followers included a large number of slaves and a few British nonconformists, most of whom were merchants and lower-level civil servants. A proposal was made to build a chapel for this congregation. But, it would take sixteen years to accomplish this work. There were the difficult problems of securing land in Port Louis for a dissident chapel, gaining the services of design and construction, and finding the funds to support the project.

With Jay's arrival in 1836, there was an able architect at hand, and as a bonus there was the promise of the attention of the Reverend Jay who could

---

[16] Rev. Jay, to [John Le Brun], Mar. 17, 1839, autograph letter, VJD.

[17] Toussaint, "Jean Lebrun," 212. In reports from the London Missionary Society, he is identified as John Le Brun; in other contexts, he is Jean Lebrun.

prompt fund-raising among the membership of the LMS. In 1837 a prospectus for this new chapel on Mauritius was published. The plan was "to erect an appropriate and commodious place of worship…of sufficient dimensions to seat 400 persons, and capable of admitting a gallery when required."[18] Accompanying this document were drawings of Jay's designs for the building rendered by Ruth Baker, who with her husband, Edward, were LMS missionaries recently diverted from service in Madagascar.

By late 1840, the building was turned over to its trustees. The final report of the chapel committee recounted the adventures and misadventures of this endeavor. First, "In the death of Mr. Jay [in 1837], late civil architect to government, who had undertaken to superintend the building, your committee lost, not only an able coadjutor [assistant], but also the interest which, as the son of The Rev. Wm. Jay of Bath, it was hoped he would create in England on behalf of this chapel." Then, costs of construction required that "Mr. Jay's plans…[be] laid aside, and a plainer stile [*sic*] of architecture adopted." Promised grants from Mauritius officials were withdrawn, but an appeal to the London Missionary Society did result in substantial donations.[19]

In 1850 John Joseph Freeman, an officer of the LMS, attended a prayer meeting in the chapel. He observed, "The chapel I liked much.… It is a substantial building, and well situated, for quietness and for the convenience of the population attending."[20] Jay's design had been "laid aside" for the usual reason of lack of funds, but elements of his plan survive in the structure which was completed in 1840 and stands today.[21]

As Jay proposed, this is a masonry building, rectangular in plan and one story in elevation, with a three-bay front and five-bay flanks. His scheme for the facade was a classical pedimented temple front with a shallow porch supported by four Doric columns (or piers). At the back of this porch were three large arched doors, and on each side of the building were five tall round-headed windows. But, rectangular doors and windows were substituted for

---

[18] Le Brun, et al., "Prospectus of a Protestant Chapel," 1837, London Missionary Society Archives, Reports of the Protestant Chapel at Port Louis, Mauritius (1837–1840), Library of the School of Oriental and African Studies, University of London (hereafter cited as LMS)..

[19] Le Brun, et al., "Report of the Committee," Sept. 10, 1840, LMS.

[20] J. J. Freeman, 371.

[21] Eglise Saint-Jean at 11 rue Poudrière, Port Louis, is now a French congregation of the Presbyterian Church of Mauritius.

the arches that would have been difficult and expensive to render, and only an abbreviation of the classical portico frames the entry. What remains of Jay's plan for Le Brun's chapel are the siting and scale, the general configuration of the building, and elements of classical composition and ornament.

EPILOGUE: LOUISA'S JOURNEY

The return to England of Jay's widow and her two small children (Louisa at age five and Ernest at age one) was complicated, snarled in the unhappy history of Jay's inadequate salary and in the ordinary morass of government paperwork. On April 25, 1837, just eight days after Jay's death, Lloyd appealed to George Dick, the colonial secretary,

> The family of Mr. Jay, late Assistant Architect in this department, being left by his decease totally unprovided for, and with unsettled claims to the amount of some hundred dollars; and Mrs. Jay being anxious to proceed with her two children & a female Servant to England by the first opportunity, I beg respectfully to solicit that, as Mr. Jay was sent out by His Majesty's Government on so insufficient a salary and died so soon after his arrival, thereby having no chance of retrieving his first heavy expenses, that His Excellency will be pleased to permit that the means of returning be afforded to His family.[22]

Eight days later, Lloyd's request was granted, and Louisa returned with her children to her family in Henley-on-Thames.[23]

Late in 1837, the first edition of *Little Willy, A Widowed Mother's Memorial of a Beloved Child* was published. In the following year, a second edition appeared with an introduction by the Reverend Jay. By the accounts of both the Reverend Jay and his son Cyrus, the book passed through several editions and thousands of copies were sold. In 1865 "a new and improved edition" was printed "enriched with a portrait of 'Little Willy,' never before published," an artist's rendering guided by the memories of a mother whose child had been dead for almost thirty years.[24]

Soon after she returned to Henley, Louisa took up the work of managing

---

[22] J. A. Lloyd to G. Dick, Apr. 25, 1837, NAM/SGD.
[23] G. Dick to the Harbour Master, Port Louis, May 3, 1837, NAM/SGD.
[24] Rev. Jay, *Autobiography*, 95; C. Jay, *Recollections*, 205–206; L. Jay, vi.

a boarding and day school for young women, and later her unmarried daughter became a teacher there. Jay's surviving son, Ernest, attended New College, London, a prominent dissenting academy, and in 1858 he was appointed to the pulpit of Hanover Chapel in Stockport, an enterprising town in the northwest of England near Manchester. According to a history of that chapel, Ernest's service was "characterized by considerable energy and activity."[25]

In 1861 a census reported that Ernest was twenty-five years old, married with two very young daughters.[26] Then, late in that year came alarming news. After only three and a half years of service, Earnest had resigned the pastorate of Hanover Chapel and would leave the ministry. Surviving accounts do not give the reason, but it is likely that he was suffering the effects of the disease that would kill him fourteen years later. He died at the age of thirty-eight on January 8, 1875, the cause of death given as "Phthisis Pulmonalis" (tuberculosis).[27] In the last ten years of his life, Ernest enjoyed a measure of success as an editor and manager for the Central Press, a news agency based in London at which national reports were collected and written for distribution to provincial newspapers. He was remembered by his colleagues as "remarkable for his business ability, and much liked and respected by all who came into contact with him." And this, "He was grandson of one of the most celebrated Dissenting ministers of the past generation, the Rev. William Jay, of Bath."[28]

In the year following the demise of her son, Louisa died. The death certificate stated that she was seventy-four years old, living in Kensington Town, Middlesex, now a district of West London. The cause was recorded as "morbus cordis," terms then used to refer to death from heart disease or unspecified natural causes. Present was her unmarried daughter, Louisa.[29]

---

[25] "Intelligence," *Christian Witness and Church Members Magazine*, 1858:237; Hanover Chapel, 25.

[26] "Ernest Coulson Jay," *Census Returns of 1861...Stockport*, London Public Record Office, London, England.

[27] "Entry of Death for Ernest Coulson Jay," *Registration District of...Lyme*, Jan. 8, 1875, London General Register Office, London, England.

[28] "Obituary—Ernest Coulson Jay," *Publishers' Circular and General Record of British and Foreign Literature*, Feb. 1, 1875:79.

[29] "Deaths" [Mrs. William Jay], *Times*, London, Apr. 3, 1876; "Louisa Jay—Entry of Death," *Registration District of Kensington*, Mar. 31, 1876, London General Register Office, London, England.

PART SEVEN

CONCLUSION

SAVANNAH'S ARCHITECT

Born in Bath, trained to the profession of architect in London but failing to establish a practice there, Jay made the journey to Savannah, Georgia. This was a place with family ties reaching back to the 1769 journey of his father's mentor Cornelius Winter to prepare for the establishment of a black church. Jay arrived in Savannah in late 1817, and in less than five years he accomplished a prodigious amount of work in the design and construction of several public buildings and private residences.

Lost for a time in a muddled history, Jay is now restored to prominence in Savannah. He was, and remains, the architect who defined a style of elegance and charm for the city. Though only three of his buildings survive here, and only one of them in a condition very like the original, much that came after him was influenced by his work. Savannahians value Jay's contributions to the city, and visitors hear his name over and over as testimony to a moment in history when the work of one architect gave expression to a particular place.

It is right to remember that Jay's career was longer and wider than his stay in Savannah. Even during the very brief time he spent in the United States, he drew plans for structures in Augusta and Darien, Georgia towns at the north and south of Savannah. And in South Carolina he prepared plans and guidelines for the construction of a number of district courthouses and jails. In Charleston, Jay designed an art academy and at least three residences. Back home in England, he worked for several years at Cheltenham and Cirencester, producing ample evidence of his competence and artistry. And finally, in Mauritius his contribution to at least two major projects (a new jail and a design for a central market) offered the promise that he might have made a significant imprint on that place had his life not ended so soon. Still, nowhere did circumstances convene to allow his art to flourish as it did in Savannah.

JAY'S SAVANNAH

Jay's career as an architect began with one remarkable success. The Albion Chapel was a prominent structure in a region of new development in London and a creative solution for a nonconformist meeting house, a neglected building type. In Charleston and Cheltenham, he designed buildings which challenged local precedent and convention. Nonetheless, it is true that Jay's most compelling work was done in Savannah, and there his legacy has been sustained. In this one city in the American South, there were the following conditions congenial to Jay's ambition, industry, and talent: *the spirit of the place,* emanating from its founding in the early eighteenth century; *a time of prosperity*, an extraordinary moment for the city in the early decades of the nineteenth century; *the distinctive town plan*, the unique plan set in place in 1733 at the beginning of the colony; and *wealthy and obliging patrons*, men who embraced Jay's work.

THE SPIRIT OF THE PLACE

Savannah was founded as a place where persons needing and wanting opportunity were offered the chance to succeed. This motive encouraged an independent and entrepreneurial cast of mind. Here ways were not set, and effort and ingenuity were rewarded. Further, as the last of the English colonies in North America, Georgia enjoyed a kind of adolescence, a character of youth and promise, restive and anxious, ready to rush ahead. And here, as nowhere else in the colonies, was a place in which it had been known from the beginning that slavery was a moral disease and a danger to the culture, a realization that would shape the character of many Georgians even when the courage to resist slavery failed.

Elements of this founding spirit were certainly alive during Jay's tenure in 1817–1822, and they were still evident in the reports of a remarkable visitor to this place in 1850. Fredrika Bremer was a Swede, born to aristocracy, resolutely unmarried, and free to travel and write about the need to expand opportunities for women. In 1849–1851 she visited the U.S. and relayed her experiences in *Homes of the New World: Impressions of America* (1853).

Bremer abhorred slavery. But, almost against her better instincts, the American South pleased her. She described Charleston as a city of "peculiar charm, so delightful, so rich, and to me so novel." She painted this picture of the place, "I see a feeble Southern beauty reposing upon a luxurious bed of flowers in a nectarine grove, surrounded by willing slaves, who at her nod bring to her the most precious fruits and ornaments in the world. But all her beauty...can not conceal the want of health and vigor...This, weak luxurious beauty is—*South Carolina*."[1]

In Savannah, Bremer experienced a city shaped by men and women of sturdy character. This was her estimate of this place,

> I find here [Savannah] a more vigorous spiritual life, a more free and unprejudiced looking at things and circumstances, in particular at the great question of slavery, than in Charleston, and I have here become acquainted with some excellent, true people—people who will look the question directly and fairly in the face; who, themselves slaveholders from the more remote time, are yet laboring for the instruction of the slave, for emancipation and free colonization.[2]

She credited Savannah's sensibilities to the character of James Edward Oglethorpe, who had set upon "a grand scheme for human happiness." And, while elements of the "grand scheme" had not survived, core values endured. She said, "After his [Oglethorpe's] death, many of his high-minded laws were annulled; intoxicating liquors were introduced into Georgia, and, by degrees, even negro slavery. But the spirit of freedom and hospitality which was the life [*sic*] of Oglethorpe's life, which was the animating influence of the earliest settlers of Georgia, lives still in Georgia. I see it, I hear it, I feel it."[3]

A TIME OF PROSPERITY

At the beginning, Savannah had struggled and nearly failed. But, in the early decades of the nineteenth century, the city enjoyed a great commercial success as an international center of the cotton trade. What Jay found when he arrived in late 1817 was a bustling place, as described here in an atlas of 1819:

> The population of the city in 1787, was about 2300; in 1800, 5146; and in 1810…5215; in 1819, upwards of 8000. There are 1200 dwelling houses, and about 1800 buildings of other descriptions. This city is the centre of the trade of the state, and owns 13, or 14,000 tons of shipping. Its grand staples are cotton, rice and tobacco. In 6 months, ending March 30, 1818, there were shipped for market about 62,000 bales of cotton, 14,000 tierces

---

[1] Bremer, 1:268.

[2] Ibid., 340.

[3] Ibid., 343–44, 351.

of rice, and 1500 hogsheads of tobacco.[4]

Savannah was flourishing. The city was growing in population, succeeding in business, and frequently visited by traders and travelers. There was an appetite to build buildings, both public and private. And important structures were understood by prominent members of the community to be symbols of achievement and prosperity. Fine architecture would declare Savannah to be a place that valued industry and art.

THE DISTINCTIVE TOWN PLAN

Savannah's unique town plan, plotted by Oglethorpe, was well known and admired by the time Jay arrived here. The 1819 atlas described the scheme in these words: "The town is laid out in the form of a parallelogram; and contains 10 public squares of one acre, at equal distances from each other, inclosed [*sic*] and planted with trees, and having wells with pumps in the centre."[5]

In March 1916, nearly a century after Jay's arrival in Georgia, Edward Hungerford, a well-known journalist, wrote what has come to be an enduring description of Savannah. His article in a prominent travel magazine was occasioned by Savannah's resurgence as a North Atlantic port with the opening of the Panama Canal in 1914. Once again Savannah was destined to be an important part of the economic engine of the country. But, Hungerford argued that there was more to Savannah than commerce. He admonished his readers to "begin by understanding that Savannah is a rarely beautiful town," a place of exceptional beauty, lovely in an uncommon degree.[6]

Hungerford discerned that Savannah was remarkable not because of its site—there were no grand ocean or mountain vistas. He said, "It is a beauty not dependent upon a rare location.... It is a beauty self-contained and almost self-created."[7] For visitors to comprehend this special quality of Savannah, he proposed an adventure still recommended to tourists in this place. He suggested a walk down the central avenue of Bull Street from the commercial

---

[4] J. Morse, 1:538–39. A bale was a compressed bundle of cotton weighing between 400 and 500 hundred pounds, a tierce of rice was a cask containing fifteen cubic feet of product, and a hogshead of tobacco was a barrel containing forty cubic feet of product.

[5] Ibid., 538.

[6] Hungerford, 35.

[7] Ibid.

district at the north to Forsyth Park at the south. He believed that this route would offer an experience of a city that was uniquely humane and gracious.

This was Hungerford's tour:

> [If] you would see what beauty and tenderness and dignity may actually do for a city, turn your path up Bull Street [still the center north/south passage through the city]...[Y]our toes point up a broad street whose path is constantly interrupted by small, immaculate, velvety-green open squares. No course for automobiles, this Bull Street.... It is to the pedestrian, the man who walks slowly and ruminatingly, that the ancient thoroughfare makes its appeal and invitation. The paths for him are straight as ruler edges; they thread the tiny squares in steady sequence. And at each of those open places he may pause and rest his limbs and eyes and thoughts alike.[8]

When Jay arrived, Savannah's squares were, as Hungerford described them, open spaces where one might "pause and rest." As certain proof of the esteem in which these spaces had come to be held, in 1817 members of city council asserted as one of their responsibilities to protect the perimeters of these squares from intrusions. Jay's mark on Savannah came as he populated this man-made landscape with distinguished public buildings and elegant houses in an architectural style and scale suited to this unique setting.

Bremer, who visited in 1850, was besotted by the plan and the fine residences of Savannah. She said, "Savannah is the most charming of cities, and reminds me of 'the maiden in the green-wood.'"[9] The specific source for this "maiden" is unknown. Because Bremer was writing to her sister Agatha, who was at home in Sweden, this may have been a reference to a poem or a song known to both of them. Likely this was simply an evocation of a common image of Swedish folklore, the *skogsrå*, known as the Lady of the Woods, a beautiful woman with magical powers who lives deep in the forest (the green wood). An enchanted place.

Bremer concluded,

> It [Savannah] is, even more than Charleston, an assemblage of villas which have come together for company. In each quarter is a green market-place, surrounded with magnificent, lofty trees; and in the centre of each verdant market-place leaps up a living fountain, a spring of fresh water, gushing forth, shining in the sun, and keeping the green-sward [green sod] moist

[8] Ibid.

[9] Bremer, 1:340.

> and cool....[T]here can not be, in the whole world, a more beautiful city than Savannah![10]

Surely no one contributed in greater measure than Jay to the creation of this "assemblage of villas...come together for company" at the sides of these lovely squares.

WEALTHY AND OBLIGING PATRONS

In 1985 the flowering of Jay's art in Savannah drew the attention of Roger G. Kennedy, then director of the Smithsonian's National Museum of American History. He offered this analysis of the extraordinary confluence of this artist, at this moment, and in this place:

> It was not just money that came into Savannah at this time [1817]. Talent and sympathy, boldness and esthetic sensitivity, economic competence and artistic genius came too. This is the context conducive to art. In Savannah, for half a decade, there existed the reinforcing relationship of an architect of genuine genius, just into his twenties, and a group of clients who valued his gifts and were able to pay for an expression of those gifts. These clients were, in their way, as amazing as the artist.[11]

Central to Kennedy's explanation for Jay's success in Savannah was the existence of wealthy and obliging patrons. Architecture is always a collaboration between the architect and the client. The work is dependent on the skill of the architect, but it is sustained and held aloft by the aesthetic sensibility, financial resources, and passion of the person who will occupy the building. In particular, Jay's Savannah houses were the result of partnerships, and we would know more about these structures if we could learn more about these clients and the circumstances of the lives they expected to enjoy in these homes.

Sadly, the historical record tells us too little about Jay's patrons to gain more than a few general observations. We know about the pretentious ambitions of William and Julia Scarbrough and the sedate demeanors of Alexander Telfair, his mother, and his sisters. But, there are no records of how they guided Jay in the design of their residences.

The generosity of Jay's first client, Richard Richardson, can be traced in

---

[10] Ibid.

[11] R. Kennedy, 163.

his support of the young English architect for other important projects in the city, including a theater and a bank. The character of Richardson's own home and the timing of its construction suggest that he was very much involved in the design and building of the house on Oglethorpe Square. Kennedy remembered this particular relationship of artist and patron in this way: "Nothing like the splendors he [Jay] now wrought for this most sympathetic of clients [Richardson] had appeared in Savannah before. Indeed, the curving interior walls, the serpentine portico and the semicircular stairs of the Richardson House were so sophisticated that the best Charleston work of the time seemed a little amateur and provincial by comparison."[12]

JAY'S ACCOMPLISHMENTS

Jay was born into a world made small by sailing ships and the adventures and misadventures of wars and commerce. His England had been transformed by an Industrial Revolution, bringing wealth to a rapidly expanding professional class and relentless poverty to laborers. His own father stood in the wake of these events, as one who had been recruited to the evangelical movement and its initiatives to transform society by rescuing the dissolute upper classes and ministering to the needs of the poor. Jay chose as his own path the professional practice of the art of architecture at a time when much building was needed.

To Savannah, Jay brought a distinctively elegant style of architecture, just as civic leaders wished to promote the achievements of this place. And very soon notice came. Here was a coastal city, located on a busy river, having a unique town plan, with a flourish of tropical greenery and a number of exceedingly handsome buildings. In almost every decade from the beginning of the nineteenth century forward, it is possible to find commentary on the special architectural character of this place.

Often travelers remarked on the fine houses of Savannah. One of these was Achille Charles Louis Murat, Crown Prince of Naples and nephew of Napoleon, whose own claim to a throne had expired with the exile of his uncle and the execution of his father in 1815. Murat emigrated to the United States in 1822, becoming a partisan of the Southern states. In an 1832 account of his adopted country, he wrote that "in the south particularly, there are many

[12] Ibid., 166.

[houses] remarkable for their elegance." For Murat, self-proclaimed "*ci-devant* [former] Prince Royal of the Two Sicilies," Savannah possessed "many private dwellings which are truly little palaces."[13]

In 1959 Pauline Corson Coad paid a tribute to Jay that seems the best neat summary of his life as an artist. Coad was the author of a booklet published by the Telfair Academy for distribution at the Owens-Thomas House, which had been opened to the public in 1954. One of her goals was to explain, as others had tried to do, the meaning of Jay's life and art. She observed that in a "brief span of years he had made more beauty than most men make in a long lifetime."[14] In fewer than five years, Jay set the course for "showy Savannah," a city that would come to be known as an uncommonly beautiful place. What is now certain is that Jay's story did not begin or end here. But, it is clear that Savannah offered both opportunity and inspiration to Jay, prompting the realization of his art.

[13] Murat, 366.

[14] Coad, 10.

ACKNOWLEDGMENTS

In 1965 I came to Savannah as an assistant professor of history at a local college, later Armstrong State University. Shortly after I arrived, I was invited to attend a meeting in the dining room of the Richardson-Owens-Thomas House, a residence designed by William Jay in 1816 which had opened as a house museum in 1954.

This occasion was my introduction to Jay, and I was dazzled by this room. Here were curved walls and doors, a ceiling border of free-standing anthemia, and a narrow window of Greek key pattern where light streamed through amber glass and fell on a richly-carved built-in sideboard. I soon learned that Jay was legendary in Savannah, although little was known of his life, his training, and the work he accomplished in other places. For me, Jay was a puzzle that an historian might solve.

In the decades that followed, I took every opportunity to explore the questions of just who Jay was, how he had conceived his elegant style, and what had become of him after his time in Savannah. My research took me to archives and libraries in Georgia and South Carolina and then to the National Archives and the Library of Congress in Washington, D.C. In the 1980s, my wife Ginger and I followed Jay's steps from Bath to London, Cheltenham, Cirencester, and Henley-on-Thames; and then to the island of Mauritius in the Indian Ocean.

Over the years, many contributed to my research on Jay, including colleagues and students at Armstrong State University; and legions of archivists, librarians, and curators in the U.S., the U.K., and on Mauritius. Now, at the end of a very long road, there are these few to whom I owe special thanks: Lisa Grove, Director of the Telfair Academy, for her generous provision of images for this publication; Marc Jolley, Director of Mercer University Press, for his recognition of this as a worthy project; Sandy Underwood, an art historian who allowed me to cajole her into helping me drag Jay over the finish line; and finally, my wife Ginger, my true research assistant, who has lived with me and Jay for nearly forty years.

—John Duncan

My husband John and I retired to Savannah in 2002. We had spent most of our working lives at St. Mary's College of Maryland at St. Mary's City—John was Executive Vice President and I was a professor of art history. To relocate from Maryland's colonial capital to that of Georgia seemed happily symmetrical.

I met John Duncan in 2007, and I volunteered to help him complete his work on Jay, not imagining that this project would take several years. But, we were aided by Beth Moore, Assistant Curator at the Telfair, an expert at finding things in the museum's archives; and by Richard Leo Johnson, a skilled architectural photographer who has documented the surviving Jay houses in Savannah and Charleston. Catherine Cardarelli, a professor of photography at the Savannah College of Art and Design, photographed John's enormous collection of images; and, before she retired to the wilds of Wyoming, she was my companion on scores of "Jay walks" across Savannah to find and photograph the unique features of Jay's work.

Finally, my husband John did whatever was necessary to keep this work going—he delivered documents, repaired computers, edited rambling drafts, and contributed his own deep knowledge of architecture. But, perhaps John Duncan and I will remember most that, at critical moments in our collaboration, we were sustained by heaping plates of John's scones.

—Sandy Underwood

CREDITS FOR THE ILLUSTRATIONS

Unless otherwise noted, all of these materials come from the V & J Duncan Collection, Savannah, Georgia, and were photographed for publication by Catherine Cardarelli, Professor of Photography (retired), Savannah College of Art and Design. Professor Cardarelli also contributed a number of views of Jay's work in Savannah, cited below as "CC/JD" (Catherine Cardarelli for John Duncan).

Richard Leo Johnson of Atlantic Archives Architectural Photography, Inc., Savannah, was commissioned to record surviving Jay facades and selected interiors in Savannah and Charleston, South Carolina. This work is cited below as "RLJ/JD © Atlantic Archives, Inc. " (Richard Leo Johnson © Atlantic Archives, Inc., for John Duncan).

The Telfair Museum of Art, authorized by Director and CEO Lisa Grove, provided a number of images and granted permission for their use. That credit, with the thanks of the authors, is noted in the list below as "courtesy of the Telfair."

The William Jays of Tisbury: "The Cottage in Which Mr. Jay Was Born," R. Bolton del., W. Holl engr., in *Autobiography of the Revd. William Jay*, London, 1854; "Revd. Mr. William Jay, Aged 19," pinxt Peat, sculpt. J. Goldar, stipple engr., n.d.; and "Fonthill Abbey, Wilts, S.W.," J. C. Buckler del., J. Barnett fe., steel engr., 1822.

The Family of the Reverend Jay: "Revd. William Jay," aft. W. Etty, engr. James Thomson, for *European Magazine*, pub. J. Asperne, London, 1819; and "Mrs. Robert Bolton (Anne Jay Bolton) and Her Two Eldest Children, William and Anne" by William Etty, oil on canvas, ca. 1817, Coll. New-York Historical Society, NYC, #1942.350, loan to Telfair, courtesy of the Telfair.

The Regent and the Regency: "George IV," aft. T. Lawrence, in D. Hume and T. Smollett, *History of England*, London, 1859; and "The Pavilion, Brighton," drawn by W. Westfall, A.R.A., engr. by __ [sic] Francis, in *Great Britain Illustrated*, pub. C. Tilt, London, 1830.

The Grecian Style: "The Wellington Rooms, Mount Pleasant," del. G. and C. Pyne, engr. Jas. Allen, in *Lancashire Illustrated*, pub. H. Fisher, Son, & Jackson, London, steel engr., 1829; and "Haberdasher's Alms Houses, Hoxton," drawn by Thos. H. Shepherd, engraved by John Rolp, in James Elmes, *Metropolitan Improvements*, pub. Jones & Co., London, steel engr., 1828.

Dissident Chapels: "South West View of the Albion Chapel, Moorgate," Robt. Buttery, aquatint, ca. 1816; and "The Reverend Jay's First Meeting Hall at Christian-Malford, Wiltshire," H. E. H., pub. Hollway & Son, Bath, litho., n.d.

Independent Presbyterian Church, Savannah, Georgia: "The Independent Presbyterian Church," in *Art Work of Savannah*, pub. W. H. Parish, Chicago, photogravure, 1893.

The Georgia Connections: "Rev. Cornelius Winter, Painswick, Gloucestershire," Ridley sculp., for *Evangelical Magazine*, Aug. 1789; "The Reverend Mr. George Whitefield, A.M., Chaplain to the Countless of Huntingdon," N. Hone pinxt., J. Greenwood fecit, mezzotint, ca. 1769; "John Wesley," fr. group caricature, pub. J. & J. Cundee, London, litho., ca. 1840; "Hannah More," aft. H. W. Pickersgill, A.R.A., steel engr., 1873; and "Reverend Robert Bolton (Robert Bolton, Liverpool Agent for the Bolton Cotton House in Savannah)" by William Etty, oil on canvas, ca. 1817, Coll. New-York Historical Society, NYC, #1942.349, loan to Telfair, courtesy of the Telfair.

Features of Jay's Savannah Houses: Set-back corner at the Telfair House, CC/JD; Arched window in deep reveal with apron panel at the Scarbrough House, CC/JD; Coade

Stone balusters at the Richardson-Owens-Thomas House, CC/JD; Coade Stone Ionic capital of the Propylaea of the Acropolis, Athens, fr. the Bulloch-Habersham House, Telfair Archives, photo., courtesy of the Telfair; and Coade Stone Corinthian capital of the Choragic Monument of Lysicrates, Athens, at the Telfair House, CC/JD.

Richardson-Owens-Thomas House, Savannah: Porch, CC/JD; and John Retan's inscription of construction dates behind the stairs to the porch, photo. David L. Kaminsky, courtesy of the Telfair.

Scarbrough House, Savannah: Porch, CC/JD; First floor plan of the Scarbrough House, in *"The Georgian Period,"* Part 12, ed. W. R. Ware, New York, 1902; South porch ironwork, CC/JD; "Eaton Hall, Cheshire," drawn by W. Westfall, A.R.A., engr. by Edward Finden, in *Great Britain Illustrated*, pub. C. Tilt, London, steel engr., 1830; "President James Monroe," aft J. Vanderlyn, engr. H. B. Hall, steel engr., ca. 1875; "Steam Ship *Savannah*, Capt. Moses Rodgers," G. Hayward, litho., ca. 1859-72; "Scarborough [sic] Mansion, West Broad Street, Savannah, Chatham County, Georgia" by Frances Benjamin Johnston, photo., ca. 1939-44, Library of Congress, Prints and Photographs Div., Washington, D.C., retrieved 19 Dec. 2017 at www.loc.gov/item/csas20080090/.http://www.loc.gov/item/csas200800901/.

Telfair House, Savannah: Porch, CC/JD; "Alexander Telfair," drawn by Alan Clarke, aft. George Lethbridge Saunders (watercolor on ivory, 1848, Telfair); "Mary Telfair," Enrichetta Narducci, gouache on ivory, 1842, courtesy of the Telfair; "And a Little Child Shall Lead Them" by John Frazee, parlor mantelpiece, marble, ca. 1818, photo. RLJ/Telfair © Atlantic Archives, Inc., courtesy of the Telfair; and "Telfair Academy," *Harper's New Monthly Magazine*, Jan. 1888, wd. engr.

Bulloch-Habersham House, Savannah: "Habersham House," in *Examples of Colonial Architecture in Charleston, S.C,. and Savannah, Ga.*, photo. and pub. Edward A. Crane and E. E. Soderholtz, Boston, photogravure, 1895; "The Bullock [sic] House – Portico, Orleans Square, Savannah, Ga., Jay, Architect," *Architectural Record*, photo., Mar. 1907; and "Staircase in the Bulloch House," dwg., and First floor plan of the Bulloch House, in *"The Georgian Period,"* Part 12, ed. W. R. Ware, New York, 1902.

Savannah Free School: "A Lancastrian School in Operation," early 19th c. print, in Ellwood P. Cubberley, *Public Education in the United States,* Cambridge, Massachusetts, 1919.

Savannah Theater: Facade, American Views, Popular Series, stereoscopic photo., late 19th c.; and "Savannah's Sesquicentennial Celebration, Governor Stephens Delivering the Oration," del. Horace Bradley, *Harper's Weekly*, Feb. 24, 1883.

Savannah Branch of the Bank of the United States: "Georgia, Branch Bank of the United States, Savannah," William Jay, Architect, drawd [sic] by J. Shaw, engr. by W. G. Mason, in *Commercial Directory*, pub. J. C. Kayser et al., Philadelphia, 1823; and "Branch of the United States Bank, Savannah," drawn by W. Goodacre Junr., N.Y., engr. and printed by Ferrier Sons & Co., in J. H. Hinton, *History and Topography of the United States of North America*, pub. Hinton & Simpkin & Marshall, London, 1831.

Jay's Designs for South Carolina Courthouses and Jails: "Courthouse, front, Plan (a)" and "Front Elevation of Goal [sic]," drawn by William Jay, in "Plans of Court Houses & Goals furnished the Board [of Public Works]," May, 17, 1820, Department of Public Works Records, South Carolina Department of Archives and History, Columbia, South Carolina; and "Court House, Sumter, S.C.," undivided postcard, Rotograph Co., NYC, ca. 1905.

Jay in Cheltenham: "The Literary Salon, Cheltenham," Jay del., Hobson sc., in *Griffith's New Historical Description of Cheltenham and Its Vicinity*, pub. S. Y. Griffith, London, steel engr., 1826; and "Columbia-place" and "Paragon Parade," in *Rowe's Illustrated Cheltenham Guide*, pub. George Rowe, Cheltenham, wd. engr., ca. 1845.

Island of Mauritius: "The Dodo Bird," F. P. Nodder engr., in *The Naturalist's Miscellany*, London, copper engr., 1792; and "Paul et Virginie," illus., in Bernardin de Saint-Pierre, *Paul et Virginie*, Paris, aft. 1855.

Jay in Port Louis, Mauritius: Entry gate of the central market, drawn by Alan Clarke, aft. 19th c. print; and "View of the Protestant Chapel, Mauritius 1841," H. Turner, R.A., del., lith., 1841.

The Deaths of William Jay and His Son "Little Willy": Little Willy teaching a black child to read, in Louisa Coulson Jay, "Little Willy," *Ardent Spirits,* Vol. 3, New York, ca. 1851; and "Mrs. Harriet Newell," W. Doyle pinx., D. Edwin sc., pub. Samuel T. Armstrong, Boston, Massachusetts, stipple engr., aft. 1814.

An Artist's Rendering of Jay's Savannah: Christopher A. D. Murphy Jr., "Owens-Thomas House Portico," etching, n.d., courtesy of Christopher Cole Murphy.

Jay's Bank drawn by Joshua Shaw (engr. W. G. Mason, pub. J. C. Kayser, 1823), on Staffordshire pottery, fr. "Beauties of America" series, a gravy tureen, dark blue transferware, border "Medallions of Rose and Leaf," J. & W. Ridgway, Cauldon Place Works, Hanley, England, c. 1823-30.

COLOR INSERT

Architect William Jay: "William Jay" by William Etty, oil on canvas, ca. 1817, York Art Gallery (VORAG: 1366), on long loan fr. Mr. R. Hanmer, courtesy of the York Museums Trust; and Signature of the architect, retrieved fr. Savannah shipping records, Dec. 1817.

Jay's Bath in the Age of Caricature: "Stewing Alive," det., del. and engr. Robt. Cruikshank, pub. Sherwood & Co., 1825.

Jay's London in the Age of Caricature: "A Regency Affair," det., del. and engr. Robt. Cruikshank, pub. Sherwood, Jones & Co., 1825.

Richardson-Owens-Thomas House, Savannah: Facade, Entry hall, and Dining room, photos., RLJ/Telfair © Atlantic Archives, Inc., courtesy of the Telfair.; and First floor plan, Telfair Archives, courtesy of the Telfair.; and The "Lafayette Balcony" on the south flank of the house, photo., CC/JD.

Telfair House, Savannah: Facade, photo., RLJ/Telfair © Atlantic Archives, Inc., courtesy of the Telfair; "Oak Room," photo., Manzone Group, NYC, courtesy of the Telfair; and First floor plan, Telfair Archives, courtesy of the Telfair.

Wayne-Gordon House, Savannah: Facade, photo., RLJ/JD © Atlantic Archives, Inc.

Scarbrough House, Savannah: Facade, photo., RLJ/JD © Atlantic Archives, Inc

Cerveau's Savannah in 1837: "View of Savannah" by Joseph Louis Firmin Cerveau, watercolor on paper, 1837, Georgia Historical Society, Savannah, coll. #A-1361-623, det. ruins of Jay's Custom House and det. City Hotel, courtesy of the Georgia Historical Society.

William Mason Smith House, Charleston, South Carolina: Facade and View of piazzas, photo., RLJ/JD © Atlantic Archives, Inc.

McBee House at Ashley Hall School, Charleston: Facade, photo., RLJ/JD © Atlantic Archives, Inc.

Watermoor House, Cirencester, England: "Watermoor House," sepia photo. by W. Dennis Moss, Cirencester, ca. 1915, det. Jay's original structure, Philip Griffiths Coll., courtesy David Viner.

BIBLIOGRAPHY

ARCHIVES

Bath Central Reference Library, Reverend William Jay Archives, Bath, England

Chatham County Records Office, Deed Books (1818-1823), Savannah, GA. Cited as CCRO.

Chatham County Superior Court, Court Records (1818-1823), Savannah, GA. Cited as CCSC.

Cheltenham Public Library, Reference Department, Cheltenham, England

Detlef Lienau Collection, Avery Architectural Library, Columbia University, New York, NY

Georgia Archives, Collections of William Scarbrough and William Few, Morrow, GA. Cited as GAM.

Georgia Historical Society, Savannah, GA. Cited as GHS.

Gloucestershire Archives, Cheltenham Church Commissioners and Church Building Commission Records, Gloucester, England. Cited as GAG.

Gloucestershire Record Office, Papers of the Architect William Jay (1825–1830), Gloucester, England. Cited as GRO.

Historic American Buildings Survey, Library of Congress, Washington, DC. Cited as HABS.

Hull Museums Collections, Social History Archives, Hull, England. Cited as HMC.

Independent Presbyterian Church Archives, Stuart A. Rose Manuscript, Archives, and Rare Book Library, Emory University, Atlanta, GA. Cited as IPC.

Keith M. Read Collection, University of Georgia Library, Athens, GA

London General Register Office, London

London Missionary Society Archives, Reports of the Protestant Chapel at Port Louis, Mauritius (1837–1840), Library of the School of Oriental and African Studies, University of London. Cited as LMS.

London Public Record Office, London

National Archives of Mauritius, Public Record Office and Colonial Office Correspondence Collections (1835–1845), Coromandel, Mauritius. Cited as NAM/PRO-CO.

National Archives of Mauritius, Surveyor General's Department Collection (1836–1837), Coromandel, Mauritius. Cited as NAM/SGD.

Savannah Municipal Archives, City Council Minutes (1817–1819), Savannah, GA. Cited as SMA.

South Carolina Department of Archives and History, Legislative Papers and Petitions Collection (1817–1827, 1837–1841), Columbia, SC. Cited as SCDAH/L.

South Carolina Department of Archives and History, Superintendent of Public Works and Internal Improvements Papers (1820–1821), Columbia, SC. Cited as SCDAH/SPW.

Thomas Gamble Collection, Live Oak Public Library, Savannah, GA

Thomas Rickman Collection, Royal Institute of British Architects Library, London. Cited as RIBA.

U.S. Census of Population and Housing, Census Bureau, Suitland, MD

U.S. Circuit Court for the Southern District of Georgia, Eastern Division (Savannah), National Archives at Atlanta, Morrow, GA

U.S. Custom Service, Baggage Entries at Savannah, GA (1817), National Archives, Washington, D.C. Cited as USCS/BE.

U.S. Custom Service, Inward Coastwise Manifests, Savannah, GA (1819), National Archives, Washington, D.C. Cited as USCS/IC.

U.S. Custom Service, Inward Foreign Cargo Manifests, Savannah, GA (1817–1819), National Archives, Washington, D.C. Cited as USCS/IFC.

U.S. Military Library Archives, Joseph G. Swift Papers, U.S. Military Academy, West Point, NY

U.S. Treasury Department Archives, Custom House at Savannah, GA, Records (1817–1822, 1836), National Archives, Washington, D.C. Cited as USTA/CH.

Virginia and John Duncan Collection, Savannah, GA. Cited as VJD.

William Etty Collection, British Library, Manuscript Collections, London. Cited as BLMC.

BOOKS, ARTICLES, DISSERTATIONS

*This list includes selected journal and newspaper articles. Other periodicals and some sundry materials are cited in full in the notes.

Act for Better Paving, Lighting, Cleansing, Watching and Improving the Town of Cheltenham in the County of Gloucester, An. Cheltenham, England: P. A. Nuttall, 1842.

Aikin, Lucy. *Memoirs, Miscellanies and Letters of the Late Lucy Aikin*. Edited by Philip Hemery Le Breton. London: Longman, Green, Longman, Roberts, & Green, 1864.

Allen, Thomas. *History and Antiquities of London, Westminster, Southwark, and Parts Adjacent*. Vols. 3 and 4. London: Cowie & Strange, 1828–1829.

———. *Lancashire Illustrated*. London: H. Fisher, R. Fisher, & P. Jackson, 1832.

Allon, Henry. *Memoir of the Rev. James Sherman*. 3rd ed. London: James Nisbet & Co., 1864.

American Academy of Arts and Sciences. *Memoirs of the American Academy of Arts and Sciences*. Vol. 11. Cambridge, MA: John Wilson & Son, 1888.

Ammon, Harry. *James Monroe: The Quest for National Identity*. Charlottesville: University of Virginia Press, 1990.

Ancient Documents of the Grand Lodge of Georgia. Macon, GA: Grand Lodge of Georgia, n.d.

Anthony, Henry Bowen. *The Fancy Ball: A Sketch*. Savannah, GA: W. T. Williams, 1837.

Avery, I. "Savannah, Georgia." *Harper's New Monthly Magazine*, January 1888.

Barber, John Warner, and Henry Howe. *Our Whole Country: Or the Past and Present of the United States*. Vol. 1. New York: George F. Tuttle & Henry M'Cauley, 1861.

Bell, M., Jr. "Ease and Elegance, Madeira and Murder: The Social Life of Savannah's City Hotel." *Georgia Historical Quarterly*, Fall 1992.

Bishop, C. [Christopher]. "Watermoor House, Cirencester: Its History and Its Architect." Report submitted to Eric Cole & Partners, Cirencester, England, March 1979. Copy, V & J Duncan, Savannah, GA.

Blake, Steven. *Pittville 1824–1860—A Scene of Gorgeous Magnificence*. Cheltenham, England: Cheltenham Art Gallery and Museum, 1988. Online as "A Short History of Pittville," edited by Fiona Clarke, www.friendsofpittville.org.

Boggs, Marion Alexander, ed. *Alexander Letters, 1787–1900*. Savannah, GA: Private printing for George J. Baldwin, 1910.

Boggs, R. "Pendleton Female Academy, 1827–1900," 1970. Copy, V & J Duncan, Savannah, GA.

Bolton, Robert, Jr. *Genealogical and Biographical Account of the Family of Bolton: In England*

and America. New York: John A. Gray, 1862.
———. *History of the County of Westchester, From Its First Settlement to the Present Time.* Vol. 1. New York: Alexander S. Gould, 1848.
———. *History of the Several Towns, Manors, and Patents of the County of Westchester: From Its First Settlement to the Present Time.* Vol. 2, rev. ed. New York: Chas. F. Roper, 1881.
Bolton, W. J. [William Jay]. *Footsteps of the Flock: Memorials of the Rev. Robert Bolton and of Mrs. Bolton.* London: Hamilton, Adams, & Co., 1860.
Bradbury, Oliver C. "Paragon Buildings, Cheltenham, Gloucestershire." *Georgian Group Journal,* 2000.
———. "William Jay's English Works After 1822." *Architectural History,* 2000.
Bremer, Fredrika. *Homes of the New World: Impressions of America.* Translated by Mary [Botham] Howitt. Vol. 1. New York: Harper & Bros., 1853.
Britton, J. [John], and A. [Augustus] Pugin, eds. *Illustrations of the Public Buildings of London.* Vol. 1. London: J. Taylor, 1825.
Bryan, John M., ed. *Robert Mills, Architect.* Washington, DC: American Institute of Architects Press, 1989.
Buckingham, J. S. [James Silk]. *Slave States of America.* Vol. 1. London: Fisher, Son, & Co., 1842.
Bulloch, Joseph Gaston Baillie. *History and Genealogy of the Families of Bulloch and Stobo and of Irvine of Cults.* Washington, DC: Byron S. Adams, 1911.
———. *History and Genealogy of the Habersham Family.* Columbia, SC: R. L. Bryan Co., 1901.
Burke, Emily P. *Reminiscences of Georgia.* Oberlin, OH: James M. Fitch, 1850.
Burnage, Sarah, Mark Hallett, and Laura Turner. *William Etty: Art and Controversy.* London: Philip Wilson Pub., Ltd., & York Museums Trust, 2011.
Byron, Lord (George Gordon). *Childe Harold's Pilgrimage, Canto IV.* London: John Murray, 1818.
Calhoun, David B. *The Splendor of Grace: The Independent Presbyterian Church of Savannah, Georgia, 1755–2005.* Greenville, SC: A Press Printing, 2005.
Candler, Allen D. [Daniel], comp. *Colonial Records of the State of Georgia.* Vol. 1. Atlanta, GA: Franklin Pub. Co., 1904.
———, and Clement A. Evans, eds. *Georgia: Comprising Sketches of Counties, Towns, Events, Institutions, and Persons.* Vol. 3. Atlanta, GA: State Historical Association, 1906.
Causton, Henry-Kent. *Kent's Original London Directory.* 91st ed. London: Henry-Kent Causton, 1823.
Chandler, James, and Kevin Gilmartin. *Romantic Metropolis: The Urban Scene of British Culture, 1780–1840.* Cambridge: Cambridge University Press, 2005.
Chatwin, Amina. *Cheltenham's Ornamental Ironwork: A Guide and History.* Cheltenham, England: Pub. by the author, 1975.
Cheltenham Art Gallery and Museum. *Cheltenham Historical Walks.* Cheltenham, England, n.d. [c. 1970].
Clark, Richard H. *Memoirs of Judge Richard H. Clark.* Edited by Lollie Belle Wylie. Atlanta, GA: Franklin Print. & Pub. Co., 1898.
Coad, Pauline Corson. *Owens-Thomas House Museum.* Savannah, GA: Telfair Academy of Arts and Sciences, Inc., 1959.
Cobbett, William. *Rural Rides.* Edited by James Paul Cobbett. London: A. Cobbett, 1853.
Coker, Clent. *Barnsley Gardens at Woodlands: The Illustrious Dream.* Atlanta, GA: Julia Pub.

Co., 2000.
Colvin, Howard M. [Montagu]. *Biographical Dictionary of English Architects, 1600–1840*. 2nd ed. London: John Murray, 1978.
Coulter, E. M. [Ellis Merton]. "Great Savannah Fire of 1820." *Georgia Historical Quarterly*, March 1939.
———. *Joseph Vallence Bevan: Georgia's First Official Historian*. Athens: University of Georgia Press, 2010. First published 1964 by UGA.
Cubberley, Ellwood. *Public Education in the United States*. Cambridge, MA: Riverside Press, 1919.
Cust, Lionel. *History of the Society of Dilettanti*. Edited by Sidney Colvin. London: Macmillan & Co., 1898.
"Custom-House—Savannah, Georgia." Report of the Committee on Commerce, May 17, 1836, House of Representatives, 24th Congress, 1st Session. In *U.S. Congressional Serial Set*, Vol. 295. Washington [DC], 1836.
———. Report of March 19, 1842. In *U.S. Congressional Serial Set*, Vol. 403. Washington [DC], 1842.
Darley, Gillian. *John Soane: An Accidental Romantic*. New Haven, CT: Yale University Press, 1999.
Darwin, Charles. *Journal of Researches into the Geology and Natural History of the Various Countries Visited by H. M. S. Beagle...from 1832 to 1836*. London: Henry Colburn, 1839.
Davies, Henry. *A View of Cheltenham, In Its Past and Present State*. 4th ed. Cheltenham: Henry Davies Pub., 1843. First pub. *The Stranger's Guide through Cheltenham*, 1832.
Dent, Ophelia Troup [Mrs. George]. "Memoirs of Ophelia Troup Dent," Aug. 6, 1902. In *Hofwyl Plantation* by Victoria Reeves Gunn. Atlanta, GA: Georgia Department of Natural Resources, Office of Planning and Research, 1976.
Dumas, Alexandre (*pére*). *George, or The Planter of the Isle of France*. Translated by G. J. Knox. Belfast, Ireland: Simms & McIntyre, 1846. First pub. *Georges*, Paris, 1843.
Duncan, Alexander McCrie. *Roll of Officers and Members of the Georgia Hussars*. Savannah, GA: Morning News, n.d. [1906].
Dunlap, William. *History of the Rise and Progress of the Arts of Design in the United States*. Vols. 1 and 2. New York: George P. Scott & Co., 1834.
Earle, John. *A Guide to the Knowledge of Bath, Ancient and Modern*. London: Longman, Green, Longman, Roberts, & Green, 1864.
Early, R. H. [Ruth Hairston]. *The Family of Early*. Lynchburg, VA: Brown-Morrison Co., 1920.
Ellis, William. *History of the London Missionary Society*. London: John Snow, 1844.
Elmes, James, ed. *Annals of the Fine Arts*. London, 1816-1820.
———. *Lectures on Architecture...Delivered at the Surrey and Russell Institutions, London, and the Philosophical Institution at Birmingham*. 2nd ed. London: Priestley & Weale, 1823.
———. *London and Its Environs in the Nineteenth Century*. London: Benjamin Blom, Inc., 1968. First pub. 1829.
———. *Metropolitan Improvements: Or London in the Nineteenth Century*. London: Jones & Co., 1827.
———. *Topographical Dictionary of London and Its Environs*. London: Whittaker, Treacher, & Arnot, 1831.
Embury, Aymar, II. *Early American Churches*. Garden City, NY: Doubleday, Page, & Co., 1914.

Evans, E. J., and W. F. Hurndall, eds. *Pulpit Memorials*. London: James Clarke & Co., 1878.

Farr, Dennis. *William Etty*. London: Routledge & Kegan Paul, 1958.

Fauber, J. Everett. "Research Archaeology and Explorations at Owens-Thomas House." Report submitted to Telfair Academy of Arts and Sciences, Savannah, GA, 1965. Copy, V & J Duncan Collection, Savannah, GA.

Faux, W. [William]. *Memorable Days in America: Being a Journal of a Tour to the United States. . . to Ascertain. . . the Condition and Probable Prospects of British Emigrants*. London: W. Simpkin & R. Marshall, 1823.

Fisher, Sidney George. *A Philadelphia Perspective: The Diary of Sidney George Fisher Covering the Years 1834–1871*. Vol. 1. Edited by Nicholas B. Wainwright. Philadelphia: Historical Society of Pennsylvania, 1967.

Forbes, John, Alexander Tweedie, John Conolly, and Robley Dunglison. *Cyclopaedia of Practical Medicine*. Vol. 4. Philadelphia: Lea & Blanchard, 1845.

Force, Peter, comp. *A National Calendar and Annals of the United States for MDCCCXXII* [1822]. Vol. 3. Washington City [DC]: Davis & Force, 1822.

Freeman, Charles. *History, Antiquities, Improvements, &c. of the Parish of Bromley, Kent*. Bromley, England: William Beckley, 1832.

Freeman, J. J. [John Joseph]. *A Tour in South Africa, With Notices of Natal, Mauritius, Madagascar, Ceylon, Egypt, and Palestine*. London: John Snow, 1851.

Gallagher, Helen Mar Pierce. *Robert Mills: Architect of the Washington Monument, 1781–1855*. New York: Columbia University Press, 1935.

Gamble, Thomas. "Jay's Reputation as 'Famous Architect' Gets Another Jolt," *Savannah Press*. March 3, 1928.

———. "Romance of Wm. Jay, Savannah Architect." *Savannah Morning News*. May 8, 1932.

———. "Savannah Theater, One of the First in America." *Savannah Morning News*. November 17, 1918.

———. "Tracking Down a Will-O'-The Wisp," *Savannah Morning News*, May 11, 1932.

Georgia Writers' Project of the Works Progress Administration. *Georgia: A Guide to Its Towns and Countryside* (1940). Revised by George G. Leckie. Atlanta, GA: Tupper Love, 1954. First pub. 1940.

Gilchrist, Alexander. *Life of William Etty, R. A.* Vols. 1 and 2. London: David Bogue, 1855.

Goding, John. *Norman's History of Cheltenham*. London: Longman, Green, Longman, Roberts, & Green, 1863.

Godley, Margaret, Lilla M. Hawes, and Thomas H. Gignilliat. *The Owens-Thomas House*. Savannah, GA: Savannah-Chatham County Historic Site and Monument Commission, 1952.

Goldsmith, Oliver. *Works of Oliver Goldsmith: Life of Richard Nash, Esq., Late Master of the Ceremonies at Bath*. 2nd ed. Vol. 4. London: John Murray, 1854. First pub. 1762.

Goodfellow, G. L. M. "William Jay and the Albion Chapel." *Journal of the Society of Architectural Historians*, December 1963.

Govan, Thomas Payne. *Banking and the Credit System in Georgia 1810–1860*. New York: Arno Press, 1978.

Granville, Augustus Bozzi. *Spas of England, and Principal Sea-Bathing Places*. Vol. 2, *Midland Spas*. London: Henry Colburn, 1841.

Graves, Algernon. *Royal Academy of Arts: A Complete Dictionary of Contributors and Their Work from Its Foundation in 1769 to 1904*. Vols. 3, 4, and 6. London: Henry Graves & Co.,

Ltd., 1905–1906.
Gregorie, Anne King. *History of Sumter County, South Carolina*. Sumter, SC: Osteen-Davis Print. Co., 1974. First pub. 1954.
Griffith, Samuel Young. *Griffith's New Historical Description of Cheltenham and Its Vicinity*. 2nd ed. Vol. 1. London: Longman, Rees, Orme, Brown, & Green, 1826.
Hall, Basil. *Travels in North America, In the Years 1827 and 1828*. Vol. 3. Edinburgh: Cadell & Co., 1829.
Hamlin, Talbot. *Architecture Through the Ages*. New York: G. P. Putnam's Sons, 1953.
———. *Greek Revival Architecture in America*. New York: Dover Pub., Inc., 1964. First pub. 1944.
Hampton, Ann Fripp. *Historic Courthouses of South Carolina*. Columbia: University of South Carolina, Southern Studies Program, 1980.
Hanover Chapel, Stockport. *Hanover Chapel and Sunday School, Stockport, Jubilee Souvenir: 1856–1906, Commemorative Record*. Stockport, England, 1906.
Hardee, Charles Seton Henry. *Reminiscences and Recollections of Old Savannah*. Savannah, GA: Private printing, 1928.
Harden, W. [William]. "Georgia Historical Society." *Georgia Historical Quarterly*, March 1917.
———. *A History of Savannah and South Georgia*. Vol. 1. Chicago: Lewis Pub. Co., 1913.
Harris, William Tell. *Remarks Made During a Tour through the United States of America, in the Years 1817, 1818, and 1819*. London: Sherwood, Neely, & Jones, 1821.
Hartridge, Walter Charlton, ed. *Letters of Robert Mackay to His Wife, Written from Ports in America and England 1795–1816*. Athens: University of Georgia Press, 1949.
———. "Magnificent Home." *Savannah Morning News*, April 20, 1956.
———. and K. Palmer. "A Beautiful Lady." *Savannah Morning News*, August 19, 1962.
Harvey, Lynn. "William Jay, A Conjectural Reconstruction of the Archibald Stobo Bulloch House, Savannah, Georgia." Chicago, IL, 1993. Revised August 1994. Unpublished manuscript. Copy, Thomas J. Watson Library, Metropolitan Museum of Art, New York.
Haupert, Michael. "Panic of 1825." In *Business Cycles and Depressions*, edited by David Glasner. London: Taylor & Francis, 1997.
Hembry, Phyllis May, Leonard W. Cowie, and Evelyn Elizabeth Cowie. *British Spas from 1815 to the Present*. Madison, NJ: Fairleigh Dickinson University Press, 1997.
Hemphill, J. C. [James Calvin], ed. *Men of Mark in South Carolina*. Vol. 1. Washington, DC: Men of Mark Pub. Co., 1907.
Hibbert, Christopher. *George IV: The Rebel Who Would Be King*. New York: Palgrave MacMillan, 2007. First published 1972 as *George IV: Prince of Wales* by Prentice Hall.
Hinton, John Howard, ed. *History and Topography of the United States of North America*. Vols. 1 and 2. London: J. T. Hinton, Simpkin, & Marshall, 1830–1832.
Hoare, Prince. *Memoirs of Granville Sharp, Esq*. London: Henry Colburn & Co., 1820.
Horton, Mrs. Thaddeus [Corinne Ruth Stocker]. "Charleston, Between Ashley and Cooper." In *"The Georgian Period": Being Measured Drawings of Colonial Work*. Edited by William Rotch Ware, Part 10. New York: U.P.C. Book Co., Inc., for the American Architect & Building News Co., 1898–1902.
———. "Classic Houses of the South." *House Beautiful*, May 1903.
———. "Georgian Houses of the Far South." *House and Garden*, December 1904.
———. "Savannah and Parts of the Far South." In *"The Georgian Period": Being Measured*

Drawings of Colonial Work. Edited by William Rotch Ware. Part 12. New York: U.P.C. Book Co., Inc., for the American Architect & Building News Co., 1898–1902.

Howard, Benjamin C. "Taylor v. Taylor et al. [Claim of Charlotte Scarbrough Taylor]." In *Reports of Cases Argued and Adjudged in the Supreme Court of the United States, January Term, 1850.* Vol. 8. Boston: Charles C. Little & James Brown, 1850.

Howard, Diana. *London Theatres and Music Halls, 1850–1950.* London: Unwin Bros., Ltd., 1970.

Howard, John. *State of the Prisons in England and Wales.* Warrington, England: William Eyres, 1777.

Howells, John Mead. *Lost Examples of Colonial Architecture.* Introduction by [Sidney] Fiske Kimball. New York: William Helburn, Inc., 1931.

Howells, W. D. [William Dean]. "In Charleston." *Harper's Magazine,* October 1915.

———. "Savannah Twice Visited." *Harper's Magazine,* February 1919.

Howes, R. K. "Joseph Pitt and Pittville." In "Essays on Local Historical Records by the University Extra-Mural Classes at Gloucester, 1972–73, 1973–74," *Gloucestershire Historical Studies VI.* Bristol, England: University of Bristol, 1974–1975. Copy, V & J Duncan Collection, Savannah, GA.

Humphris, Edith, and E. C. Willoughby. *At Cheltenham Spa; Or, Georgians in a Georgian Town.* London: Alfred A. Knopf, 1928.

Hungerford, E. "Savannah, The Pulse of the South." *Travel,* March 1916.

Hyman, Linda. "From Artisan to Artist: John Frazee and the Politics of Culture in Antebellum America." Ph.D. diss., City University of New York, 1978.

"Is Jay a Myth? *Savannah Press,* December 8, 1922.

Jackson, Henry Rootes. [Laying cornerstone of new custom house.] *Georgian,* July 19, 1848.

Jay, Cyrus. *The Law: What I Have Seen, What I Have Heard, and What I Have Known.* London: Tinsley Bros., 1868.

———. *Recollections of William Jay of Bath.* London: Hamilton, Adams, & Co., 1859.

Jay, Louisa [Coulson]. *Little Willy, A Widowed Mother's Memorial of a Beloved Child.* 2nd ed. Introduction by the Rev. William Jay. London: William Freeman, 1865. First pub.. 1837.

Jay, Rev. William. *Autobiography of the Rev. William Jay.* Edited by George Redford and John Angell James. London: Hamilton, Adams, & Co., 1854. Cited herein as *Autobiography.*

———. *Autobiography of the Rev. William Jay; With Reminiscences of Some Distinguished Contemporaries, Selections from His Correspondence, and Literary Remains.* Edited by George Redford and John Angell James. American edition. Vols. 1 and 2. New York: Robert Carter & Bros., 1855.

———. *Evening Exercises for the Closet, for Every Day in the Year.* Vol. 1. London: Hamilton, Adams, & Co., 1829.

———. *Memoirs of the Life and Character of the Late Reverend Cornelius Winter.* Bath, England: M. Gye, 1808.

Jay, William, architect. "Savannah, January 21st, 1820." *Georgian,* January 22, 1820.

———. attrib. A Friend to the Fine Arts. "For the Savannah Republican." *Savannah Republican,* February 19, 1818.

———. attrib. "A Marine Villa." *Charleston Courier,* January 3-5, 1851.

———. attrib. Peregrinus. "To the Editor of the Georgian." *Georgian,* December 9, 1818.

Johnson, Charles J., Jr. *Mary Telfair: The Life and Legacy of a Nineteenth-Century Woman.* Savannah, GA: Frederic C. Beil, 2002.

Johnson, Sherry L. Report of Archaeological Study. In "William Scarbrough House, Application for National Historic Landmark Nomination/ Renewal," submitted by the Ships of the Sea Maritime Museum, Savannah, GA, April 15, 1998. National Register of Historic Places, Department of the Interior, Washington, DC.

Jones, Charles Colcock, Jr. *Anniversary Address Delivered Before the Georgia Historical Society, in Hodgson Hall, on the 14th of February, 1881.* Savannah: Georgia Historical Society, 1881.

———. *Biographical Sketches of the Delegates from Georgia to the Continental Congress.* Boston: Houghton, Mifflin, & Co., 1891.

Kaye, Thomas. *Stranger in Liverpool.* 7th ed. Liverpool, England: Thos. Kaye, 1823.

Kayser, John C., ed. *Commercial Directory*. Philadelphia: J. C. Kayser & Co., 1823.

Kennedy, J. R. [Robie], Jr. "Georgian and Greek Revival Work in the Far South." *Architectural Record,* March 1907.

———. "Georgian Work in Charleston, South Carolina." *Architectural Record,* April 1906.

Kennedy, Roger G. [George]. *Architecture, Men, Women and Money in America 1600–1860.* New York: Random House, 1985.

Kenny, Peter M., with Frances F. Bretter and Ulrich Leben. *Honoré Lannuier, Cabinetmaker from Paris: The Life and Work of a French* Ébéniste *in Federal New York.* New York: Harry N. Abrams, Inc., for the Metropolitan Museum of Art, 1998.

Kidder Smith, G. E. [George Everard]. *Source Book of American Architecture: 500 Notable Buildings from the 10th Century to the Present.* Revised edition. New York: Princeton Architectural Press, Inc., 1996. First pub. in 1981 as *Architecture of the United States* by Anchor Press (New York).

Kimball, S. [Sidney] Fiske. *Domestic Architecture of the American Colonies and of the Early Republic.* New York: Charles Scribner's Sons, 1922.

King, Spencer Bidwell, Jr. *Darien: The Death and Rebirth of a Southern Town.* Macon, GA: Mercer University Press, 1981.

Klosky, Beth Ann. *The Pendleton Legacy.* Columbia, SC: Sandlapper Press, Inc., 1971.

Knight, Lucian Lamar. *Georgia's Landmarks, Memorials and Legends.* Vol. 1. Atlanta, GA: Byrd Print. Co., 1914.

Kohn, David, and Bess Glenn, eds. *Internal Improvements in South Carolina 1817–1828: From the Reports of the Superintendent of Public Works and from Contemporary Pamphlets, Newspaper Clippings, Letters, Petitions, and Maps.* Washington, D.C.: Private printing, 1938.

Kramer, Ellen W. "The Domestic Architecture of Detlef Lienau, A Conservative Victorian." Ph.D. diss., New York University, 1958.

Lamar, Lucius Q. C. [Quintus Cincinnatus], comp. *A Compilation of the Laws of the State of Georgia, Passed by the Legislature Since the Year 1810 to the Year 1819 Inclusive.* Augusta, GA: T. S. Hannon, 1821.

Lancaster, Joseph. *The British System of Education.* 2nd ed. Georgetown, Columbia [DC]: Joseph Milligan, 1812.

Lane, Mills B., IV. *Architecture of the Old South: Georgia.* Savannah, GA: Beehive Press, 1986.

———. *Architecture of the Old South: South Carolina.* Savannah, GA: Beehive Press, 1984.

———. *Mr. Scarbrough's House: History and Restoration.* Savannah, GA: Beehive Press for Ships of the Sea Maritime Museum, 1998.

Lawrence, Alexander A. *James Moore Wayne, Southern Unionist.* Chapel Hill: University of North Carolina Press, 1943.

Lawton, Alexander R. "Telfair Academy of Arts." *Georgia Historical Quarterly,* March 1917.

Leigh, Samuel. *Leigh's New Picture of England and Wales.* Edited by T. G. B. London: Samuel Leigh, 1820.

Lelièvre, Matthew. *John Wesley: His Life and His Work.* Translated by A. J. French. London: Wesleyan Conference Office, 1871.

Lerski, Hanna Hryniewiecka. *William Jay: Itinerant English Architect 1792–1837.* Lanham, MD: University Press of America, 1983.

Levasseur, A. [Auguste]. *Lafayette in America in 1824 and 1825.* Translated by John D. Godman. Vol. 2. Philadelphia: Carey & Lea, 1829.

Liscombe, Rhodri Windsor. *Church Architecture of Robert Mills.* Easley, SC: Southern Historical Press, Inc., 1985.

Lloyd, J. A. [John Augustus]. "Seasons [East of Madagascar]." In *Directory for the Navigation of the Indian Ocean.* Edited by Alexander G. Findlay. London: Richard Holmes Laurie, 1866.

Lockwood, Allison. *Passionate Pilgrims: The American Traveler in Great Britain, 1800–1914.* Madison, NJ: Farleigh Dickinson University Press, 1981.

Lovell, Caroline Couper Stiles. *Light of Other Days.* Macon, GA: Mercer University Press, 1995.

MacDonald, Ian [John W., Jr.]. *McBee House: A Narrative Tour.* Charleston, SC: BookSurge Pub., 2005.

Mallory, S. R. [Stephen Russell]. "Petition of Charlotte [Scarbrough] Taylor—Committee Report No. 316." In *Reports of the Committees of the Senate of the United States for the First Session of the Thirty-fifth Congress.* Vol. 2. Washington [DC]: William A. Harris, 1858.

Matero, Frank G. "A Rare Example of...Trompe L'Oeil Decoration." *Bulletin of the Association for Preservation Technology.* 1983.

———, and Zachary N. Studenroth. "Owens-Thomas House: Historic Structure Report." Submitted to Telfair Academy of Arts and Sciences, Inc., Savannah, GA, August 1984. Copy, V & J Duncan Collection, Savannah, GA.

McCord, David J. [James], ed. *Statutes at Large of South Carolina: Acts Relating to Corporations and the Militia.* Vol. 8. Columbia, SC: A. S. Johnston, 1840.

McCullough, Hollis Koons, ed. *Telfair Museum of Art: Collection Highlights.* Savannah, GA: Marquand Books, Inc., for the Telfair Museum of Art, 2005.

McDonough, James Vernon. "William Jay: Regency Architect in Georgia and South Carolina." Ph.D. diss., Princeton University, 1950.

McInnis, Maurie D. *Politics of Taste in Antebellum Charleston.* Chapel Hill: University of North Carolina Press, 2005.

Melish, John. *Travels through the United States of America, In the Years 1806 and 1807, and 1809, 1810, and 1811.* London: George Courie & Co., 1818.

Miles, Suzannah Smith. *East Cooper Gazetteer: History of Mount Pleasant, Sullivan's Island, and Isle.* Charleston, SC: History Press, 2004.

Mills, Robert. *Statistics of South Carolina.* Charleston, SC: Hurlbut & Lloyd, 1826.

Milner, John D. "Historic William Scarbrough House, Savannah, Georgia—Preliminary Study for the Restoration of the 1819 Roof and Atrium." Submitted to Historic Savannah Foundation, Inc., October 19, 1973. Copy, V & J Duncan Collection, Savannah, GA.

———. "Specifications: Restoration, William Scarbrough House, Savannah, Georgia." Submitted to Historic Savannah Foundation, Inc., August 1, 1975. Copy, V & J Duncan

Collection, Savannah, GA.
Moore, Frank, ed. "The Invasion of Georgia...A National Account." June 16, 1863. In *The Rebellion Record: A Diary of American Events.* Vol. 7. New York: D. Van Nostrand, 1864.
———. "The Invasion of Georgia...A Rebel Account." June 16, 1863. In *The Rebellion Record: A Diary of American Events.* Vol. 7. New York: D. Van Nostrand, 1864.
More, Hannah. *Poetical Works of Hannah More.* London: Scott, Webster, & Geary, 1839.
Morse, Edward Lind, ed. *Samuel F. B. Morse, His Letters and Journals.* Vol. 1. Boston: Houghton Mifflin Co., 1914.
Morse, Jedidiah. *American Universal Geography.* 7th ed. Vol. 1. Charlestown, MA: Lincoln & Edmands, 1819. First pub. 1789.
"Mr. Jay, the celebrated architect..." *Augusta Chronicle,* April 22, 1822.
Murat, Achille. *The United States of North America.* London: Effingham Wilson, 1833.
Newth, Samuel. "William Jay." In *Pulpit Memorials.* Edited by E. J. Evans and W. F. Hurndall. London: James Clarke & Co., 1878.
Newton, John. "Thoughts upon the African Slave Trade" (1788). In *Works of the Rev. John Newton.* Vol. 6. New York: Samuel Whiting & Co., 1811.
———, William Cowper, and James Montgomery. *Olney Hymns: In Three Parts.* London: T. Nelson & Sons, 1856.
Nichols, Frederick D. [Doveton]. *Early Architecture of Georgia.* Chapel Hill: University of North Carolina Press, 1957.
Nicholson, Watson. *Struggle for a Free Stage in London.* Boston: Houghton, Mifflin, & Co., 1906.
Nicoll, Maud Churchill. *The Earliest Cuylers in Holland and America and Some of Their Descendants.* New York: Tobias A. Wright, 1912.
Orr, Dorothy. *A History of Education in Georgia.* Chapel Hill: University of North Carolina Press, 1950.
Otto, William T. "Jones v. Habersham." In *Cases Argued and Adjudged in the Supreme Court of the United States, October Term, 1882.* Vol.17. New York: Banks Law Pub. Co., 1907.
Overstreet, Robert Lane. "The History of the Savannah Theater, 1865–1906." Ph.D. diss., Louisiana State University, 1970.
Parissien, Steven. *Regency Style.* London: Phaidon Press, Ltd., 2007. Reprint. Originally published 1992.
Parks, E. Taylor. *Colombia and the United States, 1765–1934.* Manchester, NH: Ayer Pub., 1970.
Parsons, C. G. [Charles Grandison]. *Inside View of Slavery: Or a Tour among the Planters.* Boston: John P. Jewett & Co., 1855.
Patrick, J. Max. *Savannah's Pioneer Theater from Its Origins to 1810.* Athens: University of Georgia Press, 1953.
Pendleton District Historical and Recreational Commission. *Pendleton Historic District: A Survey.* Pendleton, SC: Pendleton District Historical and Recreational Commission, June 1973.
Perry, Matthew Calbraith. *Narrative of the Expedition of an American Squadron to the China Seas and Japan Performed in the Years 1852, 1853, and 1854.* Edited by Francis L. Hawks. New York: D. Appleton & Co., 1856.
Peters, George H. *This Glorious Henley.* London: Independent Press, Ltd., 1950.
Peters, Linda Ellen. "A Study of the Architecture of Augusta, Georgia, 1735–1860." Ph.D.

diss., University of Georgia, 1983.
Philip, Robert. *Life and Times of the Reverend George Whitefield, M.A.* London: George Virtue, 1838.
Picton, J. A. [James Allanson]. *Memorials of Liverpool.* Vol. 2. London: Longmans, Green, & Co., 1873.
Power, W. G. [William Grattan] Tyrone. *Impressions of America, During the Years 1833, 1834, and 1835.* Vol. 2. London: Richard Bentley, 1836.
Preston, Daniel. *A Comprehensive Catalogue of the Correspondence and Papers of James Monroe.* Vol. 2. Westport, CT: Greenwood Press, 2001.
Prime, Samuel Irenaeus. *Life of Samuel F. B. Morse, LL.D., Inventor of the Electro-Magnetic Recording Telegraph.* New York: D. Appleton & Co., 1875.
Ravenel, Beatrice St. Julien. *Architects of Charleston.* 2nd ed. Charleston, SC: Carolina Art Assn., 1964. First pub. 1945.
Reps, John W. *Making of Urban America, A History of City Planning in the United States.* Princeton, NJ: Princeton University Press, 1965.
"Rev. William Jay." *European Magazine and London Review,* January 5, 1819.
"Rev. William Jay." *Methodist Quarterly Review,* April 1845.
"Rev. Wm. Jay, of Bath, At Coade's Ornamental Stone and Scagliola Marble Works." *Evangelical Magazine,* March 1822.
Robbins, G. *Robbins' Bath Directory.* Bath, England: Robbins, 1800.
Roberts, William, ed. *Memoirs of the Life and Correspondence of Mrs. Hannah More.* 3rd ed. Vol. 1. London: R. B. Seeley & W. Burnside, 1835.
Robinson, Leonard. *William Etty: The Life and Art.* Jefferson, NC: McFarland & Co., Inc., 2007.
Royal Academy of Arts. *Abstract of the Instrument of Institution and Laws of The Royal Academy of Arts in London.* London: T. Caddell, 1781.
———. *Exhibition of the Royal Academy MDCCCXVII* [1817], *The Forty-Ninth.* London: B. McMillan, 1817.
Rutledge, Anna Wells. *Artists in the Life of Charleston: Through Colony and State from Restoration to Reconstruction.* Philadelphia: American Philosophical Soc., 1949.
St. Pierre, Jacques-Henri Bernardin de. *Paul and Virginia.* London: George Routledge & Sons, 1879. First pub. as *Paul et Virginie,* 1787.
Severens, Kenneth. *Charleston Antebellum Architecture and Civic Destiny.* Knoxville: University of Tennessee Press, 1988.
Severens, Martha R., and Charles L. Wyrick Jr., eds. *Charles Fraser of Charleston: Essays on the Man, His Art and His Times.* Charleston, SC: Carolina Art Association, 1983.
Shaw, Joshua. *United States Directory for the Use of Travellers* [*sic*] *and Merchants.* Philadelphia: James Maxwell, 1822.
Shedd, Julia A. C. [Ann Clark]. *Famous Sculptors and Sculpture.* Boston: James R. Osgood & Co., 1881.
Short, Anthony. "Limestone, Lime, and Mortar." In *The Traditional Building Guide.* Edited by Sylvia Shorto. Bermuda: Department of Planning and the Bermuda National Trust, 2002. Copy, V & J Duncan Collection, Savannah, GA.
Short, Thomas. *An Essay towards a Natural, Experimental, and Medicinal History of the Principal Mineral Waters.* Sheffield, England: John Garnet, 1740.
Sidney, Edwin. *Life of the Rev. Rowland Hill* (1834). 4th ed. London: Seeley, Burnside, & Seeley, 1844. First pub. 1834.

Simons, Albert, and Samuel Lapham Jr., eds. *Early Architecture of Charleston*. Columbia: University of South Carolina Press, 1970. First pub. as *Octagon Library of Early American Architecture, Vol. I*, Charleston, South Carolina, 1927.

Smith, Alice R. [Ravenel] Huger, and D. E. [Daniel Elliott] Huger Smith. *The Dwelling Houses of Charleston, South Carolina*. Introduction by Gene Waddell. Charleston, SC: History Press, 2007. First pub. 1917 by Philadelphia, London: J. B. Lippincott Company, 1917.

Smith, Daniel E. [Elliott] Huger, Alice R. [Ravenel] Huger Smith, and Arney R. [Robinson] Childs, eds. *Mason Smith Family Letters 1860–1868*. Columbia: University of South Carolina Press, 1950.

Soane, John. *Royal Academy Lectures*. Edited and introduction by David Watkin. Cambridge: Cambridge University Press, 2000.

Sprague, William Buell, ed. *Annals of the American Pulpit*. Vols. 4 and 6. New York: Robert Carter & Bros., 1859–1860.

Stillé, Charles J. [Janeway]. *Life and Services of Joel R. Poinsett*. Philadelphia: Historical Society of Pennsylvania, 1888.

Stockton, Robert P. *The Great Shock: The Effects of the 1886 Earthquake on the Built Environment of Charleston, South Carolina*. Easley, SC: Southern Historical Press, Inc., 1986.

Stratford, Joseph. *Wiltshire and Its Worthies*. Salisbury, England: Brown & Co., 1882.

Strauch, Ileana. *Ashley Hall*. Charleston, SC: Arcadia Pub., 2003.

Street, Julian. *American Adventures: A Second Trip "Abroad at Home."* New York: Century Co., 1917.

Sullivan, Buddy. *Early Days on the Georgia Tidewater: The Story of McIntosh County and Sapelo*. McIntosh County, GA: McIntosh County Board of Commissioners, 1990.

———. *"Old Tabby": The Ashantilly Legacy of Thomas Spalding and William G. Haynes*. Darien, GA: Lower Altamaha Historical Society and the Ashantilly Center, Inc., 2009.

Sullivan, M. G. "Sir Richard Westmacott, R.A." In *Biographical Dictionary of Sculptors in Britain, 1660-1851*. Edited by Ingrid Roscoe, Emma Hardy, and M. G. Sullivan. New Haven and London: Yale University Press, 2009.

Summerson, John. *Architecture in Britain, 1530 to 1830*. 9th ed. New Haven, CT: Yale University Press, 1993. First pub. 1954.

———. *John Soane*. London: Academy Editions, St. Martin's Press, 1983.

Telfair, Mary. "Telfair Academy of Arts and Sciences: Extract from Will of Mary Telfair." *Georgia Historical Quarterly*, March 1920

Telfair Academy Board of Managers. *Report of the Committee on the Telfair Academy of Arts and Sciences to the Georgia Historical Society, January 2nd 1893*. Savannah, GA: Morning News Print, 1893.

Thomas, J. A. W. [John Alexander William]. *History of Marlboro County, With Traditions and Sketches of Numerous Families*. Baltimore, MD: Regional Pub. Co., 1971. First pub. in 1897 by Foote and Davies, Atlanta, GA.

Thompson, Henry. *Life of Hannah More*. London: T. Cadell, 1838.

Toussaint, Auguste, ed. *Dictionnaire de Biographie Mauricienne* [*Dictionary of Mauritian Biography*]. Mauritius: Société de l'Histoire de l'Ile Maurice, 1942.

Twain, Mark [Samuel Langhome Clemens]. *Following the Equator: A Journey Around the World*. Vol. 2. New York: Gabriel Wells, 1899.

Van Lemmen, Hans. *Coade Stone*. Princes Risborough, Buckinghamshire, England: Shire Pubs., Ltd., 2006.

Van Nimmen, Jane. "Telfair's Artist Statues: From Vienna to Savannah." In *Twenty-First-Century Perspectives on Nineteenth-Century Art: Essays in Honor of Gabriel P. Weisberg.* Edited by Petra ten-Doesschate Chu and Laurinda S. Dixon. Cranbury, NJ: Associated University Presses, 2008.

Vanstory, Burnette. *Georgia's Land of the Golden Isles.* Athens: University of Georgia Press, 1981. First pub. 1956.

Verey, David. "The Architect and Architecture of Watermoor House." In *Studies in the Archaeology and History of Cirencester,* edited by Alan McWhirr. *British Archaeological Reports* 30, 1976.

———. *Buildings of England: Gloucestershire 1, The Cotswolds.* 3rd ed., revised by Alan Brooks. New Haven, CT: Yale University Press, 2002. First pub. 1970 by Penguin (Harmondsworth).

———. *Buildings of England: Gloucestershire 2, The Vale and the Forest of Dean.* 3rd ed., rev. by Alan Brooks. New Haven, CT: Yale University Press, 2002. First pub. 1970 by Penguin (Harmondsworth).

Waddell, Gene. *Charleston Architecture.* Vol. 1. Charleston, SC: Wyrick & Co., 2003.

———, and Rhodri Windsor Liscombe. *Robert Mills's Courthouses and Jails.* Easley, SC: Southern Historical Press, 1981.

Wakeley, J. B. [Joseph Beaumont]. *Prince of Pulpit Orators: A Portraiture of Rev. George Whitefield, M. A.* 2nd ed. New York: Carlton & Lanahan, 1871.

Walker, George Fuller, ed. *Abstracts of Georgia Colonial Conveyance Book, Book J (1755–1762).* Atlanta, GA: R. J. Taylor Jr. Found., 1978.

Wallace, Thomas. *A Portraiture of the Late Rev. William Jay, of Bath.* London: Arthur Hall, Virtue & Co., 1854.

Ware, William Rotch, ed. *"The Georgian Period": Being Measured Drawings of Colonial Work.* Parts 1–12. New York: U.P.C. Book Co., Inc., for the American Architect & Building News Co., 1898–1902.

Wesley, John. "Thoughts Upon Slavery" (1774). In *Works of the Reverend John Wesley, A. M.,* edited by John Emory. Vol. 6. New York: T. Mason & G. Lane, 1839.

Whiffen, Marcus, and Frederick Koeper. *American Architecture, Volume 1: 1607–1860.* Cambridge, MA: Massachusetts Institute of Technology Press, 1983.

Whitefield, George. *Works of the Reverend George Whitefield, M A.* Vols. 2, 3, and 4. London: Edward & Charles Dilly, 1771.

Wilkes, John, comp. *Encyclopaedia Londinensis; Or, Universal Dictionary of Arts, Sciences, and Literature... Together with a Comprehensive History of London.* Vol. 13. London: J. Adlard, 1815.

Williams, George A. *New Guide to Cheltenham.* London: Longman & Co., 1825.

Wills, A. W. *History of Argyle Congregational Church, Bath, 1781 to 1939.* Bath, England: Harding & Curtis, 1939.

Wilson, Adelaide. *Historic and Picturesque Savannah.* Illustrated by Georgia Weymouth. Boston: Boston Photogravure Co., 1889.

Wilson, A. E. [Albert Edward]. *The Lyceum.* London: Dennis Yates, 1952.

Wilson, Joshua. *Memoir of the Life and Character of Thomas Wilson, Esq.* London: John Snow, 1849.

Wood, Betty. "James Edward Oglethorpe, Race, and Slavery: A Reassessment." In *Oglethorpe in Perspective: Georgia's Founder After Two Hundred Years,* edited by Phinizy Spalding and Harvey H. Jackson III. Tuscaloosa: University of Alabama Press, 1989.

———, *Slavery in Colonial Georgia 1730–1775.* Athens: University of Georgia Press, 2007. First pub. 1984..

———, ed. *Mary Telfair to Mary Few: Selected Letters 1802–1844.* Athens: University of Georgia Press, 2007.

Woods, Leonard. *A Sermon Preached at Haverhill, Mass. in Remembrance of Mrs. Harriet Newell, Wife of the Rev. Samuel Newell, Missionary to India…To Which Are Added Memoirs of Her Life.* 9th ed. Baltimore, MD: Pub. for Abel Brown, 1830. First pub. 1814.

INDEX

NOTE: WJ = William Jay, Architect